HANDBOOK OF RESEARCH ON BORN GLOBALS

T0319606

Handbook of Research on Born Globals

Edited by

Mika Gabrielsson

Professor of International Business, University of Eastern Finland

V.H. Manek Kirpalani

Distinguished Professor and Chairman CIBER at International Management Institute, Delhi, India; Past Director, CIBER, Bloomsburg University, Pennsylvania, USA and Distinguished Professor Emeritus, John Molson School of Business, Concordia University, Canada

Edward Elgar
Cheltenham, UK • Northampton, MA, USA

Published by
Edward Elgar Publishing Limited
The Lypiatts
15 Lansdown Road
Cheltenham
Glos GL50 2JA
UK

Edward Elgar Publishing, Inc.
William Pratt House
9 Dewey Court
Northampton
Massachusetts 01060
USA

Paperback edition 2014

A catalogue record for this book
is available from the British Library

Library of Congress Control Number: 2011929456

ISBN 978 1 84844 953 4 (cased)
     978 1 78347 286 4 (paperback)

Typeset by Servis Filmsetting Ltd, Stockport, Cheshire
Printed in Great Britain by Berforts Information Press Ltd

Contents

About the editors

Mika Gabrielsson (DSc), is a well-known international business and marketing professor. He is Professor of International Business at the University of Eastern Finland. Prior to this position he has served at Aalto University School of Economics as Professor. He is also an Adjunct Professor of International Marketing at Lappeenranta University of Technology. His teaching covers areas such as internationalization of firms and global marketing management, and research interests include among others rapid globalization.

He has been active in research projects funded by the Academy of Finland and the Finnish Funding Agency to Technology and Innovation (Tekes), such as the 'Born Globals' and 'Response to Globalization' projects. He has published over 130 articles in international refereed journals or conference proceedings, many of which have been included as chapters in international business books. His articles have appeared in respected journals, such as *Industrial Marketing Management, Journal of International Marketing, International Business Review, International Marketing Review* and *Thunderbird International Business Review.* He is a frequent reviewer in many journals and serves on the editorial board of *Industrial Marketing Management.*

Before joining the academic world he held several senior positions in purchasing and marketing of global high-tech companies. He continues to act as a consultant for Finnish internationalizing or globalizing firms, which has benefited a large number of firms operating in different industries.

V.H. Manek Kirpalani (DSc HEC University of Montreal, MA and BA Hons Oxford University, UK), is a widely recognized authority in the field of international business and marketing. He is Distinguished Professor Emeritus of Marketing and International Business at Concordia University, Montreal where he was also a member of the board of governors. He is currently Distinguished Professor and Chairman CIBER at International Management Institute, Delhi, India; Past Director of CIBER and a member of the Marketing Department, College of Business, Bloomsburg University, Pennsylvania. He is also Visiting Distinguished Professor at the Aalto University School of Economics and the Faculty of Management, Warsaw University, Honorary Professor, University of the West Indies, and has been Visiting Fellow at Templeton College, Oxford.

He was a member of the board of directors of the American Marketing Association for four years, and Head of their Global Marketing Division. He is a Distinguished Fellow of the Academy of Marketing Science (one of 35). He is the author of over 150 publications, including 18 books and a number of articles in renowned journals such as *Industrial Marketing Management*, *International Business Review*, *Journal of the Academy of Marketing Science, Journal of Business Research, Journal of Global Marketing, Journal of International Business Studies, Journal of International Marketing* and *Journal of Marketing.* Prior to joining academe, he was managing director of an Electrolux AB subsidiary and manager of a trading company subsidiary of the Swedish Match Company, Sweden.

Contributors

Arild Aspelund holds a PhD in international marketing from the Norwegian University of Science and Technology (NTNU). Currently, he is Associate Professor in Marketing at NTNU and teaches courses related to marketing, entrepreneurship, and international business development. His primary research focus is on internationalization of new industry and especially on the phenomenon of international new ventures. He also does research within general theories of economic development with special interest in entrepreneurship and economic growth. More recently, his research focus has been on the establishment and management of global production systems and he is currently the leader of the research group Global Production and Communication (GP&C) at NTNU.

Matthias Baum is research assistant at the University of Giessen, Germany. He studied business administration and economics at the University of Giessen and the Institut Supérieur du Commerce (Paris, France). He is a member of the Interdisciplinary Research Unit on Evidence-based Management and Entrepreneurship (EBME) and doctoral candidate at the Department for Human Resource Management, Small and Medium-Sized Enterprises, and Entrepreneurship. Besides his research on born globals and internationalization of technology firms, his research interests include international recruitment strategies, recruitment strategies of SMEs, employer branding and e-recruitment. He has presented his research at various international conferences and published in refereed journals such as *Zeitschrift für Betriebswirtschaft* (ZfB).

Susan Freeman is Associate Professor of International Business at the Business School, University of Adelaide, Adelaide, SA, Australia. She is the Discipline Leader for International Business and Marketing. She holds a PhD (marketing), an MEdSt.s (education) and BaEco from Monash University, Melbourne; and a DipEd from Mercy College, Ascot Vale, Melbourne. Her teaching covers areas such as global business, corporate responsibility for global business, and international management. Her research interests include born global theory, knowledge transfer in rapidly internationalizing firms, services internationalization, and emerging market strategies for developed and developing market firms. She has been active in numerous research projects in these areas including 'Services Internationalization into Emerging Markets', 'Australian FDI into the UK'; and 'EU Economic Policies, Australian Firms and Global Economic and Financial Challenges', funded by bodies such as the European Commission Funding (2010–13) ME&ECC Relex Funding, UK Trade & Investment, the British Embassy, Australia, and Monash University. She has published over 70 articles in refereed international journals or conference proceedings, and authored a number of industry reports and cases on international business. She is a frequent reviewer in many journals.

Inmaculada Galván-Sánchez holds a PhD and is Assistant Professor at the Department of Business Economics and Management of the University of Las Palmas de Gran Canaria, Spain. She is the author and/or co-author of chapter books and/or papers in both international and national journals such as *European Management Journal, Información Comercial Española*, and *Cuadernos de Estudios Empresariales*. She also serves as reviewer board member of *Revista Internacional de la Pequeña y Mediana Empresa* and several EIBA annual conferences.

Minerva García is a PhD candidate at the Business Economics Department of Universitat Autònoma de Barcelona, Spain. She has been working in the IT sector during the last five years, especially in the innovation department of an internet-based firm and as CEO of a start-up company. Her experience also includes teaching at the Universidad Iberoamericana, Mexico City and research at the same university.

Pervez N. Ghauri is Professor of International Business at King's College London, UK. He completed his PhD at the University of Uppsala, Sweden, where he also taught for some years. Before joining King's he was Professor and Chair of International Business at Manchester Business School. He has published more than 20 books and numerous articles in journals such as: *Journal of International Business Studies, Journal of World Business, Management International Review, Journal of Business Research, Industrial Marketing Management* and *International Marketing Review*. He is also editor in chief of *International Business Review* and editor for Europe for *Journal of World Business*.

Ruey-Jer (Bryan) Jean is Assistant Professor of International Business at National Chengchi University, Taiwan. He received his PhD from Manchester Business School, UK and his MSc in international trade from National Dong-Hwa University, Taiwan. His teaching covers areas such as marketing, management and international business strategy. He previously worked as a post-doctoral research fellow at Manchester Business School and his research focuses on interorganizational relationship management, with particular focus on online and international contexts. His work has appeared in *Journal of International Business Studies, Journal of International Marketing, International Business Review, Critical Perspectives of International Business, International Marketing Review*, and *Journal of Business Research.*

Rüdiger Kabst is Professor of Business Administration specializing in human resource management, small and medium-sized enterprises, and entrepreneurship at the University of Giessen, Germany. He is academic head of the Entrepreneurship Cluster Mittelhessen (ECM), director of the Interdisciplinary Research Unit on Evidence-based Management and Entrepreneurship (EBME), as well as the German representative of the Cranfield Network on International Human Resource Management (CRANET). He was formerly a visiting research scholar at the University of Illinois/Urbana-Champaign in 1996, at the University of California/ Berkeley in 2001, and at EWHA University in Seoul (South Korea) in 2006. His current research interests include international comparative human resource management, expatriate management, human resource practices between market and hierarchy (for example, outsourcing, down-sizing, interim management, working-time flexibility and so on), inter-firm cooperation (for example, joint ventures), trust between organizations, young technology start-ups, international entrepreneurship, and interna-tionalization of medium-sized enterprises.

Olli Kuivalainen has a DSc in economics, and is Professor of International Marketing at the School of Business, Lappeenranta University of Technology, Finland. He normally teaches classes focusing on inter-national business strategy and marketing. His research interests are in the areas of international entrepreneurship, and strategic management, marketing and internationalization of knowledge-intensive firms, with a focus on firms operating in the domains of media and information and communication technologies. He has published articles in *Journal of World Business, Journal of International Marketing, Technovation, Internet Research, International Journal of Production Economics*, and *Journal of International Entrepreneurship*, among others. He has also contributed to many books and has presented his research at various academic confer-ences. Before joining academia he worked in a professional service firm.

Leonidas C. Leonidou has a PhD and an MSc from the University of Bath and is Professor of Marketing at the School of Economics and Management of the University of Cyprus. He is also a visiting Principal Research Fellow in Marketing at Leeds University Business School. Before joining academia, he worked as a marketing analyst/consultant for numerous companies in the Middle East, Eastern Europe, and the

Eastern Mediterranean. His current research interests are in the areas of international marketing/purchasing, relationship marketing, strategic marketing, and marketing in emerging economies. He has published extensively in these fields in both academic journals (for example, *Journal of Business Research*, *Journal of International Business Studies*, *Journal of International Marketing*, *Journal of the Academy of Marketing Science*, *Journal of World Business*, and *Management International Review*) and practitioner-oriented journals (for example, *European Management Journal*, *Journal of the Market Research Society*, *Long Range Planning*, *Management Decision*, *Marketing and Research Today*, and *Thunderbird International Business Review*). He has also contributed chapters to and written books on marketing. He is on the editorial boards of *Industrial Marketing Management*, *International Marketing Review*, *Journal of Management Studies*, *Journal of Strategic Marketing*, and *Management International Review*.

Nicolai Løvdal has an MSc and has been a research fellow at the Norwegian University of Science and Technology (NTNU) since 2005. Currently he is working on his PhD thesis 'International entrepreneurship within offshore renewable energy'. Through industry involvements, empirical studies and as founder of a global research network on offshore renewable energy (INORE) he has developed a thorough industry insight within these industries. His research interests include variants of entrepreneurship (international, sustainable, energy) and industry innovation research. His main research focus is on international entrepreneurship in technology-based renewable energy industries where he investigates different aspects of the entrepreneur, on the firm and industry context levels. More recently, he has focused his research on technology transfer and international business related to energy and sustainability issues.

Rod McNaughton is Eyton Chair in Entrepreneurship and Director of the Conrad Centre for Business, Entrepreneurship and Technology at the University of Waterloo, Canada. He holds a PhD in marketing from Lancaster University Management School, and in economic geography from the University of Western Ontario. His specialty is international marketing strategy, focusing on the rapid entry into overseas markets by knowledge-intensive new ventures. The results of his research on export channel selection, industrial clusters, networks and internationalization, export policy, the venture capital industry, strategic alliances, and foreign direct investment are published in numerous refereed journals and books. Prior to joining the faculty at UW, he was Professor in Marketing at the University of Otago School of Business, Dunedin, New Zealand.

Jukka Partanen has a PhD and is a researcher and project manager in the Department of Marketing and Management at the School of Economics Aalto University, Finland. His research interests include inter-organizational networks, high-growth SMEs, and industrial service business. He has been active in teaching and executive education in the Small Business Center of Aalto University, and has contributed to several research projects funded by the Finnish Funding Agency for Technology and Innovation (Tekes). He has published in *Industrial Marketing Management* and in several conference proceedings as well as acted as a reviewer in, for example, the *Journal of International Business Studies*.

Noemi Pezderka holds a master's degree from the Vienna University of Economics and Business (WU-Wien), Austria and is currently a PhD candidate in comparative and international business at Manchester Business School, Manchester, UK. Her research focuses on international entrepreneurship, ICT, and economic development issues and she contributes actively to research projects in the MBS-CIBER. She has contributed book chapters to international business books and published in *International Business Review*.

Alex Rialp has a PhD and is Associate Professor of Business Organization at the Business Economics Department of the Universitat Autònoma de Barcelona, Spain. He is author and/or co-author of various books, chapter books, and papers published in both national and international scientific journals such as *International Business Review*, *International Marketing Review*, *Advances in International Marketing*, *Journal of International Entrepreneurship*, *Journal of Euromarketing*, *European Management Journal*, and *Journal of Global Marketing*. He also serves as an editorial review board member of *Journal of International Marketing* and *International Business Review*.

Sami Saarenketo holds a DSc in economics and is Professor of International Marketing at the School of Business, Lappeenranta University of Technology, Finland. He teaches on international marketing and international entrepreneurship. His primary areas of research interest are international marketing and entrepreneurship in technology-based small firms. He has published on these issues in *Journal of World Business*, *International Business Review*, *European Business Review*, *European Journal of Marketing*, and *Journal of International Entrepreneurship*, among others. He has also contributed to many books and presented his research at various academic conferences.

Saeed Samiee holds a PhD from Ohio State University and is the Collins Professor of Marketing and International Business at the University of

Tulsa, OK, USA. He has contributed to scholarly journals in marketing and international business, including the *Journal of Marketing, Journal of the Academy of Marketing Science*, and *Journal of International Business Studies*. He serves on the editorial review and advisory boards of 12 scholarly journals, including *Journal of the Academy of Marketing Science* and *Journal of International Business Studies*. He has also actively contributed to the annual conferences of the AIB, the American Marketing Association, and the Academy of Marketing Science (AMS) in various capacities. He initiated the dissertation competition for AMS and served as its first chairperson, and was appointed as the first chair of the AIB Best Paper Award and Haynes Prize Committee (2002–04). He has lectured or served as a visiting scholar at business schools internationally including in Austria, Brazil, China, Cyprus, Finland, France, Hong Kong, Korea, Mexico, Iran, Japan, Russia, and Switzerland.

Christian Schwens is a post-doc at the University of Giessen, Germany. He studied business administration at the University of Paderborn and at the University of Stockholm. In 2006 he was visiting scholar at the Carlson School of Management, University of Minnesota, MN, USA. He is a member of the Interdisciplinary Research Unit on Evidence-based Management and Entrepreneurship (EBME). His research interests include the internationalization of technology firms, international entrepreneurship, market entry mode choices of small and medium-sized enterprises (SMEs), foreign institutions, international staffing, and internationalization of SMEs. His research has been presented at various international conferences and in academic as well as managerial journals such as *International Business Review* (*IBR*), *International Journal of Human Resource Management* (*IJHRM*), *Journal of International Entrepreneurship* (*JIE*), and *Zeitschrift für Betriebswirtschaft* (*ZfB*).

Per Servais holds a PhD, and is Associate Professor of Marketing at the University of Southern Denmark. His research interests are: international entrepreneurship, the formation and growth of international new ventures, industrial marketing in small industrial firms, e-business in industrial firms, branding on industrial markets, outsourcing activities in industrial firms, and relationships and de-internationalization in small firms. He has published a number of book chapters and articles, for example in *Industrial Marketing Management, International Marketing Review, Journal of International Marketing, Advances in International Marketing*, and *International Business Review*.

Michael Sheppard is Assistant Professor at the F.C. Manning School of Business, Acadia University, Canada. He holds a PhD in management sciences from the University of Waterloo. His research focuses on high-growth firms, especially the conditions that lead to rapid growth, managing the challenges of growth, and the overlap between high growth and rapid internationalization. Before completing his PhD and joining the Faculty at Acadia University, he worked for many years in consulting and management of information technology while also gaining considerable entrepreneurial experience in the software industry.

Rotem Shneor is a research fellow and lecturer at the University of Agder in Norway, specializing in international marketing, e-marketing, and the internationalization process of the firm. Additional research interests include e-business, brand management, and cross-cultural management. Currently, he is engaged in teaching international marketing, international strategy, and entrepreneurship courses. He is a former graduate of the Hebrew University in Jerusalem as well as the Norwegian School of Economics and Business Administration (NHH) in Bergen.

Vitor Corado Simões is a professor at ISEG–Instituto Superior de Economia e Gestão (Technical University of Lisbon, Portugal). His main research areas are international management and innovation management. He has lectured at several universities abroad (Autónoma of Madrid, Complutense of Madrid, Strasbourg, Strathclyde, Toulouse and Rio de Janeiro-COPPEAD). He has researched extensively on MNCs, on MNC subsidiaries, and on born globals. He was responsible for the report on globalization, commissioned by Portugal's Economic and Social Council. He co-coordinated the research project on COTEC Portugal Innovative SME Network (2010). He has a wide international experience as consultant to the European Commission, the OECD, and UNIDO. He chaired the CREST/EU Working Group on SMEs and Innovation. He is national correspondent to PROINNO/TrendChart on Innovation and to the ERAWATCH network. He served as a member of Portugal's Technological Plan Steering Committee and is a member of COTEC Portugal Consultative Council. Before joining the university as a full-time professor, he worked for 11 years at the Foreign Investment Institute of Portugal, namely as research director. He served as President of the European International Business Academy in 1993, and is now a member of the Fellows of the Academy.

Rudolf R. Sinkovics is Professor of International Business at Manchester Business School, UK, where he is currently Head of the Comparative and International Business Group and Director of the MBS-CIBER (Centre of International Business Research). He has previously held a number of visiting scholar positions, including at Michigan State University, the University of Oklahoma, USA, and at the University of Otago in Dunedin, New Zealand. His research centers on inter-organizational governance, the role of ICT, and research methods in international business. He received his PhD from Vienna University of Economics and Business (WU-Wien), Austria. His work has been published in international business and international marketing journals such as *Journal of International Business Studies, Management International Review, Journal of World Business, International Business Review, Journal of International Marketing*, and *International Marketing Review*. He also serves on the editorial boards of international journals including *International Business Review, Journal of World Business, Critical Perspectives of International Business*, and *der Markt*. He teaches in the areas of global marketing, multinational management and research methodology.

Carl Arthur Solberg is Professor of International Marketing at BI Norwegian School of Management, Oslo, Norway. He holds a Licencié ès Sciences Économiques from L'Université de Neuchâtel, Switzerland and a PhD from Strathclyde University, Glasgow, UK. His teaching covers areas such as international marketing, international contract negotiations, and international market research. His research interests cover marketing strategies in globalizing economies, cultural impact on buyer behaviour, information behaviour of internationalizing firms, and exporter–middleman relationships. His publications include more than 80 papers, articles, and book chapters in refereed conferences, journals, and books. He has twice received the best paper award in the *Journal of International Marketing* and has been nominated in the *Asia Pacific Journal of Management* – 2007 among the 30 most published researchers in international business in the 1996–2006 period. He is a reviewer for several management journals and sits on the editorial board of the *Journal of International Marketing*. He has 10 years of previous experience with the Export Council of Norway and in the petrochemical industry. He also serves as the chairman of the board of two companies.

Kadri Ukrainski holds a PhD and an MA degree from the University of Tartu and is currently working as a Senior Researcher of Innovation Management at the Faculty of Economics and Business Administration at the University of Tartu (Estonia). She is teaching courses on the economics and management of the public sector and also technology and innovation policy, but her main research has been focused more on innovation policy issues and innovation in firms. She has conducted research in knowledge economics, with particular emphasis on knowledge as a source of innovation; sectoral innovation systems with the focus on low- and medium-technology industries; but also science and innovation policy.

She has actively participated in international research projects such as the EU 6th FP Project 'Understanding the Relationship between Knowledge and Competitiveness in the Enlarging European Union', the PRIME Network of Excellence projects 'Public Funding of Research in CEEC countries' and 'EUMIDA: European Universities MIcro DAta Feasibility Study for Creating a European University Data Collection'. She has also participated in several sectoral studies of the timber and machinery industries in Estonia.

Terhi J. Vapola holds a DSc in international business from Aalto University, Finland, an MSc degree in industrial economics, and a BSc in electrical and electronic engineering. Her research focuses on the strategic management of partnerships between MNCs and born globals. She gives special emphasis to research questions related to generating competitive advantage through external innovation in global high-velocity industries. Currently, she is CEO of a start-up in a global high-tech industry. Prior to founding her start-up, she had 15 years' successful and broad leadership experience in various director positions at Nokia, focusing on strategic partnerships and tech-oriented acquisitions.

Tiia Vissak holds a PhD and an MA degree from the University of Tartu and is currently working as a senior researcher of international economics and business at the Faculty of Economics and Business Administration at the University of Tartu (Estonia). She teaches courses on different issues in international economics and business. Her main research interests are different forms of linear and nonlinear internationalization (the pace, country, and market entry/operation mode selection, success factors, reasons for de- and re-internationalization), international entrepreneurship issues (the role of managers and other actors in internationalization, the role of subsidiaries in foreign owners' networks, and the factors impacting on that role), networks and strategic alliances (the roles of different actors and factors, the reasons for relationship dissolution), transition economies and case studies as a research methodology. She has been active in several research projects. She is a reviewer for several journals including *International Business Review* and the *Journal of East–West Business*. She is a supervisor of X. Zhang.

Xiaotian Zhang has been a PhD student at the Faculty of Economics and Business Administration, University of Tartu (Estonia) since 2009. He holds an MA degree from the Belarus State Economic University and has also studied architecture in China. He lectures on doing business in China. His main research interests are different definitions and forms of internationalization, deviations from conventional internationalization paths, entry/operation mode and target country selection in internationalization, and the activities of Chinese SMEs in Central and Eastern European transition economies and vice versa. He is the founder and CEO of OÜ Raatuse International Trade (offering business consulting to Baltic and Belorussian firms entering China and Chinese firms entering the Baltic and Belorussia). He has also worked with the International Relations Office of the University of Tartu in developing the university's cooperation with Chinese universities. In addition, he is a part-time columnist of Asian business for an Estonian business paper *Aripaev*, a business weekly *Ärileht* and a Latvian business weekly *Lietiska Diena*.

Huan Zou is a senior lecturer in international management in the Department of Financial and Management Studies at the School of Oriental and African Studies, University of London, UK. She completed her PhD at Manchester Business School, University of Manchester (UK). Her research focuses on international market entry strategies, internationalization of knowledge-intensive firms from emerging economies, knowledge acquisition and learning in international investment, and new venture financing, networks with venture capitals and growth strategies. She has published in journals such as the *Journal of World Business, Management International Review, International Journal of Research in Marketing, International Marketing Review,* and *Asia Pacific Journal of Management.*

Foreword

I am delighted to have been asked to write the Foreword for this Handbook of Research on Born Globals. 'Born Globals' in the sense of firms that internationalize at a much faster pace than other firms have always existed. However, increased globalization in recent decades with much more cross-border interaction has created better conditions and even more stimuli for faster internationalization. Accordingly we are seeing more and more firms that are born with a global mindset and start internationalization right from their inception.

The research on born globals can be traced back to the seminal article by Oviatt and McDougall, 'Toward a theory of international new ventures' (1994), where they conceptualized the phenomenon and developed a theoretical foundation for understanding the uniqueness of born globals. Since then we have seen a cottage industry of research on born globals that includes many different definitions, operationalizations, and conclusions.

It is time to take stock of this immense literature and reflect on what kind of insights we have gained through the study of born globals, which is precisely the aim of this Handbook. The Handbook will fill a gap in the literature. I was very pleased to read it as the editors have succeeded in putting together a volume that presents born global research at its best and demonstrates, if not all, then most dimensions of such research. The volume comprises many chapters that have increased my level of understanding of born globals.

The editors and authors are to be commended for an appealing, useful, and well-crafted end product. I am sure that this volume will find its way into classrooms where born globals are scrutinized as well as stimulate even further research on born globals in the future.

Torben Pedersen
Department of Strategic Management and Globalization
Copenhagen Business School

Preface

The *Handbook of Research on Born Globals* is the result of a book project undertaken by Mika Gabrielsson and V.H. Manek Kirpalani after discussion with Ben Booth of Edward Elgar. All three of us recognized that the born global research field had reached a growth point where definitions, parameters, and more theory needed to be developed for the field to expand. Researchers, practitioners, and policy makers were increasingly showing keen interest in such expansion. Also Mika and Manek had been working and publishing articles in this field for about a decade, and were widely known for their work.

This Handbook offers a very good coverage of the origin and evolution of born globals (BGs) and the changing history of this sector. It then discusses the various research areas still to be investigated in this field; looks at the training involved in developing international intellectual entrepreneurs who can found and/or manage BGs; studies the effects of different cultures on the origin and growth of BGs; and outlines the strategies BGs can adopt individually or as part of MNC networks. The text focuses on the different types of BGs that emerge from the general set of SMEs: ranging from the pure BG to born-again globals, born regionals and their subgroup of born-again regionals. It also differentiates these from internationalizing SMEs and international new ventures.

The text also analyses the growth paths of BGs as affected by different factors. These factors include the interactions of entrepreneurship and internationalization growth, aspects of knowledge accumulation, application and management, and the influence of the internet. Also the impact of utilization of large channels, of alliances and networks, and of large partner MNCs is covered. Further, the institutional support available in selected countries is discussed.

A chosen group of leading researchers have contributed to this book. They were invited due to their expertise and to reflect diversity of perspectives. The book comprises three parts. Each part commences with an overview synopsis of the intellectual area, written by Mika Gabrielsson and Manek Kirpalani, the two author/editors of the book.

In Part I, Chapter 1 deals with the historical origin of BGs and the development of theoretical and empirical research. Chapters 2–6 deal with whether these small firms are BGs or simply rapidly internationalizing firms (Chapter 2); the determinants of different types of BGs (Chapter 3);

the differences and commonalities between BGs and born-again globals (Chapter 4); the BG firm dilemma as to how to trade off between rapid growth and maintenance of control (Chapter 5); and lastly an inquiry into the BG firm's learning process (Chapter 6).

In Part II, Chapter 7 surveys the research areas that are still to be covered more fully with regard to BGs. This is very important information for both researchers and potential researchers. Chapters 8–12 discuss the use of networks/alliances by BGs and a social dynamic perspective on those (Chapter 8); Sourcing networks of BGs (Chapter 9); the BG use of the internet and new vehicles for internationalization (Chapter 10); the question of whether BGs reap more benefit from ICT use than other internationalizing SMEs (Chapter 11); and finally, there is a contribution from the viewpoint of an institutional perspective on the strategic behavior of Chinese new ventures by SMEs (Chapter 12).

In Part III, Chapter 13 analyzes the trends in the development of intellectual entrepreneur founders/managers, and in other research areas. This is followed by a discussion on new international pathways for software BGs (Chapter 14). Two contributions relate to the influence of culture on the formation and growth of BGs; one is from Portugal, which deals with the BG founders' linkages and the influence of that on the firms' evolution in regard to its international geographical pattern (Chapter 16), and the other concerns the growth and evolution of Chinese BGs as influenced by their culture (Chapter 18). Part III also draws attention to two other developing vectors. One is about the battleship strategy of a large MNC utilizing affiliated BGs as scouts and specialists in different research areas (Chapter 17) and the other introduces a new phenomenon of whole industries displaying the characteristics of a BG and thus could be turning into de facto BGs in their evolutionary globalization patterns (Chapter 15). Part III also includes an Annotated Bibliography for Researchers (Chapter 19). This comprehensive but selective bibliography contains what we with the cooperation of a number of experienced researchers have chosen as the most useful publications for BG and potential BG researchers to use. We make comments in the Bibliography as to whose publications deal with which different research subareas in order to facilitate the user. We think it will be of substantial benefit to researchers, and will help them to probe into areas more deeply.

Overall we are happy to present the book to all who are interested in the new and growing BG field. These firms confer significant knowledge, skill, and ability to the societies and economies in which they flourish.

Mika Gabrielsson and V.H. Manek Kirpalani
2011

Acknowledgements

Our deepest appreciation is expressed to the people who have helped in the development of this book. The first group is the numerous talented professionals who have contributed various chapters and those whose names are noted in the text. We also wish to thank our institutions, the College of Business at Bloomsburg University Pennsylvania, the John Molson School of Business, Concordia University Montreal, Aalto University School of Economics, and the LIITO-program of the Finnish Funding Agency for Technology and Innovation (Tekes). Also we wish to thank an academic administrator for his direct encouragement of this book project: Dr Michael Tidwell, Dean of the College of Business at Bloomsburg University, Pennsylvania.

We are indebted to Susan Krieger, Associate Professor at Mansfield University Pennsylvania who helped to organize the manuscript. We are grateful to Elizabeth Williams, MLIS, Librarian at Mansfield University, who did an excellent job in proofreading and correcting the entire manuscript and formatting it in the style required by the publishers. Our sincere appreciation and thanks to Ben Booth, Commissioning Editor at Edward Elgar for his continuous encouragement of our ideas and thoroughness in helping us to bring the manuscript to publication. Also to Jennifer Wilcox, editor at Edward Elgar, who helped the work along by her questions, effectiveness, and efficiency, and in ensuring that the work was 'correct' in all needed aspects.

Finally our warmest thanks to our wives, children, their spouses, and grandchildren for their understanding throughout the project:

Mika Gabrielsson: wife Janika, children Joakim and Nicole

V.H. Manek Kirpalani: wife Pachi, children Tara and Arjun, Tara's spouse Sundeep and children Siona, Rahul and Sarina, Arjun's children Melina and Natasha

PART I

BORN GLOBALS: ORIGIN, AND EVOLUTION OF RESEARCH

1 Overview, background and historical origin of born globals; development of theoretical and empirical research
Mika Gabrielsson and V.H. Manek Kirpalani

OVERVIEW, BACKGROUND AND HISTORICAL ORIGIN OF BORN GLOBALS

A new breed of company, the born global (BG) firm, has increased in importance during the last two decades. Evidence of emergence of firms that globalize rapidly since their establishment was first brought to the attention of the broader public by a report published by McKinsey & Company (1993). This research reported on Australian firms that behaved differently when compared to the domestic-based small and medium-sized firms or conventionally internationalizing firms with regard to their globalization behavior. These firms did not focus solely on domestic markets and did not internationalize slowly, but rather virtually from inception competed successfully in the global marketplace. Most importantly, these firms were found to be extremely important from the national standpoint since they constituted almost 20 percent of Australia's high-value-added manufacturing exports (Rennie 1993). Although attention to and importance of BGs has increased lately, they have likely existed for centuries. Trading houses, such as the East India Company in the seventeenth century, the American cotton traders in the nineteenth century, and Ford Motor Company founded in 1903 are examples of firms that traded globally early on (Oviatt and McDougall 1994). In addition, Vaisala Corporation, a global market leader in meteorological forecasting systems established in 1936 in Finland, is another good example of an early BG firm (Luostarinen and Gabrielsson 2004). What is new now is that such firms have become increasingly common and important.

BGs have recently emerged in several countries across Europe, in both North and South America, and in Asia, and these companies have increasingly been studied (see, for example, Jolly et al. 1991; McDougall et al. 1994). Given the number of studies being carried out, the increase in importance of this relatively new breed of companies in many parts of the world is clear (see a review by Rialp et al. 2005). It is important to note that these firms have been reported to exist not only in high-tech (Preece et al. 1999) and software (Bell 1995), firms but also in areas such as high innovative design (Falay et al. 2007), high-quality service and high sophisticated systems (Luostarinen and Gabrielsson 2004). BGs can also be found in traditional food, apparel, shoes, furniture, and other low-tech industries (Gabrielsson et al. 2008).

Naming and Definitions

Depending on the school of thought and characteristics of the investigated companies, scholars have used different names and definitions for BG types of firms. In their review, Luostarinen and Gabrielsson (2004) find them referred to as (a) deviations, inconsistencies, variations to the stages models of internationalization; (b) new technology-based firms; (c) high-technology start-ups; (d) born internationals; (e) born globals; (f) international new ventures; (g) global start-ups; (h) instant internationals; and (i) global, knowledge-intensive firms, among others.

The following criteria have been used when defining BGs (Gabrielsson and Kirpalani 2004): (i) vision and strategy to become global/international; (ii) small technology-oriented companies; (iii) time to become global/international, varying from immediate to three years; (iv) geographical expansion in terms of a minimum of 25 percent of foreign sales or a minimum number of countries served outside the home country; and (v) geographical expansion outside the home continent with a minimum of 50 percent external sales. The variety of definitions used in earlier studies is naturally a problem with regard to the comparability of the results. See Table 1.1 for a comparison of various definitions used.

In line with Oviatt and McDougall (1994, p. 49) we define a born global as an entity that 'from inception, seeks to derive significant competitive advantage from the use of resources and the sales of outputs in multiple countries'. Exact age, export ratios, or global growth figures are not included as decisive criteria since they are influenced by the size of the BG's country of origin and economy, the country's common market neighbors, and other factors such as the type of industry. There are two dimensions that must be acknowledged when comparing different research results, namely speed and precocity. 'Precocity' is sometimes used for the early starting issue of international business operations, whereas 'speed' is demonstrated in fast foreign growth (Zuchella et al. 2007). Nevertheless, it is obvious that there are BGs whose degree of 'globality' varies (Kuivalainen et al. 2007).

Table 1.1 Born global definitions

Dimension/ author	Vision	Precocity (Time before starting export)	Speed (Foreign growth/age)
Oviatt and McDougall* (1994)	A business organization that, from inception, seeks to derive significant competitive advantage from the use of resources and the sale of outputs in multiple countries		
McKinsey & Company (1993); Rennie (1993)	Management views the world as its marketplace from the outset of the firm's founding	Began exporting, on average, only 2 years after foundation	Achieved 76% of total sales through exports at an average age of 14 years
Knight and Cavusgil (1996)	Management views the world as its marketplace from the outset of the firm's founding	Began exporting one or several products within 2 years of establishment.	Tend to export at least a quarter of total production
Chetty and Campbell-Hunt (2004)		Within 2 years of inception.	80% of sales outside New Zealand; markets are worldwide
Luostarinen and Gabrielsson (2006)	Global vision and/or at a global growth path	At the outset entered global markets	Over 50% of sales outside home continent. Established after 1985
Servais, Madsen and Rasmussen (2007)		Within 3 years of establishment	More than 25% of foreign sales or sourcing outside home continent
Zhou, Barnes and Lu* (2010)		An international market entry process that occurs within 3 years of firm's inception	Generating at least 20% of total sales from multiple countries. Founded in 1990 or later

Note: * Authors use the term 'international new venture' rather than 'born global'.

Source: Adapted from Gabrielsson et al. (2008).

Reasons for Emergence of Born Globals

The reasons why BGs are gaining in importance and are increasingly common can be traced to the following trends:

- *Globalization of market conditions* This can be increasingly witnessed in many industries, such as the software, mobile phone, automobile, and medical industries.
- *Development of technology* for example, the increased role of the internet, mobile messaging, and automated manufacturing.
- *Capability development of people and small firms* This is enabled by higher educational levels and increased online teaching.
- *Home market conditions*, for example, the smaller the home market, the higher the probability of emergence of BGs.

Looking more closely at these trends, first, due to the globalization of market conditions, the number of niche segments has increased in which customer needs have homogenized across world markets (Levitt 1983; Yip 1989). Under these conditions, many of the smaller firms have no other choice than to specialize in relatively narrow niches in order to successfully compete against the large Multinational Corporations (MNCs). This is particularly true for BGs emerging from smaller economies (Madsen and Servais 1997; Luostarinen and Gabrielsson 2004), but also holds for firms originating in larger developed economies. Furthermore, the integration of the financial markets, increase of technology cooperation, as well as the possibility of benefiting from global networks, has enabled firms to globalize much more rapidly (Knight and Cavusgil 1996). Second, the developments in technology, for example, production process and communication technology, have enabled scale and cost advantages that allow even small firms to compete globally (ibid.). Also, transportation of people and goods has become more frequent, reliable, and cheaper (Madsen and Servais 1997). Third, human capabilities have developed in terms of enhanced usage of the newest technology, an increase in international mobility and international experience, and an increase in the number of more competent and ambitious entrepreneurs (ibid.). These factors have enabled BGs increasingly to benefit from being quicker, more flexible and more adaptive to the foreign market requirements than larger firms (Knight and Cavusgil 1996). Finally, the small and open economies (SMOPECs) have higher push and pull factors, encouraging the emergence of BGs compared to firms originating in larger economies (Luostarinen and Gabrielsson 2006). Empirical results show that the probability of new ventures going international at birth is higher when they originate from smaller rather than larger economies. Also, the capacity allocation of BGs is affected by the language of the home country, since they have been found to favor same-language markets (Fan and Phan 2007).

DEVELOPMENT OF THEORETICAL AND EMPIRICAL RESEARCH ON BGS

Academic attention to these new firms can be traced to three fields that are increasingly becoming interlinked: (i) international business researchers have noticed that the emergence of BG firms may challenge traditional internationalization theory (Knight and Cavusgil 1996; Madsen and Servais 1997; Luostarinen and Gabrielsson 2006); (ii) international entrepreneurship research has developed from entrepreneurship researchers who have noticed accelerated internationalization even among the smallest and newest organizations (Oviatt and McDougall 1994; McDougall and Oviatt 2000); and (iii) international management researchers have found that BGs may require different capabilities from conventional firms (Sapienza et al. 2006). A more detailed examination of these three streams, including their theoretical and empirical contribution into the field, follows.

International Business Research and Revised Stages Models

There has been an ongoing debate among international business researchers as to what extent BG firms deviate from conventionally internationalizing firms (Johanson and Vahlne 2003; Luostarinen and Gabrielsson 2006). Much of the research seems to claim that BGs deviate significantly in their behavior from the conventional ones (Wolff and Pett 2000). However, several researchers believe that traditional models are still valid at some level as complementary models, but they need to be extended with new insights (Madsen and Servais 1997; Sharma and Blomstermo 2003; Laanti et al. 2007). In addition, some researchers have brought up the issue that there are a number of stages models that are not equally suited to the examination of BG behavior. It seems evident that BGs do not follow the stages model in different target countries, but deviate less if investigated from the company-level pattern behavior point of view (Luostarinen and Gabrielsson 2006).

The stages models all feature an element of risk-averse behavior, which quite often is not an ingredient of BGs. The proponents of this research stream have addressed this by increasingly emphasizing the more prevalent role of BG networking than that of conventionally internationalizing firms (Madsen and Servais 1997; Johanson and Vahlne; 2003; Gabrielsson and Kirpalani 2004; Coviello 2006; Laanti et al. 2007). This has also been acknowledged by original stages model developers. The original Uppsala stages model (Johanson and Vahlne 1977) was extended to incorporate the existence of networks in the market and the firms' position within it (Johanson and Mattsson 1988), and lately the entire Uppsala stages model has been revised to incorporate the relationship aspects (Johanson and Vahlne 2009). Also, the original Helsinki stages model (Luostarinen 1979) has been developed further to incorporate the cooperative stage in addition to the inward and outward internationalization processes (Luostarinen 1994; Korhonen et al. 1996). Another criticism that has been made with regard to the stages model is that it does not incorporate strongly enough the role of the founder and/or the founding team (Madsen and Servais 1977; Laanti et al. 2007). This is probably one of the reasons for the rapid growth of research in the international entrepreneurship stream that will be reviewed next.

International Entrepreneurship Research and International New Venture Theory

International entrepreneurship researchers are increasingly arguing that the deviations of BG firms are so significant that existing internationalization theories do not explain them, and entirely new theories are needed that better address international new ventures (McDougall et al. 1994). This is because these firms are suffering from three liabilities: smallness, newness, and foreignness. Oviatt and McDougall (ibid.) developed a framework in which they assert that BGs (international new ventures) do not need to own their assets by internalizing their business operations, since, compared to mature organizations, they can rely on alternative governance structures, such as licensing, franchising, and networking. Furthermore, they emphasize that such entrepreneurial firms must possess a unique advantage over indigenous local firms, which is often based on mobility of knowledge and best protected with secrecy. International entrepreneurship research is drawing attention to the characteristics and orientation of the entrepreneur as an important aspect to be studied in order to understand BG behavior (Jones and Coviello 2005). This behavior, which Covin and Slevin (1989) identified to be innovative, proactive, and risk seeking, has become a cornerstone in research. This is well reflected in McDougall and Oviatt's (2000, p. 903) definition of international entrepreneurship as 'a combination of innovative, proactive and risk seeking behavior that crosses national borders and is intended to create value in organizations'.

Furthermore, Oviatt and McDougall (1994) develop a matrix, which results in four types of BG firms based on two dimensions: level of coordination of value chain activities across countries, and number of countries involved. This leaves us with four types: export/import start-ups (minor coordination, few countries addressed), multinational traders (minor coordination, many countries addressed), geographically focused start-ups (many activities coordinated, few countries addressed), and global start-ups (many activities coordinated, many countries addressed). The first two types have received less attention in BG research due to the fact that export/import behavior and MNC behavior are better understood by earlier theories, whereas the last ones have captured more attention. International entrepreneurship researchers have, however, increasingly called for all four types to be studied so that their prevalence under different industry-market conditions, firm capabilities, and entrepreneur-related characteristics could be understood (Zahra 2005). International entrepreneurship researchers maintain that the entrepreneur and his/her level of innovativeness, risk tolerance, and managerial competence is crucial in determining firm internationalization behavior and performance over time (Jones and Coviello 2005). However, the role of industry-market conditions and, particularly, firm capabilities with regard to BG behavior and performance, is an area that international management has started to increasingly address.

International Management Research and Importance of Capabilities

The ability to internationalize early on and succeed in foreign markets can be largely traced back to the capabilities of the firm (Knight and Cavusgil 2004). Management researchers have postulated that there are so-called 'learning advantages of newness', which are particularly important for BG firms (Autio et al. 2000). In other words, an earlier internationalization age will enable faster international growth. The other two attributes that management research is emphasizing are the positive influence of managerial experience and the existence of resource fungibility (Sapienza et al. 2006). The recognition of the importance of managerial experience for BG growth is not a novel finding (Reuber and Fischer 1999). However, what is an important finding is that their adaptability is more important than the amount of resources. This is in line with what dynamic capabilities-based research (Teece et al. 1997) has concluded. Firms must constantly be able to reconfigure their capabilities. Similarly, learning processes should be seen from a dynamic perspective, in other words, learning, but also unlearning, is key to firm capability development (Saarenketo et al. 2004). The latest research in the BG field has started to examine the conditions under which firms can both grow and survive (Sapienza et al. 2006;

Gabrielsson and Gabrielsson 2009). This is an area in which BG research-ers can benefit from international management research.

Empirical Research and Methods Applied

When we examine the empirical research of the early contributors and look at its development, we can identify the following aspects (see also Coviello and Jones 2004 and Rialp et al. 2005):

- a transfer from conceptual and explorative research toward more robust proposition-and hypothesis-based research;
- use of both qualitative and quantitative approaches with some cultural influence–for instance, Scandinavian researchers tend to use more qualitative methodologies than US researchers. A trend toward use of mixed or multiple methods can be seen;
- a transfer of research from single-country-focused research to multiple-country comparative research; and
- a transfer from cross-industry sector research to longitudinal research.

COMMENT ON CHAPTERS WRITTEN BY INVITED AUTHORS

Chapter 2 (Leonidou and Samiee), 'Born global or simply rapidly inter-nationalizing? Review critique, and future prospects', provides a state-of-the-art summary of the historical development, definitions, and key drivers behind the BG phenomenon, and the challenges that this presents to the traditional internationalization theories, and provides useful future research suggestions. These authors note that the research field is still in its early stage of development and much of the research has addressed the BG phenomenon simply as rapid internationalization when setting the criteria on starting time, speed, scale, market scope, and mode of entry. They state that 'although true BGs do exist, they constitute only a very small proportion of firms studied in the extant literature'. We agree with the authors that the current development phase of research has led to the existence of numerous definitions that are not necessarily comparable, and that a commonly agreed-upon definition would be beneficial for compara-tive reasons. However, the different countries and industrial fields from which the BGs originate call for some flexibility. One way, therefore, is to use the criteria provided by the authors for measuring the degree of 'born globalness'. The authors provide a good summary of the aspects in which

BGs typically differ from those firms for which the traditional internation-alization model was developed. Indeed, the gradual acquisition of market knowledge is often replaced by a more rapid pace, successive stages are replaced by suitability of operation mode, the pre-engagement stage on the domestic market may no longer exist, and psychic distance is not dic-tating the order or number of countries entered. The authors progress to explaining the key drivers for this deviating behavior under the grouping of environmental, organizational, and managerial factors. It is easy to agree that this new business environment calls for new theory develop-ment, which can build on existing theories, such as entrepreneurship theory, innovation theory, the resource-based view, the knowledge-based view and dynamic capabilities, but also may call for building a particular BG theory. We welcome the suggestions by the authors to expand the research diversity of countries, industries and research methods to increase the ability to generalize the findings. The pinpointed research suggestions on the changing role of the BG's managerial team, organizational struc-ture and, particularly, marketing function during BG development and performance implications, are important areas to be addressed in future research.

Chapter 3 (Baum, Schwens and Kabst), 'Determinants of different types of born globals,' points out that limited attention has been given to the original four types suggested by Oviatt and McDougall (1994), namely global start-up, geographically focused start-up, multinational trader, and export start-up. The authors examine the differences between these types and postulate propositions on what factors determine their foundation. Based on earlier research, they contend, for instance, that for the emer-gence of global start-ups, prior international experience and social capital stemming from international network contacts is essential. Geographically focused start-ups are found to emerge when a high knowledge-intensive firm is serving a restricted market scope with extensive scale. Multinational traders can benefit from managers that have prior experience of working in international firms, whereas managers of export start-ups require learn-ing capabilities similar to those suggested by the stages model. We believe that the authors are right in suggesting that future research should control for the type of BG under investigation and that the full potential of the original classification by Oviatt and McDougall has not yet been utilized. For instance, research should investigate the dimensions behind this clas-sification, consisting of the number of countries in which the BG firm is involved and the level of coordination that they seek across the foreign countries in which they operate.

Chapter 4 (Sheppard and McNaughton), 'Born global and born-again global firms: a comparison of internationalization patterns', provides insights into the characteristics of a 'born-again global' firm type that, after a long domestic period, 28 years in their Canadian firm-based data, starts to rapidly internationalize/globalize. Their preliminary findings indicate a tendency of born-again global firms to be larger, serve a greater number of foreign markets and have lower proportional R&D investments *vis-à-vis* their revenues than BG firms. Both types of firms are found to invest a relatively high share of revenues in their sales and marketing. We agree with the authors' notion that there are many similarities between these two types of BG firms, but also dissimilarities. We appreciate their conclusion that, resource wise, the born-again globals may be better equipped than born globals. However, they face the challenge of overcoming path dependency and the administrative heritage that BGs do not typically suffer from because of their young age when going abroad and the consequent advantages of learning.

Chapter 5 (Solberg), 'The born global dilemma: trade-off between rapid growth and control', deals with the strategic operation mode and investor timing options of the BG firm, which is confronted by global competition and constrained by its resources. A matrix is developed around two dimensions: level of growth activity and control. The strategic options range from the extreme of active growth and much control to passive growth and little control. Analysis reveals that, whichever strategic quadrant the BG selects, it is facing challenges. The chapter then presents theoretical propositions to be further explored, but also deals with managerial implications. With regard to operation modes, the author suggests avoiding overdependence on one partner without having an option to build up later control. Furthermore, Solberg suggests that BG founders should carefully consider the timing of inviting external investors into the venture to enable effective growth. We welcome this investigation into the speed of growth with respect to the control perspective in mind. We also agree that it is highly important to tie in the timing of inviting external investor finance to the investigation, since this may, in the best case, lead to sufficient finance for the BG firm to gain control of international markets and operations, but at the other extreme risk losing control of the entire firm.

Chapter 6 (Rialp, Galván-Sanchez and García), 'An inquiry into the born global firms' learning process: a case study of information technology-based SMEs', argues that knowledge and learning are essential elements for BG firms' construction of organizational capabilities. Based on a case study of four Spanish BGs, it was concluded that these firms have knowledge-based dynamic capabilities. This was evidenced by the finding that the more advanced knowledge and learning mechanisms the firms possessed, the more favorable was market and customer base expansion. The research area of organizational capabilities, learning, and knowledge patterns is still in an early phase and hence this contribution is very welcome. Future research could benefit from a more parsimonious use of concepts and further development of testable frameworks.

REFERENCES

Autio, E., H. Sapienza and J. Almeida (2000), 'Effects of age at entry, knowledge intensity, and imitability on international growth', *Academy of Management Journal*, **43**(5), 909–24.
Bell, J. (1995), 'The internationalization of small computer software firms: a further challenge to "stage" theories', *European Journal of Marketing*, **29**(8), 60–75.
Chetty, S. and C. Campbell-Hunt (2004), 'A strategic approach to internationalization: a traditional versus a "born-global" approach', *Journal of International Marketing*, **12**(1), 57–81.
Coviello, N.E. (2006), 'The network dynamics of international new ventures', *Journal of International Business Studies*, **37**(5), 713–31.
Coviello, N.E. and M.V. Jones (2004), 'Methodological issues in international entrepreneurship research', *Journal of Business Venturing*, **19**(4), 485–508.
Covin, J.F. and D.P. Slevin (1989), 'Strategic management of small firms in hostile and benign environments', *Strategic Management Journal*, **10**(1), 75–87.
Falay, Z., M. Salimäki, A. Ainamo and M. Gabrielsson (2007), 'Design intensive born globals: a multiple case study of marketing management', *Journal of Marketing Management*, **23**(9–10), 877–99.
Fan, T. and P. Phan (2007), 'International new ventures: revisiting the influences behind the "born global" firm', *Journal of International Business Studies*, **38**(7), 1113–31.
Gabrielsson, Mika and Peter Gabrielsson (2009), 'Survival and failure of born globals: the case of software firms', in Kevin Ibeh and Sheena Davies (eds), *Contemporary Challenges to International Business*, Basingstoke, UK: Palgrave Macmillan, pp. 106–25.
Gabrielsson, M. and V.H.M. Kirpalani (2004), 'Born globals: how to reach new business space rapidly', *International Business Review*, **13**(5), 555–71.
Gabrielsson, M., V.H.M. Kirpalani, P. Dimitratos, C.A. Solberg and A. Zucchella (2008), 'Born globals: propositions to help advance the theory', *International Business Review*, **17**(4), 385–401.
Johanson, Jan and Lars Gunnar Mattsson (1988), 'Internationalization in industrial systems – a network approach', in Neil Hood and Jan-Erik Vahlne (eds), *Strategies in Global Competition*, London: Croom Helm, pp. 287–314.
Johanson, J. and J.-E. Vahlne (1977), 'The internationalization process of the firm– a model of knowledge development and increasing foreign market commitments', *Journal of International Business Studies*, **8**(1), 23–32.
Johanson, J. and J.-E. Vahlne (2003), 'Business relationship learning and commitment in the internationalization process', *Journal of International Entrepreneurship*, **1**(1), 83–101.
Johanson, J. and J.-E. Vahlne (2009), 'The Uppsala internationalization process model revisited: from liability of foreignness to liability of outsidership', *Journal of International Business Studies*, **40**(9), 1411–31.
Jolly, V.K., Matti Alahuhta and Jean-Pierre Jeannet (1991), 'Challenging the incumbents: how high technology start-ups compete globally', *IMD Working Paper Series*, WP 91-003, Institute for Management Development, Lausanne, 1–17.
Jones, M.V. and N.E. Coviello (2005), 'Internationalisation: conceptualising an entrepreneurial process in time', *Journal of International Business Studies*, **36**(3), 284–303.
Knight, G.A. and S.T. Cavusgil (1996), 'The born global firm: a challenge to traditional internationalization theory', in S. Tamer Cavusgil (ed.), *Advances in International Marketing*, Vol. 8, Bingley, UK: Emerald Group Publishing, pp. 11–26.

Knight, G.A. and S.T. Cavusgil (2004), 'Innovation, Organizational Capabilities and the born-global firm', *Journal of International Business Studies*, **30**, 124–41.

Korhonen, H., R. Luostarinen and L. Welch (1996), 'Internationalization of SMEs: inward–outward patterns and government policy, *Management International Review*, **36**(4), 315–29.

Kuivalainen, O., S. Sundqvist, and P. Servais (2007), 'Firms' degree of born-globalness, international entrepreneurial orientation and export performance', *Journal of World Business*, **42**(3), 253–67.

Laanti, R., M. Gabrielsson and P. Gabrielsson (2007), 'The globalization strategies of business-to-business born global firms in the wireless technology industry', *Industrial Marketing Management*, **36**(8), 1104–17.

Levitt, T. (1983), 'The globalization of markets', *Harvard Business Review*, **61**(3), 92–101.

Luostarinen, Reijo (1979), 'Internationalization of the Firm', Doctoral dissertation Helsinki School of Economics, Helsinki.

Luostarinen, Reijo (1994), *Internationalization of Finnish Firms and Their Response to Global Challenges, Research for Action*, WIDER Report, Forssa: United Nations University/WIDER.

Luostarinen, Reijo and Mika Gabrielsson (2004), 'Finnish perspectives of international entrepreneurship', in Léo-Paul Dana (ed.), *Handbook of Research on International Entrepreneurship*, Cheltenham, UK and Northampton, MA, USA: Edward Elgar, pp. 383–403.

Luostarinen, R. and M. Gabrielsson (2006), 'Globalization and marketing strategies of born globals in SMOPECs', *Thunderbird International Business Review*, **48**(6), 773–801.

Madsen, T. and P. Servais (1997), 'The internationalization of born globals – an evolutionary process', *International Business Review*, **6**(6), 1–14.

McDougall, P. and B. Oviatt (2000), 'International entrepreneurship: the intersection of two research paths', *Academy of Management Journal*, **43**(5), 902–6.

McDougall, P.P., S. Shane and B.M. Oviatt (1994), 'Explaining of international new ventures: the limits of theories from international business research', *Journal of Business Venturing*, **9**(6), 469–87.

McKinsey & Co. (1993), *Emerging Exporters: Australia's High Value-added Manufacturing Exports*, Melbourne: McKinsey Company and Australian Manufacturing Council.

Oviatt, B.M. and P.P. McDougall (1994), 'Toward a theory of international new ventures', *Journal of International Business Studies*, **25**(1), 45–64.

Oviatt, B.M. and P.P. McDougall (1995), 'Global start-ups: entrepreneurs on a worldwide stage', *Academy of Management Executive*, **9**(2), 30–43.

Preece, S.B., G. Mills and. M.C. Baetz (1999), 'Explaining the international intensity and global diversity of early-stage technology-based firms', *Journal of Business Venturing*, **14**(3), 259–81.

Rennie, M.W. (1993), 'Global competitiveness: born global', *The McKinsey Quarterly*, **4**, 45–52.

Reuber, A.R. and E. Fischer (1999), 'Understanding the consequences of founders' experience', *Journal of Small Business Management*, **37**(2), 30–45.

Rialp, A., J. Rialp and G. Knight (2005), 'The phenomenon of early internationalizing firms: what do we know after a decade (1993–2003) of scientific inquiry?', *International Bsuiness Review*, **14**(2), 147–66.

Saarenketo, S., K. Puumalainen, O. Kuivalainen and K. Kyläheiko (2004), 'Dynamic knowledge-related learning processes in internationalizing high-tech SMEs', *International Journal of Production Economics*, **89**(3), 363–78.

Sapienza, H.J., E. Autio, G. George and S. Zahra (2006), 'A capabilities perspective on the effects of early internationalization on firm survival and growth', *Academy of Management Review*, **31**(4), 914–33.

Servais, P., T.K. Madsen and E.S. Rasmussen (2007), 'Small manufacturing firms' involvement in international e-business activities', *Advances in International Marketing*, **17**, 297–317.

Sharma, D. and A. Blomstermo (2003), 'The internationalisation process of born globals: a network view', *International Business Review*, **12**(6), 739–53.

Teece, D.J., G. Pisano and A. Shuen (1997), 'Dynamic capabilities and strategic management', *Strategic Management Journal*, **18**(7), 509–33.

Wolff, J.A. and T.L. Pett (2000), 'Internationalization of small firms: an examination of export competitive patterns, firm size, and export performance', *Journal of Small Business Management*, **38**(2), 34–47.

Yip, G.S. (1989), 'Global strategy . . . in a world of nations?', *Sloan Management Review*, **31**(1), 29–41.

Zahra, S.A. (2005), 'A theory of international new ventures: a decade of research', *Journal of International Business Studies*, **36**(1), 20–28.

Zhou, L., B.R. Barnes and Y. Lu (2010), 'Entrepreneurial proclivity, capability upgrading and performance advantage of newness among international new ventures', *Journal of International Business Studies*, **41**(5), 882–905.

Zuchella, A., S. Danicolai and G. Palamara (2007), 'The drivers of the early internationalization of the firm', *Journal of World Business*, **42**(3), 268–80.

2 Born global or simply rapidly internationalizing? Review, critique, and future prospects
Leonidas C. Leonidou and Saeed Samiee

INTRODUCTION

The technological, social, and corporate transitions predicated some three decades ago by Levitt (1983) in his influential and controversial *Harvard Business Review* article, 'The globalization of markets', appear to have served as instrumental levers in setting the tone, manner, and direction for patterns of the internationalization of firms. It is noteworthy that a number of key international institutional transformations that are now a reality were not even planned when Levitt's publication appeared in print.[1] Collectively, these changes serve to further solidify the basic principles he advocated. A consequence of the relatively rapid changes in the business environment along technological (for example, transportation, communications), competitive (for example, market entry by new competitors, including electronic commerce), and regulatory and trade (for example, lower tariffs, ease of conducting cross-border business) dimensions has been the intensification of international business activities, particularly exporting, by an increasing number of firms.

In the late 1980s, business publications were perhaps the first to report on the shifting tides and emergence of ventures that were essentially international from the start. Attention was initially drawn to the phenomenon when the first articles referring to successful cases of early and rapidly internationalizing firms appeared in the popular business press (Gupta 1989; Mamis 1989). Although it is less clear exactly when the terms 'born international' or 'born global' were coined, observers attribute them to academic scholars who investigated the topic in the late 1980s and early 1990s. The earliest academic use of the term 'born international' is likely to have been by Ray (1989) in a conference paper. Later, the use of 'born international' and its variations, such as 'global start-ups', 'international new ventures', and 'instant internationals', was intensified (for example, McDougall and Brush 1991; McDougall and Oviatt 1991; Oviatt et al. 1993; McDougall et al. 1994; Preece et al. 1999).

The born global (BG) phenomenon has aroused a great deal of enthusiasm, leading to a growing list of scholarly publications in academic journals. However, despite two decades of scholarly inquiry about BGs, the nature of the topic and its future remain tenuous, leading some scholars to believe that there is still more to be learned about their international business involvement (Rialp et al. 2005; Zahra 2005). A key issue clouding the BG phenomenon, which we shall address later, is the lack of convergence in the definitions and operationalization of BG as a separate and unique entity. Hence, our goal is first, to examine the BG phenomenon and its treatment in the extant literature and, second, to broadly review and present a critique of the BG literature, suggesting future directions for exploration of the topic. To achieve this, we shall focus exclusively on scholarly contributions with a BG theme.

HISTORICAL BACKGROUND

The BG phenomenon has received increasing attention since the late 1980s and much scholarly effort has been devoted to exploring, understanding, and explaining the concept (for example, Brush 1992; McDougall et al. 1994; Oesterle 1997; Autio et al. 2000; Freeman and Cavusgil 2007). Oviatt and McDougall (1994, p. 29) give an excellent historical account of the BG phenomenon:

> Since the late 1980s, the popular business press has been reporting, as a new and growing phenomenon, the establishment of new ventures that are international from inception (Brokaw 1990; *The Economist* 1992, 1993; Gupta 1989; Mamis 1989). These start-ups often raise capital, manufacture, and sell products on several continents, particularly in advanced technology industries where many established competitors are already global.

The term 'born global' refers to firms that have globalized their business activities by the use of methods that circumvent the traditional approach to international business engagement (Knight and Cavusgil 1996; Autio et al. 2000). In much of the writing to date, globalization, or at least the internationalization of the firm from its inception, is either stated or implied. The use of the word 'born', for example, is indicative of globalization from the firm's inception. As described, from the time they are established, these organizations try to gain competitive advantage by exploiting business opportunities in multiple foreign markets (Oviatt and McDougall 1994, p. 46). In other words, they are *not* characterized by an incremental progression on the internationalization path, as suggested by various 'stages models', whereby firms are first fully devoted to the home market, then begin their international operations with a low level of involvement, and subsequently increase their commitment to international markets (Johanson and Wiedersheim-Paul 1975; Johanson and Vahlne 1977).

Since BGs are by definition new firms, as such, they tend to be smaller than their rivals until some time has passed. There is some evidence, however, that the more internationally energized firms which begin exporting activities earlier, as is the case for BGs, achieve greater success than their counterparts (Moen and Servais 2002). A study by McKinsey & Co. (1993), conducted in Australia, revealed that a notable number of small firms are engaged in international operations from their inception, competing successfully against large firms which are already established in global markets. According to OECD (1997), approximately 1–2 percent of newly established business units are international at inception, while the internationalization of the activities of these emerging firms grows at an accelerating pace.

This has prompted some scholars (for example, McDougall 1989; Brush 1992) to systematically examine the BG phenomenon from an academic perspective. It is widely acknowledged that the foundation of this new stream of research has been set by the landmark study by Oviatt and McDougall (1994). Since then, numerous studies on the subject in different contexts (for example, countries, industries, products), have promoted the growing role that BGs play in many parts of the world.

DEFINING AND OPERATIONALIZING OF 'BORN GLOBAL'

Although the term 'born global' is the common terminology for referring to firms that do not seem to fit the traditional internationalization models (for example, Knight and Cavusgil 1996; Kirpalani and Luostarinen 1999; Autio et al. 2000), as noted earlier, other terms have also been used in the international business literature: 'international new ventures' (for example, McDougall et al. 1994), 'global start-ups' (for example, Oviatt and McDougal' 1994), 'born internationals' (for example, Majkgård and Sharma 1999), 'instant internationals' (for example, Dana 2001), 'gazelles' (for example, Birch 2001), 'global knowledge-intensive firms' (for example, Almor 2000), 'new technology-based firms' (for example, Autio 1995), and 'high-technology start-ups' (for example, Alahuhta 1990). Obviously, this differentiation in the terms used to describe BGs creates unnecessary confusion and, for the purposes of this study, we use 'born global', which shares similar characteristics with other terms.

The most commonly used definition of a BG firm is that proposed by Oviatt and McDougall (1994, p.46), who state that: 'it is a business organization that, from inception, seeks to derive significant competitive advantage from the sales of outputs in multiple countries'. This essentially expresses a vision and strategy by the management team of viewing the world as the firm's marketplace from its outset, which has also been used in the BG definitions offered by other researchers (for example, Rennie 1993; Knight and Cavusgil 1996; Gabrielsson and Kirpalani 2004). Selecting a definition for their study, Gabrielsson and Kirpalani observe that scholars have used a variety of criteria to operationalize BGs, including:

> (1) vision and strategy to become global/international (for example, Knight and Cavusgil 1996; Oviatt and McDougall 1994), (2) small technology-oriented companies (for example, Bell 1995; Knight and Cavusgil 1996), (3) time to become global/international, varying from immediate to three years (for example, Knight et al. 2001; Knight and Cavusgil 1996), (4) geographical expansion in terms of a minimum of 25% of foreign sales (for example, Knight and Cavusgil 1996) or a minimum number of countries served outside the home country (for example, Oviatt and McDougall 1994), and (5) geographical expansion outside the home continent with a minimum of 50% external sales (Luostarinen and Gabrielsson 2004). (p. 557)

Assuming that these studies are indeed investigating BGs, a BG firm can be defined as one that meets all of these criteria. However, to a large extent, these criteria seem arbitrary and attempting to meet all of them would make the sample rather small. A problem posed by the lack of convergence in defining and operationalizing the unit of analysis, on the other hand, is that it becomes difficult to compare results and generalize the reported findings to a larger population (Gabrielsson and Kirpalani 2004).

A number of researchers (for example, Rennie 1993; Knight and Cavusgil 1996; Chetty and Campbell-Hunt 2004; Luostarinen and Gabrielsson 2004) have used more quantitative definitions for BGs, centering on four major criteria: (a) the time that elapses between a company being set up and becoming international (ranging from immediate up to eight years); (b) percentage of foreign sales as part of total corporate sales (ranging from 75 to 100 percent); (c) percentage of foreign sales generated outside the home continent (ranging from 25 to 50 percent); and (d) minimum number of countries served beyond the home market.

Our examination of the BG literature reveals no convergence in either the definition or operationalization of BGs. As stated earlier and implied by the word 'born', as per Oviatt and McDougall (1994), BGs by definition should be international at inception. Although such cases tend to be more of an exception, international activities from inception constitute just one indication of rapid internationalization. Clearly, the magnitude of international involvement must carry an even greater weight than, say, small-scale sporadic exporting at inception. Greater involvement in international sales is dependent on much higher degrees of procedural matters, market knowledge, and resource commitment, including the start-up's organizational structure, than ventures that derive the vast majority of their revenues and profits from their domestic markets.

Given that few firms are actually born international, the 'rapid internationalization' slant pursued in a number of studies is a reasonable alternative for culling firms that are truly different from their counterparts. Clearly, a definition that incorporates foreign sales growth rate and a minimum threshold for foreign sales can assist in homing in on rapidly internationalizing firms, generically referred to as BGs.

CHALLENGES TO TRADITIONAL INTERNATIONALIZATION THEORIES

For the most part, studies focusing on BG firms or international new ventures challenge the traditional process-based view (for example, Hedlund and Kverneland 1985; Turnbull 1987; Sullivan and Bauerschmidt 1990; Samiee and Walters 1991; Bell 1995; Coviello and Munro 1995; Knight and Cavusgil 1996; Oviatt and McDougall 1997; Chetty and Campbell-Hunt 2004). Although the process-based view of internationalization advocated by Luostarinen (1970), Johanson and Wiedersheim-Paul (1975), Bilkey and Tesar (1977), Johanson and Vahlne (1977), Cavusgil (1980), and others is widely accepted, it has not been without its critics. Hedlund and Kverneland (1985) demonstrated that the export pattern of Swedish firms in Japan did not follow the Uppsala model, concluding that firms can potentially bypass some critical stages in the model, due largely to the changes in the external environment. For example, one-half of the Swedish firms studied by Hedlund and Kverneland transitioned from using a local agent to establishing manufacturing facilities in Japan, thereby bypassing the sales subsidiary stage advocated by the Uppsala model (Johanson and Vahlne 1977). Thus, it is argued that such firms had already acquired the necessary knowledge to make a more serious commitment to Japan and, therefore, it was not necessary for them to go through this stage. A number of other studies examining the internationalization patterns of firms have confirmed that there is virtually always a subset of firms that internationalize more rapidly. Brush (1992), for example, demonstrated that 13 percent of US firms included in her sample began exporting during their first year of operation. Whether these observations debase the stages model of internationalization is open to debate. The stages models are indeed intuitively sound and have the backing of numerous empirical studies. On the other hand, the emergence and perhaps the proliferation of rapidly internationalizing enterprises, as well as firms skipping certain stages of internationalization advocated by the stages models, are also a reality.

Traditional theory views the firm's involvement in international activities as a sequential process, which is the outcome of the interplay between the development of foreign experiential knowledge and the increasing commitment of organizational resources (Johanson and Vahlne 1977, 1990). Specifically, the internationalization mechanism assumes that gradually market knowledge and commitment affect commitment decisions and the way current activities are performed, and these in turn influence market knowledge and commitment. Such a gradual approach to international markets is not applicable in the case of BGs, where organizational learning occurs at a rapid pace, due to the possession of superior knowledge about foreign markets from a very early stage (Chetty and Campbell-Hunt 2004).

Another dimension challenged by BGs has to do with the several identifiable and distinct *successive stages* characterizing the firm's movement along the internationalization path, with higher-level stages indicating greater foreign involvement. For instance, Johanson and Wiedersheim-Paul (1975) suggest that firms pass through four distinctive stages in their internationalization, beginning with no regular export activities, export via independent representatives (agent), sales subsidiary, and ending with manufacturing via foreign direct investment (FDI). However, in the case of BGs, such stages do not exist and the initial foreign market entry mode may take any form, ranging from exporting, licensing, joint ventures, and even FDI.

Traditional theories of internationalization also stress the role of the pre-engagement phase to internationalization, whereby the firm first *develops its domestic market* and then thinks about the possibility of selling abroad (Leonidou and Katsikeas 1996). In fact, some scholars posit that before its début in international operations, the firm undergoes an 'extra-regional domestic expansion', that is, it begins selling in one region of the home market and gradually expands to other regions until saturation is reached (Wiedersheim-Paul, et al. 1978; Welch and Wiedersheim-Paul 1980). However, the domestic market for BGs is largely irrelevant because the majority of, if not all, corporate sales is derived from international business activities.

A key concept underlying traditional internationalization theory is that of 'psychic distance' which is defined as the sum of factors interrupting the flow of information between the firm and the specific foreign market (Johanson and Wiedersheim-Paul 1975; Johanson and Vahlne 1977). Psychic distance leads firms to initially target countries that they perceive as being closer to their home markets, and are therefore presumably less risky to enter. This distance is gradually reduced due to increased market-specific knowledge, which in turn allows the firm to extend its activities to more psychologically distant countries. Thus, the firm approaches international markets in a cautious manner in order to minimize uncertainty, reduce costs, and avoid mistakes (Welch and Luostarinen 1993). In the case of BGs, the concept of psychic distance is likely to be affected by the urgency and speed with which they internationalize. In the electronics industry, for example, the urgency to internationalize is greater and, therefore, firms take much greater risks by entering psychologically distant markets.

Traditional theory claims that during the early stages of internationalization firms tend to concentrate on a few foreign markets, but as they advance in their international operations there is a tendency to diversify to a larger number of markets (Piercy 1981). This is because: (a) there is greater availability of organizational resources as the firm advances to higher levels of internationalization, allowing for a broader market focus; (b) the market spreading strategy helps to diversify risks and exploit opportunities better than a market concentration approach; and (c) the problems associated with handling different foreign markets tend to decline as the firm acquires more international experience (Naidu and Prasad 1994; Dalli 1995). The gradual increase in the number of foreign markets is not applicable in the case of BGs, since from their very inception they serve multiple foreign markets simultaneously.

KEY DRIVERS BEHIND THE BG PHENOMENON

The emergence and existence of BG organizations could be ascribed to numerous factors, which can be classified as environmental, organizational, and managerial.

Environmental Factors

The changes in environmental forces (Levitt 1983), particularly over the last three decades, are to a large extent responsible for the emergence of firms that can rapidly internationalize or even be international at inception. The transformation of external forces was initially slow, but has accelerated as, for example, more nations have joined the WTO, or as the European Union expanded. As more nations join the world trade body, others find it desirable, if not necessary, to also join the organization.

The growing *convergence of consumer tastes and needs* around the world, as a result of rising disposable incomes, increasing consumer mobility, and intensifying economic trade integration, offers fertile ground for instant internationalization (Gabrielsson et al. 2008). As noted earlier, Levitt (1983) acknowledged the presence of conditions that permit globalization of markets. Clearly, when customer needs converge, firms can leverage off the uniformity in demand and develop strategies for concurrent market entry in multiple markets. As a result, BGs tend to view the world from the very beginning as a potential market, instead of confining themselves to the home market. The economies of scale associated with simultaneously selling to multiple foreign markets are very attractive, leading to reduced costs per unit, while allowing the firm to achieve increased sales. This does not imply that the BG firm will always adopt a blanket approach to all foreign markets, but rather that they will choose those that have the greatest potential (Berry et al., 2002).

The *regulatory environment* of a firm's home market may also force it to go global from inception. In fact, this is perhaps the key reason why some firms go international from their establishment. In the pharmaceutical industry, for example, each new product must undergo an extensive testing and approval procedure that in some countries, for example, the United States, can take many years. Such procedures vary considerably in the time required from one country to the next and in some cases drugs can be approved much more quickly. Thus, newcomers to this industry are often truly BGs.

Competitive pressure on a global scale and the need to confront competitors proactively and quickly in their strong markets, as well as the increasing requirements of customers for global sourcing, are other factors responsible for the growing *dynamism* of many of the markets today. In these markets, firms have to operate in a quick, efficient, and holistic manner if they want to successfully exploit any international business opportunities (Crick and Spence 2005; Dimitratos and Jones 2005). The dynamic situation of foreign markets provides fertile ground for BGs, since right from inception they attempt to move rapidly in order to take advantage of opportunities that can emerge and disappear rapidly.

An impetus to BG internationalization has also been given by significant advancements in *production, transportation, and communication technologies* (Zahra et al. 2000; Moen and Servais 2002). New manufacturing technologies allow for more economically small-scale production of goods, as well as for a more specialized, customized, and niche approach to the market, which characterizes BGs. Transportation improvements have also allowed BGs to have more frequent, reliable, and cheaper movement of products between countries. Finally, the widespread diffusion of communication technologies (for example, internet, cellular phones, facsimile) has been helpful to BGs by facilitating access to foreign market information, initiating and building business relationships beyond national boundaries, and developing and implementing strategies at a global level.

BGs also tend to flourish in countries with *small and open economies*, such as Australia (Rennie 1993), Ireland (Knight et al. 2001), and Finland (Kirpalani and Luostarinen 1999). In these countries, the founders of BGs recognize the limited potential of the domestic market (for example, for corporate growth, sales generation, and economies of scale) and therefore seek, from the very beginning, to identify and exploit opportunities in international markets (Luostarinen and Gabrielsson 2004). The small size of the domestic market in such nations has been cited as one of the reasons for small firms to begin exporting (Leonidou et al. 2007), but the prevailing conditions in these markets have also given rise to a disproportionate number of BGs.

The prevailing *conditions in a given industry* can also be highly influential in forcing firms to internationalize rapidly or simply to internationalize at inception. Although the literature has examined BG firms belonging to a range of industries (Moen 2002; McDougall and Oviatt 2003), the high-technology sectors (for example, information technology, biotechnology) appear to be dominant (Knight and Cavusgil 1996; Madsen and Servais 1997; Sharma and Blomstermo 2003; Rialp et al. 2005). In some high-technology sectors, it is essential to internationalize rapidly for access to a broader market, simply because that is the only way to survive. Not surprisingly, technology-based firms have been shown to derive a larger proportion of their revenues from international markets when management holds positive views towards internationalization (Preece et al. 1999). In particular, to be financially viable, high-technology electronics firms require rapid sales growth through international expansion. Capital outlays associated with each generation of microchip platforms, for example, are very high and tend to change rapidly. Newer platforms have a higher yield, which significantly increases the fabrication rate. Concurrently, the technologies for which manufacturing platforms are designed tend to have relatively short life cycles. These conditions virtually force firms to go international, either from inception or very shortly afterwards (Freeman et al. 2006). In other words, internationalization is not an option, rather it is a must if the firm wishes to remain viable. In some high-technology electronics firms, such as communications chips, business viability is also dependent on the setting of international standards. This can be achieved through global collaboration with other parties (for example, Philips and Sony setting the standards for audio CD), or an advanced technology and rapid global introduction of the innovation. It is therefore not surprising that research indicates that high-technology firms internationalize rapidly, irrespective of size or inception date (Burrill and Almassy 1993).

One environmental change that is seldom mentioned in the BG literature is associated with the *internationalization of higher education*. As more schools and universities promote internationalization and offer international courses, encourage students to spend a semester abroad, offer international business or management degrees, and incorporate an international flavor in their expanding MBA programs, they heighten awareness, interest, knowledge, and experience in international business during students' formative years. As a result, students entering the job market today are relatively more 'international' in perspective and knowledge than their predecessors. Governments have also had a hand in the educational transformation. In the US, for example, the Department of Education has been offering large, multi year grants to universities to expand their international business education, research, and related activities. Likewise, the United States Information Agency has been funding international educational endeavors in many countries and across multiple disciplines.[2] Taken together, it then seems natural that newer firms, presumably established by a new generation of 'internationalized' entrepreneurs, would more rapidly embrace overseas expansion (Moen and Servais 2002).

Organizational Factors

The possession of an *innovative product* (that is, unique characteristics, superior design, high-quality focus, or other highly specialized competence) is also a key characteristic of BG firms (Gabrielsson and Kirpalani 2004; Knight and Cavusgil 2004). This is because an innovative product, which is aesthetically, functionally, and strategically superior to competing products, is a necessary ingredient when adopting a niche business strategy (Kirpalani and Luostarinen 1999). Due to their small size, BGs find it less risky and costly to protect themselves; they are narrow segments in global markets (Madsen et al. 2000). Studies have shown that the innovative capability of the BG firm has a powerful effect on achieving a successful globalization process (Madsen and Servais 1997; Karagozoglu and Lindell 1998; Yip 2000; Jones and Coviello 2005).

The extent to which a firm is *customer oriented* may also influence the speed of its international market entry. Successful technology start-ups attract large customers, who tend to have an extensive international market presence. As such, high-tech start-ups may enter international markets simply to serve customers who require their suppliers to accompany them abroad and supply them with raw materials/components wherever they operate (Oviatt and McDougall 1997).

Successful BGs are characterized by an *organizational culture*, which consists of four major dimensions: (a) *proactiveness*, that is, actively pursuing foreign market opportunities rather than simply reacting to competitors' movements; (b) *risk-taking*, that is, a tendency to undertake risk associated with business ventures in overseas markets; (c) *innovativeness*, that is, the ability to develop new ideas, products, and services, as well as finding creative solutions to business problems; and (d) *flexibility*, that is, the ability to adjust quickly to different environments and accommodate unexpected problems that may arise in international markets. Most of these dimensions have often been found among young as opposed to established firms, because the former are more receptive to new knowledge, practices, and operations than the latter (Oviatt and McDougall 1994; Barkema and Vermeulen 1998; Autio et al. 2000).

Another important organizational characteristic of BGs is their networking ability with distributors, financiers, subcontractors, sellers, and customers in international markets (Oviatt and McDougall 1995; Knight and Cavusgil 1996). Such networks offer commercial, technical, financial, and allied resources that are vital for the globalization of BGs, which under other circumstances would take many years to develop (Madsen and Servais 1997; Karagozoglu and Lindell 1998; Baum et al. 2000). BG networks can be of either a formal or an informal nature (McAuley 1999), as well as take place in either a local or an international context. Irrespective of its nature and origin, networks possess valuable market and experiential knowledge, which is crucial for BGs when assessing the potential of operating successfully in foreign markets.

Managerial Factors

A key factor conducive to the appearance of BGs is the *entrepreneurial behavior* of the manager, which incorporates elements of innovativeness, proactiveness, and a risk-taking approach (Knight and Cavusgil 1996; Madsen and Servais 1997; McAuley 1999; McDougall and Oviatt 2000; Zahra and George 2002). Such behavior is crucial to offering new products, entering new markets, and introducing new ideas, which are vital for the establishment, development, and sustainment of BG operations (Oviatt and McDougall 1994).

The tendency of the manager to have a *global mindset*, the latter implying his/her propensity to engage in visionary and proactive behavior in order to realize strategic objectives in foreign markets, is also a key feature of many BGs (Harveston et al. 2000; Knight and Cavusgil 2004). Such a global mindset is more likely to develop among managers who have been educated abroad, have lived in foreign countries, and are good linguists (Reuber and Fischer 1997).

A number of studies also point to the fact that BGs have *managers* with a high level of *experience in international matters*, which is gained before the firm's inception in the market (Oviatt and McDougall 1994; Madsen and Servais 1997; McDougall et al. 2003). Although the international experience of managers has often been cited as facilitating the engagement of firms in international business in general (Leonidou et al. 1998), it is particularly important in the case of BGs, due to the lack of any previous knowledge at the firm level (Autio 2005). The facilitating role of managerial experience is more evident when it is related to the specific industry in which the BG firm is operating (Madsen and Servais 1997). The manager is able to take advantage of personal contacts, customer links, and the market knowledge acquired during his/her previous work experience (Oviatt and McDougall 1997; Crick and Jones 2000; Moen and Servais 2002; Sharma and Blomstermo 2003).

BG INTERNATIONALIZATION CONFIGURATION

Six major dimensions have been used by researchers in the field to describe a firm as a BG. The first has to do with the *starting time*, that is, the time that elapses between the establishment of the BG firm and its début in international markets. Although early definitions of BGs refer to the initiation of international operations from the moment the firm is founded, most empirical studies define a specific time period, ranging from two (Rennie 1993; Moen and Servais 2002) to eight (McDougall et al. 1994) years. Obviously, such diversity in specifying the time span between a company's inception and its internationalization indicates the absence of an objective definition for BGs and/or arbitrariness in the operationalization of the BG phenomenon, rather than an absolute, theoretically-based measure (see Chetty and Campbell-Hunt 2004).[3]

Another configuration dimension is the *speed* with which the firm *internationalizes*, usually depending on the company's ability to accommodate the problems and complexities involved in foreign markets (Vermeulen and Barkema 2002). BGs are characterized by rapid internationalization growth, which is largely attributed to the low organizational inertia associated with their youthful nature (Autio et al. 2000). In measuring internationalization speed, most researchers take the time period between the moment the firm entered international markets and the moment data were collected from sample firms.

The *scale of internationalization*, that is, the extent to which the firm's activities are related to international operations, has also been used to define a BG firm. To measure this scale dimension, most researchers have used the proportion of sales derived from international activities as the proportion of total corporate sales. Although there is no consensus in the literature as to the level of international sales intensity, the most common ratio used in many BG studies (for example, Knight and Cavusgil 1996; Madsen et al. 2000; Moen 2002) is 25 percent. However, this cut-off point has been criticized on several grounds. First, it is arbitrary and probably reflects the exploratory status of this line of research. It is also relatively low, especially in the case of BGs originating from small countries and operating knowledge-intensive industries. McKinsey & Co. (1993) considers 75 percent export intensity within two years of inception as the appropriate scale of internationalization for BGs.

Another dimension is *market scope*, that is, the number of countries to which the BG sells its products. Almost from inception, BGs sell to multiple countries, indicating that their international activities are more than just a few export accounts (see Oviatt and McDougall 1994). However, there are no clear definitions in the extant empirical literature as to the number of countries and the geographical locations to which BGs are expected to sell.

The final configuration dimension concerns the *mode of entry* into foreign markets. The limited resources and knowledge intensity characterizing BGs imply that most would opt to enter international markets using the exporting mode (which can range from domestic export houses to direct export sales) (Madsen et al. 2000). The BG firm is also very likely to cultivate collaboration with various partners in the foreign market, such as agents and distributors, as well as through piggybacking. For BGs, the FDI venue is not particularly attractive as a foreign market entry mode, although other less resource-intensive options, such as contract manufacturing, licensing, and joint venturing, are more plausible.

CONCLUSIONS AND FUTURE DIRECTIONS

Despite the relatively recent nature of the BG phenomenon, research on the subject has grown significantly, establishing a body of knowledge within the wider sphere of international business. However, this line of research appears still to be in an early stage of development, as demonstrated by the lack of theoretical underpinnings, the absence of a relatively uniform definition and operationalization, the descriptive and exploratory nature of most of the studies, the existence of many unexplored issues, and the appearance of different (and sometimes contradictory) findings.

Our conclusion from the review of the extant literature is that the term 'born global' is almost invariably used to refer to rapidly internationalizing firms. Although true BGs do exist, they constitute only a very small proportion of firms studied in the extant literature. Nevertheless, the literature has prompted scholars to consider an increasing number of pertinent dimensions and to design more objectively angled studies, as would be expected while the area of inquiry begins to establish itself. However, there is still much to be done before this area reaches maturity.

First, research on BGs has been atheoretic in general, largely owing to the fact that it is a relatively new and unknown phenomenon (Madsen and Servais 1997; Rialp et al. 2005). Some theories that have been proposed, at times, to explain the BG phenomenon are: entrepreneurship theory (Kirzner 1973), innovation theory (Miller and Friesen 1982), the resource-based view (Barney 1991; Collis 1991), the knowledge-based view (Grant 1996), and the dynamic capabilities view (Teece et al. 1997). However, these have only been used tangentially to back conceptual thinking and empirical models on the subject. Thus, it is important to embark on a more systematic use of relevant theories in future research, as well as gradually build a theory of BGs themselves.

As mentioned earlier, there is great discrepancy among researchers as to the criteria used to classify a firm as a BG, which poses serious problems when attempting to draw comparisons among the findings of empirical studies. Researchers in the field need to embark on a commonly agreed definition of BGs (for example, starting time, speed of internationalization, market scope, and so on) to be used in future studies on the subject. It is also important to identify and properly operationalize key constructs associated with the BG phenomenon that can be systematically employed to assess the validity of relevant conceptual models.

Most BG research has been conducted in small, developed countries, which may question the generalizability of their findings to other countries. It would be useful to extend this research to larger countries (for example, Germany), newly industrialized countries (for example, Brazil), and countries with a high involvement in international trade (for example, China). The fact that the emphasis of most studies was on specific industrial sectors relating mainly to high technology, poses some problems as regards the generalization of research findings to other industrial settings. It is important therefore to extend the investigation into the BG phenomenon to more traditional industries (for example, food and beverages), as well as draw comparisons across different industrial sectors.

With a few exceptions, the bulk of BG empirical studies have used the case study rather than the survey approach to collect data. Although this method produces in-depth information of high quality, the fact that most studies focused on a small number of firms (sometimes falling as low as six) also causes a generalization problem. More large-scale, quantitative surveys would yield more representative information on BGs. This would also allow a more sophisticated statistical analysis of the data collected and reveal any causal associations among the key parameters describing the BG phenomenon.

Another weakness of extant research on BGs relates to the cross-sectional approach adopted by almost all empirical studies on the subject. However, by definition, the nature of the BG phenomenon is very dynamic, which needs to be captured by the use of a longitudinal approach. Some of the reasons cited in support of this approach are: (a) the changing synthesis of the BG firm's managerial team during the rapid internationalization process and business growth; (b) the changing organizational resources and capabilities required by the BG firm to succeed along the internationalization path; and (c) the changing conditions in the international economic, political–legal, technological, and other environments surrounding the BG firm's operations (Falay et al. 2007).

Finally, empirical research in the field deals exclusively with BGs, without substantiating existing differences between ordinary exporters and BGs as regards the firm and managerial characteristics and strategies deployed. The identification of such differences is vital to segmenting BG firms and defining the profile of each group. It is also crucial to link the BG phenomenon to other key functional areas in international business. In particular, marketing is a critical function in such firms, but little is known about how these firms develop their international marketing so rapidly, how they identify and establish distribution network connections, the extent to which their strategy is standardized or adapted, and the implications of the BG marketing strategy choice on business performance.

NOTES

1. Some major developments that have accelerated globalization moves include: the Uruguay Round of GATT (General Agreement on Tariffs and Trade) negotiations which began in 1986, paving the way for the creation of the World Trade Organization (WTO) in 1995; the European Commission's White Paper published in 1985 and the Single European Act, leading to the creation of an economically more unified Europe in 1993, which was passed in 1987; MERCOSUR (Southern American Common Market) becoming a functioning trade body in 1991; NAFTA (North American Free Trade Agreement) eventually becoming reality in 1994; and the rapid expansion of the internet as a means of fast and relatively inexpensive communications for firms and their customers.
2. The European Union offers financial backing for a range of international education activities and most EU members independently pursue similar goals. Austria, for example, has a significant educational commitment for Eastern European nations that

is implemented through various educational institutions. Indeed, a number of MBA and undergraduate programs within Europe are taught on multiple university campuses and in several languages, even though increasingly English is the language of choice. The Korean government offers significant internationalization grants to both state and private universities. Virtually all major universities offer graduate and executive MBA programs that are entirely in English and many include visiting professors and short international field trips.

3. The lack of attention given to this critical conceptual and method-related dimension was evident in our review of the BG literature. For example, none of the studies we reviewed defines and operationalizes 'born global', as reflected by its label, that is, international at inception (see Oviatt and McDougall 1994). As a result, much of the research to date is focused on rapidly internationalizing firms. In other words, the BG term is used as a convenient label to broadly refer to all firms that rapidly internationalize.

REFERENCES

Alahuhta, Matti (1990), 'Global growth strategies for high technology challengers', doctoral dissertation, Helsinki University of Technology, Helsinki Electrical Engineering Series, No. 66.

Almor, T. (2000), 'Born global: the case of small and medium-sized born global knowledge-intensive Istaeli firms', in T. Almor and T. Hashai (eds), *FDI International Trade, and Economic peacemaking*, Rishon Le Zion, Israel: College of Management, Academic Studies Division.

Autio, Erkoo (1995), 'Symplectic and generative impacts of new, technology-based firms in innovation networks: an international comparative study', doctoral dissertation, Helsinki University of Technology, Helsinki.

Autio, E. (2005), 'Creative tension: the significance of Ben Oviatt's and Patricia McDougall's article "Toward a theory of international new ventures"', *Journal of International Business Studies*, **36**(1), 9–19.

Autio, E., H.J. Sapienza and J.G. Almeida (2000), 'Effects of age at entry, knowledge intensity, and imitability on international growth', *Academy of Management Journal*, **43**, 909–24.

Barkema, H.G. and F. Vermeulen (1998), 'International expansion through start-up or acquisition: a learning perspective', *Academy of Management Journal*, February, **41**(1), 7–26.

Barney, J. (1991), 'Firm resources and sustained competitive advantage', *Journal of Management*, **17**(1), 99–120.

Baum, J.A.C., T. Calabrese and B.S. Silverman (2000), 'Don't go alone: alliance network composition and startups' performance in Canadian biotechnology', *Strategic Management Journal*, **21**(3), 267–94.

Bell, J. (1995), 'The internalization of small computer software firms: a further challenge to "Stage" theories', *European Journal of Marketing*, **29**(8), 60–75.

Berry, Maureen, Pavlos Dimitratos and Michael McDermott (2002), 'Globalisation and the smaller firm: reconcilable notions?', in Frank McDonald, Heinz Tuselmann and Colin Wheeler (eds), *International Business: Adjusting to New Challenges and Opportunities*, Basingstoke, UK and New York: Palgrave, pp. 247–57.

Bilkey, W.J. and G. Tesar (1977), 'The export behavior of smaller-sized Wisconsin manufacturing firms', *Journal of International Business Studies*, **8** (spring/summer), 93–8.

Birch, D. (2001), 'Small business 2001: the gazelles theory', *Small Business*, **23**(7), 28–9.

Brokaw, L. (1990), 'Foreign affairs', *Inc.*, November, 92–104.

Brush, Candida G. (1992), 'Factors motivating small companies to internationalize: the effect of firm age', doctoral dissertation, School of Management, Boston University, Boston, MA.

Burrill, G.S. and S.E. Almassy (1993), 'Electronics, 93', The New Global Reality: Ernst & Young's Fourth Annual Report on the Electronics Industry, San Francisco, CA: Ernst & Young.

Cavusgil, S.T. (1980), 'On the internationalization process of firms', *European Research*, **8** (November), 273–81.

Chetty, S. and C. Campbell-Hunt (2004), 'A strategic approach to internationalization: a traditional versus a "born-global" approach', *Journal of International Marketing*, **12**(1), 57–81.

Collis, D. (1991), 'A resource-based analysis of global competition', *Strategic Management Journal*, **12**, 49–68.

Coviello, N.E. and H.J. Munro (1995), 'Growing the entrepreneurial firm: networking for international market development', *European Journal of Marketing*, **29**(7), 49–61.

Crick, D. and M.V. Jones (2000), 'Small high-technology firms and international high-technology markets', *Journal of International Marketing*, **8**(2), 63–85.

Crick, D. and M. Spence (2005), 'The internationalisation of "high performing" UK high-tech SMEs: a study of planned and unplanned strategies', *International Business Review*, **14**(2), 167–85.

Dalli, D. (1995), 'The organization of exporting activities: relationships between internal and external arrangements', *Journal of Business Research*, **34**(2), 107–15.

Dana, L.P. (2001), 'Introduction: networks, internationalization, and policy', *Small Business Economics*, **16**(2), 57–62.

Dimitratos, P. and M.V. Jones (2005), 'Future directions for international entrepreneurship research', *International Business Review*, **14**(2), 119–28.

Economist, The (1992), 'Go West, young firm', May 9, 88–9.

Economist, The (1993), 'America's little fellows surge ahead', July 3, 59–60.

Falay, Z., M. Salimäki, A. Ainamo and M. Gabrielsson (2007), 'Design-intensive born globals: a multiple case study of marketing management', *Journal of Marketing Management*, **23**(9/10), 877–99.

Freeman, S. and S.T. Cavusgil (2007), 'Toward a typology of commitment states among managers of born-global firms: a study of accelerated internationalization', *Journal of International Marketing*, **15**(4), 1–40.

Freeman, S., R. Edwards and B. Schroder (2006), 'How smaller born-global firms use networks and alliances to overcome constraints to rapid internationalization', *Journal of International Marketing*, **14**(3), 33–63.

Gabrielsson, M. and V.H.M. Kirpalani (2004), 'Born globals: how to reach new business space rapidly', *International Business Review*, **13**(5), 555–71.

Gabrielsson, M., V.H.M. Kirpalani, P. Dimitratos, C.A. Solberg and A. Zucchella (2008), 'Born globals: propositions to help advance the theory', *International Business Review*, **17**, 385–401.

Grant, R.M. (1996), 'Toward a knowledge-based theory of the firm', *Strategic Management Journal*, **17** (Winter Special Issue), 109–22.

Gupta, U. (1989), 'Small firms aren't waiting to grow up to go global', *The Wall Street Journal*, December 5, B2.

Harveston. P.D., B.L. Kedia and P.S. Davis (2000), 'Internationalization of born global and gradual globalizing firms', *Advances in Competitiveness Research*, **8**(1), 92–9.

Hedlund, G. and A. Kverneland (1985), 'Are strategies for foreign market entry changing? The case of Swedish investment in Japan', *International Studies of Management and Organization*, **15**(2), 41–59.

Johanson, J.A. and J.-E. Vahlne (1977), 'The internationalization process of the firm: a model of knowledge development and increasing foreign market commitment', *Journal of International Business Studies*, **8**(1), 23–32.

Johanson, J.A. and J.-E. Vahlne (1990), 'The mechanism of internationalisation', *International Marketing Review*, **7**(4), 11–24.

Johanson, J.A and F. Wiedersheim-Paul (1975), 'The internationalization of the firm: four Swedish case studies', *Journal of Management Studies*, **12**(3), 305–22.

Jones, M.V. and N.E. Coviello (2005), 'Internationalization: conceptualizing and entrepreneurial process of behavior in time', *Journal of International Business Studies*, **36**(3), 284–303.

Karagozoglu, N. and M. Lindell (1998), 'Internationalization of small and medium-sized technology-based firms: an exploratory study', *Journal of Small Business Management*, **36**(1), 44–59.

Kirpalani, V.H. Manek and Reijo Luostarinen (1999), 'Dynamics of success of SMOPEC firms in global markets', Proceedings of the 25th Annual Meeting of the European International Business Academy, Manchester, Manchester School of Management, 12–14 December.

Kirzner, Israel M. (1973), *Perception, Opportunity, and Profit: Studies in the Theory of Entrepreneurship*, Chicago, IL and London: University of Chicago Press.

Knight, G.A. and S.T. Cavusgil (2004), 'Innovation, organizational capabilities, and the born-global firm', *Journal of International Business Studies*, **35**(2), 124–41.

Knight, Garry, Jim Bell and Rod McNaughton (2001), 'The "born global" phenomenon: a re-birth of an old concept?', in M.V. Jones and P. Dimitratos (eds), *Researching New Frontiers*, Vol. 2, 4th McGill Conference on International Entrepreneurship, University of Strathclyde, Glasgow, 21–23 September, pp. 1–15.

Knight, G.A. and S.T. Cavusgil (1996), 'The born global firm: a challenge to traditional internationalization theory', in S. Tamer Cavusgil (ed.), *Advances in International Marketing*, Vol. 8, Bingley, UK: Emerald Group Publishing, pp. 11–26.

Leonidou, L.C. and C.S. Katsikeas (1996), 'The export development process: an integrative review of empirical models', *Journal of International Business Studies*, **27**(3), 517–51.

Leonidou, L.C., C.S. Katsikeas, D. Palihawadana and S. Spyropoulou (2007), 'An analytical review of the factors stimulating smaller firms to export: implications for policy-makers', *International Marketing Review*, **24**(6), 735–70.

Leonidou, L.C., C.S. Katsikeas and N.F. Piercy (1998), 'Identifying managerial influences on exporting: past research and future directions', *Journal of International Marketing*, **6**(2), 74–102.

Levitt, T. (1983), 'The globalization of markets', *Harvard Business Review*, May–June, 92–102.

Luostarinen, Reijo (1970), *Foreign Operations*, Helsinki: Helsingin Kauppakorkeakoulun Kuvalaitos.

Luostarinen, Reijo and Mika Gabrielsson (2004), 'Finnish perspectives of international entrepreneurship', in Leo Paul Dana (ed.), *Handbook of Research on International Entrepreurship*, Cheltenham, UK and Northampton, MA, USA: Edward Elgar, pp. 383–403.

Madsen, T.K., E. Rasmussen and P. Servais (2000), 'Differences and similarities between born globals and other types of exporters', *Globalization, the Multinational Firm*, **10**, 247–65.

Madsen, T.K. and P. Servais (1997), 'The internationalization of born globals: an evolutionary process?', *International Business Review*, **6**(6), 561–83.

Majkgård, Anders and D. Deo Sharma (1999), 'The born internationals', Workshop in International Business and Nordic Workshop on Inter-organizational Research, University of Vaasa, Finland.

Mamis, R.A. (1989), 'Global start-up', *Inc.*, **11**(8), 38–47.

McAuley, A. (1999), 'Entrepreneurial instant exporters in the Scottish arts and craft sector', *Journal of International Marketing*, **7**, 67–82.

McDougall, P.P. (1989), 'International versus domestic entrepreneurship: new venture strategic behavior and industry structure', *Journal of Business Venturing*, **4**, 387–400.

McDougall, P.P. and C. Brush (1991), 'A symposium on global start-ups: entrepreneurial firms that are born international', Paper presented at the annual Academy of Management meeting, Miami, FL, August.

McDougall, P.P. and B.M. Oviatt (1991), 'Global start-ups: new ventures without geographic limits', *The Entrepreneurship Forum*, **15**(Winter), 1–5.

McDougall, P.P. and B.M. Oviatt (2000), 'The interaction of two research paths', *Academy of Management Journal*, **43** (5), 902–6.

McDougall, P.P. and B.M. Oviatt (2003), 'Some fundamental issues in international entrepreneurship', available at: www.usabe.org/knowledge/whitepapers/index.asp.

McDougall, P.P., B.M. Oviatt and R.C. Shrader (2003), 'Comparison of international and domestic new Ventures', *Journal of International Entrepreneurship*, March **1**(1), 59–82.

McDougall, P.P., S. Shane and B.M. Oviatt (1994), 'Toward a theory of international new ventures', *Journal of International Business Studies*, **25**(1), 45–64.

McKinsey & Co. (1993), 'Emerging Exporters: Australia's High Value-Added Manufacturing Exporters', McKinsey & Co., Australian Manufacturing Council, Melbourne.

Miller, D. and P. Friesen (1982), 'Innovation in conservative and entrepreneurial firms: two models of strategic momentum', *Strategic Management Journal*, **3**, 1–25.

Moen, Ø. (2002), 'The born globals: a new generation of small European exporters', *International Marketing Review*, **19**(2), 156–75.

Moen, Ø. and P. Servais (2002), 'Born global or gradual global? Examining the export behavior of small and medium-sized enterprises', *Journal of International Marketing*, **10**(3), 49–72.

Naidu, G.M. and V. Kanti Prasad (1994), 'Predictors of export strategy and performance of small and medium-sized firms', *Journal of Business Research*, **31**(2/3), 107–15.

OECD (1997), *Globalization and Small and Medium Enterprises (SMEs)*, Paris: Organisation for Economic Cooperation and Development.

Oesterle, M. (1997), 'Time-span until internationalization: foreign market entry as a built-in mechanism of innovations', *Management International Review*, **37**(2), 125–49.

Oviatt, B.M. and P.P. McDougall (1994), 'Toward a theory of international new ventures', *Journal of International Business Studies*, **25**(1), 45–64.

Oviattt, B.M. and P.P. McDougall (1997), 'Challenges for internationalization process theory: the case of international new ventures', *Management International Review*, **37**(2), 85–99.

Oviatt, B.M. and P.P. McDougall (1995), 'Global start-ups: entrepreneurs on a worldwide stage', *Academy of Management Executive*, **9**, 30–43.

Oviatt, B.M., P.P. McDougall, M. Simon and R.C. Shrader (1993), 'Heartware International Corporation: a medical equipment company "born international"', Part A, *Entrepreneurship: Theory and Practice*, Winter, 111–28.

Piercy, N. (1981), 'Company internationalisation: active and reactive exporting', *European Journal of Marketing*, **15**(3), 26–40.

Preece, S.B., G. Miles and M.C. Baetz (1999), 'Explaining the international intensity and global diversity of early-stage technology-based firms', *Journal of Business Venturing*, **14**(3), 259–81.

Ray, Dennis M. (1989), 'Entrepreneurial companies "born" international: four case studies', paper presented at Babson Kauffman Entrepreneurship Research Conference, St. Louis, MO.

Rennie, M.W. (1993), 'Born global', *McKinsey Quarterly*, **4**, 45–52.

Reuber, A.R. and E. Fischer (1997), 'The influence of the management team's international experience on the internationalization behaviors of SMEs', *Journal of International Business Studies*, **28**(4), 807–25.

Rialp, A., J. Rialp and G.A. Knight (2005), 'The phenomenon of early internationalizing firms: what do we know after a decade (1993–2003) of scientific inquiry?', *International Business Review*, **14**(2), 147–66.

Samiee, S. and P. Walters (1991), 'Segmenting corporate exporting activities: sporadic versus regular exporters', *Journal of the Academy of Marketing Science*, **19**(2), 93–104.

Sharma, D.D. and A. Blomstermo (2003), 'The internationalization process of born globals: a network view', *International Business Review*, **12**(6), 739–53.

Sullivan, D. and A. Bauerschmidt (1990), 'Incremental internationalization: a test of Johanson and Vahlne's thesis', *Management International Review*, **30**, 19–30.

Teece, D.J., G. Pisano and A. Shuen (1997), 'Dynamic capabilities and strategic management', *Strategic Management Journal*, **18**(7), 509–33.

Turnbull, Peter W. (1987), 'A challenge to the stages theory of the internationalization process', in Phillip J. Rosson and Stanley D. Reid (eds), *Managing Export Entry and Expansion*, New York: Praeger, pp. 21–40.

Vermeulen, F. and H. Barkema (2002), 'Pace, rhythm, and scope: process dependence in building a profitable multinational corporation', *Strategic Management Journal*, **23**, 637–53.

Welch, L.S. and R.K. Luostarinen (1993), 'Inward-outward connections in internationalization', *Journal of International Marketing*, **1**(1), 44–57.

Welch, L.S. and F. Wiedersheim-Paul (1980), 'Initial exports – a marketing failure?', *Journal of Management Studies*, **17**(3), 333–44.

Wiedersheim-Paul, F., H.C. Olson and L.S. Welch (1978), 'Pre–export activity: the first step in internationalization', *Journal of International Business Studies*, **9**(1), 47–58.

Yip, G.S. (2000), 'The role of the internationalization process in the performance of newly nationalizing firms', *Journal of International Marketing*, **8**(3), 1–35.

Zahra, S.A. (2005), 'A theory of international new ventures: a decade of research', *Journal of International Business Studies*, **36**(1), 20–28.

Zahra, Shaker A. and Gerard George (2002), 'International entrepreneurship: the current status of the field and future research agenda', in Michael A. Hitt, R. Duane Ireland, S. Michael Camp and Donald L. Sexton (eds), *Strategic Entrepreneurship: Creating a New Mindset*, Oxford: Blackwell, pp. 255–88.

Zahra, S., R.D. Ireland and M. Hitt (2000), 'International expansion by new venture firms: international diversity, mode of market entry, technological learning, and performance', *Academy of Management Journal*, **43**(5), 925–50.

3 Determinants of different types of born globals

Matthias Baum, Christian Schwens and Rüdiger Kabst

INTRODUCTION

Young entrepreneurial firms which act on an international level from inception, so-called 'born globals' (BGs), have been widely discussed in the international business, management, and entrepreneurship community over the last two decades (for reviews see, for example, Coviello and Jones 2004; Keupp and Gassmann 2009). This development is a consequence of BGs' importance for future economic development and their increasing empirical occurrence (Bürgel et al. 2004). The main body of BG research is directed towards the comparison between early and late internationalizing firms and which factors enable new ventures to become international directly or shortly after inception. Surprisingly, most conducted inquiries fail to scrutinize the question of whether BGs are a homogeneous or a heterogeneous group of firms.

Oviatt and McDougall (1994) were the first to create a theoretical framework based on the internationalization of new ventures, challenging the traditional international process models. Even though most of their arguments have been observed intensively, less attention has been devoted to the four types of BGs they identified on a theoretical basis. Thus, it remains unclear how firm-and entrepreneur-related conditions influence the formation of the different types of BGs. Several recently conducted studies have accommodated the differences among BGs by examining the intensity (Bloodgood et al. 1996; Reuber and Fischer 1997; Sapienza et al. 2005) and diversity (Kundu and Katz 2003; Preece et al. 1998) of international activities or modes of foreign market entry (Zahra et al. 2000), showing that BGs are not as homogeneous as they are generally considered. However, previous studies generally fail to compare explicitly defined groups of BGs. This is an important issue because varying scales and scopes of international activities mean that BGs face different impediments, have a diverging resource base, and have differentiated managerial cognitions (Pulkkinen and Larimo 2007).

This work explicitly shows that the types of BGs, adapted from Oviatt and McDougall's seminal framework (1994), indeed vary from one another in terms of firm and individually related characteristics. Specifically, this work builds a framework of influential factors based on the different BG types mentioned by Oviatt and McDougall, and deduces propositions about the effect of the proactiveness and prior international experience of the management, knowledge intensity, product differentiation, international network contacts, and learning orientation on the formation of BGs.

Recent international entrepreneurship literature uncovers prior research that generally does not include examinations of the different BG groups. Only Pulkkinen and Larimo (2007) employ a genuine demarcation between the different BG types. Their qualitative study among eight BGs highlights the importance of founding conditions, internationalization motives, and international experience of the founding managers on BGs' early-stage development.

Even though Preece et al. (1998) do not directly compare different BG types, they emphasize differences among exogenous variables' influence on international diversity and the scale of international action. They state that managerial proactiveness, governmental assistance, resource base, and age, significantly account for the intensity of international actions, whereas only the available resources and the firms' age significantly contribute to the diversity of internationalization of young high-tech firms. Thus they show that realizing a huge proportion of foreign revenues is not the same in many foreign countries, which may mean that BGs, depending on their scale and scope of internationalization, may be influenced by diverging forces.

Oviatt and McDougall (1994) claim that the different types of BGs are determined by diverging factors and still need scientific emphasis. Therefore, the following work contributes to the understanding of how the several postulated types of BGs differ and which factors determine their foundation. Accordingly, propositions are drawn from international new venture theory (INVT) (ibid.), underpinned by further scholarly research.

THEORETICAL FRAMEWORK AND PROPOSITIONS

The predominant definition of BGs was first introduced by Oviatt and McDougall, and describes a BG as 'a business unit that, from inception, seeks to derive significant competitive advantages from the use of resources and the sale of outputs in different countries' (ibid., p. 49).

The seminal framework by Oviatt and McDougall has challenged traditional stage models of internationalization by stating that foreign markets are entered not only by large and internationally experienced multinational enterprises (MNEs), but also increasingly by start-ups directly or shortly after their inception (Autio et al. 2000). The INVT focuses on the question of how it is possible for companies to venture into foreign markets from inception. To answer this research question Oviatt and McDougall (1994), as well as further studies in the field of international entrepreneurship, identify different determinants for international new venturing. First, BGs are characterized by a highly internationally experienced management team helping the firm to overcome liabilities of foreignness when venturing abroad early in their life cycle. Second, international new ventures are driven by a strong degree of growth orientation, leading the firm to proactively pursue international growth opportunities at an early stage. Third, international new ventures are characterized by knowledge intensity and product differentiation. Due to the mobility of their knowledge, BGs find global demand in niche markets creating international sales and leading to the exploitation of international growth opportunities with more flexibility and fewer constraints than might be caused by national boundaries (Autio et al. 2000). Fourth, BGs have a strong learning orientation, which leads firms to search for new knowledge in foreign markets. Thus, due to this eclectic explanation of BGs' emergence combined with the theoretical pluralism demanded by many scholars (for example, Coviello and McAuley 1999), INVT is a good framework to explore the research question.

Besides addressing determinant factors for international new venturing, Oviatt and McDougall identify different typologies of BGs:

1. *Export-import start-ups*, which coordinate just a few activities, mostly logistics abroad, and operate in few international markets.
2. *Multinational traders*, which, on the one hand possess a limited degree of internationalization, and on the other, have a high degree of international diversification in terms of markets served.
3. *Geographically focused start-ups*, which are internationally concentrated, but coordinate plenty of operations abroad.
4. *Global start-ups*, which are characterized by a huge number of foreign markets served, as well as the coordination of many activities across countries.

The major determinants and their impact vary for the different types of BGs. The success of export start-ups depends on the ability 'to spot and act on emerging opportunities' before increased competition occurs (ibid., p. 58). Thus, a stronger learning orientation prevails for this group of BGs. Geographically focused start-ups operate in selected foreign markets on a high scale. In order to serve very specialized needs, they are characterized by highly knowledge-intensive products and services.

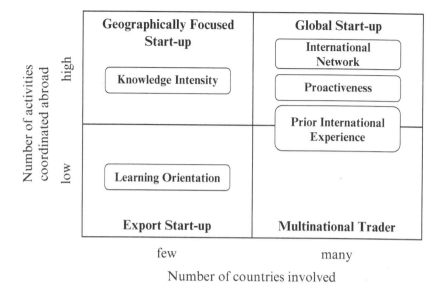

Figure 3.1   Types of BGs and their respective determinants

Global start-ups, which are the most difficult type of BG to develop, derive 'significant competitive advantage from extensive coordination among multiple organizational activities' in various countries (ibid., p. 59). Their intense international activity at a young age predominantly results from a distinctive growth-oriented attitude of the management, and is facilitated if a high degree of previous international experience of the management team prevails. Previous international experience is also a major issue for multinational traders, as they need experience to efficiently govern multiple international engagements. These relationships are elaborated in more detail in the following proposition section. Figure 3.1 illustrates how the different determinants influence the specific types of BGs.

PROPOSITIONS

The pivotal role of the management on new ventures' development has often been asserted in previous research (Coviello and McAuley 1999; Saarenketo et al. 2001; Zahra and George 2002; Nummela et al. 2004; Dimitratos and Jones 2005). Characteristics of the top management team (TMT) include not only capabilities but also attitudes, such as the proactiveness by which international activities are approached (Chetty and Campbell-Hunt, 2004). Oviatt and McDougall state that 'new ventures begin with a proactive international strategy' (1994, p. 49). Thus, the INVT suggests that founders or decision makers possess a distinctive and proactive orientation to spot windows of opportunity on a global scale (Knight and Cavusgil 1996). By definition, global start-ups are characterized by a high scale and scope of international activities, that is, a higher commitment towards foreign markets than other BG types. This in turn may result in higher risks, in particular for young, financially constrained ventures (Acedo and Jones 2007). In order to achieve such intense and diverse international operations in spite of their connected risks of failure, a proactive cognition towards internationalization is essential (Preece et al. 1998) compared to other BGs, especially to export start-ups. This leads to the first proposition:

Proposition 1: Global start-ups will more likely have a more proactive attitude towards internationalization than other types of BGs.

Another key variable linked with BGs is the previous international experience of the TMT (Bloodgood et al. 1996; Bürgel et al. 1998; Kundu and Katz, 2003; McDougall et al. 2003) which, due to BGs' infancy, is rooted on the individual level rather than on an organizational one (Saarenketo et al. 2001; Schwens and Kabst 2009). According to Cohen and Levinthal (1990), previous international experience can be seen as a proxy for a new venture's absorptive capacity, which increases the 'ability to identify, value, select and assimilate new knowledge' to existing knowledge (Zahra 2005, p. 25). This reduces the uncertainty of operating abroad, resulting in an increased probability of entering additional countries (Autio et al. 2000; Oviatt and McDougall 2005). Conversely, new ventures that are internationally concentrated, even if on a high scale, will depend less on the previous international experience of their managers. Accordingly, the necessary market knowledge may be obtained more easily if only a few different countries have to be studied, reducing the need for a higher absorptive capacity in comparison to other, more internationally dispersed acting new ventures. So, previous international experience is particularly important for globally dispersed BGs, rather than for geographically focused BGs. Therefore, the second proposition can be asserted:

Proposition 2: BGs acting in many countries, namely global start-ups and multinational traders, will more likely have an internationally experienced management.

In Oviatt and McDougall's INVT (1994), knowledge has been identified as a unique resource and one of the four necessary and sufficient elements of sustainable BGs. Knowledge intensity is recognized as a key source of international competitive advantage by several international entrepreneurship scholars (for example, Coviello and McAuley 1999; Jones 1999; Autio et al. 2000; Bell et al. 2003), enabling firms to exploit international growth opportunities with more flexibility and fewer constraints from national boundaries, due to the mobility of knowledge (Autio et al 2000; McNaughton 2001, 2003). Although knowledge intensity is important for all BGs, Oviatt and McDougall's INVT suggests that it is particularly crucial for geographically focused start-ups, since they serve highly specialized needs which in turn requires a high knowledge base. Additionally, knowledge-intensive products entail the risk of product piracy and illegal replication, resulting in a trade-off for the BG. On the one hand, BGs have to internationalize in order to manage opportunities due to their knowledge-intensive product or services. On the other, they must protect their inherent knowledge. Therefore, BGs that are characterized by high knowledge intensity will intensively serve a low number of markets rather than a large number of markets. This leads to the third proposition:

Proposition 3: Geographically focused start-ups will more likely have a higher knowledge intensity than other BG types.

As already mentioned, knowledge is an eminent determinant for the creation and development of BGs (Oviatt and McDougall, 1994). Both existing knowledge and the attitude towards knowledge creation play a pivotal role and impact on the 'process of assimilating new knowledge into the organization's knowledge-base' (Autio et al. 2000, p. 911).

Export start-ups, which act on a low international scale and scope, especially need to build up specific knowledge about the few markets they serve. Only then can they spot emerging opportunities before other ventures do so, and, combined with their knowledge about the market structure and suppliers, build up sustaining competitive advantages (Oviatt and McDougall, 1994). Additionally, export start-ups might be most in similar to incrementally internationalizing enterprises, described by Johanson and Vahlne (1977). Therefore, export start-ups tend to learn more intensively about existing markets before increasingly committing to further foreign markets. This leads to the fourth proposition:

Proposition 4: Export start-ups will more likely have a high learning orientation compared to other types of BGs.

A number of scholars believe that networks are a powerful tool to facilitate early internationalization (Selnes and Sallis 2003; Oviatt and

McDougall 2005). Social ties are meant to help BGs identify international business opportunities (Oviatt and McDougall, 1995) and to 'contribute to lowering risk and uncertainty inherent in international operations' (Weerawardena et al. 2007, p. 301). Hence they are a powerful tool to facilitate early internationalization by providing security and financial back-up (Shane and Cable 2002). By providing information and trust (Uzzi 1997), social ties reduce transaction costs and environmental uncertainty and, thus, protect the distribution of knowledge-intensive products and services abroad. Moreover, strong international social ties provide opportunities for market development and to identify international business opportunities (Oviatt and McDougall 1995). International network contacts may be helpful to acquire foreign customers, resulting in an increased intensity of international operations. Moreover, the international network contacts will allow for stepping into foreign markets, since liabilities of foreignness can be surmounted more easily with the help of foreign network partners.

Therefore, international social capital increases opportunities for internationalization by providing increased market knowledge and higher security. Social ties help firms to overcome the barriers of internationalization and to increase both international intensity and international diversity. This leads to the fifth proposition:

Proposition 5: Global start-ups will more likely have more international network contacts than other types of BGs.

DISCUSSION

The goal of this work is to contribute to the understanding of BGs by observing how organizational and entrepreneur-related factors lead to differences among the BG types identified by Oviatt and McDougall. Therefore, predictor variables were deduced from INVT. Thereby, it was demonstrated how separate predictor variables affect the four BG types differently. BGs are a more heterogeneous than homogeneous group of enterprises and, depending on the scale and scope of their international activities, different aspects become important. Global start-ups, for example, predominantly depend on a very proactive and internationally experienced management to succeed in international markets. In forming such a BG, obstacles are encountered that require a proactive management. However, in order to overcome the risks due to extensive internationalization at an early stage, proactiveness alone will not be sufficient. In addition, to previous international experience and international network contacts are pivotal for becoming a global start-up. By contrast, geographically focused start-ups are mainly established if high knowledge intensity characterizes the new venture. Therefore, acting on an extensive international scale but on a restricted scope seems to be the appropriate strategy to exploit the knowledge and simultaneously protect against patent infringements and product piracy. Accordingly, this work contributes to the discussion about the impact of knowledge intensity on early internationalization (Autio 2003) by emphasizing that the influence among internationalization behavior is not equal for all kinds of BGs. Knowledge intensity is a driver for the scale of international expansion, but not for the scope. Multinational traders, who pursue a high-scope, low-scale internationalization strategy (thus acting in numerous countries) profit from managers who worked in international operating firms. Managers from those firms have higher capabilities in coordinating multiple country operations since they are more likely to have been exposed to global operations in their previous employment. This experience, therefore, will also forward the international operations of multinational traders. Even though learning orientation is often associated with a higher propensity to internationalize (for example, Oviatt and McDougall 2005; Chetty and Campbell-Hunt 2004), it can also be restricting for international expansion. One may conclude that export start-ups in particular need to learn intensively in order to better serve the few markets they are operating in and to identify opportunities more efficiently. Taking all these findings into consideration may help practitioners find the most appropriate internationalization strategy according to the firm's profile, and advise researchers (at least) to control for the types of BGs since results may vary depending on which BG types are predominantly observed.

REFERENCES

Acedo, F.J. and M.V. Jones (2007), 'Speed of internationalization and entrepreneurial cognition: insights and a comparison between international new ventures, exporters and domestic firms', *Journal of World Business*, **42**, 236–52.

Autio, E. (2003), 'Creative tension: the significance of Ben Oviatt's and Patricia McDougall's article "Toward a theory of international new ventures"', *Journal of International Business Studies*, **36**, 9–19.

Autio, E., H.J. Sapienza and J.G. Almeida (2000), 'Effects of age at entry, knowledge intensity, and imitability on international growth', *Academy of Management Journal*, **43**(5), 909–24.

Bell, J., J. McNaughton, R. Young and D. Crick (2003), 'Towards an integrative model of small firm internationalization', *Journal of International Entrepreneurship*, **1**, 339–62.

Bloodgood, J.M., H.J. Sapienza and J.G. Almeida (1996), 'The internationalization of high-potential U.S. ventures: antecedents and outcomes', *Entrepreneurship: Theory and Practice*, **20**(4), 61–76.

Bürgel, O., A. Fier, G. Licht and G. Murray (2004), 'The internationalization of young high-tech firms: an empirical analysis in Germany and the United Kingdom', *ZEW Economic Studies*, **22**, Physica-Verlag, Heidelberg.

Bürgel, O., G. Murray, A. Fier, G. Licht and E. Nerlinger (1998), 'The internationalization of British and German start-up companies in high technology industries', ZEW Discussion Papers, **98**(34), ZEW – Zentrum für Europäische Wirtschaftsforschung/Center for European Economic Research.

Chetty, S. and C. Campbell-Hunt (2004), 'A strategic approach to internationalization: a traditional versus a 'born-global' approach', *Journal of International Marketing*, **12**(1), 57–81.

Cohen, W.M. and D.A. Levinthal (1990), 'Absorptive capacity: a new perspective on learning and innovation', *Administrative Science Quarterly*, **35**, 128–52.

Coviello, N.E. and M.V. Jones (2004), 'Methodological issues in international entrepreneurship research', *Journal of Business Venturing*, **19**, 485–508.

Coviello, N.E. and A. McAuley (1999), 'Internationalization and the smaller firm: a review of contemporary empirical research', *Management International Review*, **39**(3), 223–56.

Dimitratos, P. and M.V. Jones (2005, 'Future directions for international entrepreneurship research (Guest Editorial)', *International Business Review*, **14**, 119–28.

Johanson, J. and J.E. Vahlne (1977), 'The internationalization process of the firm: a model of knowledge development and increasing foreign market commitment', *Journal of International Business Studies*, **4**, 20–29.

Jones, V.M. (1999), 'The internationalization of small high-technology firms', *Journal of International Marketing*, **7**(4), 15–41.

Keupp, M.M. and O. Gassmann (2009), 'The past and the future of international entrepreneurship: a review and suggestions for developing the field', *Journal of Management*, **35**(3), 600–633.

Knight, G.A. and S.T. Cavusgil (1996), 'The born global firm: a challenge to traditional internationalization theory', in S. Tamer Cavusgil (ed.), *Advances in International Marketing*, Bingley, UK: Emerald group publishing, pp. **8**, 11–26.

Kundu, S.U. and J.A. Katz (2003), 'Born-international SMEs: bi-level impacts of resources and intentions', *Small Business Economics*, **20**, 25–47.

McDougall, P.P., B.M. Oviatt and R.C. Shrader (2003), 'A comparison of international and domestic new ventures', *Journal of International Entrepreneurship*, **1**, 59–82.

McNaughton, R.B. (2001), 'The export mode decision-making process in small knowledge-intensive firms', *Market Intelligence and Planning*, **19**, 12–20.

McNaughton, R.B. (2003), 'The number of export markets that a firm serves: process models versus the born-global phenomenon', *Journal of International Entrepreneurship*, **1**, 297–311.

Nummela, N., S. Saarenketo and K. Puumalainen (2004). 'Global mindset – a prerequisite for successful internationalization?', *Canadian Journal of Administrative Sciences*, **21**(1), 51–64.

Oviatt, B.M. and P.P. McDougall (1994), 'Toward a theory of international new ventures', *Journal of International Business Studies*, **25**(1), 45–64.

Oviatt, B.M. and P.P. McDougall (1995), 'Global start-ups: entrepreneurs on a worldwide stage', *Academy of Management Executive*, **9**(2), 30–43.

Oviatt, B.M. and P.P. McDougall (2005), 'Defining international entrepreneurship and modeling the speed of internationalization', *Entrepreneurship: Theory and Practice*, **29**(5), 537–53.

Preece, S.B., G. Miles and M.C. Baetz (1998), 'Explaining the international intensity and global diversity of early-stage-technology-based firms', *Journal of Business Venturing*, **14**, 259–81.

Pulkkinen, J. and J. Larimo (2007), 'Variety in international new ventures: typological analysis and beyond', *Journal of Euromarketing*, **16**(1), 37–57.

Reuber, A.R. and E. Fischer (1997), 'The influence of the management team's international experience on the internationalization behavior of SMEs', *Journal of International Business Studies*, **28**(4), 807–25.

Saarenketo, S., O. Kuivalainen and K. Puumalainen (2001), 'Emergence of born global firms: internationalization patterns of the infocom SMEs as an example', in proceedings of 4th McGill Conference on International Entrepreneurship, 21–23 September, University of Strathclyde, Glasgow, Vol 2, pp. 442–68.

Sapienza, H.J., D.D. De Clercq and W.R. Sandberg (2005), 'Antecedents of international and domestic learning effort', *Journal of Business Venturing*, **20**, 437–57.

Schwens, C. and R. Kabst (2009), 'Early internationalization: a transaction cost economics and structural embeddedness perspective', *Journal of International Entrepreneurship*, **7**(4), 323–40.

Selnes, F. and S. Sallis (2003), 'Promoting relationship learning', *Journal of Marketing*, **67**(3), 80–89.

Shane, S. and D. Cable (2002), 'Network ties, reputation and the financing of new ventures', *Management Science*, **48**(3), 364–81.

Uzzi, B. (1997), 'Social structure and competition in interfirm networks: the paradox of embeddedness', *Administrative Science Quarterly*, **42**, 35–67.

Weerawardena, J., G.S. Mort, P.W. Liesch and G. Knight (2007), 'Conceptualizing accelerated internationalization in the born global firm: a dynamic capabilities perspective', *Journal of World Business*, **42**, 294–306.

Zahra, S.A. (2005), 'A theory of international new ventures: a decade of research', *Journal of International Business Studies*, **36**, 20–28.

Zahra, S.A. and G. George (2002), 'International entrepreneurship: the current status of the field and future research agenda', in M. Hitt, R. Ireland, M. Camp and D. Sexton (eds), *Strategic Leadership: Creating a New Mindset*, London: Blackwell, pp. 225–88.

Zahra, S.A., R.D. Ireland and M.A. Hitt (2000), 'International expansion by new venture firms: international diversity, mode of market entry, technological learning, and performance', *Academy of Management Journal*, **43**(5), 925–50.

4 Born global and born-again global firms: a comparison of internationalization patterns
Michael Sheppard and Rod McNaughton

INTRODUCTION

This chapter reports the results of research that identifies and compares two patterns of internationalization that may be found among smaller firms: born global firms (which internationalize rapidly soon after their founding), and born-again global firms (which exist as domestic firms for a long time before rapidly internationalizing). Both patterns share the characteristic of rapid and intensive internationalization, but the first type of firm enters foreign markets as a new venture, while the latter does so much later in its life cycle.

Recent literature on patterns of internationalization focuses on the phenomenon of 'born global' firms, also called 'international new ventures' (Oviatt and McDougall 1994) and 'rapid internationalizers', and contrasts this internationalization pathway with the traditional model of incremental (or staged) internationalization. However, researchers such as Bell et al. (2003) point out that there are multiple pathways and variants of the archetypal born global and incremental internationalizing firm. As a specific example, Bell et al. (2001) introduced the notion of 'born-again global' firms to the literature. Such firms focus on their domestic market for many years before beginning rapid and dedicated internationalization.

As yet, there are few empirical descriptions of born-again global firms, and few investigations of how they may differ from their more studied born global counterparts. Bell et al. reported cases that illustrate potential motives for shifting from a focus on the domestic market to rapid internationalization. However, they did not provide guidance on how to identify born-again global firms in terms of specific criteria (for example, how long after founding qualifies a firm as 'born again', or the rapidity or intensity of their internationalization).

This chapter uses data from a cross-sectional survey of small Canadian firms to identify and then compare characteristics of born global and born-again global firms. There is disagreement in the literature as to the criteria for classifying the internationalization pathway of firms. In general, born

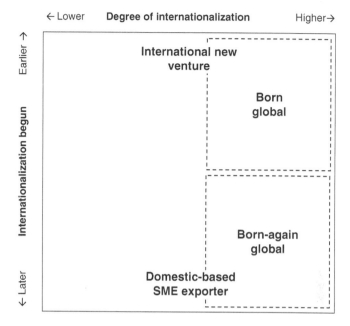

Figure 4.1   SME internationalization patterns

global firms are recognized as a type of international new venture (INV), based on Oviatt and McDougall's (1994) seminal explanation of the necessary and sufficient conditions for this organizational form. What differentiates born global firms from other INVs, is implied in the name: 'global' firms have a broader market scope than merely 'international' firms, which may only export to a few neighboring countries. Despite dispute around this distinction, and its implication for firms located in regions of varying access to multiple national markets, many studies simply focus on two easily measured factors: the time a firm takes to begin internationalizing and the extent to which it develops international markets, or 'degree of internationalization' (Sullivan 1994). All small and medium-sized enterprises (SMEs) that enter foreign markets fall somewhere in a two-dimensional space defined by these factors. (See Figure 4.1.)

Given the ambiguity around the definition of 'global', the focus of this study is primarily on the period between a firm's founding and when it begins to internationalize. To emphasize possible differences between early and late internationalization, Knight and Cavusgil's (1996) widely cited definition of 'born global' as a firm that realizes at least 25 percent of its revenues from outside its national market within three years of its formal founding is used. Bell et al. (2001) offer a time threshold for a firm to

---

BOX 4.1   CASE A: INTERNATIONAL NEW VENTURE (WWW.ARGONSECURITY.COM)

Within a year of founding, this Canadian military communications equipment manufacturer was receiving 90 percent of its revenue from exports mainly through direct sales to the US, though it reported sales in three countries. Like many INVs, it is a knowledge-based firm with half of its 25 employees in research and development and several patents based on 'first in North America' innovation. While its strategic focus is profitability, it has achieved strong growth in employment and sales in the last three years, with current sales in the $1–5 million range.

---

become 'born again'. Thus, this study investigates the distribution of time periods before internationalization begins, and selects the most extreme 10 percent – firms that served only their domestic market for their first 28 years of existence. From within this set of firms, those firms that achieve an export intensity of at least 25 percent within three years of beginning to internationalize were selected. The next subsections describe the born global and born-again global pathways, and provides brief cases that illustrate each pattern of internationalization.

International New Ventures and Born Global Firms

Oviatt and McDougall (1994, p. 49) defined an INV as 'a business organization that, from inception, seeks to derive significant competitive advantage from the use of resources and the sale of outputs in multiple countries'. Firms that quickly achieve a global presence are considered to be 'born global' firms, a special case of INV. Other INVs may achieve a lesser degree of internationalization, or globalize at a slower pace. A case example is provided for each type of firm described in Figure 4.1. Case A (Box 4.1) describes a firm that would be considered an INV by the above definition. However, this company did not achieve the global status attained by the firm described in Case B (Box 4.2).

Domestic-based SME Exporters and Born-again Global Firms

The lower half of Figure 4.1 corresponds to the internationalization path normally associated with 'incremental internationalizers', or the domestic-

---

BOX 4.2 CASE B: BORN GLOBAL (WWW.ESG.CA)

This firm provides innovative technology used to enhance workplace safety in mining operations and has sales of between 5 and 10 million dollars. It employees more than 40 people, with some located outside of Canada, and approximately one-third in research and development. The firm began in its founding year with direct exports to the US, followed by a number of European countries, to exceed 25 percent of total sales in the first year and 50 percent within four years. Currently approximately two-thirds of its sales are international through locations across seven continents. Over the last three years the company has doubled in size, in terms of both sales and employment.

BOX 4.3 CASE C: DOMESTIC-BASED SME EXPORTER (WWW.RIDEAU.COM)

Founded more than 90 years ago, this company established a strong reputation in Canada as a jeweller before undergoing a transformation of its core business in the 1980s which led to entry into the US market. The firm's successful new offering, which comprised a turnkey corporate rewards package with an online component added in the late 1990s, led to the expansion of its direct exports to the US. This accounted for more than half of its total sales by 2008. The company has 250 employees, with 20 located in offices across the US. Its workforce has increased by one-third and sales have more than doubled in the last three years.

---

based SME exporters described by Rennie (1993). Case C (Box 4.3) gives an example of such a firm. Beginning with the domestic market, the focus gradually expands outward, normally beginning with one or more geographically, or 'psychically', close 'lead' markets as documented by Bell et al. (2001).

However, Bell et al. also found that some companies go for a number of years without any international activity until some critical incident leads them to internationalize rapidly later in life. These companies follow the

---

**BOX 4.4   CASE D: BORN-AGAIN GLOBAL
(WWW.CANPROGLOBAL.COM)**

Founded in the 1970s, this investigation services company employs over 200 people and has sales of between 5 and 10 million dollars. The firm began to internationalize later in life with services provided to clients in the US then the Middle East. Corporate restructuring and branding, as well as a number of acquisitions, preceded a period of growth in which international sales exceed 25 percent of the total within a year. Currently the company provides services in 14 countries with sales growth exceeding 300 percent in the last three years.

'born-again' global pattern of internationalization (lower-right quadrant of Figure 4.1) and can be considered a special case of domestic-based SME exporter which succeeds in its efforts to establish a truly global presence. Case D (Box 4.4) is an example of such a born-again global firm.

RESEARCH METHOD

Data for the study were gathered from a survey administered to a cross-industry sample of Canadian businesses that measured internationalization patterns and growth of employment and sales, along with a number of demographic variables. A sample of 1,665 responses was received from the 16,099 contacts selected from the *Canadian Company Capabilities Directory* (Industry Canada), *Scott's Directory* as well as firms listed in *Profit Magazine's* annual publication of Canada's fastest-growing companies. Of the responses, those having up to 250 employees (following the EU definition of an SME) were selected. There were 837 such firms, of which 347 (42 percent) reported having international sales at some point.

Figure 4.2 shows the distribution of these firms by the number of years after founding that they first received revenue from outside of Canada. The distribution is strongly right skewed, with a mean of approximately 11 years (median = 6 years) and standard deviation of 13.8 years. Approximately 25 percent of the firms internationalized within three years of founding, and 50 percent within six years. The 90th percentile is 28 years. (There are 35 firms that began selling internationally after focusing on the domestic market for at least 28 years.) Combining these criteria with Knight and Cavusgil's (1996) threshold of achieving at least

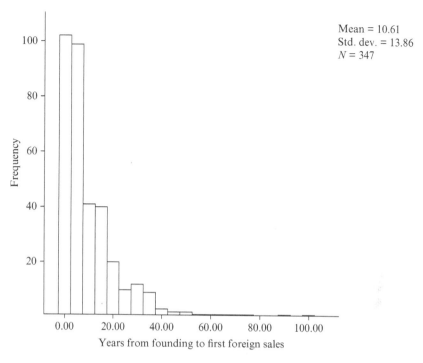

Figure 4.2   *Distribution of number of years between founding and first
international sales*

25 percent of revenue from outside the domestic market within three years,
the sample includes 130 firms classified as born global and 20 firms that are
born-again global.

These cases were analyzed using descriptive statistics and tests of differences in means to compare characteristics of firms that internationalize
early and rapidly versus those that internationalize quickly, but much
later in their life cycle. As the samples of born global and born-again
global firms are very different in size, and the tests for equality of variances
showed significant differences for several of the independent variables, a
robust measure of differences between means that does not assume equality of variances (the Brown–Forsythe test) is reported. The data collected
by the questionnaire allowed the comparison of firm size, proportion of
sales from products (versus services), investment in R&D and sales and
marketing, proportion of sales from new products, proportion of international sales of total, proportion of sales outside North America, as well as
growth of employment and sales over the last three years, and knowledge
intensity.

FINDINGS

Tables 4.1 and 4.2 report the findings. Born global firms significantly differ from born-again global firms on two of the independent variables – number of employees and R&D intensity. Born-again global firms are much larger (a mean of 78 compared with 18 employees), and spend a smaller proportion of revenue on R&D (5 percent compared with 17 percent). In all other respects, firms following these two internationalization paths are statisti-

Table 4.1   Means comparison: born global versus born-again global firms

	Born global (N = 130)	Born-again global (N = 20)	Brown–Forsythe
Employees	18 (33.8)	78 (81.6)	10.4**
% revenue from sale of products (vs. Services)	43 (41.7)	62 (41.3)	3.4
R&D/revenue	17 (23.7)	5 (4.7)	26.8***
Sales & marketing/revenue	28 (31.5)	23 (32.0)	0.3
% Sales from new products (last three years)	13 (22.3)	10 (16.1)	0.6
% Growth in sales (last three years)	18 (32.4)	13 (20.8)	1.1
% Growth in number of employees (last three years)	6 (30.4)	4 (9.9)	0.3
Number of national markets (current)	6 (9.6)	17 (36.8)	1.5
% Sales from international markets	52 (35.1)	40 (32.4)	2.3
% Sales from the United States	33 (28.6)	37 (27.4)	0.3

Notes: $* = p < 0.05$, $** = p < 0.01$, $*** = p < 0.001$; standard deviations appear in parentheses below means.

Table 4.2   Comparison of knowledge intensity between born global and born-again global firms

	Born global, no. (%)	Born-again global, no. (%)	Total
Knowledge producers	4 (3)	2 (7)	6
Knowledge users	59 (49)	12 (40)	71
Other	67 (56)	6 (20)	73
Total	120 (100)	30 (100)	150

Note: Fischer's Exact Test = 4.72, $p = 0.080$.

cally indistinguishable. There is a tendency for the born-again global firms to serve a greater number of international markets and for the overall proportion of revenue from outside Canada to be lower. However, given the sample sizes, these differences are not significant.

Table 4.2 compares the knowledge intensity of the two groups of firms, using a classification of knowledge-based sectors developed by Clendenning & Associates (2000). The first group includes a number of science and technology-related industries considered to be *knowledge producers,* while the second group of sectors characterizes companies that are innovative *knowledge users.* Sectors not included in either of these two categories form the final group. Fischer's Exact Test shows that there is no statistically significant association between knowledge intensity and internationalization pattern p = 0.05). However, the pattern is for a much higher proportion of born global firms to be outside the two knowledge-intensive groups.

DISCUSSION

This brief empirical comparison reveals few differences between born global and born-again global firms. Born-again global firms are on average much larger (and by definition are much older), as would be expected given the longer period over which they have grown within the domestic market. They spend a smaller proportion of revenue on R&D, which again may be a function of age. As born global firms are also on average much smaller, a small denominator (revenue) makes their R&D expenditures relatively larger. Knowledge-based theory has been used to explain how born global firms use their networks to develop knowledge-intensive products (for example, Autio et al. 2000; Mort and Weerawardena 2006), supported by a high level of resource commitment to R&D. Many of these small innovative firms offer market-leading products or services that challenge the status quo. However, the cross-tabulation in Table 4.2 shows no statistically significant association between knowledge intensity and internationalization pattern. If anything, a higher proportion of born global firms may be in sectors that are not typically thought of as either significant producers or users of new knowledge. Whether they internationalize early or late, smaller companies face the difficulty of creating consumer awareness and overcoming the liability of newness when competing with larger global players. Thus, the mean expenditure on sales and marketing is high (28 and 23 percent of sales, respectively), and these proportions are not significantly different between the two groups of firms.

The discussion has so far avoided the contentious issue of the use of the term 'global' which relates to the scale and scope of internationalization.

Figure 4.1 indicates a difference between born global firms and other early firms in terms of the degree to which they have developed international markets (Bell et al. 2001) and suggests that rapid and dedicated internationalization typifies the born global firm. Firms are thus considered to be 'born global' (or 'born-again' global as the case may be) if they achieve a high degree of internationalization soon after they have begun to internationalize. Degree of internationalization can be measured in terms of the proportion of international sales, the number of markets, and whether these markets are outside the firm's region or continent. In this study, the criteria of achieving at least 25 percent of sales from outside the country within three years was used as an indication of rapid and significant internationalization for both born global and born-again global firms.

Kuivalainen et al. (2007) and Johanson and Vahlne (2009) claim that most born global firms are actually 'born regional' or 'born international' without having truly global activity. While a number of authors have proposed definitions that address the issue of global scope, it is still an area of debate. For example, exports to five or more countries could be used to qualify a firm as global, however for companies in EU nations this may not be as impressive as for those based in North America. The former often start out at least with a regional presence in neighboring countries. The latter, unless they occupy a small niche, normally have a large domestic market to penetrate before an internationalization strategy would make sense. It follows, then, that exports outside the continent may provide a more comparable definition of global, as suggested by Gabrielsson et al. (2004).

Within the sample of firms, the number of markets (countries) served was not significantly different between the two groups. There are 'international' and 'global' firms among both early and later internationalizing firms. While the difference is not statistically significant, there is a tendency for born-again global firms to sell to more countries, and there is much greater variability in their experience (the standard deviation is 37 countries for born-again global firms, compared with 10 countries for born global firms). For Canadian firms, the largest and most attractive 'international' market is usually the United States. Both types of firm receive about one-third of their revenues from the US, and the variances are also very similar.

CONCLUSIONS

This chapter explored possible differences between firms that internationalize earlier and those that internationalize later. Born global and born-again global firms are considered as a special case of each of these types of firm, characterized by rapid and intensive internationalization. In the sample of Canadian SMEs, there are few statistically significant differences between these internationalization paths. Born-again global firms are rare – using the admittedly extreme criterion of the 90th percentile of the age when a firm first internationalizes its market – only 20 (5.8 percent of firms in the sample that export) were identified as born-again global firms. This compares with 130 (37.5 percent) born global firms, and 197 (56.8 per cent) exporting firms that do not fit into either category. Only 41.5 per cent of firms in the total sample (837) reported any revenue from outside Canada.

In the sample, born global and born-again global firms differ significantly only in terms of size (and, by definition, age), and in the proportion of revenue they spend on R&D. There is a tendency for born-again global firms to sell to more countries, and for born global firms to be less knowledge intensive, but these differences are not statistically significant. Given the small sample size, and discrepancy in the number of firms representing each internationalization path, our statistical tests lack power. The important observation, however, is that despite their substantial difference in age and size, born global and born-again global firms share many characteristics in common. This reinforces the basic point made by Bell et al. (2001), that the born global phenomenon is not necessarily only experienced by new ventures. Events may occur much later in a firm's life cycle that set off a similar process of rapid and intensive internationalization, for example, as illustrated by Case D.

Future research should take this into account, and acknowledge that the born global internationalization path is not necessarily unique to new ventures. However, the processes that born global and born-again global firms go through, and the challenges that they must overcome during internationalization may be qualitatively different. For example, we might expect that born global firms have greater resource constraints, but benefit from their learning advantage, while born-again globals may have to overcome path dependency and administrative heritage but have greater access to resources.

REFERENCES

Autio, E., H. Sapienza and J. Almeida (2000), 'Effects of age at entry, knowledge intensity, and imitability on international growth', *Academy of Management Journal*, **43**(5), 909–1014.

Bell, J., R. McNaughton and S. Young (2001), '"Born-again global" firms – an extension to the "born global" phenomenon', *Journal of International Management*, **7**(3), 173–89.

Bell, J., R.B. McNaughton, S. Young and D. Crick (2003), 'Towards an eclectic model of small firm internationalisation', *Journal of International Entrepreneurship*, **1**(4), 339–62.

Clendenning & Associates (2000), 'Comparison and Reconciliation of SIC and NAICS: Industry Codes Used to Define Knowledge-Based Industries (KBIs)', Industry Canada.

Gabrielsson, M., V. Sasi and J. Darling (2004), 'Finance strategies of rapidly-growing Finnish SMEs: born internationals and born globals', *European Business Review*, **16**(6), 590–604.

Johanson, J. and J.-E. Vahlne (2009), 'The Uppsala internationalization process model revisited: from liability of foreignness to liability of outsidership', *Journal of International Business Studies*, **40**, 1411–31.

Knight, G.A. and S.T. Cavusgil (1996), 'The born global firm: a challenge to traditional internationalization theory', in S. Tamer Cavusgil (ed.), *Advances in International Marketing*, Vol. 8, Bingley, Uk: Emerald Publishing Group, pp. 11–26.

Kuivalainen, O., S. Sundqvist and P. Servais (2007), 'Firms' degree of born-globalness, international entrepreneurial orientation and export performance', *Journal of World Business*, **42**(3), 253–67.

Mort, G.S. and J. Weerawardena (2006), 'Networking capability and international entrepreneurship – how networks function in Australian born global firms', *International Marketing Review*, **23**(5), 549–72.

Oviatt, B. and P. McDougall (1994), 'Toward a theory of international new ventures', *Journal of International Business Studies*, **25**(1), 45–64.

Rennie, M. (1993), 'Born global', *The McKinsey Quarterly*, (4), 45–52.

Sullivan, D. (1994), 'Measuring the degree of internationalization of a firm', *Journal of International Business Studies*, **25**(2), 325–42.

5 The born global dilemma: trade-off between rapid growth and control
Carl Arthur Solberg

INTRODUCTION

Conventional wisdom advocates a stepwise approach to international markets: the firm should learn how to 'creep before it runs'. The theoretical underpinnings for such advice are provided by writers in the incremental internationalization tradition (for example, Johanson and Vahlne 1977, 1990, 2009; Luostarinen 1979; Bilkey and Tesar 1977; Cavusgil 1984). However, the description of the 'traditional' pathway to international markets through a gradual process of building experience, starting in neighboring markets and progressively expanding to markets further away and increasingly engaging in more committing operation modes, was challenged by many writers. Reid (1983), Rosson (1987) and Turnbull (1987), all challenged the traditional pathway for being too deterministic. Benito and Gripsrud (1992) and Nordström (1990) challenged the lack of empirical support concerning the geographical dimension of the model. Furthermore, other explanations to international market involvement such as 'follow-thy-customer', oligopolistic behavior, networks or supply orientation have been observed (Engwall and Wallenstål 1988; and Johanson and Mattsson 1988; see Terpstra and Yu 1988). Welch and Luostarinen (1988) suggested that leapfrogging stages in the internationalization process was possible given certain resources. But most of all, the incremental internationalization model was challenged by the emerging literature on international new ventures and born globals (Rennie 1993).

The incremental internationalization model was, however, mainly developed at a time when firms operated in multi-domestic markets (Porter 1985) where they could slowly and confidently develop their international operations taking one step at a time, 'sneaking unobserved by competitors' into new markets (Solberg 1997) where management was most comfortable, without fearing retaliation or being copied on a global scale. For many firms, this no longer seems to be the case. The new breed of new ventures that go international right after inception was particularly conspicuous after the late 1980s, in great part spurred by globalization drivers such as increasing international trade and investment flows in the wake of liberalization of trade barriers and ease of communication across borders (Oviatt and McDougall 1995; Knight and Cavusgil 1996; Coviello and Munro 1997; Madsen and Servais 1997; Autio 2005; Rialp et al. 2005; Aspelund et al. 2007; Karlsen 2007; Laanti et al. 2007). One new dimension of the economic environment is the interdependence between players in national markets, leading to a more complex competitive situation with firms from all corners of the world offering novel and competitive solutions to both new and old problems.

Thus, born globals (BGs) are not only confronted with the challenges of scarcity of resources but they are also under extremely demanding circumstances. Often their products are introduced in markets where global incumbents have a firm market position, giving the latter leverage in the contest for market shares through their dominance of both distribution channels and industrial solutions. In spite of this, BGs elbow their way into markets, exploiting networks and using a range of different entry modes to capture customers in a diversity of markets. The advent of the internet has provided them with a powerful channel, although the use of this channel for marketing purposes has not always yielded the expected results (Sinkovics and Pezderka 2010).

This chapter delves into the compounded challenge of scarcity of resources and global competition confronting the BG firm. The internationalization literature is discussed and contrasted to the new string of BG research. Then internationalization strategies, with particular emphasis on entry modes, available to the BG are reviewed and a model that outlines 'the born global dilemma' is presented and discussed. At the conclusion, a number of propositions to be tested and implications for management are suggested.

BORN GLOBALS AND INTERNATIONALIZATION PROCESS THEORY

Early contributions on the internationalization process of firms suggest that firms start out with an agent or distributor, then, after some years of experience, replace the independent middleman by their own subsidiary, and eventually end up investing in a manufacturing unit to more deeply service the foreign market. This gradual trajectory to international markets seems to yield better returns than a more direct route to international foreign direct investment (FDI) in production capacity (Newbold et al. 1978). The trade-off between risk and growth in international markets is at the center of this discussion (Andersen 1993).

Market knowledge acquired through years of experience will reduce the risk of committing more resources to the international venture, at the expense of rapid international growth. All the same, the time it takes to accumulate the necessary insight into and understanding of local market conditions – thus reducing the investment risk – may jeopardize the development of the firm pursuing the cautious path to international markets, simply because competitors with more muscle are better placed to exploit the opportunities offered. Also, as the BG develops, it will need additional financing and with that, more often than not, new investors will be invited in, creating a new atmosphere inside the boardroom of these firms, and possibly also different expectations and demands on management (Gabrielsson et al. 2008, Solberg and Bretteville forthcoming).

There is a question whether BG is a theory in its own right or whether it is a special case of internationalization theory. Certainly, there are differences: BGs begin exporting at the very start or soon after inception, the pace of internationalization is different, their resource base is generally limited and the two streams of literature were developed in two very different contexts – multilocal versus global markets. But this is a question of geography and context more than one of a growth or business model. On the other hand, both the traditional school of internationalization process and BG contributions at large, consider factors such as uncertainty and risk, experience, commitment, entry mode strategies, and so on.

The Uppsala school model suggests that export activities are being triggered, the firm engages in export activities, experience is accumulated, and the exporter is then committing more resources to the export venture based on that very experience, hence, at lower risk (Johanson and Vahlne 1977). Gabrielsson et al. (2008) suggest that some of the mechanisms are the same, but their details may vary and they may come in a different order. For instance, both BGs and traditional exporters start their international activities because they are triggered, either by external forces (unsolicited orders, competition, limited home market, trends such as improved access to world markets) or by internal drivers (that is, global vision by management/founders, economies of scale, defense of home market). The detailed content of these drivers may, however, vary. In the case of traditional exporters, the triggers are possibly limited to scale economies, competition, and unsolicited orders, whereas BG drivers such as global vision of the founder(s) and access to markets (through the internet, lower trade barriers, and so on) may prevail. Furthermore, the commitment of BGs actually precedes any export activity. This, however, is a different kind of commitment.

We shall term this 'affective commitment', which is triggered by identification with the goal of the BG venture (Meyer and Allen 1991). The essence in this context is that the initial commitment is created by the global perspectives of the entrepreneur and the opportunities represented by them. It is not created by market activities, experiential knowledge, and specific investments. This kind of commitment of the BG entrepreneur will also permeate the staffing of the firm, which will in turn strengthen the affective commitment (Gabrielsson et al. 2008). After the initial phases of the BG export life, the circular model presented by Johansson and Vahlne (1977) is being caught up by the BG, then becoming a 'normal company' (Gabrielsson et al. 2008).

Attempts have been made to understand the mechanisms of export performance. This research is important in that it seeks to help our understanding of sustainable growth of firms in international markets. In one of the first reviews of the literature, Aaby and Slater (1989) found that one factor prevailed in explaining export performance: commitment by top management to the export venture. Another early contribution by Kamath et al. (1987) plainly concludes that 'any strategy goes', shotgun or rifle; fast or slow; extensive or limited management experience; high or low R&D effort (except in high-tech industries); and excellent or poor financial strength. In other words, success hinges on other factors. This conclusion may still hold, but new research has completed the picture with a much richer variety of impacting factors being studied.

Over the last 20 years, more than 250 articles have been published on export performance. The general impression is that whereas it is difficult to find a general pattern of agreement on strategy variables leading to superior performance, other factors such as learning effectiveness and capabilities (Phromket and Ussahawanitchakit 2009), market orientation (Cadogan et al. 2009; Tantong et al. 2010), proactive attitudes (Okpara and Kabongo 2009), innovation (Lages et al. 2009) and proactive strategies (Solberg and Durrieu 2008) seem to prevail in explaining export performance. It may be inferred that softer and less perceptible variables impact on exporters' financial and market performance, whereas superficial (but easily observable) indicators such as size, financial strength, R&D intensity and so on are much less consequential. This stream of research is important in that it also has relevance for BGs at large. For instance, it parallels BG literature in its emphasis on the role of attitudes, learning, and proactive strategies as key elements for sustainable growth (Gabrielsson et al. 2008). These effects are directly linked to the choice of entry mode by way of impacting on the decision itself (attitudes guiding the entry mode decision) or what consequences the choice of entry mode has on learning and control (Solberg and Nes 2002).

BORN GLOBALS AND ENTRY MODES

Choice of entry mode is one of the most important decisions made by international marketers (Young et al. 1989). This decision determines many other variables of the international marketing effort such as monitoring and control, use of financial and managerial resources, and financial risk (Solberg 2006). Entry mode decisions are therefore of particular interest in BG research as most BGs lack resources – thus constraining the alternative entry mode options – and are confronted with the compounded risk of new (often fast-growing) markets and new products (Ansoff 1957). Over the last 30–40 years, two theoretical approaches have dominated the discussion: transaction cost economics (TCE) and the internationalization process (IP) model. The basic premise of TCE is that a foreign middleman behaves opportunistically. The need to contain transaction costs and to control partner opportunism (Williamson 1985), and the need to address market imperfections and reduce uncertainty about pricing (Buckley and Casson 1976) speak in favor of integrating international operations rather than choosing an independent intermediary (market). The IP model, based on the theory of the growth of the firm (Penrose 1959), explains entry mode by the accumulation of experience over the years. The focus here is on risk and resources of the exporter. The exporter typically starts its foreign operations with little experience and few resources through a low commitment mode (independent trading partner), and then, having gradually gained experience in the specific market (and also in exporting in general), and accumulating more resources, changes to a more committed mode of operation, such as a sales subsidiary; (Johanson and Vahlne 1977). Whereas TCE is concerned with structure, IP studies the internal processes of the firm that lead to a build-up of resources allowing bolder steps in its international ventures.

In our present context, given the resource constraints of BGs we may exclude some entry modes, for example, FDI in production capacity. On the other hand we may identify a number of less committing entry modes that BG firms may realistically pursue. The list below, partly inspired by Gabrielsson and Kirpalani (2004), is organized according to increasing degrees of control of the firm's international operations:

- new owners taking over, funnelling the product/service through its own international distribution network;
- alliance with a large independent licensing or distribution partner;
- gradual international involvement through agents/distributors in individual countries;

- franchising to partners in individual markets; and
- setting up sales subsidiaries in individual markets.

Other strategies may certainly be conceivable, but the above list covers many of the most-relevant approaches to international markets available to BGs.

New Owners

This strategy may be seen as the easy way out for many founders of BGs. They realize that the task is too formidable or they simply want to capitalize on the values created in the firm. We may perceive that founders have a proclivity to pursue their business idea to reap the fruits of their work and to make sure that the firm is true to its original ideas. The stubbornness of founders to stick to their company is a well-known phenomenon in new ventures; often when new owners come in, it is despite the will of the founders rather than by virtue of a deliberate strategy (Solberg 1997). This may be a good strategy for the firm if its new owner(s) is/are ready and able to follow up on the business idea without the initial founder(s) at the helm. Examples abound of both successful takeovers and more dubious takeovers where the whole venture is doomed (Solberg and Bretteville forthcoming).

Licensing/Distribution Partner

Licensing involves the transfer of production rights, know-how or patent (licensing object) to a partner that takes on the task of developing a market for the object (Welch et al. 2007). The advantage for the entrepreneur of pursuing this strategy is that (s)he does not need to build a marketing organization to ascertain the market introduction of the products. This part is taken over by the licensee. This entry mode in international markets is often seen in research parks or universities where top researchers have created an innovation with substantial commercial value, but they do not have the resources or the willingness to bring it to the market (Macho-Stadler and Pérez-Castrillo 2010). New ventures (often emanating from these milieus) may also need to resort to a partnership with a large, often dominant partner that can take care of the commercial part of the venture. Whereas the upside is evident (relatively few resources needed, royalties, rapid market deployment using the network and distribution channels of the licensee), the risks are equally imminent: the licensor forecloses its own development of the commercial potential of the invention and it risks that the licensee takes over the whole product idea and becomes a competitor rather than a partner (Welch et al. 2007).

Licensing does not normally involve the transfer of brand names and business concepts, the licensee then achieving full control of the marketing – including its brand name or own trade mark. In cases of a narrow window of opportunity this may be the only conceivable strategy for the resource-poor BG, but it comes at a price: loss of control. Licensing rights may also be given to a number of *different* licensees in different countries. In this way the BG does not confer the rights to one sole partner, but disperses the risk of rights transfer to several licensees. Much of the same reasoning put forth for licensing to a large partner may also apply to a distribution relationship with a large OEM (original equipment manufacture) partner, the main difference being that the firm (BG) is taking charge of the supply of the products or services, either by producing them itself or through contract manufacturing arrangements. In this way, they have more control over greater parts of the value chain, although not branding or marketing.

Gradual Internationalization

According to the discussion above, this approach is generally seen as a safe way to enter international markets – but again may also be paved with challenges that make the BG firm particularly vulnerable. There is a risk that market introduction is proceeding too slowly and competitors may enter the window of opportunity, thus precluding the BG from taking advantage of its potential.

Franchising

Franchising entails the handover of the rights to exploit the commercial value of a business system and/or trademark (Welch et al. 2007). This strategy is being deployed at an increasing pace in international markets, often in service industries. The emergence of Zara (affordable fashion) and Starbucks (coffee shops) are cases in point. In both cases, the firms have resorted to a strategy of franchising and have built up a system of control and monitoring of their franchising partners' activities in world markets. In the case of franchising, the firm has more control of its operations through full ownership of its trademark. This control does not come without investments in monitoring systems so as to avoid opportunistic behavior such as free-riding by the franchisee (Kidwell et al. 2007). Therefore, this business solution is not necessarily for the unproven entrepreneur. On the other hand, BGs with the necessary resources to venture into international franchising may well be rewarded.

Sales Subsidiary

In principle, sales subsidiaries give the BG full control of the foreign marketing operations. However, setting up sales subsidiaries is wrought with challenges concerning staffing the local unit with competent personnel, financing it, and not least, monitoring and controlling its activities in the market. The lack of experience and local network may therefore make investing in local sales subsidiaries a costly endeavor for the BG. Examples abound of firms that wanted to take control early on and have then suffered because they bit off more than they could chew. Cases in Norway suggest that even with large financial resources and professional boards, firms that expand rapidly in international markets by means of sales subsidiaries may overstretch their limited managerial resources which either have inadequate experience in monitoring international marketing activities or do not yet have the routines and systems in place to properly address the task (Borsheim and Solberg 2002; Solberg and Bretteville forthcoming). In some of the cases mentioned above, the BGs had invested in about 10 markets in order to tap into a window of opportunity over a period of less than a year or two, only shortly thereafter to retract when problems piled up because of a lack of understanding of local marketing conditions or because the firm did not have a satisfactory subsidiary monitoring system in place. Evidently, this is a case of a trade-off between control and the risk inherent in rapid growth of the firm.

THE DILEMMA

We may infer that the BG needs to mold its strategy in the tension between control of its international expansion and its level of activity in order to grow and acquire new customers in international markets. BGs with the vision of servicing global markets need first and foremost to relinquish control of marketing and distribution in order to achieve the desired growth because they lack resources to wield the necessary clout to independently cover a broad range of markets. On the other hand, the need for rapid market introduction, which is inherent in BGs, is imminent for many firms, because they are confronted with a window of opportunity. If they do not exploit it and actively deploy market operations in key countries, then they risk being exploited by competitors. But rapid international market expansion may lead the newcomer to make fatal decisions because of lack of local market understanding. Using a maritime metaphor it may be said that they lack a proper chart to navigate,

Table 5.1   The trade-off between too much and too little

Issue	Effect on strategy	Possible outcomes
Too little control	Market control left to partner(s)	Loss of learning effects and control of own development
Too much control	Requires resources and market insight that the BG does not have	Stigmatizes smooth and efficient development of international market expansion
Too passive	Too careful, invests too little in market development and positioning	Competitors will exploit the unique window of opportunity and the BG is left with marginal customers in marginal markets
Too active	Too impatient and too eager to conquer world markets without the necessary financial or managerial clout	Risky path to retraction and potential bankruptcy

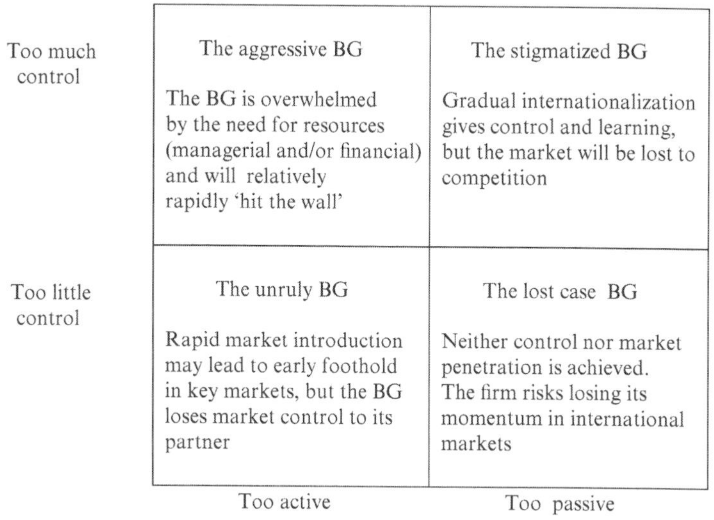

Too much control	**The aggressive BG** The BG is overwhelmed by the need for resources (managerial and/or financial) and will relatively rapidly 'hit the wall'	**The stigmatized BG** Gradual internationalization gives control and learning, but the market will be lost to competition
Too little control	**The unruly BG** Rapid market introduction may lead to early foothold in key markets, but the BG loses market control to its partner	**The lost case BG** Neither control nor market penetration is achieved. The firm risks losing its momentum in international markets
	Too active	Too passive

Figure 5.1   The born global dilemma

and their navigation skills leave something to be desired. Table 5.1 sums up the discussion above.

Placing these two dimensions – control and level of activity – in a matrix we get the following taxonomy (Figure 5.1).

IMPLICATIONS FOR RESEARCH AND MANAGEMENT

Research Implications

The main research streams on BGs have until recently focused on why and how BGs grow in international markets, but not so much on the trade-off between control and growth. This is an important dilemma of many BGs. One research avenue is to identify companies in each of the above categories, and carry out case studies in order to understand the pattern of decisions leading to the different strategies, and to explore how companies solve the proposed dilemma. Four propositions to be explored in this context may flow from the above model:

- Rapidly expanding BGs seeking marketing control in international marketing channels (through, for instance, their own sales subsidiaries) will sooner or later have to retract because of financial and managerial resource constraints.
- Rapidly expanding BGs leaving marketing control in international marketing channels to one major partner will lose touch with the market and eventually either be taken over by the partner or be outcompeted by the partner (the latter taking over the technology or developing a competing technology).
- BGs that are less expansive but nevertheless seek marketing control in international marketing channels will be confronted with competitors with greater resources that exploit the window of opportunity, thus precluding them from reaping the market potential.
- BGs that expand gradually in international markets, leaving marketing control in international marketing channels to independent partners, will lose touch with and, thereby, clout in, international markets, and risk eventually being taken over by one of its trading partners.

Such a project needs to be carried out over several years in order to study the effects over time.

Management Implications

Managers can draw important lessons from this discussion. The following factors are considered critical for both the short-and long-term success of the BG:

- early access to key customers in the industry in several countries to help the BG to get references, set the industry standard and obtain the necessary cash flow;
- rapid deployment in the market to pre-empt competition to capture market shares; and
- control so that the long-term interests of the founders and BG share-holders are ascertained.

But how then to eat the cake and still have it? The keyword here is flex-ibility. For instance, the BG needs to make sure that it is not getting stuck in contractual obligations with a dominant partner that it may not easily change. For newcomers to international markets, it may be tempting to sign contracts that apparently secure sales growth and market coverage. However, the firm may risk ending up in the trap of getting too depend-ent on the partner without having had the opportunity to build necessary competence enabling it to take control at a later stage (Solberg and Welch 1996). Furthermore, if the firm has a unique technology, design or product which is either patented or difficult to copy, the firm may have a great potential to draft an alliance package with a future partner that pays due attention to the above concerns. For instance, it is conceivable to invite a licensing partner to set up a company (the licensee) financing the bulk of the investment, and where the licensor (the BG) has an option to gradually increase its share, for example, by gradually substituting part of the royal-ties due with new shares in the company.

Another issue is that of timing: when should the BG invite new investors to take a stake in the venture? If they are invited too early, the BG and its founder(s) risk either ending up with a partner that takes over the firm or its technology without the original investors being able to reap the profits from its real potential, or receiving investments that are insufficient to finance the necessary expansion of the firm. If they are invited to invest in the company too late, the window of opportunity may be closed.

CONCLUSIONS

The control–growth dilemma is haunting management of many BGs in their strategic deliberations. Firms with a narrow window of opportunity in world markets are particularly vulnerable to the caprices of the situa-tion, and the right answer to the dilemma is not obvious though it will be decisive for the future development of the firm. This chapter has endeav-ored to cast light on the dilemma, thereby elucidating likely outcomes and, hopefully, guiding management to viable solutions. In addition, this is an under-researched area of study, and the proposed model may serve as a roadmap for further exploring the phenomenon.

REFERENCES

Aaby, Nils-Erik and Stanley F. Slater (1989), 'Management influences on export perform-ance: a review of the empirical literature 1978–88', *International Marketing Review*, **6**(4), 7–27.

Andersen, O. (1993), 'On the internationalization process of firms: a critical analysis', *Journal of International Business Studies*, **24**(2), 209–32.

Ansoff, H. Igor (1957), 'Strategies for diversification', *Harvard Business Review*, **35**(5), 113–24.

Aspelund, A., T.K. Madsen and Ø. Moen (2007), 'A review of the foundation, international marketing strategies, and performance of international new ventures', *European Journal of Marketing*, **41**(11/12), 1423–48.

Autio, E. (2005), 'Creative tension: the significance of Ben Oviatt's and Patricia McDougall's article "Toward a theory of international new ventures"', *Journal of International Business Studies*, **36**(1), 9–19.

Benito, G.R.G. and G. Gripsrud (1992), 'The expansion of foreign direct investments: discrete location choice or a cultural learning process?', *Journal of International Business Studies*, **23**(3), 461–76.

Bilkey, W.J. and G. Tesar (1977), 'The export behavior of smaller-sized Wisconsin manufac-turing firms', *Journal of International Business Studies*, **8**(1), 93–8.

Borsheim, J.H. and C.A. Solberg (2002), 'The internationalization of born global internet firms', Cahiers de Recherche, Bordeaux École de Management, Talence, France.

Buckley, Peter J. and Mark C. Casson (1976), *The Future of the Multinational Enterprise*, London: Macmillan.

Cadogan, J.W., O. Kuivalainen and S. Sundqvist (2009), 'Export market-oriented behavior and export performance: quadratic and moderating effects under differing degrees of market dynamism and internationalization', *Journal of International Marketing*, **17**(4), 71–89.

Cavusgil, S.T. (1984), 'Organizational characteristics associated with export activity', *Journal of Management Studies*, **21**(1), 3–22.

Coviello, N. and H. Munro (1997), 'Network relationships and the internationalization process of small software firms', *International Business Review*, **6**(4), 361–86.

Engwall, L. and M. Wallenstål (1988), 'Tit for tat in small steps: the internationalization of Swedish banks', *Scandinavian Journal of Management*, **4**(3/4), 157–9.

Gabrielsson, M. and V.H.M. Kirpalani (2004), 'Born globals: how to reach new business space rapidly', *International Business Review*, **13**(5), 555–71.

Gabrielsson, M., V.M. Kirpalani, P. Dimitratos, C.A. Solberg and A. Zucchella (2008), 'Born globals: propositions to advance the theory', *International Business Review*, **17**(4), 385–401.

Johanson, Jan and Lars Gunnar Mattsson (1988), 'Internationalization in industrial systems – a network approach', in *Strategies in Global Competition*, Neil Hood and Jan-Erik Vahlne (eds), New York: Croom Helm, pp. 287–314.

Johanson, J. and J. -E. Vahlne (1977), 'The internationalization process of the firm', *Journal of International Business Studies*, **8**(1), 23–32.

Johanson, J. and J. -E. Vahlne (1990), 'The mechanism of internationalization', *International Marketing Review*, **7**(4), 11–24.

Johanson, J. and J. -E. Vahlne (2009), 'The Uppsala internationalization process model revisited: from liability of foreignness to liability of outsidership', *Journal of International Business Studies*, **40**, 1411–31.

Kamath, Shyam, Phillip J. Rosson, Donald Patton and Mary Brooks (1987), 'Research on success in exporting: past, present and future', in Stanley D. Reid and Phillip J. Rosson (eds), *Managing Export Entry and Expansion*, New York: Praeger, pp. 398–421.

Karlsen, S.M.F. (2007), 'The born global – redefined – on the determinants of SMEs pace of internationalization', unpublished PhD thesis, Department of Marketing, BI Norwegian School of Management, Oslo.

Kidwell, Roland E., Arne Nygaard and Ragnhild Silkoset (2007), 'Antecedents and effects of free riding in the franchisor–franchisee relationship', *Journal of Business Venturing*, **22**(4), 522–44.

Knight, G.A. and S.T. Cavusgil (1996), 'The born global firm: a challenge to traditional internationalization theory', in S. Tamer. Cavusgil (ed.), *Advances in International Marketing*, Vol. 8, Bingley, UK: Emerlad group Publishing, pp. 11–26.

Laanti, R., M. Gabrielsson and P. Gabrielsson (2007), 'The globalization strategies of business-to-business born global firms in the wireless technology industry', *Industrial Marketing Management*, **36**(8), 1104–17.

Lages, Luis Filipe, G. Silva and C. Styles (2009), 'Relationship capabilities, quality, and innovation as determinants of export performance,' *Journal of International Marketing*, **17**(4), 47–70.

Luostarinen, R. (1979), 'Internationalization of the firm', doctoral thesis, Marketing Department, International Marketing, Helsinki School of Economics, Series A: 30.

Macho-Stadler, I. and D. Pérez-Castrillo (2010), 'Incentives in university technology transfers', *International Journal of Industrial Organization*, **28**(4), 362–7.

Madsen, T.K., and P. Servais (1997), 'The internationalization of born globals – an evolutionary process', *International Business Review*, **6**(6), 1–14.

McDougall, P.P. and B.M. Oviatt (2000), 'International entrepreneurship: the intersection of two research paths', *Academy of Management Journal*, **43**(5), 902–6.

Meyer, J.P. and N.J. Allen (1991), 'A three-component conceptualization of organizational commitment', *Human Resource Management Review*, **1**(1), 61–89.

Newbold, Gerald D., Peter J. Buckley and Jane Thurwell (1978), *Going International*, London: Associated Business Press.

Nordström, K. (1990), 'The internationalization of the firm in a new perspective', PhD dissertation, Institute of International Business, Stockholm.

Okpara, J.O. and J.D. Kabongo (2009), 'Entrepreneurial export orientation, strategy and performance of SMEs in an emergent African economy', *African Journal of Business Economic Research*, **4**(2/3), 34–54.

Oviatt, B.M. and P.P. McDougall (1995), 'Global start-ups: entrepreneurs on a worldwide stage', *Academy of Management Executive*, **9**(2), 30–44.

Penrose, Edith T. (1959), *The Theory of the Growth of the Firm*, Oxford: Basil Blackwell.

Phromket, C. and P. Ussahawanitchakit (2009), 'Effects of organizational learning effectiveness on innovation outcomes and export performance of garments business in Thailand', *International Journal of Business Research*, **9**(7), 6–31.

Porter, Michael E. (1985), *Competition in Global Industries*, Boston, MA: Harvard Business School Press.

Reid, S.D. (1983), 'Firm internationalization, transaction costs and strategic choice', *International Marketing Review*, **1**(2), 44–57.

Rennie, M.W. (1993), 'Global competitiveness: born global', *McKinsey Quarterly*, **4**, 45–52.

Rialp, A., J. Rialp and G.A. Knight (2005), 'The phenomenon of early internationalizing firms: what do we know after a decade (1993–2003) of scientific inquiry?', *International Business Review*, **14**(2), 147–66.

Rosson, Philip (1987), 'The overseas distributor method: performance and change in a harsh environment', in Stan Reid and Rosson (eds), *Managing Export Entry and Expansion*, New York: Praeger, New York, pp. 296–315.

Sinkovics, R. and N. Pezderka (2010), 'Do born-global SMEs reap more benefits from ICT use than other internationalizing small firms?', in C.A. Solberg (ed.), CIMaR 2010 Conference Proceedings, Oslo, Norway, May 26–28.

Solberg, C.A. (1997), 'A framework for strategy development in globalizing markets', *Journal of International Marketing*, **5**(1), 9–30.

Solberg, Carl Arthur (2006), 'Relationship between exporters and their foreign sales and marketing intermediaries: Introduction', in Solberg (ed.) *Advances in International Marketing*, vol 16, pp. xvii–xxvi.

Solberg, Carl Arthur and Trine Bretteville (forthcoming), 'Inside the boardroom of born globals', *International Journal of Entrepreneurship and Small Business*.

Solberg, Carl Arthur and François Durrieu (2008), 'Strategy development in international markets: a two tier approach', *International Marketing Review*, **25**(5), 520–43.

Solberg, Carl Arthur and Erik B. Nes (2002), 'Exporter trust, commitment and marketing control in integrated and independent export channels', *International Business Review*, **11**(4), 385–406.

Solberg, C.A. and L.S. Welch (1996), 'Strategic alliances for SMEs: a path for internationalization?', Proceedings 9th Nordic Conference on Small Business Research, Lillehammer, Norway, May.

Tantong, P., K. Karande, A. Nair and A. Singhapakdi (2010), 'The effect of product adaptation and market orientation on export performance: a survey of Thai managers', *Journal of Marketing Theory Practice*, **18**(2), 155–69.

Terpstra, V. and C.M. Yu (1988), 'Determinants of foreign investment of US advertising agencies', *Journal of International Business Studies*, **19**(1), 33–46.

Turnbull, Peter W. (1987), 'A challenge to the stages theory of the internationalization process', in Stanley D. Reid and Phillip J. Rosson (eds), *Managing Export Entry and Expansion*, New York: Praeger, pp. 21–40.

Welch, Lawrence S., Gabriel R.G. Benito and Bent Petersen (2007), *Foreign Operation Modes: Theory, Analysis, Strategy*, Cheltenham, UK and Northampton, MA, USA: Edward Elgar.

Welch, Lawrence S. and Reijo Luostarinen (1988), 'Internationalization: evolution of a concept', *Journal of General Management*, **14**(2), 34–55.

Williamson, Oliver E. (1985), *The Economic Institutions of Capitalism: Firm, Market, Relational Contracting*, New York: Free Press.

Young, Stephen, James Hamill, Colin Wheeler and J. Richard Davies (1989), *International Market Entry and Development*, London: Harvester.

6 An inquiry into born global firms' learning process: a case study of information technology-based SMEs

Alex Rialp, Inmaculada Galván-Sánchez and Minerva García

INTRODUCTION

According to several authors, an outstanding orientation towards organizational learning and knowledge management constitutes a useful platform for getting into hyper-competitive markets (Argyris and Schon 1978; Kim and Kogut 1996; Prencipe and Tell 2001).

Traditional internationalization theories consider firms' internationalization as a gradual process of commitment that is the consequence of an incremental learning curve. However, some firms, specially those in the information and communication technology (ICT) sector do not necessarily follow this general path. It is possible to find processes of quick internationalization from inception, based on different resources such as networks (external resources) or capabilities (internal resources) and with a special orientation towards organizational learning (Autio et al. 2000; Bell and McNaughton 2000; Zahra et al. 2000; Zahra and George 2002; Knight and Cavusgil 2004). Firms implementing this internationalization process have received different names in the literature (born globals, international new ventures, global start-ups, instant internationals, high-technology start-ups, global high-tech firms), and are usually defined as 'a business organization that, from inception, searches for earning a significant competitive advantage from the use of its resources, and from the sale of products, in multiple countries' (Oviatt and McDougall 1994, p. 49). Zahra and George (2002, p. 11) conceive the mechanism of creation of international firms as 'the creative process of discovering and exploiting opportunities that reside outside of the domestic markets, searching for competitive advantage'. These born globals and international ventures, among other labels, are currently following early and rapid internationalization processes, especially, but not only, in the high-tech sector.

To date there are a few studies that address the phenomenon of born global firms, and although a constant reference to the learning capability is made in several studies (Autio et al. 2000; Dimitratos and Plakoyiannaki 2003; Knight and Cavusgil 2004; Rialp et al. 2010), almost none have gone deeper either in the analysis of this aspect or in the generation of capabilities – with the relevant exceptions of Prashantham (2005) and Weerawardena et al. (2007). Rialp et al. (2005, p. 162) mention that the perspective of organizational capabilities can constitute 'one of the more promising theoretical frames to explain and interpret not only the appearance of rapidly internationalized firms, but their future development through a sustainable and fast international growth'.

In addition, according to several researchers (Autio et al. 2000; Knight and Cavusgil 2004; Rialp et al. 2005) more research is needed on early internationalizing firms, particularly from a knowledge-based perspective. To address this, this study implements a qualitative methodology based on case studies of firms in the ICT sector. This case-based study explores organizational learning mechanisms allowing some purposefully selected Catalan born globals acting in the Spanish information technology (IT) sector to develop dynamic capabilities in the context of three key decision-making processes: new product development, the search for an exploitation of foreign market knowledge, and development of the business strategy.

The chapter is organized as follows. The next section describes the theoretical framework of the study (organizational capabilities and the learning theories) and it summarizes the literature review of born global firms, referring to their learning process and knowledge development. The methodology section explains some peculiarities of the ICT sector, followed by the methodology implemented in this study. The subsequent section analyzes the obtained results. The final section discusses the conclusions based on the study.

LITERATURE REVIEW AND THEORETICAL FRAMEWORK

Organizational Capabilities

Firm capabilities and/or competencies are referred to as the skills that a firm possesses for generating any type of output. Just as different levels of knowledge exist, different levels of capabilities also exist. In particular, those allowing firms to generate some competitive advantage, a strategy of growth or that provide a value added, have been called 'dynamic capabilities' (Teece et al. 1997; Teece 2000), 'main competencies' (Prahalad and Hamel 1990), 'high-level capabilities' (Winter 2000), or 'combinative' ones

(Kogut and Zander 1992). These different capabilities create alternatives of growth, because they represent opportunities for liberating earned skills in the work with certain type of technologies, products or processes for other types of managerial applications (Lei et al. 1996).

From a hierarchically structured perspective (Grant 1991, 1996), organizational capabilities can be categorized into:

- Basic knowledge or skills and rules simply guiding action.
- Organizational routines (Nelson and Winter 1982): sequential behavior patterns made by individuals and formed by tacit knowledge. That is the reason why their transfer becomes difficult without a previous process of knowledge articulation. Routines are learned by doing and observing, through mechanisms of socialization (Nonaka 1991; Nonaka and Takeuchi 1995).
- High-level, dynamic capabilities developed through complex mechanisms of coordination such as codification, articulation, and experience-based organizational learning (Zollo and Winter 2002).

Grant (1998) distinguishes among capabilities according to their functionality in: corporative or firm headquarters, information management, research and development, production, product design, and marketing, sales, and distribution (Figure 6.1).

In a dynamic environment, the capability of a firm for integrating, building, and reconfiguring internal and external competences, has been called 'dynamic capabilities' (Teece et al. 1997). These capabilities of a series of strategic and organizational processes such as the development of new products, alliances, opening of branch offices, and so on that create value from knowledge based on experience (Prahalad and Hamel 1990; Eisenhardt and Martin 2000; Zollo and Winter 2002). Prahalad and Hamel's 'main competences' constitute the set of collective learning in the organization, specifically addressed to determining how to coordinate diverse productive skills and integrate multiple technologies. For Kogut and Zander (1992), combinative capabilities are organizational processes through which firms acquire knowledge resources and with them generate new resources. Likewise, Winter (2000, p. 983) defines capabilities as 'high level routines' (or collections of routines) which, together with their input fluxes, confer to the management of the organization a series of decision alternatives to produce significant outputs of a certain type. The difference with routines is that capability effects are known and intended and some control on them exists. Emphasis is made on learning and what is considered to be a dynamic capability, if such a learning capability is systematic and persistent inside the organization.

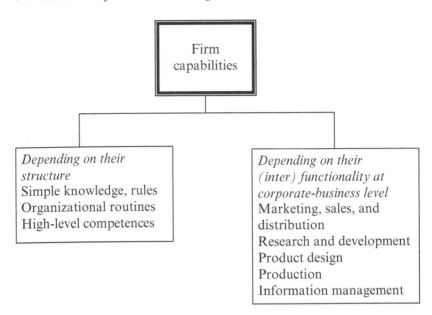

Source: Adapted from Grant (1996).

Figure 6.1   Types of capabilities

Eisenhardt and Martin (2000) have also considered that dynamic capabilities can be identified as 'the best practices'. However, the important point is not just their result, but the process promoting their development. A learning-oriented organization is characterized by being capable of articulating its experience in practices and replicable processes, and not by the simple fact of carrying out an effective and efficient process. It would be the difference between 'to know how to do' and 'to be conscious of knowing how to do'. To have a certain skill or knowledge of tacit character does not imply necessarily that the owner of that knowledge is capable of transferring it. For building dynamic capabilities, Zollo and Winter (2002) point out the importance of the 'cyclic evolution of knowledge', where the articulation and codification are superior mechanisms of organizational learning. The result of exercising a capability is multidimensional, because the results have enormous variations. Capabilities cannot be represented simply as dichotomy variables, in the sense that they are possessed or not. The capability represents the measure to which results are near the desired result or above expectations in an objective (McGrath et al. 1995).

Accordingly, high-level, dynamic, combinative capabilities configure those core competencies, allowing firms to generate some level of competitive advantage, usually by means of a growth-based strategy, providing higher added value to the firm (Prahalad and Hamel 1990; Kogut and Zander 1992; Teece et al. 1997; Eisenhardt and Martin 2000). In essence, such core competencies are usually related to a company's multidimensional learning capability needed to develop new and distinctive products/ processes and/or (foreign) markets in which integration of internal and external resources and interfunctional coordination is paramount.

Theories of Learning and Knowledge

Learning has been defined as the change of state of knowledge of an individual or organization. 'Change of state' is defined as the adoption of a new belief, the giving up of a previous belief, or the change in the confidence level which an individual or group of individuals have in the ideas of an organization (Sánchez and Heene 1997; Sadler-Smith, et al. 2001). Therefore, knowledge represents a pile of beliefs and learning represents the process that can modify it. Knowledge is part of the capabilities and they are the indispensable elements that allow us to develop actions or practice functions.

From the cognitive perspective, people skills, as well as organization skills, are the result of the degree of expertise developed along time in a process of continuous experimentation and interpretation, the so-called 'learning process' (Albino et al. 2001). March (1991) identifies two types of processes informing learning: the exploration and the exploitation of knowledge. Exploration is a mechanism of searching whereby individuals or organizations try to identify how to solve a problem, and it includes variation, experimentation, discovery, and innovation. Exploitation implies using learning in activities such as election, production, selection, implantation, and execution. To be involved continuously in exploration activities suggests that the acquired knowledge cannot be improved because it is not exercised enough, while to be involved only in exploitation activities supposes that organizations develop neither innovations nor improvements so they remain obsolete. March (1991, p. 71) states: 'the right balance between exploration and exploitation is the main factor for the survival of the system and its prosperity'.

In the searching, or exploration mechanisms, experience has been identified as a very important source of the so-called 'learning by doing', a kind of inductive learning (Pisano 2000). On the other hand, deductive learning, 'learning before doing', is defined as that technique whereby situations that could arise are simulated, and the results are studied before operations begin. In fact, both types of learning are used in parallel depending on the degree of previous knowledge possessed. In order for 'learning before doing' to be effective, a more solid knowledge base is needed, because without it, to design a simulation and furthermore, to interpret the variations, is difficult.

So, knowledge acquisition and its exploitation are functions of the organizational learning process. The activity allowing knowledge to return value for the organization is called 'knowledge management' (Prencipe and Tell 2001). Knowledge management includes all those processes aimed at creating new knowledge, capturing individual knowledge and disseminating it (Obeso 1999). When knowledge is disseminated within the organization, this influences other members, implying acquisition and sharing of knowledge, as a learning mechanism. Accordingly, knowledge management and organizational learning are intimately tied to and need each other.

The 'spiral of knowledge' concept, developed by Nonaka (1991) and Nonaka and Takeuchi (1995), explains the processes followed by knowledge to transfer it from the individual level to the organizational level, and the learning processes implying the conversion of tacit knowledge into explicit knowledge, and vice versa. The cycle begins with the transmission and teaching of knowledge from tacit to tacit, by using observation, imitation and practice as mechanisms of socialization. In this context, the communities of practice (Brown and Duguid 1991) illustrate how this process is carried out. The conversion of knowledge from explicit to explicit is fulfilled through the combination of knowledge, basically through the synthesis of information. The conversion from tacit to explicit knowledge is generated by articulating it in a more systematic way. And finally, the transformation from explicit knowledge into tacit knowledge is carried out by internalizing it; that is, using the explicit knowledge to increase the base of tacit knowledge.

Bearing in mind the difficulty of transmission and replication of tacit knowledge, Prencipe and Tell (2001) developed a 3×3 matrix for characterizing several learning mechanisms in different projects (Table 6.1). The horizontal dimension is referred to as the accumulation of the experience, articulation, and codification, while in the vertical dimension, the learning typologies are identified, that is, the methods for characterizing each one of these processes, their results, and economic benefits.

In addition, Albino et al. (2001) propose a classification of knowledge according to the degree of formalization of the norms and procedures the knowledge is based upon. Then, it is possible to distinguish between intuitive knowledge versus scientific (experience-based, qualitative or quantitative) knowledge. Intuitive knowledge is the more basic level, founded upon simple learning mechanisms such as common sense, intuition, and analogies. Experience-based or tacit knowledge is developed

Table 6.1 Learning typologies: results and economic benefits

	Accumulation of experience	Articulation of knowledge	Codification of knowledge
Learning typologies	Learning by doing Learning by using	Learning by: reflection, thought, discussion, confrontation	Learning by: writing and rewriting, implantation, replication, adaptation
Results	Local experts and knowledge based on individual experience	Symbolic representations and communication Better understanding of the report of the results (predictive knowledge)	Organizational handbooks and codified processes
Economic benefits	Economies of specialization	Economies of coordination	Economies of information (diffusion, replication, and re-using information)

Source: Prencipe and Tell (2001, p. 1378.

through learning by doing (action), learning by observation, and learning by interaction with others. This type of knowledge is what comprises most organizational routines (Nelson and Winter 1982). Qualitative knowledge is created and transferred generally by means of socialization processes. Quantitative knowledge is the most highly formalized and most controlled by the individual/organization. Among these four types of knowledge, both qualitative knowledge and quantitative scientific knowledge help to identify casual relations and the measurement of results.

Kogut and Zander (1992, 1996) consider that what firms do better than markets is to share and transfer knowledge of individuals and groups inside an organization, so the competitive dimension of these processes is to carry them out efficiently. Learning inside the organization can be obtained in two different ways: learning through the existing members, or integrating new members possessing knowledge that the organization does not have (Simon 1991). Kogut and Zander (1992, 1996) suggest that organizations should be seen as social communities where their expert knowledge is transformed into products and services applying high-level organizational principles. This evolution coincides with the statement of evolutionary theory (Nelson and Winter 1982), which considers that the firm's skills or routines are sources of knowledge and, to the extent that these are developed and replicated, the firm will be able to survive and grow. Organizational learning is then the mechanism for developing a knowledge base (Shrivastava, 1983; Kogut and Zander 1992). Kogut and Zander (ibid.) argue that the differences in firms' results lie in the transfer and imitation problems associated with knowledge. Knowledge is not always transmitted and replicated easily, due to the degree to which it can be codified and its degree of complexity. As has been explained, the whole knowledge cannot be codified, so its transmission and replication can become difficult.

From this perspective, the firm is a system whereby actions are addressed to produce certain outputs through the coordination and integration of its resources and capabilities. It is important to detect where the knowledge resides and who has acquired it, because it must be available for strategic choices (Simon 1991). Organizational effectiveness depends on the quality of the available and tested 'knowledge base' to carry out appropriate strategic decisions, organizational learning being the crucial mechanism for developing such a knowledge-related base. A firm with very basic and simple knowledge will be at a clear disadvantage compared to another firm with more experience and tested knowledge. Organizational knowledge is intimately tied with the interpretive managerial processes of problem-solving, thus it is important for managers to be able to trace the development of new capabilities. To keep this an ongoing process, organizational learning systems (learning by versus before doing, single versus double loop learning, exploration and exploitation of both tacit and explicit knowledge, and so on) can be, at least partly, institutionalized through formal mechanisms and informal practices (Shrivastava 1983).

From this perspective, the 'absorptive capability' concept, developed by Cohen and Levinthal (1990) becomes relevant. The idea underlying this concept is that: 'the skill to evaluate and use external knowledge is, in great measure, a function of the previous level of related knowledge' (ibid., p. 128). In other words, the more that previous knowledge is related to some phenomenon or situation, the larger the interpretive capacity and, therefore, the more an organization can learn from external stimuli. This skill is considered an important capability for the development of new products (Stock et al. 2001). So, in this study 'knowledge base' will be the firm's absorptive capability.

Learning and Knowledge Patterns in Born Global Firms

Considering the assumptions of the more traditional internationalization models, small and recently created firms would tend to start their activities abroad through less risky modes characterized by low resource commitment, and gradually move towards modes with a major degree of risk and resource commitment (Johanson and Vahlne 1977, 1990; Luostarinen and Gabrielsson 2002). From this gradual internationalization perspective, it is generally understood that when the firm acquires knowledge and experience abroad, it will gradually compromise more resources and will be able to introduce itself into more distant cultural markets. As can be observed, in general, those models depart from the assumptions of lack of resources, market knowledge, and risk aversion. Based on these facts, they explain the introduction to foreign markets as a time-consuming process.

However, compared to more traditional internationalizing firms, born global and international new ventures are mostly characterized by becoming international almost from inception (Madsen and Servais 1997), thus avoiding incremental and time-consuming acquisition of experiential knowledge abroad. Their geographical coverage seems to be more determined by the founders' experiences as well as by their economic capacity and their clients (Andersson and Wictor 2003). Born global firms tend to take advantage of the competencies obtained from their partners or strategic alliances, especially those in distribution channels (Madsen and Servais 1997; Bürgel and Murray 2000). In particular, their learning capabilities allow them to develop knowledge-based intangible assets, products or services, and also business processes that can be internally replicated and transferred by means of diversification and/or international expansion (Stalk et al. 1992; Teece et al. 1997; Zahra and George 2002).

Accordingly, the phenomenon of born global firms has captured the attention of academicians in the internationalization and entrepreneurship areas because the behavior of these firms is opposite to that expected for a gradually internationalizing firm (Rialp et al. 2005). New firms used to almost always suffer the disadvantages of being new and small because they lacked both resources and experience, however, some of them now are developing capabilities that allow them to overcome these impediments. Autio et al. (2000) consider that the disadvantages of being new, small, and foreign are compensated by the learning capability these firms possess. Firms performing in international environments from inception do not need to unlearn habits or routines established for operating in national markets (Nelson and Winter 1982). They generate structures and forms to operate successfully in international markets directly. Accordingly, their absorption capacity (Cohen and Levinthal 1990) is better and, therefore, they assimilate the knowledge coming from diverse sources faster than other firms. Erikkson et al. (2000) and Zahra et al. (2000) point out that to have access to different markets allows firms to learn faster because they become involved in diverse sources of experience and knowledge.

Learning and knowledge are two basic elements in the construction of organizational capabilities. Learning is the form in which knowledge is acquired and becomes the base for building competencies. Several authors in this field (Autio et al. 2000; Bell and McNaughton 2000; Zahra et al. 2000; Zahra and George 2002; Knight and Cavusgil 2004) point out that born global firms show a special orientation towards developing intensive organizational learning and knowledge patterns which become crucial for building stronger organizational competences. Bell and McNaughton (2000) developed an eclectic model and distinguished between born global firms and traditional ones. These authors refer to the former as 'based on knowledge' and/or 'knowledge intensive'. The 'knowledge-intensive' born global firms' use knowledge as an instrument for improving their processes, while 'based on knowledge' born globals involve knowledge in their product directly, that is, they develop high-tech products.

A distinctive characteristic of firms based on knowledge and/or knowledge intensive is their innovation capability (Knight and Cavusgil, 2004). The explanation of growth and business development based on organizational knowledge resides in evolutionary theory (Nelson and Winter 1982), where innovation and knowledge processes are described in depth. Knowledge created through innovation processes provides the needed capacities for technological development, probably the key resource that born global firms use to develop unique products. Recently created firms usually lack tangible resources, however born global firms are able to develop products and services through the use of capabilities based on knowledge and intangible assets. Moreover, these firms possess a strong market orientation and make use of technological strategies to develop unique products by putting great emphasis on quality (Knight and Cavusgil 2004).

Today, born global firms are being studied from the perspective of both internationalization and entrepreneurship theories, creating a research field called 'international entrepreneurship' (Zahra and George 2002). Several of the distinctive characteristics of a new firm can be comparable to those of a born global firm. However, Dimitratos and Plakoyiannaki (2003) point out that a characteristic culture of this type of born global firm includes orientation towards international markets, learning and innovation, risk and networking, and an international managerial motivation that shapes and facilitates their early foreign activities.

Thus according to the literature review and theoretical framework, the main research proposition in this study, using Catalan born global small and medium-sized enterprises (SMEs), is to analyze whether those processes aimed at articulating, codifying, and transferring knowledge inside and outside the organization are crucial for leveraging the extant knowledge base in a more effective way and for transforming it into core competences. In addition, the associated learning mechanisms (at both the formal and informal levels) may also help show that the investigated born global firms develop, exploit, and convert knowledge into such dynamic capabilities.

METHODOLOGY

Empirical Context: ICT Sector in Catalonia

This study focuses on analyzing a selected number of SME cases in the ICT sector established in Catalonia (Spain). The main reasons for justifying the analysis of this type of firm in this particular sector are the following:

- First, DIRCE (2004), states that 99.87 percent of Spanish firms are SMEs. In Catalonia this picture is reproduced. IDESCAT (2000), reports that SMEs represent 99.85 percent of the total number of Catalan firms. These figures evidence the importance of studying SMEs because they represent the large majority of firms in this particular economy.
- Second, the ICT sector is composed of computer science, telecommunications, audiovisual and electronics; consequently, it configures the nucleus of the digital era. Without ICT knowledge, society would simply not exist. The knowledge society or 'knowledge-based economy' recognizes the role that knowledge and technology play in economic growth. It is estimated that more than 50 percent of GDP (gross domestic product) of the bigger economies of the OECD has been created in industries based on knowledge (OECD 1996). In fact, knowledge investments can increase productive capacity, as well as transforming it into new products and processes. As these knowledge investments are characterized by growing performance, they become key for long-term economic growth (ibid.). In addition, the new economic model for Catalonia is currently focused on transforming its productive base into a knowledge-based economy (Trullén et al. 2001).

One of the more important industries representing this type of knowledge economy is the ICT sector, since it has a multiplying effect in the innovation, productivity, and competitiveness of many other industrial sectors. The ICT sector, particularly software firms, can be distinguished because it can exploit scale economies easily. The main characteristic of the software that permits these scale economies is the possibility of using certain components again in new products (Diaz-Herrera et al. 2000).

Research Methodology: Case Selection, Data Collection, and Analysis

The case study methodology has been implemented (Eisenhardt 1989; Yin 1994) to analyze the development of the firms' learning capability. Case study allows a dynamic analysis, understanding the path followed by new and/or young international firms. One of the strengths of using a qualitative methodology is that the analysis can be centered on events in their natural environment, so data collection occurs very close to the situation being studied (Miles and Huberman 1994).

This study is focused on a qualitative, case-based analysis of a selected number of ICT Catalan firms. In order to select a sufficient number of eligible firm cases, the first contacts were carried out by means of a directory of exporting firms on COPCA's (the Catalan public institution in charge of promoting Catalan firms' internationalization) web page. Other firms were initially contacted through Barcelona Activa (a business incubator center) and others through one of the managers who agreed to participate in the study.

Apart from the fact that any eligible firm had to belong to the ICT sector, other criteria were considered for determining whether a specific firm was a born global one. One necessary condition was mostly based upon the time that had elapsed between the birth of the firm and its first international activity (Rennie 1993; Autio et al. 2000; Shrader et al. 2000). In line with other studies in this field (Oviatt and McDougall 1994, 1995), the six-year convention between start-up and internationalization of the firm was adopted. Also, by checking firm data related to the year of business creation, year of start-up operations abroad, and the number of markets subsequently approached, it was possible to decide whether a particular firm fulfilled the requirements to be eligible for further research. Accordingly, we used the combination of a theoretical framework focused on the interplay between organizational learning and knowledge management processes, together with the consideration of ICT-related Catalan exporting firms meeting the operational definition of born global firms. This resulted in the selection of four case firms, thus complying with the appropriate range of cases required to conduct this type of study, according to Eisenhardt (1989), whose anonymity condition is expressly preserved.

Two of the firms participating in the study are highly specialized in the development of software (referred to as A and C, respectively). Firm B performs ICT-related specialized services for the banking sector and firm D also applies software as an important business tool.

Data collection was carried out during November 2007 and March 2008; the series of interviews conducted with the selected firms' managers and/or directors was the richest source of information. The research protocol was the main tool implemented in order to ensure that the compiled data were useful to carry out a comparison between these four cases. In the interviews with the different informants, special emphasis was put on obtaining information regarding the products' nature for better understanding the learning processes and the type of knowledge behind them.

The analysis of information started with an individual examination of cases. All the available information was integrated, according to some previously codified categories. Then each of the four cases was rewritten and returned to those interviewed for their own revision and approval. At the same time, a cross-case analysis was carried out using matrix analysis for detecting the most common and distinct factors among the selected cases.

Operationalization of Key Conceptual Constructs

Due to the fact that capabilities replication is reinforced with more sophisticated knowledge bases and formal learning mechanisms (Shrivastava 1983; Kogut and Zander 1992, 1996; Pisano 2000; Zollo and Winter 2002), the study took into consideration that a special orientation towards these aspects would exist in these firms. The learning capability was explored in three dimensions that are considered important for expansion: market knowledge, product development, and business strategy. Market knowledge facilitates the geographical expansion, while product development and business strategy allow a product line diversification (Stalk et al. 1992; Stock et al. 2001).

The main focus of the study lay in understanding the different learning systems as well as the available knowledge base of the case firms. To evaluate the type of knowledge base, Albino et al.'s (2001) categorization was adopted, eliminating the category of intuitive, non-scientific knowledge, because it was not clearly observable in any selected case firm. The result is the following classification of scientific knowledge-based capabilities: E: experience-based knowledge; Q: qualitative knowledge; C: quantitative knowledge. In addition, two main organizational learning systems were also analyzed, distinguishing between formal and informal mechanisms.

Following Yin (1994) and Maxwell (1996), validity and reliability requirements were conveniently satisfied by means of applying a complete research protocol, triangulation of sources of data, cross-comparison

BOX 6.1   METHODOLOGICAL DESIGN

Research context	The Autonomous Community of Catalonia is capitalizing the impulse for establishing a truly knowledge-based economy in Spain (Trullén et al. 2001)
Type of case study	Multiple case-based research was applied basically aimed at obtaining analytic, non-statistical generalization (Eisenhardt, 1989; Yin, 1994)
Case selection and sample	Purposeful, theory-driven sample of Catalan SMEs in IT sector. Operational criteria conventionally applied to assure both the IT-oriented activity and the born global condition of potentially eligible firms resulted in the final selection of 4 case firms
Data collection process	Triangulation of information sources, lasted around five months to complete (November 2007 and March 2008)
Data analysis	Individual analysis of the 4 firms and cross-case comparisons, based upon pre-codified categories and matrix analyses, were performed
Operation-alization of key research constructs	Each firm's learning-based capabilities were explored in terms of 3 key dimensions: (foreign) market knowledge, product development and business strategy (product line and/or geographic diversification) Partially following Albino et al. (2001), to evaluate the type of firm's extant scientific knowledge base, the following classification was used: E (experience knowledge), Q (qualitative knowledge) and C (quantitative knowledge) Two main organizational learning systems, distinguishing between formal and informal ones, were also analyzed
Validity and reliability requirements	Following Yin (1994) and Maxwell (1996), validity and reliability requirements were conveniently satisfied by means of applying a complete research protocol, triangulation of sources of data, cross-comparison techniques, and feedback from firms' interviewed informants and from other specialists not directly involved

techniques, and feedback from the firms' interviewed informants and from other specialists not directly involved.

Box 6.1 presents a summary of the methodological design of this research.

RESULTS

Table 6.2 summarizes the main characteristics of the four analyzed firms, and shows that firm B is the oldest one, created in 1987, and firms A and C are the youngest ones, both set up in 2002. In general the four companies are characterized by having a management team with deep knowledge in their specific area of specialization and for favoring internal environments that tend to impact positively on the generation of organizational learning.

Base of Available Scientific Knowledge

According to the theoretical framework, the research findings are discussed in the context of three main decision-making processes: product development, market knowledge, and the business strategy (Table 6.3).

Product/technical knowledge

In terms of (new) product development, the base of extant technological knowledge (algorithms and programming) underlying this capability was found to be solid enough in these four case companies.

Firm A has been able to develop an algorithm that generates the base for a product that has great acceptance in the marketplace (software for e-procurement). This knowledge serves for its replication in almost all new situations that firm A faces. After the initial knowledge creation, the particular knowledge required for each single project has been generated. Knowledge generated by its clients is codified in a database that any member of the firm can easily check to solve new problems. Firm B also has some standardized mathematical models which serve as a base to solve problems for different clients. In this sense, firm B carries out some adjustments because each client has particular databases and specific needs.

On the other hand, firms C and D have a relatively less replicable knowledge base between clients. Although some applications inside their programs can be replicated, many of their products must be developed for each specific client. Firm C is selling its applications mostly to satisfy soccer referees' communication needs, because the product does not require so many adaptations in this particular context. When firm C develops some new applications for institutions or firms, these are only partially

Table 6.2 *Firm cases characteristics*

	Firm A	Firm B	Firm C	Firm D
Year of establishment/Year of internationalization	2002/2003	1987/1989	2002/2003	1995/2001
Main IT-related activity	Specialized software for e-procurement solutions. Its specialized software complements well the functions of an ERP system. Client-related information is also codified	Develops standard mathematical models (algorithms) for assessing risk associated with products usually commercialized by financial entities (banks, etc.)	Develops software for applications in PDA. Two main business lines: software for managerial applications and for sports as, for example, soccer referees, match statistics, etc.	Develops portals in Internet, focused on the creation of markets of classified ads. By working on the 3-layers development different web pages can be generated very quickly. The firm has more than 25 large websites on the internet
Product/s nature	Software product (essentially an algorithm) with very few modifications across their clients based upon very high technical knowledge replicability	Some specific developments for each particular client are always needed to adjust the model to their usually different databases. Product models have been subsequently refined by the firm	Business-related new applications are only 50% replicable. However, sport-oriented applications, specifically statistics, are more replicable	Currently, all its portals essentially share the same business strategy and fully replicable technical applications, only changing the markets in which this firm operates

Foundation act	The firm was created as a spin-off of a larger company and it is owned by three main partners	A technical specialist in this activity was the person who decided to create and run the firm	It was the implemented result of an entrepreneurial project developed for a doctorate course in e-commerce in a university in Barcelona (URL)	The firm started in 1995 as a provider of ISP services. In 1997 its first portal was created. In 2000, the firm changed the business strategy: ISP-related were sold and, since then, the company focused on the creation of portals of classified ads
Employees	5 people in total, three partners and 2 full-time contracted employees	Around 80 people, 60 of whom work in Barcelona and 20 in the rest of branches opened in Portugal, Mexico, and Argentina, among others	4 partners work in the company. There are 4 other full-time employees and, depending on each project, some scholars are hired	About 200 employees
Expansion towards foreign markets and modes of entry until 2005	2003 Germany, France and England 2004 Latin America — Licence agreement/ export via foreign distributors	1989 Portugal, 1994 Mexico, 1995 Argentina, 2001 Chile, US, Austria, Poland and other Latin American countries — Subsidiaries Direct export	2003 Netherlands 2004 Belgium and Chile — Export via foreign distributors	2001 Poland (1 portal) Strategic Agreement 2001 Mexico Subsidiary 2003 Italy Subsidiary 2005 Poland (3 portals) Subsidiary

Table 6.3   Analysis of scientific knowledge base for product/business strategy/foreign market knowledge development

Product development	Experience-based knowledge	Qualitative knowledge	Quantitative knowledge
Firm A		Highly replicable technical knowledge across product line	Algorithms
Firm B			Algorithms
Firm C			Programming
Firm D		Highly replicable technical knowledge across portals	3 layers (stages) programming
Business strategy development			
Firm A		Partnerships with service (consulting) firms	
Firm B		Network relationships with clients (financial entities)	
Firm C	Disperse experiences according to the 2 different lines of business		
Firm D		9 basic corporate principles 36 marketing principles	High-level capabilities for developing its business model (Metcalfe networks)
Foreign market knowledge			
Firm A		Internationalized domestic partners (consulting firms)	
Firm B			Headquarter-foreign subsidiaries formal relationships
Firm C	Foreign distributors' network		
Firm D	Direct visits		Headquarter-foreign subsidiaries formal relationships

replicable, so the core element of the application must be developed ad hoc for any particular client.

Something similar happens in firm D. Currently, this firm applies the so-called 'three layers' (or stages) development, which allows it to generate web pages very quickly. However, for the time being, this is only applied to some of its e-business models.

Thus with regard to (new) product development or technical solutions across cases, firms A and D quickly develop new, related products based upon a high level of (technical) knowledge replicability. However, although also meaningful, technical knowledge replicability seems to be a significantly lower capability for B and C than for A and D.

Market knowledge

In terms of gaining (international) market knowledge, this capability is largely externalized in cases A and C and more internalized in cases B and D. Firm A's domestic internationalized partners (consulting firms) usually possess this foreign market knowledge base. On the other hand, Firm C heavily depends on foreign independent distributors with experience-based knowledge of their own local markets. On the other hand, firm B directly and internally obtains knowledge from international markets through its networks of commercial branches/subsidiaries abroad. Finally, the internet-based firm D, whose portals are addressed to rather small (foreign) market niches in terms of users, requires the most specific market knowledge which is usually obtained through internal means (foreign subsidiaries and direct travels/market visits).

Business strategy

Regarding competitive strategy development, some commonalities and differences also emerged among these four case firms.

Firm D shows the most solid knowledge base useful to develop new business models in the form of internet portals. This firm, with its nine well-established corporate principles of strategy, 36 principles of marketing, the application of 'Metcalfe networks' and its web pages based upon architecture in three layers, can be considered as the one with more dynamic capabilities for the development of new businesses. This can be clearly seen when its evolution is analyzed, because in 1995 it had only one portal, three in 1998 and at the time of the study, around 30 portals are being managed.

Firms A and B are highly specialized firms whose strategy development to achieve sustained growth mostly depends on networking with consulting firms (A) and key financial clients (B). Firm A's high specialization allows it to avoid entry barriers and to achieve quick growth. Its business strategy is focused on qualitative knowledge and based upon the possibility of replication. However, its managers have detected that consulting firms must be their key strategic partners. In this way, firm A could expand very rapidly as a consequence of potential synergies, resulting firm reputation, brand management, and constantly adding new products into its portfolio of services. Firm B is also a specialist that attends a very specific market segment (risk assessment software) whose growth strategy in order to get new clients is based upon socialization processes by means of establishing network relationships with key financial entities. Firm C's business strategy development is mostly dependent upon experience-based knowledge. So far, this firm has been acting in very diverse sectors, but without the capability of unifying such concrete experiences into a more consolidated strategic knowledge base. Its current challenge, thus, is to develop mechanisms for gaining feedback from the different single projects managed so far.

Organizational Learning Mechanisms

Two different, but at the same time complementary, forms of organizational learning mechanisms were also explored within this research: formal and informal. In fact, both formal and mostly informal learning mechanisms existed in all four firms.

Formal mechanisms

Formal mechanisms usually imply knowledge articulation through programmed meetings for information exchange and codification of knowledge stored in databases, distribution lists and so on. Firm A has a database in which relevant case experiences are stored and easily retrievable. Firm B also has, a database of clients. Firm D possesses a directory with PowerPoint presentations and documents that are useful for the different lines of business. Moreover, in this particular firm, regular meetings between the different business directors are periodically carried out, in which everyone presents his/her key strategies and results, thus favoring knowledge transfer and the development of new ideas.

Informal mechanisms

Informal communication flows, involving direct contact/interaction, daily meetings and e-mails, were highly supported by an open and collaborative work environment presented in most of these Catalan born global firms.

The most used informal mechanism is natural and spontaneous conversations among the firm's members during daily activities. In firm B, for example, there are only 10 project managers, and normally they have lunch together, so learning transfer is informally favored. Firm C has only eight employees and the office is an open space, so communication flows easily. Although firm D has more employees, the physical characteristics of the space are very similar to firm C, and so is the learning mechanism. On the other hand, other communication mechanisms such as distribution lists and e-mails were generally used. Thus, in all the investigated case firms there seems to be a friendly internal environment promoting cooperation and interaction.

CONCLUDING REMARKS

From the interplay between theory and case-based research, this study has analyzed to what extent possessing more tested and replicable bases of knowledge facilitates product, strategy, and foreign market development. A tested base of knowledge facilitates a quicker development of new products, and/or diverse applications for the same products (Kogut and Zander 1992, 1996; Pisano 2000; Stock et al. 2001; Zollo and Winter 2002), thus enlarging the possibility of exploring new markets by exploiting the existent knowledge base (March 1991).

Interestingly, in spite of their relatively small size, all of the firm cases investigated in this research show rather sophisticated dynamic capabilities supported by scientific, not merely intuitive-based, knowledge. The four investigated born globals are generally characterized by showing diverse and shared knowledge domains in their specific areas of activity. Those showing a more tested base of product/market development knowledge, as a key dynamic capability, may enlarge the number of clients more easily. When the innovation/product development capability, sustained in technical and technological knowledge, is favorably complemented with marketing and network capabilities, early penetration into different markets is facilitated, thus increasing market knowledge capability (Knight and Cavusgil 2004). Moreover, when strategy development knowledge is higher, the possibilities of growth are increased even more. Born global D may be the most outstanding case, with knowledge-based dynamic capabilities supporting quicker development of new products (portals), foreign markets, and of its strategic business model.

In addition, all of them show a certain level of 'business international culture' (Dimitratos and Plakoyiannaki 2003) as demonstrated by entering into international markets at a very young age. Their key managers also seem to have promoted an internal environment stimulating the generation of organizational learning mechanisms, both formal and informal, within their respective companies. Thus, Shrivastava's (1983) categorization of formal and informal learning mechanisms applies in all four firm cases whose respective organizational cultures tend to favor organizational learning promoting problem-solving (Barney 1991; Autio et al. 2000; Bell and McNaughton 2000; Zahra et al. 2000; Dimitratos and Plakoyiannaki 2003).

Moreover, this study also provides evidence related to organizational capabilities. In this sense, as final concluding remarks, the evidence suggests the following:

First, the concept of 'core competence' development according to Prahalad and Hamel (1990) applies in all investigated cases. Considering the limitations to size and age that these firms face, they generally concentrate on what they know how to do and, in general, externalize other tasks.

Second, the more solid scientific knowledge bases (qualitative and quantitative) favor the expansion of markets, and make a product's replication for new clients easier. These knowledge-based capabilities have a major degree of reliability and require a high level of organizational learning, promoting knowledge articulation and codification.

However, this exploratory study is not free of several limitations often characterizing qualitative research approaches: first, only a limited number of firms belonging to the ICT industry in one particular region (Catalonia) are researched, thus only analytical but not statistical generalization can be achieved. Regarding the sector limitations, the study could only be transferred – with caution – to other sectors of the 'knowledge economy' to the extent to which a common element could be shared, namely scientific, knowledge-based capabilities.

REFERENCES

Albino, V., A.C. Garavelli and G. Schiuma (2001), 'A metric for measuring knowledge codification in organisation learning', *Technovation*, **21**(7), 413–22.
Andersson, S. and I. Wictor (2003). 'Innovative internationalisation in new firms: born globals – the Swedish case', *Journal of International Entrepreneurship*, **1**(3), 249–76.
Argyris, Chris and Donald A. Schon (1978), *Organisational Learning: A Theory of Action Perspective*; Reading, MA: Addison-Wesley.
Autio, E., H. Sapienza and J. Almeida (2000), 'Effects of age at entry, knowledge intensity, and imitability on international growth', *Academy of Management Journal*, **43**(5), 909–23.
Barney, J. (1991), 'Firm resources and sustained competitive advantage', *Journal of Management*, **17**(1), 99–120.
Bell, J. and R. McNaughton (2000), 'Born global firms: a challenge of public policy in support of internationalization', in J. Pels and D.W. Stewart (eds), *Marketing in Global Economy*, Conference Proceedings CD ROM, Buenos Aires: American Marketing Associacion (AMA), pp. 176–85.
Brown, J. and P. Duguid (1991), 'Organizational learning and communities of practice: toward a unified view of working, learning, and innovation', *Organizational Science*, **2**(1), 40–57.

Bürgel, O. and G. Murray (2000), 'The international market entry of start-up companies in high-technology industries', *Journal of International Marketing*, **8**(2), 33–62.

Cohen, W.M. and D.A. Levinthal (1990), 'Absorptive capacity: a new perspective on learning and innovation', *Administrative Science Quarterly*, **35**, 128–52.

Diaz-Herrera, J., P. Knauber and G. Succi (2000), 'Issues and models in software product lines', *International Journal of Software Engineering and Knowledge Engineering*, **10**(4), 527–39.

Dimitratos, P. and E. Plakoyiannaki (2003), 'Theoretical foundations of an international entrepreneurial culture', *Journal of International Entrepreneurship*, **1**(2), 187–215.

DIRCE (Spanish National Statistics Institute) (2004), database.

Dosi, Giovanni, Richard R. Nelson and Sidney G. Winter (eds) (2000), *The Nature and Dynamics of Organizational Capabilities*, Oxford and New York: Oxford University Press.

Eisenhardt, K. (1989), 'Building theories from case study research', *Academy of Management Review*, **14**(4), 532–50.

Eisenhardt, K. and J. Martin (2000), 'Dynamic capabilities: what are they?', *Strategic Management Journal*, **21**, 1105–21.

Eriksson, K., J. Johanson, A. Majkgård and D. Sharma. (2000), 'Effect of variation on knowledge accumulation in the internationalization process', *International Studies of Management and Organization*, **30**(1), 26–45.

Grant, R. (1991), 'The resource-based theory of competitive advantage: implications for strategy formulation', *California Management Review*, **33**(3), 114–35.

Grant, R. (1996), 'Toward a knowledge-based theory of the firm', *Strategic Management Journal*, **17** (Winter Special Issue), 109–22.

Grant, Robert M. (1998), *Contemporary Strategy Analysis: Concepts, Techniques, and Applications*, Oxford: Blackwell.

IDESCAT (Institut d'Estadística de Catalunya) (2000) Estadística, producció i comptes de la indústria 2000–2002, available at: www.idescat.es.

Johanson, J. and J.-E. Vahlne (1977), 'The internationalization process of the firm: a model of knowledge development and increasing foreign markets commitment', *Journal of International Business Studies*, **8**(1), 23–32.

Johanson, J. and J.-E. Vahlne (1990), 'The mechanism of internationalization', *International Marketing Review*, **7**(4), 11–24.

Kim, D.J. and B. Kogut (1996), 'Technological platforms and diversification', *Organization Science*, **7**(3), 283–301.

Knight, G. and T. Cavusgil (2004), 'Innovation, organizational capabilities, and the born-global firm', *Journal of International Business Studies*, **35**, 124–41.

Kogut, B. and U. Zander (1992), 'Knowledge of the firm, combinative capabilities and the replication of technology', *Organization Science*, **3**(3), 383–97.

Kogut, B. and U. Zander (1996), 'What do firms do? Coordination, identity and learning', *Organization Science*, **7**(5), 502–18.

Lei, D., M. Hitt and R. Bettis (1996), 'Dynamic core competences through meta-learning and strategic context', *Journal of Management*, **22**(4), 549–69.

Luostarinen, R. and M. Gabrielsson (2002), 'Globalization and global marketing strategies of born globals in SMOPECs', paper presented at the Annual Conference of the European Business Academy (EIBA), Athens (Greece), December 8-10.

Madsen, T. and P. Servais (1997), 'The internationalization of born globals: an evolutionary process?', *International Business Review*, **6**(6), 561–83.

March, J. (1991), 'Exploration and exploitation in organizational learning', *Organization Science*, **2**(1), 71–87.

Maxwell, Joseph A. (1996), *Qualitative Research Design – An Interactive Approach*, Thousand Oaks, CA: Sage.

McGrath, R.G., I.C. MacMillan and S. Venkataraman (1995), 'Defining and developing competence: a strategic process paradigm', *Strategic Management Journal*, **16**, 251–75.

Miles, Matthew B. and A. Michael Huberman (1994), *Qualitative Data Analysis*, Thousand Oaks, CA: Sage.

Nelson, Richard R. and Sidney G. Winter (1982), *An Evolutionary Theory of Economic Change*, Boston, MA: Harvard University Press.

Nonaka, I. (1991), 'The knowledge creating company', *Harvard Business Review*, **69**(6), 96–109.

Nonaka, Ikujiro and Hirotaka Takeuchi (1995), *The Knowledge Creating Company: How Japanese Companies Create the Dynamic of Innovation*, Oxford and New York: Oxford University Press.

Obeso, C. (1999), 'Homo faber, homo sapiens. Estado de la cuestión', in M. Güell (ed.), *Homo Faber, Homo Sapiens. La gestión del capital intelectual*, Barcelona: ESADE, pp. 140–55.

OECD (1996), *The Knowledge-based Economy*, Paris: OECD.

Oviatt, B. and P. McDougall (1994), 'Toward a theory of international new ventures', *Journal of International Business Studies*, **25**(1), 45–65.

Oviatt, B. and P. McDougall (1995), 'Global start- ups: entrepreneurs on a worldwide stage', *Academy of Management Executive*, **9**(2), 30–44.

Pisano, Gary P. (2000), 'In search of dynamic capabilities: the origins of R&D competence in biopharmaceuticals', in Dosi et al. (eds), pp. 129–54.

Prahalad, C.K. and G. Hamel (1990), 'The core competence of the corporation', *Harvard Business Review*, May–June, 79–91.

Prashantham, S. (2005), 'Toward a knowledge-based conceptualization of internationalization', *Journal of International Entrepreneurship*, **3**, 37–52.

Prencipe, A. and F. Tell (2001), 'Inter-project learning: processes and outcomes of knowledge codification in project-based firms', *Research Policy*, **30**, 1373–94.

Rennie, M. (1993), 'Global competetiveness: born global', *McKinsey Quarterly*, **4**, 45–52.

Rialp-Criado, A., I. Galván-Sánchez and S. Suárez-Ortega (2010), 'A configuration-holistic approach to born global firms' strategy formation process', *European Management Journal*, **28**, 108–23.

Rialp-Criado, A., J. Rialp-Criado and G. Knight (2005), 'The phenomenon of early internationalizing firms: what do we know after a decade (1993–2003) of scientific inquiry?', *International Business Review*, **14**, 147–66.

Sadler-Smith, E., D. Spicer and I. Chaston (2001), 'Learning orientations and growth in smaller firms', *Long Range Planning*, **34**, 139–58.

Sanchez, Ron and Aimé Heene (eds) (1997), *Strategic Learning and Knowledge Management*, Hoboken, NJ: John Wiley & Sons.

Shrader R., B. Oviatt and P. McDougall (2000), 'How new ventures exploit trade-offs among international risk factors: lessons for the accelerated internationalization of the 21st century', *Academy of Management Journal*, **43**(6), 1227–47.

Shrivastava, P. (1983), 'A typology of organizational learning systems', *Journal of Management Studies*, **20**, 7–29.

Simon, H. (1991), 'Bounded rationality and organizational leaning', *Organization Science*, **2**(1), 125–34.

Stalk, G., P. Evans and E. Shulman (1992), 'Competing on capabilities: the new rules of corporate strategy', *Harvard Business Review*, March–April, 57–69.

Stock, G., N. Greis and W. Fischer (2001), 'Absorptive capacity and new product development', *Journal of High Technology Management Research*, **12**, 77–92.

Teece, D. (2000), 'Strategies for managing knowledge assets: the role of firm structure and industrial context', *Long Range Planning*, **33**, 35–54.

Teece, D., G. Pisano and A. Shuen (1997), 'Dynamic capabilities and strategic management', *Strategic Management Journal*, **18**(7), 509–33.

Trullén, J., J. Lladós and R. Boix (2001), 'Economia del coneixement i competitivitat internacional de la indústria de Barcelona', Perspectiva econòmica de Catalunya, Cambra de Comerç de Barcelona, pp. 83–95.

Weerawardena, J., G. Sullivan Mort, P.W. Liesch and G. Knight (2007), 'Conceptualizing accelerated internationalization in the born global firm: a dynamic capabilities perspective', *Journal of World Business*, **42**, 294–306.

Winter, S. (2000), 'The satisficing principle in capability learning', *Strategic Management Journal*, **21**, 981–96.

Yin, Robert K. (1994), *Case Study Research – Design and Methods*, Thousand Oaks, CA: Sage.

Zahra, Shaker A. and Gerard George (2002), 'International entrepreneurship: the current status of the field and future research agenda', in Michael A. Hitt, R. Duane Ireland, Donald L. Sexton and S. Michael Camp (eds) (2002). *Strategic Entrepreneurship: Creating an Integrated Mindset*, Strategic Management Series, Oxford: Blackwell, pp. 11–85.

Zahra, S., D. Ireland and M. Hitt (2000), 'International expansion by new venture firms: international diversity, mode of market entry, technological learning, and performance', *Academy of Management Journal*, **43**(5), 925–50.

Zollo, M. and S. Winter (2002), 'Deliberate learning and the evolution of dynamic capabilities', *Organization Science*, **13**(3), 339–51.

PART II

BORN GLOBALS: RESEARCH AREAS REQUIRING MORE DEVELOPMENT

7 Born globals: research areas that still need to be covered more fully

V.H. Manek Kirpalani and Mika Gabrielsson

INTRODUCTION

Born globals (BGs) are a unique breed of international entrepreneurial small and medium-sized enterprises (SMEs). BGs are obviously, and historically, a relatively new phenomenon. They are very different from the traditional SME, in their roots, choice of foreign markets to enter, and growth processes. The BG is formed by entrepreneurs who have creative and or technological knowledge of a high order. The SME is formed by entrepreneurs who do not necessarily need any particular knowledge of a high order. BG growth is very rapid and thus the growth process it follows may well involve finding large channels, large partner MNEs, or other networks/alliances. The BG from inception, or soon after, looks at a global market. The SME grows domestically and then looks at markets abroad. For the SMEs, in most cases, the markets abroad are neighboring countries, and the process of entry is dominated by the concepts of physical distance and/or short business distance. The SME growth process is more often than not a stage pattern of growth where the firm proceeds from an export stage, to sales organizations, and later, possibly, to manufacture abroad. Thus, research that would be relevant and useful to BGs has to be different.

Furthermore, it must be recognized that the BG targets a global market but there could be a number of small firms that are BGs in approach but target only the regional market. In addition, some SMEs are born-again globals (BaGs), which have been defined as firms that started off as BGs. BaGs were not successful in their initial endeavors, refocused on their domestic markets and regrouped their strategies and resources, and now are returning to invade global markets. Logically, one can split this group into BaGs and born-again regionals (BaRs) which target their regional market. Finally, research has been done on what may be termed born-global industries (Løvdal and Aspelund 2010).

With regard to the issues faced by BGs, there are a number of research areas that have been covered in the literature. But much remains to be done in most of these areas, and in new ones that have yet to be looked into. This overview separates the research areas into two groups. The first is research done on BGs *per se*, and the second is research done on the interaction and impact between external variables and BGs. A general finding is that much more research has been done on BGs *per se*, and relatively little by comparison in the area of external variables/BGs.

RESEARCH ON BGS *PER SE*

This section analyzes research and discussions on new areas that are pertinent to BGs. First, however, a fundamental issue that tends to 'cloud' much of research progress is the fact that there is no clearly agreed-upon definition of what constitutes a BG firm, which would obviously be very useful to the development of research and theory concerning BGs.

Definition of a Born Global

Depending on the school of thought and characteristics of the investigated companies, scholars have used the following criteria when defining BGs:

- vision and strategy to become global/international (for example, Oviatt and McDougall 1994; Knight and Cavusgil 1996);
- technology-oriented small firms (for example, Bell 1995; Knight and Cavusgil 1996);
- time to become global/international, varying from immediate to three years (for example, Knight and Cavusgil 1996; Knight et al. 2001);
- geographical expansion in terms of a minimum of 25 percent as foreign sales (for example, Knight and Cavusgil 1996);
- geographical expansion in terms of a minimum number of countries served outside the home country (for example, Oviatt and McDougall 1994); and
- geographical expansion outside the home continent with a minimum of 50 percent as 'external' sales (Luostarinen and Gabrielsson 2004).

One agreed-upon universal point among scholars is that BGs (many of which are from a small and open economy (SMOPEC), such as Denmark, Finland, Norway, Sweden, Australia, Ireland, Israel, New Zealand, and Taiwan) rapidly globalize their business. They generally do this by methods that circumvent many of the existing international business research paradigms. This has been highlighted through studies in different countries; for example, Australia (Rennie 1993), Ireland (Knight et al. 2001), Israel (Almor 2000), New Zealand (Dana 2001), Scandinavian countries (Kirpalani and Luostarinen 1999; Luostarinen and Gabrielsson 2004), and the USA (Oviatt and McDougall 1994; Knight and Cavusgil 1996). The underlying cause is that BGs are facing a tremendous challenge given their resource constraints and vision. Given these circumstances, selection of international marketing channels is among one of the most difficult managerial challenges. It usually takes years for multinational enterprises (MNEs) to expand and penetrate into foreign markets. Enormous amounts have been spent in setting up subsidiaries and/or building effective marketing channels. BGs lack such resources, and therefore they have to utilize 'alternative governance structures' (Oviatt and McDougall 1994) and to more often rely on hybrid structures in their distribution channels, such as close relationships and network partners.

The variety of definitions used in many studies obviously creates a problem with regard to the comparability of the results, and difficulty in developing a theory. A similar problem arose much earlier in attempts to define MNEs (Kirpalani 1985). The solution there was more or less to adopt a broad descriptive approach rather than to construct a narrower model with tighter parameters. We suggest a similar solution and define BGs in line with Oviatt and McDougall (1994, p. 49): 'from inception, [BGs seek] to derive innovation from the use of resources and the sales of outputs in multiple countries'. Furthermore, 'to qualify as a BG the firm's offering should have either unique technology and/or superior design or innovative product/service, or know-how, systems or other specialized competencies' (Gabrielsson and Kirpalani 2004, p. 557). Discussion on research areas follows. Table 7.1 outlines a grid into which research studies can be placed, and as a trigger for thought about future studies.

Another group of researchers (Gabrielsson et al. 2008) clarified the definition of a BG firm, and drew upon empirical evidence to describe the phases through which BGs progress. These phases for successful BGs were introductory, growth and resource accumulation, and break-out to independence as a major player. Further, it was found that the risks, resource development, channels or networks, and organizational learning of BGs develop in the three phases mentioned above. However, the development process deviates considerably from that followed by traditional internationalizing SMEs. Table 7.2 illustrates the areas and phases where BGs face issues as they grow.

Table 7.1   Research grid of born global kinds of enterprises and internal areas of study

Areas of study \ Types of enterprise	BG	BR	BaG	BaR	ISME	BG Industry
Rapid globalization / internationalization						
International entrepreneurship / international new ventures						
Internet						
Knowledge acquisition, application, dissemination, management						
Market orientation						
Networks, joint ventures and large channels						
Organizational learning						
Resources: financial and other						
Strategy						

Note: BG=born global, BR=born regional, BaG=born-again global, BaR=born-again regional, ISME=internationalizing small and medium size enterprise, BG Industry=born global industry.

Table 7.2   Born globals: research areas and evolutionary phases

Areas \ Phases	Introductory	Growth	Remain with large partner	Break-out
Rapid globalization / internationalization				
International entrepreneurship/ international new venture				
Internet				
Knowledge acquisition, application, dissemination, management				
Market orientation				
Networks / large channels				
Organizational learning				
Resources: financial and other				
Strategy				

SELECTED SIGNIFICANT STUDIES

The discussion turns now to analyzing selected significant studies in the areas in which research has already emerged in the literature.

Rapid Globalization/Internationalization

The degree of globalization/internationalization of firms can be conceptualized on two vectors: structural and psychological. To start with the structural, some researchers have used foreign sales in the absolute, but the more common approach has been export intensity, which is a share of total turnover from foreign markets. This is a scale dimension. The scope dimension can be brought in through the number of markets served, the significantly varying distances of foreign markets, and the number of different kinds of customers, or different kinds of target markets. Many researchers have used time, which is exemplified by the speed of globalization/internationalization. This measure, utilized in conjunction with the commencement of a firm's existence, can create two distinct categories: the born global which internationalizes rapidly, and the 'born-again global' which also internationalizes rapidly, but after years of existence in the domestic market (Bell et al. 2001).

On the psychological vector, the degree of globalization/internationalization can be studied as a spectrum of behavior resulting from the owners' or managers' attitudes towards foreign operations and towards risk. For the latter factor, the risk is not only in the foreign operations, but in the previous package of risks already being carried by a BG with regard to the finance and start-up of the firm. One research group (Melén and Nordman 2009) explored which internationalization modes BGs use in their initial and continued progress. Using longitudinal data from eight biotechnology BGs, three subsets were formed: the slow committers, the incremental committers, and the high committers. The incremental committers went from low to high commitment modes in their continued internationalization, while the high committers used both low and high modes from inception. The difference between the three modes was the speed at which these firms committed resources to foreign markets.

An Australian case-based study focused on the attitudinal orientation of senior management in BGs. It identified four states of commitment to accelerated internationalization, and suggests that delineating these states should assist management to accelerate internationalization. The strategist state adopts a more benevolent, collaborative, behavioral stance designed to preserve relationships. The other three states are the responder, the opportunist, and the experimentalist, all of which have a shorter-term orientation, are more competitive, and are self-interested. The researchers offered a theoretical explanation that integrated the network perspective and resource-based view with international entrepreneurship (Freeman and Cavusgil 2007). Psychological measures are the attitudinal drivers of international commitment, such as the causes for the development of affective commitment and global or international strategy. These causes stem from an entrepreneurial mode of thinking and a global mindset and specific competencies to overcome the barrier of newness to different facets of the business.

A taxonomy for BGs was developed by a research team (Knight and Cavusgil 2005). The study describes each firm's grouping with regard to its basic orientations and the generic strategies it uses, as well as associated international performance. The findings suggest that superior international business performance of BGs tends to be driven by entrepreneurial orientation, technological leadership, and the strategies of differentiation and focus. The findings are discussed with regard to both their practical and scholarly implications.

International Entrepreneurship

The research paths of international business and entrepreneurship are intersecting with increasing frequency (McDougall and Oviatt 2000). International business researchers typically use the term 'born globals', whereas some international entrepreneurship researchers use the term 'international new ventures' (INVs) when investigating firms of the born global type. This reflects the internationalization of the marketplace and the increasing prominence of entrepreneurial firms in the global economy. Cross-border business activity is of increasing interest to researchers studying entrepreneurship. Moreover, accelerated internationalization is being observed in even the smallest and newest organizations. International entrepreneurship is a new multidisciplinary field that has its origins in the research on BGs. Networks and relationships have become important in internationalization studies in view of the former's role in helping overcome the 'resource poverty' of BGs and other small internationalizing firms. A research study based on six cases from high-tech and low-tech industries sought to identify the role and characteristics of entrepreneurial owner-managers and the development of their 'network capability' over time (Mort and Weerawardena 2006). How such network capability helps the identification and exploitation of international market opportunities, the development of knowledge-intensive products, and BG international performance is discussed. Also, the issue of network rigidity is highlighted. Future research directions are explored, in particular the extension of network capability research and its influence on large firms exhibiting international entrepreneurship.

A picture arises of how BG research is sprouting on different tangents but related to the effect of entrepreneurship. One study investigated the interrelationships of entrepreneurial orientation, marketing strategy, tactics, and firm performance among SMEs affected by globalization (Knight 2000). Conclusions on the critical roles of entrepreneurship and marketing to assist SME managers were also drawn. Another study explored the relationship between entrepreneurial orientation and two different BG development paths: the 'true born global' and the 'apparently born global or born international' (Kuivalainen et al. 2007). The researchers studied the effectiveness of the two different development paths after ascertaining that there was an increasing amount of evidence that small entrepreneurial firms, or those at an early stage in their development and possessing limited resources, were aiming at rapid internationalization.

The empirical results from 185 Finnish exporting firms showed that those that were 'true born-globals' had better export performance. Furthermore, depending on the degree of born-globalness, different dimensions of entrepreneurial orientation were of importance. A qualitative case-based research investigated four BG firms in a specific region of Spain for the most relevant traits shown by them versus more traditional and more recently established SMEs (Rialp, et al. 2005). The results indicate that the two different types of firms have two distinctive patterns of international development. Another relevant finding is that those BGs tended to be more entrepreneurial in their export entry behavior.

Entrepreneurial research has also been drawn on to present a framework for international joint ventures as the cross-border nexus of individuals and opportunities (Di Gregorio, et al. 2008). These opportunities may be associated with cross-border combinations of resources and/or markets. The study framework accounts for the emergence of firms whose existence stems from such opportunities. This perspective has implications for whether internationalization follows competitive advantage or vice versa. It also shows how exploitation of these opportunities can contribute to economic development. The following subsections examine whether certain factors have contributed significantly to BG success: the internet; knowledge accumulation; market orientation; networks and joint ventures; organizational learning; resources; financial and other; and strategy.

Internet

Very little research has focused on the use of the internet by BGs, and how this could be used to advantage by BGs. One study focused on how small computer software exporting firms use the internet for their international marketing activities (Moen et al. 2003). In the six firms surveyed, it was found that use of the internet did not replace personal sales. The firms discovered that standardized products were most suited for internet-based sales, but this was not an incentive. Product standardization led to reduced competitive advantage and lower profit margins for the firms. The findings suggested that most such firms use the internet to search for information about customers, distributors, and partners. Most firms reported a complex purchasing process and an extensive need for communication with customers before the purchase decision. Most significantly, internet usage for post-sales service and support activities generated revenue and led to improved customer relations. Image building through the internet, plus partnership agreements with well-known firms and positive product reviews were important, and reduced the uncertainty that potential customers often experience when unknown suppliers offer unfamiliar products.

The Knowledge Accumulation

An empirical survey study of US global start-up exporting firms investigated the effects of information acquisition activities on export performance (Yeoh 2000). The study covered the firms' information search effort and the use of personal, quasi-government and documented sources. The impact of these on the variables of information source characteristics, firms' strategic orientation, and environmental and organizational characteristics was examined. The results provided mixed support in predicting the firms' information search effort and information source use. The findings support the notion that firms which engage in greater information search and those that rely on personal and quasi-government information sources tend to have higher performance levels.

Knowledge is considered an essential resource in a firm's internationalization process, both from the sequential point of view and from the perspective of international entrepreneurship. One research team explored how different kinds of prior knowledge possessed by the founders and/or managers at BGs are related to the firm's discovery and exploitation of foreign market opportunities (Nordman and Melén 2008). They dichotomized data from eight biotech BGs into two subsets: born academics and born industrials. The different combinations of technological and international knowledge held by the founders and managers impacted on their firm's proactive and reactive behavior towards foreign market opportunities. The results indicate that these BGs follow different internationalization processes. Therefore, they should not be analyzed as a homogeneous group, as has been the common perspective.

Another study explored the marketing activities of BGs that had been established with a designer(s) as a founder. The focus of the study was on the impact of the mental model of the designer-founder, in terms of the operationalizing of marketing activities and on the commercial success of the firm's internationalization (Falay et al. 2007). The analysis showed that in the first phase the designer-founder was trying to establish the designer's own brand by participating in trade fairs, personal contacts with the marketing channel representatives, and control of point of sale activities. After early growth, the design-intensive BG began to suffer through lack of sufficient marketing competencies to manage growth to the second phase leading to maturity. This led to the management directing effort to the goal of profitability. It was found that in some firms a partnership between the designer-entrepreneur and a marketing professional was a source of sustained competitive advantage. The researchers believe that these findings can be generalized, and that other such BGs need higher requirements for marketing competencies in the second phase of growth.

An increasing number of new venture firms, many of which are BGs, are internationalizing their business operations (Zahra et al. 2000). Previous explanations of this trend focused on the importance of technological knowledge, skills, and resources for such expansion. But little is known about how these firms use the technological learning. The study mentioned here examined the pattern of international expansion as measured by international diversity of markets, mode of market entry on a firm's technological learning, and the effects of this learning on the firm's financial performance.

Another research study employed knowledge-based theory concentrated on international growth in entrepreneurial firms (Autio et al. 2000). It found earlier initiation of internationalization and greater knowledge intensity to be associated with faster international growth. The results suggest that early pursuit of international opportunity induces greater entrepreneurial behavior and confers a growth advantage.

Market Orientation

One team of researchers approached the BG phenomenon by applying ideas from existing international entrepreneurship, business, and marketing literatures. Their study shows how market orientation is a relevant construct for understanding the existence of BGs (Brannback et al. 2007). Market orientation is contrasted with science-driven strategies in young, technology based firms. In markets and science, both global and local forces influence the behavior of new biotechnology-based firms. The research methodology includes interviews and multiple industry cluster surveys. Qualitative data are analyzed by categorizing and combining data into thematic interviews. Quantitative survey data are summarized through non-parametric statistics. It was found that young ventures in a global biotechnology-based industry simultaneously face forces that require a global approach and other forces that drive them towards localization. Even though both markets, as well as the science base in biotechnology products, are increasingly global, this study suggests that BGs must do more than passively adapt to the global scene. One study concentrated on what key factors result in superior export performance for small firms from small countries (Brouthers et al. 2009). The firms were selected from Greece and several Caribbean countries. Drawing on the internationalization process model and organizational learning theory, the researchers hypothesized various scenarios. They found that emphasizing international sales while restricting exports to a few foreign markets resulted in superior export performance. The small firms were able to develop expertise in those foreign markets, build strong distribution networks, and manage export activities effectively.

One researcher has pointed out that little has been written about the branding strategies of BGs (Gabrielsson 2005). His research examines the branding strategies of 30 Finnish SME BGs. The experience, qualities, and global orientation of the founder and the top management team are deemed important for the success of the branding achievements of these firms. An additional key finding is that business-to-business and business-to-consumer BGs differ as to their branding approaches and strategies. Analysis reveals that branding strategies are dynamic and depend on the degree of globalization of the firm.

Another study builds on the literature regarding market orientation and internationalization to develop a model. Hypotheses are developed regarding the relationships between market orientation, knowledge acquisition, and market commitment, plus the direct and indirect effects of these variables on the performance of SMEs in foreign markets (Armario et al. 2008). The model and hypotheses are empirically tested on a multi-industry sample of Spanish SMEs operating in foreign markets. The results, obtained by structural equation modeling, indicate a direct positive relationship between market orientation and an internationalization strategy. However, the effect of market orientation on performance in foreign markets is moderated by the variables of knowledge acquisition and market commitment.

Networks and Joint Ventures

Smaller BG firms face key constraints: lack of economies of scale, lack of resources, particularly finance and knowledge, and aversion to risk-taking. One study explores how such firms overcome these constraints and achieve rapid growth internationally. They use technology to obtain competitive advantage, and networking competencies to develop alliances with suppliers, distributors, and joint venture partnerships (Freeman et al. 2006). Another useful area explored is how these relationships change over time to meet changing needs.

Other research reports on the use of business networks to identify how small and medium-sized manufacturing firms in New Zealand deal with issues of success and rapid growth resulting from their internationalization efforts (Chetty and Campbell-Hunt 2003). The study yields information on the internationalization process of firms. It also lays out the relationships between rapid international growth and business networks. In addition, business networks and their benefits and problems are discussed.

In the joint venture sector, some 261 international joint ventures or acquisitions carried out by BGs were studied. The BGs were 124 US newly public firms, which had formed these joint ventures within the first six years of their founding (Gleason and Wiggenhorn 2007). The study indicated that the market had responded positively. It was seen that the larger and more liquid firms had a higher propensity for joint ventures rather than acquisitions. Further, the firms that opted for joint ventures were rewarded with significantly higher returns. The study also found that cultural similarity affects mode choice.

Organizational Learning

BG firms are early adopters of internationalization. This highlights the critical role of innovative culture, as well as knowledge, and organizational capabilities (Knight and Cavusgil 2004). In this research, case studies are analyzed to better understand the early internationalization phenomenon and to ascertain key orientations and strategies that lead to international success among these innovative firms. These findings are then validated through a survey-based study. Despite the scarce resources typical among small firms, the findings show that BGs leverage a distinctive mix of orientations and strategies that enable them to succeed in diverse international markets.

Some researchers have looked at organizational learning and proposed a model to integrate the influence of knowledge on internationalization behavior based on proposals taken from organizational learning literature (Casillas et al. 2009). The model comprises several phases: prior knowledge, acquisition of new knowledge, integration of both the above sets of knowledge, action, and feedback. Using the above model, different courses of action are identified for further research into firm internationalization.

Resources: Financial and Other

One study with a resource-based view looked at factors that encouraged owner-managed SMEs to enter export markets. It was able to identify categories of human and financial capital (Westhead and Wright 2001). Two Spanish researchers developed a resource-based model for analyzing the effect of several resources of an intangible character (Rialp and Rialp 2007). The model tested several intangible resources that may have influenced a representative sample of Spanish manufacturing exporters to start export activity almost from inception. Further, the model aimed to measure, through the export intensity ratio, whether the results from these exports were better than those obtained from other SMEs that were not exporting from their inception. The results seem to confirm that both human and organizational capital resources had a significant impact on highly successful BGs.

For a young resource-constrained technology-based start-up firm, the choice of entry mode into foreign markets is a strategic decision of major importance. The authors analyzed the determinants of 398 export decisions taken from a UK survey of 246 technology-based start-ups with international activities (Bürgel and Murray 2000). The findings show that the decision is a trade-off between resources available and the support requirements of the customer. Particularly strong determinants of the mode choice are the innovativeness of the technology and the channel experience of the firm domestically. The authors suggest that an organizational capability perspective offers a better explanation of entry decisions than either stage or transaction theory.

Strategy

The objective of another study was to explore linkages between the strategies of small firms and the patterns, processes, and pace of their internationalization (Bell et al. 2004). The study methodology was qualitative and involved 30 in-depth interviews with key decision makers in internationalizing small firms in Great Britain. The findings showed close relationships between product policies and market focus, with innovation of products or processes often providing an important stimulus to international expansion. Further, business policies, including those linked to ownership and management changes, had an important influence upon the international orientation of many firms.

Another strategy study investigated BGs from Denmark and the USA using case and survey-based studies (Knight et al. 2004). The hypotheses were developed from a model that represents key factors in BG international success. The results suggest that international performance is enhanced with managerial emphasis on foreign customer focus and marketing competence. Product quality and differentiation strategy also play important roles, particularly in US firms.

Another research team explored the relationship between the adoption of a global orientation and strategic thinking in small firms that internationalize (Kalantaridis 2004). The researchers pointed out that there were two schools of thought: one argued that there is a positive relationship between the above two variables, while the other contended that small firms may internationalize even though they took a passive or reactive approach to the external environment. The study set out to further this discussion by comparing the experience of small firms with their medium and large firm counterparts. It drew upon the findings of a survey of 1,000 internationalized firms in England. The results suggested that there was little disparity in the strategy development among internationalized enterprises of different sizes. However, the incidence of strategic behavior among medium and large firms increased with the complexity of international operations. This was not the case with the small firms, where the latter complexity factor was not significant.

Another research team focused on the internationalization processes of 16 New Zealand small firms, comparing the traditional approach with that of the BG (Chetty and Campbell-Hunt 2004). The researchers conducted a systematic analysis of the differences in the strategies the firms used, and in their prior motivations and capabilities. The main findings were that many attributes of the BG model also characterized firms that began their internationalization along traditional lines, but were then radically transformed in the process of achieving global reach. The study identified the consequences of rapid international growth, referred to as the 'gusher' among these firms, and the destabilizing effects of such experience as the traditional firm was taken in unexpected directions. The researchers concluded that the BG model has much in common with that of the internationalization of small entrepreneurial firms. The most distinctive elements lie in the BG's relevance to an increasingly globalized world economy, and in the more aggressive learning strategies required to follow this path.

One research study showed that, contrary to expectations, firms with more imitable technologies grew faster than others which relied on services, and thus customized their products (Autio et al. 2000). This calls into question the conventional wisdom on the role of imitable products, and of services on international growth.

Another study examined how 87 new ventures based in the US managed international risks of 212 foreign market entries by simultaneous trade-off among foreign revenue exposure, country risk, and entry mode commitment (Shrader et al. 2000).

One study on international new ventures sought to ascertain whether their international expansion path was that of a BG or the more sequential international entry path shown in older traditional literature (Fan and Phan 2007). On examination, it was found that in the absence of a specific technological advantage, the international expansion path at inception of the BG is influenced by the size of the firm's home market and the firm's production capacity. Cultural and economic forces that are prevalent, equally influence BGs and other more traditional firms that enter international markets.

One of the few studies of the strategic orientation of BGs was done in Finland (Jantunen et al. 2008). The hypotheses were drawn up from past literature on the strategic orientation and BGs, and the data tested were from 299 Finnish BGs from different industrial sectors. The findings indicate that strategic orientation is related to a BG's international performance, as moderated by its international growth strategy.

Another study discussed the globalization process of business-to-business BGs in the rapidly growing wireless technology industry (Laanti et al. 2007). Deviations of these BGs from the mainstream internalization pattern and from earlier BG literature are discussed. Furthermore, the roles of the founders and managers, the networks, the financial resources, and the innovations of the companies in the sample are analyzed. A conceptual framework and propositions explaining the product, operation, and market strategies of BGs was developed. The results suggest that BGs in the wireless sector do deviate from the traditional internationalization process in many areas. Their expansion to distant markets is rapid, and they apply advanced product strategies at an early stage, but their business operations proceed at a more conventional pace. However, a noticeable difference from traditional firms is their rapid establishment of sales and marketing subsidiaries. BG firms were found to lack the resources and capabilities accumulated by traditionally internationalizing firms. Therefore, they needed to acquire them through the founding team or from external domestic and international networks.

Another research study attempted a deeper conceptual understanding of the early and rapid internationalization of BGs by studying the impact of the strategy-making process (Rialp-Criado et al. 2010). The purpose was to stimulate more creative and integrative thinking on investigating the BG phenomenon. It is likely to be followed up by further research. We turn now to the second part of our overview: the research on external variables that directly impact on the BG.

RESEARCH ON EXTERNAL VARIABLES THAT DIRECTLY INTERACT WITH AND IMPACT ON BGS

Table 7.3 outlines a grid into which these research studies can be placed, and provides food for thought concerning future studies.

Culture

One research study was conducted on how the perceived familiarity with foreign markets of managers of international firms from Denmark, Sweden, and New Zealand, all SMOPECs, develops during a period of entry or expansion (Pedersen and Petersen 2004). It starts by pointing out that the internationalization process literature offers different predictions of how foreign market familiarity changes during these periods. These predictions are then subjected to an empirical examination on data as reported by the managers of such firms. In addition, the empirical study provides insight into the incidence and character of 'shock effects' from foreign market entry. The study data support the supposition that, in general, managers do experience shock effects. This is evident from managers' inclination to underestimate differences between the business

Table 7.3   Research grid of born global kinds of enterprises and selected external variables that directly interact with and/or impact on them

Areas of study \ Types of enterprise	BG	BR	BaG	BaR	ISME	BG Industry
Culture						
Institutional perspective: entrepreneurial capabilities						
Institutional perspective: resources and decision-making processes						
Large channels						
Networks /strategic alliances						
Public policy on SMEs						
Public policy on research and development						
Resources: financial and other						
Social capital						

Note: BG=born global, BR=born regional, BaG=born-again global, BaR=born-again regional, INV=international new venture, ISME=internationalizing small and medium sized enterprise, BG Industry=born global industry environments of home and host countries. Further, managers of entrant firms experienced shock effects in relation to entry into adjacent markets, but not into distant markets. Entrant firms also experienced shock effects with respect to tacit rather than explicit knowledge. Furthermore, shock effects befall producers of customized products but not of standardized products. In addition, the researchers found the lowest level of market familiarity among managers of entrant firms that are in the eighth year after entry or initiation of market expansion.

Institutional Perspective: Entrepreneurial Capabilities

One study explored the rapid internationalization of high-technology firms created through the commercialization of academic research (Styles and Genua 2008). In particular, the effect of entrepreneurial orientation and networks was examined. Four cases were studied. The findings suggest that the fundamental networks of the academics involved in the firms assisted in the identification and exploitation of initial opportunities to internationalize. The research also suggests that only certain dimensions of entrepreneurial orientation impacted on the internationalization of these firms. Specifically, these were risk-taking, technological innovativeness, and autonomy in certain parts of the organization. The rapid international success of the firms was assisted by their proactiveness and product-market innovativeness.

Other research considers the capabilities entrepreneurs require to create successful international new ventures (Karra et al. 2008). An in-depth study of a serial international entrepreneur and the two new ventures he founded, led to the researchers proposing three entrepreneurial capabilities: international opportunity identification, institutional bridging, and a capacity and preference for cross-cultural collaboration. They also considered how budding entrepreneurs could develop such capabilities.

Another significant theoretical study for an internationalization framework was developed by conceptualizing entrepreneurial behavior over time (Jones and Coviello 2005).

Institutional Perspective: Resources and Decision-making Processes

In another study, the authors (Bradley and Gannon 2000) examine the influence of the firm's technology and marketing profile on foreign market entry mode from a study of 105 firms in four European countries. The four most important variables found were the firm's generic marketing strategy concentration versus diversification, demand uncertainty, transaction costs, and technology value added through product patents.

Large Channels: Networks/Strategic Alliances

In the formation of BGs linked with large channels, networks, and alliances, important factors include knowledge management, knowledge application, and dissemination, that is, how to manage the flow and how to balance and control the level and degree of knowledge being circulated. Obviously, no party in the network or alliance wants to lose its proprietary intellectual and other knowledge. How, then, is one to control the intellectual property and knowledge flow? On the one hand, if control is too rigid, the network or alliance may not be optimally effective. On the other, at some point new BGs may join the system, and/or existing members of the system may desire to leave. Should newcomers pay some tariff when joining? Are non-confidential agreements enough to bind a party that is leaving the network or alliance system? Should some other financial arrangements be made? This field should be researched more fully in order to have a more sustainable system in which networks and alliances may flourish.

One study explored empirically why and how MNEs complement their in-house R&D by forming strategic alliances with innovative BGs (Vapola et al. 2008). These alliances are loose, non-equity opportunity-seeking cooperative relationships, termed the 'battleship strategy' by the authors. The critical elements include an open innovation commercialization strategy, creation of forums for facilitating open innovation, and capturing ideas generated externally. In the high-tech industries, new innovations affect an MNE's competitive advantage. The authors suggest that MNEs may externalize some of their innovation activities while gaining a competitive advantage through access to open innovation. This whole area requires more research into the benefits and costs of MNEs/large channels tying up with BGs having customized products/services. A good part of the foundation for these studies already exists in the areas of supply chain management and value-added activities. Many emerging markets with group business cultures will provide additional insights into the development of frameworks of analysis.

Resources: Financial and Other

One study explored the influence of financing strategies and the commensurate finance management capabilities on Finnish BGs and born internationals (Gabrielsson et al. 2004). The results showed that BGs had greater access to superior finance and finance-related managerial resources from the start-up phase than did born internationals. In addition, these BGs more quickly obtained global management-related skills through the use of external business partners and venture capital representatives.

The importance of top management teams to aid the development of small firms is well recognized, but their impact on the rapid internationalization of such firms is relatively under-researched (Loane et al. 2007). Loane et al.'s cross-national study of small firms in Australia, Canada, Ireland, and New Zealand made clear the significant impact of such teams in creating the core internal capabilities and leverage of external resources required for rapid and dedicated internationalization. Further, the study showed the need to augment the top management teams to help find key resources, cover knowledge gaps, and/or expand international networks. Also studied were changes in team structures on strategy and internationalization. In addition, directions for future research and implications for public policy were discussed.

Another study examined the importance of human resources in the internationalization of professional service firms (Hitt et al. 2006). Human resources were viewed as human capital and also as relational capital derived through relations with corporate clients and foreign governments. The results showed that human capital had a positive effect on firm internationalization, especially when teamed with corporate client relational capital. Furthermore, human capital moderated the relationship between internationalization and firm performance in a positive manner. However, the effect of relational capital was mixed. Corporate client relational capital had a strong positive effect, while foreign government relational capital had a negative effect on firm performance

Social Capital

One in-depth qualitative study explored how social capital influences an SME to change its internationalization mode (Chetty and Agndal 2007). The study investigated 10 New Zealand firms and 10 Swedish ones, and identified 36 internationalization mode changes. The research focused on relationships and mode change. Using the network approach, the researchers developed three categories of social capital and discussed their role in influencing mode change. The roles were efficacy, serendipity and liability, thus incorporating both the positive and negative aspects of social capital. The most frequently observed form of social capital to influence mode change is the liability role. Further, the most frequent type of mode change is toward a high-control internationalization mode.

COMMENTS ON CHAPTERS WRITTEN BY INVITED AUTHORS

Obviously the internet has helped to speed up the pace of internationalization of firms through providing greater capability in the areas of communication and information. In Chapter 10, Shneor presents some a interesting research on BGs that have emerged because of internet-enabled internationalization, and how use of the internet has powered their climb. The author uses selected literature on e-adoption, international marketing, and internationalization to conceptualize the key dimensions that were assumed to underlie the mode configurations. A mode was defined as a strategic format through which firms access, serve, and interact with their clients and partners abroad. The mode approach allows flexibility in the sense that a cluster of modes may be employed at every stage of internationalization, while if the analysis rested on a stages approach, that flexibility of studying a stage from different dimensions may be more restricted.

Shneor's dimensions are functionality, localization, and service directness. Functionality involves firms evolving along the information → communication → transaction → integration path. The integration level has cross-organizational learning and process improvements. Localization refers to addressing the world as one market with target global customer segments or addressing nationally defined target markets. Service directness refers to the internet enabling direct interface with customers, suppliers and strategic partners, or adding channel members rather than displacing them. The internet, then, does not displace intermediaries, but the latter redefine their value proposition and remain for information collection, filtering, analysis, interpretation, and dispersion mechanisms.

Three cases of 'internet-enabled internationalizion' (IEI) were analyzed. These highlighted the role of online communities as an international promotional, marketing, and distribution channel. It also extended the understanding of the uniqueness of IEI dynamics and modes. IEI leads to the formation of communities which present a new mode of internationalization activities. Furthermore, the analysis suggests that online localization depends on the cultural sensitivity of the product. This extends our knowledge into website localization decisions. However, it must be recognized that the study was of three BGs from SMOPEC countries. IEI mode configurations may well exhibit different patterns with firms that are less reliant on the internet for conducting strategic business processes other than those included in this study.

In Chapter 11, Pezderka, Sinkovics and Jean ask whether BGs reap more benefits from information and communication technology (ICT) use than other internationalizing small firms. This is a good question, but the specific impact of the internet on firm internationalization has been comparatively limited. However, recently, two major streams within the 'online internationalization' literature have emerged: the internationalization of e-commerce corporations and the impact of the internet on the internationalization of non-internet-based firms. Pezderka et al., in their research on BGs, concentrate on the latter stream. Further, they make the claim that there is no empirical study testing the impact of the internet as an alternative to physical foreign market entry mode with regard to export performance. However, they point out that BGs are relying on the Internet as a growth facilitator even though rapid growth is not necessarily equated with better financial performance. There are no studies investigating the impact of the internet as an alternative market entry mechanism on export performance. However, it has been found that internet-based multiple channels can reduce the liability of foreignness and newness.

The findings of the study support the conclusion that firms with less export experience seem to overestimate the importance of ICT investments and neglect the relevance of their offline/physical market experience. Firms with more export experience, however, have already developed the capabilities of transcending the trap of thinking that the exploration of underlying market conditions can be sufficiently carried out by the sole reliance on ICT. Overall, the authors concluded that the internet has the potential to advance the development of first-order capabilities that can contribute to enhanced export performance. Yet, when its use is not aligned with strategy, it can lead to financial damage.

What of the use of networks and alliances by BGs? In Chapter 8, Freeman identifies common triggers underpinning the increasing incidence of BGs. These include the increasing relevance of global networks and alliances, and how entrepreneurial managers in small and new firms use their personal and social networks to seek information about foreign market opportunities. It was also found that tie-based opportunities lead to better exchanges than those identified through non-network methods, such as trade fairs and advertising for international exchange. Freeman proposes that relational resources dependent on social ties are central to the internationalization of small firms from emerging economies. This new model of BG internationalization is underpinned by the social dynamic perspective that builds on the co-evolutionary approach, which sees the path of the firm as a product emerging from the co-evolution of internationalization activities, organizational resources specific to the effects of social ties and inter-firm networks and industry influences.

In Chapter 9, on networks and SMEs, Partanen and Servais point out that BGs and other smaller SME firms are recognized to be resource poor. The researchers term this the 'liability of smallness'. The research was undertaken in order to explore how networks source BGs and other smaller firms. The authors differentiate between categories of inter-firm networks such as customers, and downstream and upstream networks. The research is focused on upstream networks and is done by investigating the experiences of some small Finnish BGs. Partanen and Servais suggest that the current body of knowledge provides little conceptual understanding on the complex nature of sourcing networks of a born global firm.

Finally, in Chapter 12, Zou and Ghauri analyze the strategic behavior of international new ventures (INVs) from an institutional perspective. The institutional differences between developed and emerging markets explain variations in the entrepreneurial capabilities, resources, and decision-making processes of INVs. The results stem from an analysis of cases in the Chinese semiconductor industry.

DISCUSSION, CONCLUSIONS, AND RESEARCH AREAS

We can proceed by following the areas laid out in Table 7.1, starting with an initial discussion on theory development. The emphasis will be on suggesting new research areas, and commenting on under-researched areas that it would be useful to encourage.

Theory Development

Overall, there is a need for development of theory in all facets concerning BGs. For example, once there is a generally agreed-upon theory of what constitutes a BG, research can proceed in a more organized manner. In particular, the field needs a theoretical framework to differentiate a BG from other small firms: the 'BG' from the 'BaG' (born again global), the 'BR' (born regional), the 'BaR' (born again regional), the INV (international new venture) , or the 'traditional internationalizing SME'. Without such theory development, the pattern of past research indicates that many studies are carried out on what different authors term BGs, but which do not cover similar sets of firms. It is necessary that researchers categorize the types of SMEs that are included in their particular study. Each category of those firms has different origins and different evolutionary paths; both causal factors make those SMEs distinct from others and affect their future growth trajectory. The overall development of the BG research field can only benefit from that clarification. Moreover, a theoretical framework would be useful for constructing categories of globalization/internationalization rates, phases of growth, and to develop thoughts about relevant BG products/services, suitable brands, and network exit procedures.

Rapid Globalization/Internationalization

Past research indicates that academicians can use their networks when collaborating with BGs. This can lead to the BGs accelerating their internationalization. This research area is worth encouraging since academicians have many intellectual and social resources that could help BGs and simultaneously be useful to them. In addition, they have a large resource of better students who could supply support when needed. It is recognized that in different cultures such resources may be different or may be utilized in implementation in ways that are specific to the regions. In the US, for instance, state universities do not actively encourage consulting with private small firms, but in China, state universities often work with the private sector for commercial gain. Another area where more research will help is how to increase the effectiveness and efficiency with which BGs can commit resources to globalization/internationalization.

What can speed up the process? What government support policies can help? The rapid globalization vector is rising in importance as a result of the growing competition in the global marketplace as borders become more open, and new firms, both MNEs and SMEs, from the BRIC countries (Brazil, Russia, India, and China) are entering. These BRIC firms have not grown slowly over the years, but are the result of entrepreneurship and/or large concentrations of capital and resources from the state and from networks of private families.

International Entrepreneurship

More research is needed on how BGs can develop the capability to join networks and alliances. More research is also needed on how downstream and upstream networks and alliances can source from BGs and other smaller firms. There has been very little research done in these areas. This may be because of the limited number of business academics who receive formal training in social skill fields, but those who are qualified should increase their research in these areas.

Much more research is also necessary on what international marketing opportunities are available, or are likely to be available, on a global basis. As of yet, there is much data, information, and research on country markets, and even regional markets such as the EU, but global segments for BGs have not been studied extensively. Such global research will provide opportunity awareness to BGs, and thus help to improve their international performance.

Another research vector in this area that needs more study is the affective commitment of owners/managers of BGs to international performance, and how this commitment manifests itself. Does it help strategic thinking, or shorter-term responses, more opportunistic behavior, or the approach of an experimentalist? The kind of commitment will influence the speed, scope, and reach of the BG's internationalization performance. Furthermore, is it possible for this commitment to be directed towards another perspective to enable the BG to grow more rapidly over time?

Further, for better international performance, researchers must carry out more studies with regard to what dimensions or entrepreneurial traits BG owners/managers must have or must develop. Furthermore, there should be research into whether these traits need to change over the different phases that successful BGs pass through. In addition, we need to know more about what can influence or cause changes in such traits, and how best these traits are learned.

Internet

Internet use for international activities can only burgeon over time. What will be interesting to determine is whether that use is for information, sales, support of the buyer purchasing process or of direct selling, image building, and/or the reduction of uncertainty when dealing with the unfamiliarity of foreign environments. Much more research is needed on how BGs can benefit from the internet. Further, it must be emphasized that, so far, most BG research has focused on BGs in production as opposed to services. In the knowledge and technological world of this century, there will be more service-oriented BGs starting up. More research is warranted on such service BGs because they may well be more capable of utilizing the internet to advantage.

Knowledge Acquisition, Application, Dissemination, Management

With reference to BGs acquiring knowledge, the research question that should be explored more fully is whether technical and scientific knowledge is more important than knowledge of how to internationalize with regard to the BGs' exploitation of foreign market opportunities. This might well vary by industry. In addition, more research on the kinds of products from BG firms that achieve international success more quickly and easily would be useful.

Furthermore, it will be important to understand from research whether BG owner-managers who had prior knowledge were much more prone to succeed than those who acquired knowledge as they required it. This has importance from the knowledge learning and teaching perspectives. Moreover, research that shows how the background of different owner-managers of BGs could influence international performance can be useful to entrepreneurs and policy makers. Designer-founders of BGs may have markedly different approaches as compared with engineers, and other specialists. They also may reach very different levels of international performance.

An important additional field that is under-researched is how BGs with network and/or large channel partners should share and manage the knowledge flow, balance, and control level, including that of intellectual property, with such partners. Research on how a sustainable and flexible system can be evolved in such groups will be very useful. Additionally, research could indicate whether newcomers who join such groups later should be charged a tariff, and how confidentiality can be best protected.

Market Orientation

The BG is by nature a global firm, and our field of research is primarily the BG. Therefore, it is important that many more studies be done on the effects of enhanced market orientation in many different markets, and on the many different products/services that BGs and other categories of SMEs have. The studies which have been done thus far have mainly been in the markets of rich nations as opposed to emerging nations. There have been relatively few studies in the BRIC countries, which are almost certainly the countries that will carry substantial economic weight in the global marketplace as the twenty-first century evolves.

Additional research would be helpful about whether market orientation drives BG strategies with regard to particular organizational functions towards globalization or localization. The effect of market orientation on BG performance also needs to be researched for the intervening effects of mediators, such as knowledge acquisition and market commitment. Furthermore, much more research is needed on branding and co-branding strategies that could be effective for BGs. Co-branding is what the BG is likely to experience as it joins networks/alliances.

Large Channels, Networks, Alliances, and Joint Ventures

Much more research needs to be done on the interface of BGs with large channels and/or networks, that is, how BGs can be attracted to large channels and/or networks and alliances or vice versa. Research is needed on how to make the search process more productive. In addition, studies need to be done on the way BGs and large channels and/or their network/ alliance partners can develop the bonds that attract the BGs towards them, and vice versa, for better international performance. Furthermore, it needs to be determined how BGs can exit the partnership with minimum penalty and how large channels and/or the networks/alliances can do the same. A concomitant research must also examine what strengths the BG should acquire before deciding on such an exit.

More research is necessary on the kind of joint ventures that BGs should undertake that will enable them to gain an international presence in the short and long terms. The size and kind of partner for BGs is very important, that is, what characteristics must the joint venture partner have in order to offer BGs substantial help in their success and growth.

Organizational Learning

More research will be very helpful with regard to what organizational learning is available for BGs in their home country and how much learning takes place from forays into foreign and/or global markets. Another area of research that can be useful is how home governments can encourage programs where BG owners/managers can acquire more organizational learning. An additional aspect of organizational learning is the impact of market orientation. Yet another area where more research would be useful to BGs is how information search and use of different sources help to advance international performance.

Similarly, more research is required on how to make more capital available to BGs for organizational learning. The rich countries give organizational capital aid to projects in poorer countries. Why not carry out research into how some aid can be given beneficially to BGs? Furthermore, much more research needs to be done on how organizational capability within BGs can aid entry mode decisions and choice when entering foreign markets. This is a vital decision and choice area for BGs and influences their further growth.

Resources: Financial and Other

More research needs to be done on how BGs can raise finance from external business-related partners. This research could extend to what frameworks or regulations governments can institute to help BGs raise finance. Governments build such frameworks and/or regulations to guarantee loans to some groups, including small business, give finance and/or tax exemptions to encourage R&D, and generally aid sectors that are considered to be worth encouraging. BGs should be regarded as one such sector. Researchers could help to identify the benefits that BGs can contribute to economic development.

More research needs to be done into how more human resources can be made available to BGs and what benefits will result. Governments help SMEs to obtain human resources at subsidized cost in various ways. These measures should be extended to BGs, recognizing that BGs have few resources at inception, but could pay back later if they are successful. Some top managers who have retired from different firms are a potential useful human resource that could be persuaded to help BGs on a 'payable when able' basis. This needs to be researched. Linked to the matter of augmenting the human capital of BGs, more research is needed on social capital that accrues from certain social connections, and concerns relational capital when teamed with corporate client relations.

Strategy

BGs with a global vision linked to strategic thinking ought to have better international performance globally than traditional SMEs. More research needs to be done in this area to validate this proposition. Further, the research should test different strategic approaches in this context.

Another facet of BG strategy research that would prove useful, is to what extent a foreign customer focus linked to improving products and/or product policies can improve international performance. Further, what strategic approaches are better for BGs when they want to tie up with large networks and large MNEs. This involves research on the degree of independence that BGs should maintain in different contexts. Additionally, more research is needed in areas that can be complementary and useful when BGs develop strategies, such as global branding strategies, and how to accelerate learning in this regard. We hope our discussion will spark a plentitude of research studies on BGs and their adjacent neighbor firms in the SME subsets, as well as many studies on BGs as they travel through different phases of evolution. They are a vital resource for the innovativeness and growth of modern economies.

REFERENCES

Armario, J.M., D.M. Ruiz and E.M. Armario (2008), 'Market orientation and internationalization in small and medium-sized enterprises', *Journal of Small Business Management*, **46**(4), 485–511.

Almor, T. (2000), 'Born global: the case of small and medium-sized born global knowledge-intensive Israeli firms', in Almor and T. Hashai (eds), *FDI, International Trade, and Economic Peacemaking*, Rishon Le Zion, Israel College of Management Economic Studies Division.

Autio, E., H.J. Sapienza and J.G. Almeida (2000), 'Effects of age at entry, knowledge intensity and imitability on international growth', *Academy of Management Journal*, **43**(5), 909–24.

Bell, J.D. (1995), 'The internationalisation of small computer firms, a further challenge to 'stage' theories', *European Journal of Marketing*, **29**(8), 60–75.

Bell, J., D. Crick and S. Young (2004), 'Small firm internationalization and business strategy: an exploratory study of "knowledge-intensive" and "traditional" manufacturing firms in the UK', *International Small Business Journal*, **22**(1), 23–56.

Bell, J., R. McNaughton and S. Young (2001), 'Born-again-global firms – an extension to the born-global firm', *Journal of International Management*, **7**, 173–89.

Bradley, F. and M. Gannon (2000), 'Does the firm's technology and marketing profile affect foreign market entry?', *Journal of International Marketing*, **8**(4), 12–36.

Brannback, M., A. Carsrud and M. Renko (2007), 'Exploring the born global concept in the biotechnology context', *Journal of Enterprising Culture*, **15**(1), 70–100.

Brouthers, L.E., G. Nakos, J. Hadjimarcou and K.D. Brouthers (2009), 'Key factors for successful export performances for small firms', *Journal of International Marketing*, **17**(3), 21–38.

Bürgel, O. and G. Murray (2000), 'The international market entry choices of start-up companies in high-technology industries', *Journal of International Marketing*, **6**(2), 33–62.

Casillas, J.C., A.M. Moreno, F. Acedo, M.A. Gallego and E. Ramos (2009), 'An integrative model of the role of knowledge in the internationalization process', *Journal of World Business*, **44**(3), 311–22.

Chetty, S. and H. Agndal (2007), 'Social capital and its influence on changes in internationalization mode among small and medium-sized enterprises', *Journal of International Marketing*, **15**(1), 1–29.

Chetty, S. and C. Campbell-Hunt (2003), 'Explosive international growth and problems of success amongst small to medium-sized firms', *International Small Business Journal*, **21**(1), 5–27.

Chetty, S. and C. Campbell-Hunt (2004), 'A strategic approach to internationalization: a traditional versus a "born-global" approach', *Journal of International Marketing*, **12**(1), 57–81.

Dana, L.P. (2001), 'Introductions networks, internationalization, and policy', *Small Business Economics*, **16**(2), 57–62.

Di Gregorio, D., M. Musteen and D.E. Thomas (2008), 'International new ventures: the cross-border nexus of individuals and opportunities', *Journal of World Business*, **43**(2), 186–96.

Falay, Z., M. Salimäki, A. Ainamo and M. Gabrielsson (2007), 'Design-intensive born globals: a multiple case study of marketing management', *Journal of Marketing Management*, **23**(9/10), 877–99.

Fan, T. and P. Phan (2007), 'International new ventures: revisiting the influences behind the "born-global" firm', *Journal of International Business Studies*, **38**(7),1113–31.

Freeman, S. and S.T. Cavusgil (2007), 'Toward a typology of commitment states among managers of born-global firms: a study of accelerated internationalism', *Journal of International Marketing*, **15**(4), 1–40.

Freeman, S., R. Edwards and B. Schroder (2006), 'How smaller born-global firms use networks and alliances to overcome constraints to rapid internationalization', *Journal of International Marketing*, **14**(3), 33–63.

Gabrielsson, M. (2005), 'Branding strategies of born globals', *Journal of International Entrepreneurship*, **3**(3), 199–222.

Gabrielsson M. and V.H.M. Kirpalani (2004) 'Born globals: how to reach new business space rapidly', *International Business Review*, **13**(5), 555–71.

Gabrielsson, M., V.M. Kirpalani, P. Dimitratos, C.A. Solberg and A. Zucchella (2008), 'Born globals: propositions to advance the theory', *International Business Review*, **17**(4), 385–401.

Gabrielsson, M., V. Sasi and J. Darling (2004), 'Finance strategies of rapidly-growing Finnish SMEs: born internationals and born globals', *European Business Review*, **16**(6), 590–604.

Gleason, K.C. and J. Wiggenhorn (2007), 'Born globals, the choice of globalization strategy, and the market's perception of performance', *Journal of World Business*, **42**(3), 322–35.

Hitt, M.A., L. Bierman, K. Uhlenbruck and K. Shimizu (2006), 'The importance of resources in the internationalization of professional service firms: the good, the bad, and the ugly', *Academy of Management Journal*, **49**(6), 1137–57.

Jantunen, A., N. Nummela, K. Puumalainen and S. Saarenketo (2008), 'Strategic orientations of born globals – do they really matter?', *Journal of World Business*, **43**, 158–70.

Jones, M.V. and N.E. Coviello (2005), 'Internationalization: conceptualizing an entrepreneurial process of behavior in time', *Journal of International Business Studies*, **36**(3), 284–303.

Kalantaridis, C. (2004), 'Internationalization, strategic behavior, and the small firm', *Journal of Small Business Management*, **42**(3), 245–62.

Karra, N., N. Phillips and P. Tracey (2008), 'Building the born global firm: developing entrepreneurial capabilities for international new venture success', *Long Range Planning*, **41**(4), 440–58.

Kirpalani, V.H. Manek (1985), *International Marketing*, New York: Random House.

Kirpalani, V.H. Manek and Reijo Luostarinen (1999), 'Dynamics of Success of SMOPEC films in global markets', Proceedings of the 25th Annual Meeting of the European International Business Academy, Manchester, 12–14 December.

Knight, G. (2000), 'Entrepreneurship and marketing strategy: the SME under globalization', *Journal of International Marketing*, **8**(2), 12–32.

Knight, J., J. Bell and R. McNaughton (2001), 'The "born-global" phenomenon: a re-birth of an old concept?', *Researching New Frontiers*, Vol. 2, McGill Conference on International Entrepreneurship, Glasgow, 21–23 September.

Knight, Gary A. and S. Tamer Cavusgil (1996), 'The born global firm: a challenge to traditional internationalization theory', in Cavusgil (ed.), *Advances in International Marketing*, Vol. 8, Bingley, UK: Emerald puplishing group, pp. 11–26.

Knight, G.A. and S.T. Cavusgil (2004), 'Innovation organizational capabilities and the born-global firm', *Journal of International Business Studies*, **35**(2), 124–41.

Knight, G.A. and S.T. Cavusgil (2005), 'A taxonomy of born-global firms', *Management International Review*, **45**(3), 15–35.

Knight, G., T.K. Madsen and P. Servais (2004), 'An inquiry into born-global firms in Europe and the USA', *International Marketing Review*, **21**(6), 645–65.

Kuivalainen, O., S. Sundqvist and P. Servais (2007), 'Firms' degree of born-globalness, international entrepreneurial orientation and export performance', *Journal of World Business*, **42**, 253–67.

Laanti, R., M. Gabrielsson and P. Gabrielsson (2007), 'The globalization strategies of business-to-business born global firms in the wireless technology industry', *Industrial Marketing Management*, **36**(8), 1104–17.

Loane, S., J. Bell and R. McNaughton (2007), 'A cross-national study on the impact of management teams on the rapid internationalization of small firms', *Journal of World Business*, **42**(4), 489–504.

Løvdal, N.S. and A. Aspelund (2010), 'International entrepreneurship in the offshore renewable energy industry', Chapter 7 in R, Wüstenhagen and R. Wuebker (eds), *Handbook of Research on Energy Entrepreneurship*, Cheltenham, UK and Northampton, MA, USA: Edward Elgar.

Luostarinen, Reijo and Mika Gabrielsson (2004), 'Finnish perspectives of international entrepreneurship', in L.P. Dana (ed.), *Handbook of Research on International Entrepreneurship*, Cheltenham, UK and Northampton, MA, USA: Edward Elgar, pp. 383–403.

McDougall, P.P. and B.M. Oviatt (2000), 'International entrepreneurship: the intersection of two research paths', *Academy of Management Journal*, **43**(5), 902–6.

Melén, S. and E.R. Nordman (2009), 'The internationalization modes of born globals: a longitudinal study', *European Management Journal*, **27**(4), 243–54.

Moen, Ø., I. Endresen and M. Gavlen (2003), 'Executive insights: use of the internet in international marketing: a case study of small computer software firms', *Journal of International Marketing*, **11**(4), 129–49.

Mort, G.S. and J. Weerawardena (2006), 'Networking capability and international entrepreneurship: how networks function in Australian born global firms', *International Marketing Review*, **23**(5), 549–72.

Nordman, E.R. and S. Melén (2008), 'The impact of different kinds of knowledge for the internationalization process of born globals in the biotech business', *Journal of World Business*, **43**(2), 171–85.

Oviatt, B.M. and P.P. McDougall (1994), 'Toward a theory of international new ventures,' *Journal of International Business Studies*, **25**(1), 45–64.

Pedersen, T. and B. Petersen (2004), 'Learning about foreign markets: are entrant firms exposed to a "shock effect"?', *Journal of International Marketing*, **12**(1), 103–23.

Rennie, M.W. (1993), 'Born global', *Mekinsey Quarterly*, **4**, 45–52.

Rialp, A. and J. Rialp (2007), 'Faster and more successful exporters: an exploratory study of born global firms from the resource-based view', *Journal of Euromarketing*, **16**(1/2), 73–86.

Rialp, A., J. Rialp, D. Urbano and Y. Vaillant (2005), 'The born-global phenomenon: a comparative case study research', *Journal of International Entrepreneurship*, **3**, 133–71.

Rialp-Criado, A., I. Galván-Sánchez and S.M. Suárez-Ortega (2010), 'A configuration-holistic approach to born-global firms' strategy formation process', *European Management Journal*, **28**(2), 108–23.

Shrader, R.C., B.M. Oviatt and P.P. McDougall (2000), 'How new ventures exploit trade-offs among international risk factors: lessons for the accelerated internationalization of the 21st century', *Academy of Management Journal*, **43**(6), 1227–47.

Styles, C. and T. Genua (2008), 'The rapid internationalization of high technology firms created through the commercialization of academic research', *Journal of World Business*, **43**(2), 146–57.

Vapola, T.J., P. Tossavainen and M. Gabrielsson (2008), 'The battleship strategy: the complementing role of born globals in MNC's new opportunity creation', *Journal of International Entrepreneurship*, **6**(1), 1–20.

Westhead, P. and M. Wright (2001), 'The internationalization of new and small firms: a resource-based view', *Journal of Business Venturing*, **16**(4), 333–58.

Yeoh, P. (2000), 'Information acquisition activities: a study of global start-up exporting companies', *Journal of International Marketing*, **8**(3), 36–60.

Zahra, S.A., R.D. Ireland and M.A. Hitt (2000), 'International expansion by new venture firms: international diversity, mode of market entry, technological learning, and performance', *Academy of Management Journal*, **43**(5), 925–50.

8 Born global firms' use of networks and alliances: a social dynamic perspective
Susan Freeman

INTRODUCTION

The identification of key internal and external driving forces, as well as trends underpinning the increasing incidence of born globals or 'fast internationalizers' (that is, development of small firms seeking international expansion at or near inception) reveals four common triggers. The forces comprise: new market conditions across diverse economic sectors; technological developments in functional areas such as production, transportation, and communication; increasing relevance of global networks and alliances; and finally, the presence of more skilled and entrepreneurial-oriented people, including those who establish the early internationalizing firm (Freeman et al. 2010; Rialp-Criado et al. 2010). While earlier born global research focused on the first two factors, more recent studies address the last two. Thus, recent research has focused on the increased importance of global networks, building on earlier studies on exporting firms and the importance of 'contact systems' and 'personal networks' (Welch and Welch 1996) and alliances (Johanson and Mattsson 1988). Specifically, the focus has been on the study of personal and social networks of managers operating in emerging and transitional economies (Zhou et al. 2007; Ellis 2008; Casillas et al. 2009; Manolova et al. 2010).

Some researchers have argued that the network approach is too deterministic and ignores the role of the individual decision maker (Chetty and Blankenburg-Holm 2000). This is because network research focuses on how networks determine the firm's strategic opportunities (Meyer and Skak 2002). Far less research has focused on the 'entrepreneurial discovery and exploitation of those opportunities' (Ellis 2008, p. 4). More recently, studies have addressed this gap and have examined how entrepreneurial managers in small and new firms use their personal and social networks (for example, relationships with existing and former customers, friends, relatives living in foreign markets) to seek information about foreign market opportunities (Loane and Bell 2006; Ellis 2008; Manolova et al. 2010). Firms derive benefits from direct links with customers and suppliers or indirect links with customers' customers or former suppliers. Business or industrial networks include vertical networks, for example, distribution channels and subcontracting arrangements, and horizontal networks, for example, joint action groups such as export marketing cooperatives (Welch and Welch 1996). Access to foreign markets is also facilitated by indirect links, adding to the manager's social capital through possible scenarios including previous employment in the host market or living in the host market (Ellis 2008). Thus, awareness of foreign market opportunities is obtained by entrepreneurs through their social or interpersonal ties (Loane and Bell 2006). Therefore, examining 'social ties independently of interorganizational networks' (Ellis 2008, p. 4) does seem to be important.

Moreover, earlier research focused on advanced economies, yet it is now in the emerging economies (Lu, et al. 2010) that we are observing increasing numbers of manufacturing and services firms, in both high- and low-technology sectors, entering global supply chains. This development is driving more-flexible cross-border links and alliances (Freeman et al. 2010). What is especially noticeable in this very recent research is that firms rely on domestic and personal networks in transitional and emerging economies, which studies confirm have a positive effect on internationalization of entrepreneurial ventures from Eastern Europe (Manolova et al. 2009) and China (Lu et al. 2010). Manolova et al. (2010) confirm the key role of the founder's social and interpersonal ties and emergent inter-firm networks as essential links to the internationalization of new and small firms. In particular, they demonstrate the critical role that interpersonal ties have on alliance formation with evidence that 'partnerships and connections with other [managers in] firms established early in the life span of the new venture are most productive for its internationalization' (p. 262). However, it is the founder-manager's heavy reliance on domestic personal ties and inter-firm networking which is especially important for small and new ventures in emerging transitional economies, because they usually lack internally generated resources and thus sources of competitive advantage (Meyer and Skak 2002). This is because they 'face a daunting triple challenge in competing abroad: the simultaneous liabilities of newness, smallness, and foreignness' (Manolova et al. 2010, p. 262). This challenge is more than their advanced economy small and medium-sized enterprise (SME) counterparts face as they are less resource-endowed (Aulakh et al. 2000) with fewer internally generated sources of competitive advantage (Uhlenbruck et al. 2003). These small and new venture alliances are operating in intensely competitive domestic economies because of increasing market reforms and trade liberalization in Central and Eastern Europe (Manolova et al. 2010) and Asia (Zhou et al. 2007; Ellis 2008).

However, as Ellis (2008) points out, while social networks with 'known others' might be especially helpful in exchange settings where institutional inadequacies raise costs of identifying, evaluating, and conducting business with exchange domestic partners, 'there are good reasons to suspect that transitional economy managers will be at a disadvantage when it comes to using social ties to foster *international* exchange' (p. 8; original italics). The historic period of managed pre-reform trade by a few large foreign trade corporations, meant that Chinese managers had little or no outside contact with foreign buyers, which denied them the opportunity to cultivate 'boundary-spanning' networks. Despite the increasing liberalization in China since the 1980s, many Chinese managers are still learning how to develop international contacts to link into global supply networks. Manolova et al. (2010) confirm that this is also the case for managers in other transitional economies such as Bulgaria. Ellis (2008) found that opportunity identification is fundamentally affected by network structure, with entrepreneurs in mature, open economies better able to rely on their ties with others than entrepreneurs in transitional economies. Further, he found that network benefits increase with international experience of managers as evidenced by increasing reliance on social ties over time by managers. Finally, tie-based opportunities lead to better exchanges than opportunities identified through non-network methods such as trade fairs and advertising for international exchange.

Despite this acknowledged phenomenon,

> [The] effect of personal networking on the internationalization of entrepreneurial ventures from transitional economies has been relatively under-researched. Further, the role of domestic inter-organizational networks for new-venture internationalization in the context of transition economies has so far remained outside the focus of research attention. (Manolova et al. 2010, p. 257)

More particularly though, we lack a depth of understanding about the founder-manager's reliance on home-based social networks, 'believed to be a critical factor in mediating the performance impact of internationalization (both outward and inward)' (Zhou et al. 2007, p. 674). Home-based social networks have been virtually ignored because they are largely considered informal and outside the domain of inter-organizational networks (Hallen 1992; Ellis 2008). This research oversight needs urgent attention if we are to advance our understanding of the rise in small and new venture internationalization from emerging economies, as this 'mediating effect would suggest that there is an underlying network-based mechanism through which a firm's international orientations contribute to its superior performance' (Zhou et al. 2007, p. 674).

Thus, the increased prevalence of born globals is accredited to the skill and strategic behavior of entrepreneurial-oriented founders who can utilize more developed alliances globally. In the last few decades, increas-

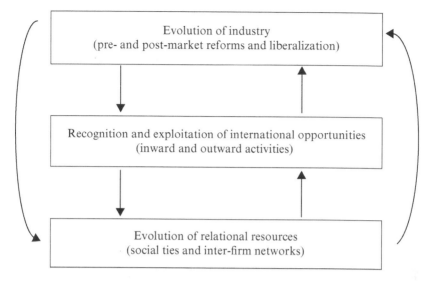

Figure 8.1   Co-evolutionary model of industry, internationalization, and relational resources: a social dynamic perspective

ing numbers of people are now internationally educated and experienced (Andersson 2000).This enhanced mobility between economies creates employees and managerial staff with the ability to interact in cross-border environments, and an international orientation (ability and desire to make international connections). This ability is basic to managers wishing to seek opportunities and take advantage of the new technologies across production, communication, and transportation. More specific to born globals is the increase in mobility, cross-cultural education, and international experience of staff. Increasingly, research is now focusing on the importance of past experience, both technological and international (Nordman and Melén 2008), ambitions, motivations, attitudes, and orientations (Freeman and Cavusgil 2007) and capabilities (Pajunen and Maunula 2008) of the born global founder/entrepreneur-manager.

Relying on social network theory (Zhou et al. 2007; Ellis 2008), this chapter moves beyond the earlier network-based level of analysis (Axelsson and Johanson 1992). It focuses on the more recent social 'tie-level' perspective argued as 'less restrictive and better suited to examining the dynamics of opportunity recognition' (Ellis 2008, p. 1) for the study of the internationalization of born global SMEs from emerging economies, such as China. Thus, the fundamental role of social capital and international entrepreneurship and other related theories is incorporated into the conceptual model (see Figure 8.1). This provides a much-needed relational orientation (social ties and links to international inter-firm boundary-scanning networks), to our understanding of small and new ventures' international opportunity recognition and performance from emerging economies.

In summary, central to the internationalization of small firms from emerging economies are *relational* resources dependent upon social ties (Zhou et al. 2007; Ellis 2008; Michailova and Wilson 2008; Freeman et al. 2010), which is often underemphasized (Ellis 2008; Freeman et al. 2010) and (business) inter-firm network relationships (Johanson and Mattsson 1988; Freeman et al. 2006). For this reason, a co-evolutionary view of internationalization is included in the conceptual model in recognition that two or more processes have a noticeable influence on each other's evolution (Lewin and Volberda 1999; Pajunen and Maunula 2008). It is argued that these co-evolutionary interactions are influenced by the founder-manager's attitude towards internationalization (Freeman and Cavusgil 2007; Welch and Welch 2009), that is, his/her international orientation. Thus, a dynamic conceptual model is provided that first assumes that opportunities are recognized by individuals and not by firms (Mort and Weerawardena 2006). Second, it demonstrates the strategic value of leveraging social or interpersonal ties as well as inter-firm networks, and the alliances they bring, to enhance a firm's performance. This is arguably the most efficient means of doing business in turbulent environments for newly internationalizing SMEs from emerging economies. A review of internationalization and strategy literature, with emphasis on social network theory and a co-evolutionary perspective is presented, together with a conceptual model. Finally, in the discussion and conclusion, a new social dynamic perspective for explaining the process of newly internationalizing SMEs from emerging economies is provided.

THE STRATEGY PROCESS FOR INTERNATIONALIZATION OF BORN GLOBALS IN EMERGING ECONOMIES

Relying on a more integrative approach to conceptualizing organizations as configurations of differing characteristics and behaviors, based on the premises of Mintzberg (1990) and Rialp-Criado et al. (2010), different approaches to strategy formation can be clustered. Under circumstances most frequently associated with advanced economies, where conditions of relative environmental stability prevail, planning–analytical approaches to strategy make more sense. On the other hand, in contexts of dynamic configurations of start-up and turnaround, more in keeping with the context of emerging and transitional economies, other approaches to strategy formation include entrepreneurial, political, cultural, and environmental. These last approaches are underpinned by theories from a range of disciplines focusing on strategic management issues and problem-solving tools. While a more prescriptive planning–analytical approach will provide insights into how the firm's strategy-making process should be – one that is based on a highly rational-oriented, formal and intended process, described as 'deliberate strategy' – a contrary view is offered, an emergent strategy, with the more descriptive, organizational-oriented approaches. This might conceivably include entrepreneurial–visionary, cognitive–clinical, learning–dynamic, political–interpretive, cultural, and environmental approaches, where the focus is examining how strategy-making actually occurs (Rialp et al. 2005; Rialp-Criado et al. 2010).

Despite the research shift and increased attention on managerial-rather than firm-level analysis and on social ties, not only inter-organizational networks (Ellis 2008), comprehensive theoretical explanations and causal models of born global phenomena are still underdeveloped, with mixed results providing a challenge. This is a challenge 'because internationalization in SMEs is a complex phenomenon that may involve some intermediate steps that do not directly influence firm performance' (Zhou et al. 2007, p. 674). Regardless of the direction of internationalization – outward (exporters, joint ventures and foreign direct investment) or inward (importers and licensors, exclusive resellers), – 'the particular information benefits of social networks can be more or less equally critical [as both directions can] make use of key sources of social networks for . . . knowledge . . . advice and experiential learning . . . and referral endorsement to build trust' (ibid., p. 674). This social reality has not been acknowledged by the separate research streams in born global literature in international business and marketing on the one hand and entrepreneurship on the other. Recent literature suggests that the benefit and full potential of integrating international entrepreneurship and strategic management is unrealized (Rialp-Criado et al. 2010). However, current theoretical developments in international entrepreneurship tend to focus on how and why the dynamics of born global internationalization leads to superior performance (Knight and Cavusgil 2004; Oviatt and McDougall 2005a). This trajectory assumes a linear relationship between increasing commitment to internationalization and performance. It is argued that the gap might reflect the tendency in many studies to focus on the direct influence of internationalization on firm performance without fully appreciating the indirect mediated effects or underlying mechanisms that drive the process (Zhou et al. 2007). It is argued that this is especially relevant for small firm internationals *per se*, essential to the understanding of the born global, and fundamental to the born global process in emerging economies.

This chapter addresses this gap by shifting the research focus and theorizing internationalization as a process that is dynamic, where internationally oriented firms are participating in diverse and multiple cross-border relations and exchanges (Welch and Luostarinen 1993), which are not always linear (Welch and Welch 2009) and recognizes the central role of informal home-based social networks, perceived as a mediating factor which links internationalization orientation to firm performance (Zhou et al. 2007; Manolova et al. 2010). Social networks are viewed as distinct from the formal structure of business relationships and thus become the focus. It is argued that the social network research stream is especially important for international entrepreneurial SMEs from emerging economies such as China, 'where personal connections such as *guanxi* (relationships) serve as the metaphor for doing business and understanding economic transactions' (Zhou et al. 2007, p. 674). Rialp-Criado et al. (2010) argue that 'there seems to be scope for developing an improved theoretical framework of reference on the born global phenomenon by means of linking entrepreneurial and strategic process-oriented approaches' (p. 113). The next section recognizes the importance of the emergent strategy and organizational-oriented entrepreneurial–visionary, cognitive–clinical, learning–dynamic, political–interpretive, and cultural and environmental approaches to born global internationalization in emerging economies and their link to performance. It provides support for the conceptual model (Figure 8.1), underpinned by the social dynamic perspective, for explaining the process of newly internationalizing SMEs from transitional and emerging economies.

ENTREPRENEURIAL-VISIONARY APPROACHES AND BORN GLOBAL PERFORMANCE IN EMERGING ECONOMIES

International entrepreneurship has undergone various iterations of definitional understanding in the last few decades (Ellis 2008). Initially, it was conceived as organizations international from inception (Oviatt and McDougall 1994). Then definitional discussions moved beyond new ventures to innovative, proactive, and risk-seeking behavior across national borders to create value (McDougall and Oviatt 2000). The next iteration defined entrepreneurial behavior as discovery, evaluation, and exploitation of opportunities (Shane and Venkataraman 2000), with the realization that entrepreneurs are best defined by their opportunity-seeking behavior rather than their differences in personality type or risk preferences (Eckhardt and Shane 2003; Freeman et al. 2006). This prompted a further redefining as the 'discovery, enactment, evaluation and exploitation of opportunities – across national borders – to create future goods and services' (Oviatt and McDougall 2005b, p. 7). However, to understand more completely the social dynamics of born global managers from emerging economies, it is argued in this chapter that this later approach (Eckhardt and Shane 2003) ignores the interaction between behavior and personality.

Assuming that opportunity recognition is central to entrepreneurship, two questions follow. First, how and why do some managers and not others discover and exploit opportunities? The usual response is that opportunity recognition is influenced or mediated by the managers' participation in social and business networks (Lu et al. 2010; Oviatt and McDougall 2005b). Second, a related but very different question is, why do some managers manage social and business networks better than others? This question requires a more intricate answer which recognizes first, that managing relationships, both social and business, is not only a capability (behavior), but also an attitude which includes personality and risk profile. Second, there needs to be the recognition that not all managers are the same. Capabilities and personality are heterogeneous in their distribution across a population. In particular, the mediating role of social networks in the form of *guanxi* means that managers operating in emerging economies, such as China, must consider more aspects of relationships, both inter-organizational and inter-personal in nature, than those perceived from a network-based perspective (Zhou et al. 2007; Ellis 2008). From a tie-level perspective (ibid.), however, social ties go far beyond business networks in an emerging economy context. This requires a relational orientation by managers which recognizes that while networks are self-serving, managers must consider the obligations and the reciprocity that social and business networks bring, suggesting a long-term rather than short-term behavioral orientation view of relationships (Freeman and Cavusgil 2007). This capability, however, does not alone explain why some managers are better than others at managing successful social and business relationships. At an attitudinal level, some managers are more comfortable with risk. Even faced with considerable environmental uncertainty and inexperience, some managers will respond to the discovery recognition of an opportunity and exploit it while others will not.

This chapter draws attention to the need to broaden our understanding of the opportunity recognition process and acknowledge both behavioral and attitudinal elements in the identification and exploitation of opportunities. Thus, the conceptual model provides an important understanding underpinning the dynamics of *relational orientation* by born global

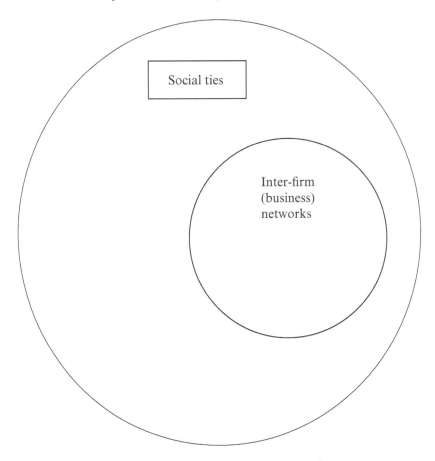

Figure 8.2   Social ties and inter-firm (business) networks

managers. It recognizes their differences, and accordingly, emphasizes their heterogeneity (Freeman and Cavusgil 2007; Freeman et al. 2010), rather than homogeneity, which is the focus of most studies. It also elevates the importance of the social ties of the entrepreneur-manager over the (business) inter-firm network, with the latter a subset of the former, in the emerging economy context (see Figure 8.2).

Cultural and Environmental Approaches and Born Global Performance in Emerging Economies

Recent research has looked at the relationships between capabilities, resources, and international performance among entrepreneurial firms from emerging economies, such as China (Zhou et al. 2007; Ellis 2008; Lu et al. 2010). It is increasingly acknowledged that a pre-emptive strategy to access information and deploy resources timely and flexibly through relational networks in emerging economies (Ellis 2008) such as the informal social network (that is, *guanxi* in China, *kankei* in Japan, *immak* in Korea, or *blat* in Russia), is imperative for internationally oriented SMEs (Zhou et al. 2007). These economies are well known for the relational embeddedness that permeates all social and business activity, and which is deeply ingrained at the cultural level of societal interaction. Recent studies suggest that the attributes and capabilities of entrepreneur-managers of born globals are neither homogeneous nor static (Freeman et al. 2010), with some managers showing more relational capability than others and recognizing the importance of long-term over short-term orientation where the duration of social and organizational relationships is recognized as more important than short-term rent-seeking behavior (Freeman and Cavusgil 2007). Further, that a relational orientation encompassing relational capabilities of the entrepreneur-manager, more specifically, social ties (Ellis 2008), is a mediator, linking resources and international performance of entrepreneurial firms from emerging economies, such as China (Lu et al. 2010).

Inward International Activity

Additionally, a co-evolutionary understanding of internationalization is incorporated into the conceptual model. Very recent research concludes that 'internationalization is essentially an evolutionary process, although not necessarily an incremental or a progressive one' (Pajunen and Maunula 2008, p.247). In this sense, internationalization includes 'the role of inward international activity as potentially a key part of companies' international development – including international re-entry' (Welch and Welch 2009, p. 568). These activities provide a platform which comprises the firm's 'international heritage' of prior international activities, and includes 'its retained knowledge, networks (including relationship sediments), key management and staff, and *attitudes*' (ibid. p. 575; added italics). As social ties of the founder-manager are also used to seek international information and access opportunities in international locations, the informal and indirect effects, as well as formal, direct inter-firm networks, are both included in understanding the opportunity recognition and access by founder-managers. Co-evolutionary interaction of internationalization with the evolution of industry (Andersson 2000), especially seen in the sweeping and intensely competitive environment found in the liberalization of transitional economies, together with the core resources of the firm (Pajunen and Maunula 2008) provides a partial explanation of the complex internationalization process of firms. The co-evolution of industry and internationalization explains why the direction and speed of internationalization are dependent upon the industrial context and that how industries evolve will influence internationalization and vice versa (Liesch et al. 2002). The co-evolution of core resources and internationalization supports the view of the central role of internal resources and organizational capabilities in the early internationalization of born globals (Knight and Cavusgil 2004). The resource-based view (Barney 1991) has been supported more recently by the dynamic capabilities view (Helfat and Peteraf 2003), which provides an evolutionary aspect to the understanding of capabilities by providing a model of a capability life cycle: founding stage; development stage; stage of maturity; and maintain/harvest/discontinue stage.

Personal Ties and Home-based Social Networks

In the organizational context, social networks might encompass social relationships (ties) between individuals within the formal structure of business connections, for example, buyer–seller relationships or strategic alliances (Bjorkman and Kock 1995; Zhou et al. 2007). Social networks are perceived as a 'network of personal connections as well as relationships, which can be used to secure favors' for personal and business gain (Burt 1992; Zhou et al. 2007), and are the crux of network resources of the firm.

Weidenbaum and Hughes (1996) highlighted the remarkable and pervasive cross-border movement of people and goods in Southeast Asia and coined the term 'bamboo network' as a result of the economic reforms and trade liberalizations in the last two decades, a factor not adequately understood in the West. These economic pressures are making political borders less important. The last decade or two has seen an increasing flow of goods, services, capital, and people across the Southeast Asian region, despite concerns raised in Beijing, Hong Kong, and Taiwan. The bamboo network of overseas Chinese family-oriented businesses has provided a partial explanation of the rapid movement of mainland China towards private enterprise. The bamboo network provides a mechanism for Chinese manager-entrepreneurs' personal ties and home-based social networks to form direct and indirect links to ethnic inter-firm (business) networks in foreign markets. Based on this understanding, it is theorized that a relational capability life cycle similarly exists alongside other resource capabilities for founder-managers of born globals from transitional and emerging economies (see Figure 8.3).

In the founding stage, recognition of international opportunities by

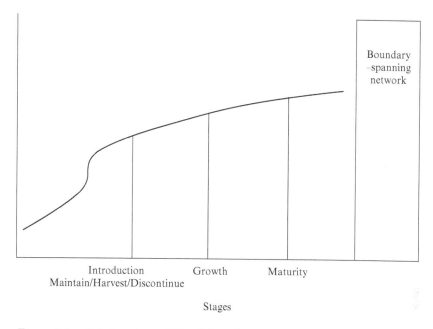

Boundary
-spanning
network

Introduction   Growth   Maturity
Maintain/Harvest/Discontinue

Stages

Figure 8.3   Relational capability life cycle

founder-managers of born globals relies on formal, government-organized trade activities (through trade fairs and advertising). They have little or no chance to access international activities through personal ties and must rely on their home-based social networks and inter-firm networks during the pre-market reforms and pre-trade liberalization phase in transitional economies.

In the development stage, recognition of international opportunities by founder-managers of born globals again relies heavily on formal, government-organized trade activities, but also begins to rely more on personal ties. They have increasing opportunities to access international activities through a few personal ties and are now able to rely less on their home-based social networks and inter-firm networks during the early market reforms and initial trade liberalization phase in transitional economies, with variations across industry sectors, as some are liberalized ahead of others. They are experiencing increasing presence of foreign com-petition via exports, as the economies begin opening themselves to foreign entrants, mostly from firms from advanced economies, providing further founder-manager access to international opportunity recognition.

In the stage of maturity, recognition of international oppor-tunities by founder-managers of born globals relies little on formal, government-organized trade activities, and instead relies heavily on personal ties. Founder managers have excellent opportunities to access international activities through many trust-based personal ties, built up over time, relying on their boundary-spanning social networks and inter-firm networks during the post-market reforms and advanced trade liberalization phase in emerging economies across most industry sectors. They are experiencing increasing presence of foreign competition through foreign direct investment, mostly from advanced economies and some from other transitional and emerging economies, which is expanding founder-managers' recognition of international opportunities. In the 'maintain, harvest, and discontinue stage', recognition of international opportunities by founder-managers of born globals relies very rarely on government-organized trade activities and almost exclusively relies on many strong and numerous weak personal ties. They have exceptional opportunities to access international activities through many trust-based personal ties, built up over very long periods of time (even through prior international work experience) relying exclusively on their boundary-spanning social networks and inter-firm networks enhanced by the bilateral and multilateral government agreements in their advanced open trade economies across all industry sectors. They experience the presence of foreign competition through foreign direct investment from all types of economies, which increases the reach, depth, and scope of the founder-manager's personal ties and inter-firm networks through rich global boundary-spanning networks with an unlimited 'opportunity horizon' (Ellis 2008). There is little constraint in terms of geographical and linguistic distance. In this final stage, tie-based opportunities lead to better exchanges than opportunities identified via non-network means such as trade fairs and advertising.

DISCUSSION AND CONCLUSION

Earlier research has provided understanding of a number of organizational and contextual factors relating to small and new firm internationalization, yet it has failed to explain the relations between these factors over time and in the emerging economy context. This new conceptual model underpinned by the *social dynamic perspective*, builds on Pajunen and Maunula's (2008) co-evolutionary approach, which sees the path of the firm as a product emerging from the co-evolution of internationalization activities (inward and outward), organizational resources (specifically the indirect effects of social ties and direct effects of inter-firm networks), and industry influences (pre- and post-market reforms and liberalization).

First, it shows new understanding of born global internationalization by revealing the added complexity of internationalization comprising both inward and outward activities (chances for *international* opportunities recognition and access by founder-managers), and thus the significance of the founder-entrepreneur's international orientation to this dynamic process.

Second, for founder-managers in the early phase of liberalization in transitional and emerging economies, it highlights the fundamental importance of cultural and personal social networks, and the initial reliance on few social ties and primarily on home-based inter-firm networks, both of which provide very limited chances for them to recognize international opportunities and develop international alliances. The new market reforms and industry liberalization cycle have major positive implications for the boundary-spanning capabilities of the founder-manager's tie-based opportunities, captured in the new relational capability life cycle. Thus, the conceptual model demonstrates the importance of the cyclical nature of the relational orientation of the founder-entrepreneur.

Third, the conceptual model provides a tie-based explanation for the relationships between international orientation, relational orientation, and born global performance. At the founder-entrepreneurial tie-based level of analysis, performance of the small and new firms is a complex interchange between sales (short term), profit (long term) and survival (evolution of the firm). For founder-entrepreneurs from emerging economies where culturally and socially embedded domestic personal ties are part of the expected norm and behavior of 'doing business', the mediating effect of the industry factors and relational orientation of the founder-entrepreneur on the speed of international alliance formation is fundamental. Founder-entrepreneurs from traditional and emerging economies, initially, are not likely to have social ties that are rich in boundary-spanning networks that provide them with chances for recognition of international opportunities. Rather, they will be relying on personal home-based social ties and inter-firm networks. The co-evolution of relationships, industry factors and international activities may result in activities that are traditionally defined as short-term performance measures, namely sales, as relational dimensions might require a long-term orientation by the manager to ensure the firm's survival. In addition, while the relational orientation (social ties and links to international inter-firm boundary-scanning networks) of the founder-entrepreneur will determine the quality (knowledge, advice, referred trust, obligation) of the relationship and, therefore, the benefit of the inter-firm (business) network and the speed of the alliance formation, it is the *international orientation* (ability and desire to make international connections) of the founder which will determine the scope of the small venture's cross-border activity.

Finally, the conceptual model provides a managerial tie-based-level explanation of the relationship between international and relational orientation. Performance of small rapidly internationalizing firms from emerging economies is conceived as survival, and internationalization is the outcome of inward and outward activities underpinned by attitudinal dimensions and cultural domestic social ties that link founder-entrepreneurs to inter-firm (business) networks, revealing dynamic and co-evolutionary processes.

REFERENCES

Andersson, S. (2000), 'The internationalization of the firm from an entrepreneurial perspective', *International Studies of Management and Organization*, **30**(1), 63–92.

Aulakh, P.S., M. Kotabe and H. Teegan (2000), 'Export strategies and performance of firms from emerging economies: evidence from Brazil, Chile, and Mexico', *Academy of Management Journal*, **43**(3), 342–61.

Axelsson, Björn and Jan Johanson (1992), 'Foreign market entry: the textbook vs. the network view', in Björn Axelsson and Geoff Easton (eds), *Industrial Networks: A New View of Reality*, London: Routledge, pp. 218–34.

Barney, J. (1991), 'Firm resources and sustained competitive advantage', *Journal of Management*, **17**(1), 99–120.

Bjorkman, I. and S. Kock (1995), 'Social relationships and business networks: the case of Western companies in China', *International Business Review*, **4**(4), 519–35.

Burt, R.S. (1992), *Structural Holes*, Cambridge, MA: Harvard Business School Press.

Casillas, J.C., A.M. Moreno, F.J. Acedo, M.A. Gallego and E. Ramos (2009), 'An integrative model of the role of knowledge in the internationalization process', *Journal of World Business*, **44**(3), 311–22.

Chetty, S. and D. Blankenburg-Holm (2000), 'Internationalization of small to medium-sized manufacturing firms: a network approach', *International Business Review*, **9**(1), 77–93.

Eckhardt, J.T. and S.A. Shane (2003), 'Opportunities and entrepreneurship', *Journal of Management*, **29**(3), 333–49.

Ellis, P.D. (2008), 'Social ties and international opportunity recognition', Working Paper Series, draft, Department of Management and Marketing, Hong Kong Polytechnic University, Hung Hom, Kowloon, Hong Kong, April 11.

Freeman, S. and S.T. Cavusgil (2007), 'Entrepreneurial strategies for accelerated internationalization of smaller born globals', *Journal of International Marketing*, **15**(4), 1–40.

Freeman, S., R. Edwards and B. Schroder (2006), 'How smaller born-global firms use networks and alliances to overcome constraints to rapid internationalization', *Journal of International Marketing*, **14**(3), 33–63.

Freeman, S., K. Hutchings, M. Lazarius and S. Zyngier (2010), 'A model of rapid knowledge development: the smaller born-global firm', *International Business Review*, **19**(1), 70–84.

Hallen, Lars (1992), 'Infrastructural networks in international business', in Mats Forsgren and Jan Johanson (eds), *Managing Networks in International Business*, Philadelphia, PA: Gordon & Breach, pp. 77–92.

Helfat, C.E. and M.A. Peteraf (2003), 'The dynamic resource-based view: capabilities lifecycles', *Strategic Management Journal*, **24**(10), 997–1010.

Johanson, Jan and Lars-Gunnar Mattsson (1988), 'Internationalization in industrial systems – a network approach', in Neil Hood and Jan-Erik Vahlne (eds), *Strategies in Global Competition*, New York: Croom Helm, pp. 287–314.

Knight, G.A. and S.T. Cavusgil (2004), 'Innovation, organizational capabilities, and the born global firm', *Journal of International Business Studies*, **35**(2), 124–41.

Lee, S.-G., C. Koo and K. Nam (2010), 'Cumulative strategic capability and performance of early movers and followers in the cyber market', *International Journal of Information Management*, **30**(3), 239–55.

Lewin, A.Y. and H.W. Volberda (1999), 'Prolegomena on coevolution: a framework for research on strategy and new organizational forms', *Organization Science*, **10** (5), 519–34.

Liesch, P.W., L.S. Welch, D. Welch, S.L. McGaughey, B. Petersen and P. Lamb (2002), 'Evolving strands of research on firm internationalization: an Australian–Nordic perspective', *International Studies of Management and Organization*, **32**(1), 16–35.

Loane, S. and J. Bell (2006), 'Rapid internationalization among entrepreneurial firms in Australia, Canada, Ireland and New Zealand: an extension to the network approach', *International Marketing Review*, **25**(5), 467–85.

Lu, Y., L. Zhou, G. Brunton and L. Weiwen (2010), 'Capabilities as a mediator linking resources and the international performance of entrepreneurial firms in an emerging economy', *Journal of International Business Studies*, **41**(3), 419–36.

Manolova, T., I.M. Manev and B.S. Gyoshev (2010), 'In good company: the role of personal and inter-firm networks for new-venture internationalization in a transition economy', *Journal of World Business*, **45**(3), 257–65.

McDougall, P. and B. Oviatt (2000), 'International entrepreneurship: the intersection of two research paths', *Academy of Management Journal*, **43**(5), 902–6.

Meyer, K. and A. Skak (2002), 'Networks, serendipity and SME entry into Eastern Europe', *European Management Journal*, **20**(3), 179–88.

Michailova, S. and H.I.M. Wilson (2008), 'Small firms' internationalization through experiential learning: the moderating role of socialization tactics', *Journal of World Business*, **43**(2), 243–54.

Mintzberg, Henry (1990), 'Strategy formation: schools of thought', in James W. Fredrickson (ed.), *Perspectives on Strategic Management*, New York: Harper & Row, pp. 105–235.

Mort, G.S. and J. Weerawardena (2006), 'Networking capability and international entrepreneurship: how networks function in Australian born global firms', *International Marketing Review*, **23**(5), 549–72.

Nordman, E.R. and S. Melén (2008), 'The impact of different types of knowledge for the internationalization process of born globals in the biotech business', *Journal of World Business*, **43**(2), 171–85.

Oviatt, B. and P. McDougall (1994), 'Toward a theory of international new ventures', *Journal of International Business Studies*, **25**(1), 45–64.

Oviatt, B. and P. McDougall (2005a), 'Defining international entrepreneurship and modeling the speed of internationalization', *Entrepreneurship: Theory and Practice*, **29** (5), 537–53.

Oviatt, B. and P. McDougall (2005b), 'The internationalization of entrepreneurship', *Journal of International Business Studies*, **36**(1), 2–8.

Pajunen, K. and M. Maunula (2008), 'Internationalization: a co-evolutionary perspective', *Scandinavian Journal of Management*, **24**(3), 247–58.

Rialp, A., J. Rialp and G. Knight (2005), 'The phenomenon of early internationalizing firms: what do we know after a decade (1993–2003) of scientific inquiry?', *International Business Review*, **14**(2), 147–66.

Rialp-Criado, A., I. Galván-Sánchez and S.M. Suárez-Ortega (2010), 'A configuration–holistic approach to born-global firms' strategy formation process', *European Management Journal*, **28**(2), 108–23.

Shane, S. and S. Venkataraman (2000), 'The promise of entrepreneurship as a field of research', *Academy of Management Review*, **26**(1), 13–17.

Uhlenbruck, K., K. Meyer and M.A. Hitt (2003), 'Organizational transformation in transition economies: resource-based and organizational learning perspectives', *Journal of Management Studies*, **40**(2), 257–82.

Weidenbaum, Murray L. and Samuel Hughes (1996), *The Bamboo Network: How Expatriate Chinese Entrepreneurs are Creating a New Economic Superpower in Asia*, New York: Free Press.

Welch, C.L. and L.S. Welch (2009), 'Re-internationalization: exploration and conceptualization', *International Business Review*, **18**(6), 567–77.

Welch, D.E. and L.S. Welch (1996), 'The internationalization process and networks: a strategic management perspective', *Journal of International Marketing*, **4**(3) 11–28.
Welch, L.S. and R. Luostarinen (1993), 'Inward and outward connections in internationalization', *Journal of International Marketing*, **1**(1), 46–58.
Zhou, L., W.-P. Wu and X. Luo (2007), 'Internationalization and the performance of born-global SMEs: the mediating role of social networks', *Journal of International Business Studies*, **38**(4), 673–90.

9   Sourcing networks of born global firms
Jukka Partanen and Per Servais

INTRODUCTION

Rapidly growing small and medium-sized enterprises (SMEs) are known for their highly important role for generating new knowledge, innovations, and employment, and, as consequence, their contribution to the well-being of society (Storey 1994). Small growth-oriented firms are also resource-poor actors, which often have to adopt a niche strategy, that is, focus on their core competency and a few key customer segments (Knight and Cavusgil 2004). Since domestic markets can be limited in terms of sufficient number of customers, growth-oriented firms often need to seek new growth opportunities on international markets and to form 'born global' firms (Madsen and Servais 1997).

In order to overcome this resource scarcity or 'liability of smallness' (Stinchcombe 1965; Hannan and Freeman 1984), small firms complement their resources by engaging in different kinds of inter-firm networks (Hoang and Antoncic 2003; Maurer and Ebers 2006). Indeed, the current body of knowledge on SME networks recognizes several categories of inter-firm networks including customers (Shaw 2006), downstream networks (Lechner and Dowling 2003; Schutjens and Stam 2003), R&D networks (McGee and Dowling 1994; Lechner and Dowling 2003; Rickne 2006) and upstream networks (Lipparini and Sobrero 1994; Schutjens and Stam 2003).

While the recent literature on born globals recognizes the utilization of networks as a distribution channel strategy (Gabrielsson and Kirpalani 2004), export arrangements (Chetty and Holm 2000) or more generally 'alternative governance structures' (Oviatt and McDougall 1994), previous studies have not examined the role of networks in sourcing of born global firms (Ratti 1994). Indeed, in the context of small firms, the concept of upstream or sourcing networks, that is, vertical business relationships related to outsourcing and manufacturing, has remained fairly vague. Previous studies have identified only a few broad categories of upstream networks, namely suppliers (Lipparini and Sobrero 1994; Chetty and Holm 2000; Schutjens and Stam 2003), subcontractors (Chetty and Campbell-Hunt 2003) and outsourcing partners (Schutjens and Stam 2003). While some of the more recent studies have investigated the supply chain management (SCM) in the context of SMEs (Arend and Wisner 2005) and the phenomenon of SME sourcing (Morrissey and Pittaway 2006), the current body of knowledge provides little conceptual understanding on the complex nature of sourcing networks of a born global firm. This lack of research attention is somewhat surprising since it is essential that rapidly growing born globals are capable of scaling up their production in order to meet the demand of their global customers (Knight and Cavusgil 2004).

This research gap can be addressed by the following research question: what are the types and roles of different sourcing networks of rapid growing born global firms? Wynarczyk and Watson (2005, p. 49) state that 'further research is required to determine the role played by [supply chain] partnerships [in the SME context]'. To answer this research question, a case study of three born global SMEs in Finland was conducted. This contributes to the literature on networks of born globals (Chetty and Holm 2000) and new international ventures (Coviello 2006) by developing a theoretical framework, which distinguishes the different types of upstream network partners as well as the roles they play in the business concepts of born global firms.

THEORETICAL BACKGROUND

Previous Studies on Sourcing in the SME Context

Rooted in the literature on transaction cost economics (Coase 1937; Williamson 1975) and inter-firm relationships (Gulati 1995; Dyer and Singh 1998), strategic sourcing or SCM has been achieving increasing attention among academics and practitioners since its formalization in the mid-1980s (Bradley et al. 1998; Ayers 2000; Miller 2001). A literature review on the buying behavior of entrepreneurs (Ellegaard 2006) shows that remarkably little research has been done in this field. Only a few papers deal with the purchasing activities of newly started firms. As has been seen in the born global literature, sales and export have received much attention, but purchasing and the import phenomena have received only very little attention (Quayle 2002). Quayle's survey of 400 SMEs on the establishment of purchasing priorities and practices of small companies represents one contribution. Quayle found that 65 percent of the responding companies perceived purchasing to be unimportant but argued that this could be due to a lack of understanding of the value potential of the purchasing task. Quayle furthermore argued that effective purchasing requires resources, which the resource-poor entrepreneur does not often possess. Hence, most previous studies focused on the context of large firms (Buvik 2001).

Only a handful of studies have examined the sourcing operations of smaller firms (Morrissey and Pittaway 2006). On a general level, it has been argued that power asymmetry and dependency are the key factors which make the sourcing operations of SMEs distinctive compared to their larger counterparts. In order to circumvent these factors, previous studies suggest that SMEs rely on soft factors and trust in managing their supplier relationships (ibid.). In addition, earlier studies suggest that SMEs do not implement formal SCM systems as deeply as larger firms, and, as a consequence, do not gain profitability benefits from their SCM efforts (Arend and Wisner 2005).

Although previous studies have developed supplier categories and port-folios for larger firms (for example, Kraljic 1983; Olsen and Ellram 1997), there are only a few classifications on sourcing networks for small firms. Schutjens and Stam (2003, p. 122), for instance, distinguish two types of sourcing networks: suppliers are firms that supply input (parts, units) needed for the product/service of the focal firm, subcontractors are firms that deliver services not directly related to the product/service of the focal firm (accountants, cleaners, catering). The remaining studies on SME sourcing simply refer to sourcing networks by using one broad term such as 'supply chain partnerships' (Wynarczyk and Watson 2005), 'upstream vertical alliances' (Arend 2006), suppliers (Lipparini and Sobrero 1994; Chetty and Holm 2000) and 'subcontractors' (Chetty and Campbell-Hunt 2003).

As to the role of sourcing networks, previous literature suggests that supplier relationships contribute to the cost-efficiency (Johnson and Houston 2000), quality and responsiveness (Dean and Terziovski 2001), and innovation activity (Lipparini and Sobrero 1994; Pittaway et al. 2004) of an SME, and that SMEs that adopt an explicit strategy of devel-oping close partnerships with other supply chain members achieve higher growth and performance rates than non-collaborative firms (Wynarczyk and Watson 2005; Arend 2006). In brief, the specific types and roles of different sourcing networks have been a relatively unexplored research topic.

Theoretical Framework

In order to examine the sourcing networks of born globals, it is neces-sary to develop a framework of different types of sourcing network partners (Figure 9.1). The vertical dimension of the continuum assesses the replaceability of the sourcing partner. This dimension is theoretically

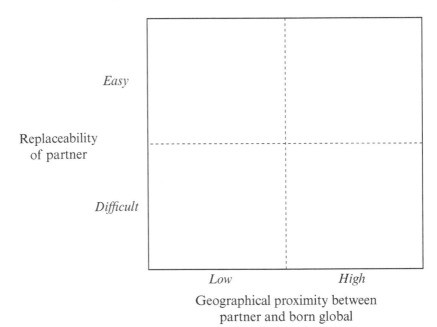

Figure 9.1   Location and replaceability of the partner

well-justified since previous studies on SME sourcing emphasize that the replaceability of the supplier or dependency between the supplier and the firm is one of the key factors that distinguishes suppliers (Morrissey and Pittaway 2006). Replaceability of the supplier has also been a widely used variable in the previous literature on buyer–seller relationships (Kumar et al. 1995).

The horizontal dimension refers to the geographical location of the sourcing partner. This dimension is theoretically in line with the previous studies on SME sourcing (Wynarczyk and Watson 2005; Arend 2006) and supplier selection (Hoetker 2005). In addition, the geographical proximity is especially suitable for examining born global firms since earlier studies suggest that the internationalization process can also include manufacturing collaboration with international partners (Kaufmann 1995; Kirby and Kaiser 2003; Lu and Beamish 2006).

It should be emphasized that the framework used here is not a two-by-two matrix with clear-cut boundaries providing four distinctive sourcing partners, but a continuum or 'production space' (Ratti 1994) of small firms, which can include several different types of sourcing partners.

METHOD

This study was conducted in Finland, which is a small open economy where a large proportion of businesses are SMEs; 99.8 percent of the firms have fewer than 250 employees (Finnish Ministry of Economy 2007; see Hyrsky 2007). A qualitative multiple case study of three case firms was conducted. A multiple case study is a suitable approach since the aim is to develop theories on born global networks (Eisenhardt 1989, 1991; Yin 1989; Chetty 1996; Garnsey et al. 2006). In a similar vein, the recent studies on SME sourcing propose that a more qualitative research approach is needed in the field (Morrissey and Pittaway 2006).

Selection of Case Firms

The case firms were selected from the environmental technology industry. This industry is considered to be a dynamic and complex environment offering a strong potential for global expansion and rapid growth. The case firms were selected using the following criteria. First, all of the cases are SMEs. The European Union definition of an SME was adopted. This definition states that an SME has 10–250 employees and turnover below €50,000,000 (European Commission 2003). Second, the selected case firms can be qualified as born global firms. Thus, all of the cases have entered global markets within three years from their inception (Knight et al. 2001) and generated at least 25 percent turnover from their global operations (Knight and Cavusgil 1996). Currently, most of the turnover of the firms is generated from global markets such as Asia, the US and Russia. The third criterion was a recordable rapid growth. Turnover was used as the basic measurement of firm growth, since it is the most common growth indicator used in previous studies (Brush and Vanderwerf 1992).

With regard to rapid growth, the view of studies conducted in the OECD countries was used: SMEs with a minimum of 150 percent increase in the four-year cumulative turnover are characterized as rapid (or hyper) growth companies (Parsley and Halabisky 2008). The final supportive criterion of the successfulness of a firm is the different kinds of awards received by the firms. Thus, most of the case firms have received awards for their innovativeness, export performance, and growth success. The profiles and the turnover development of the case firms are depicted in Tables 9.1 and 9.2.

Data Collection and Analysis

The primary data of the study consist of six semi-structured interviews with the senior managers (CEOs, CFOs) of the case firms. The scope of

Table 9.1   Profiles of case firms

Firm	Offering	Number of employees	Year of inception	Number of int'l markets	Awards
BG1	Emission control systems	15	1994[1]	Worldwide	Innovation (1996, 2003), Export (2008)
BG2	Oil spill recovery equipment	35	1982[2]	Worldwide	Export (2002), National Entrepreneur Award (2002)
BG3	Wind turbines	120	2000	Worldwide	Entrepreneurship (2007)

Notes:
1. In its early days, BGI was a small dockyard serving mainly Russian customers. In 1989 after the Soviet Union collapsed, the firm focused solely on oil recovery business. In early 1990s BG1 employed only three persons. The rapid global expansion of the oil recovery business started in mid-1990s.
2. In its early days BG2 delivered its products to European co-carting centers. The strategic re-focus and consequent rapid global expansion started in 2001.

Table 9.2   Turnover development of case firms

Year	BG1			BG2			BG3		
	Turn-over	%	C% (4)	Turn-over	%	C% (4)	Turn-over	%	C% (4)
1996	*			*					
1997	*			*					
1998	*			*					
1999	0.15			3.43					
2000	0.37	142		5.95	74	74			
2001	0.40	9		13.14	121	284			
2002	0.40	−1		11.40	−13	233	4.94		
2003	1.79	348		18.17	59	430	4.26	−14	
2004	1.52	−15	−15	13.78	−24		7.35	73	73
2005	3.40	124	90	16.51	20		14.25	94	235
2006	5.70	68	218	33.00	100		32.50	128	664
2007	16.70	193	833	38.00	15		60.00	85	1310
2008									

Notes:
% = annual growth of turnover.
C% (4) = cumulative growth of turnover over four years.
* = data not available.

the interviews was twofold. First, they provided rich descriptions of the current business models of the firms. Second, the respondents were asked to describe their network environments and its key actors in detail, as well as draw the network maps i.e. illustrations of the firm and its linkages to other firms and organizations. In addition, an extensive set of secondary data was collected. This included internal documents such as business plans, memos, collaborative contracts, and presentation materials as well as public material such as newspaper and industry magazine articles, brochures, publicly available statistics, business reports, and the firm websites. These secondary data were used as background material to gain understanding of the current business environment of the firms as well as for triangulation of information by comparing the respondent's comments to written, secondary sources of information.

The interviews were carefully transcribed, and the transcripts were corrected and commented on by the respondents. The unit of analysis was a sourcing partner rather than a firm. The analysis included two phases. First, the sourcing partners were analyzed by evaluating them according to the dimensions of the framework (replaceability and geographical distance). Second, the role of each partner was analyzed by assessing it in terms of its operational tasks and activities (for example, crucial versus complementary activities), and complexity of exchanged resources (for example, R&D competence, market information, new business contacts), and in terms of the intensity and characteristics of the collaboration (for example, the level of trust, frequency of communication, long-term versus project-based relationships). The network maps were also included in the analysis as they were compared to the transcripts. By utilizing the transcripts and network maps, tables were constructed which helped to analyze the data of the three firms and find patterns, similarities, and dissimilarities between the cases (Miles and Huberman 1984).

EMPIRICAL FINDINGS

Figure 9.2 shows the framework that represents the different types of sourcing networks of a born global firm. It should be emphasized that the analysis of the case firms' sourcing networks is not inclusive. It does not include marginal and non-strategic actors such as lawyers, accountants, and ad agencies. The reason for this narrow focus is that when the respondents were asked to describe the network partners that were contributing to their global business concepts, they rarely mentioned these supporting actors. Consequently, only those relationships that were emphasized by respondents, and so have strategic relevance, are reported.

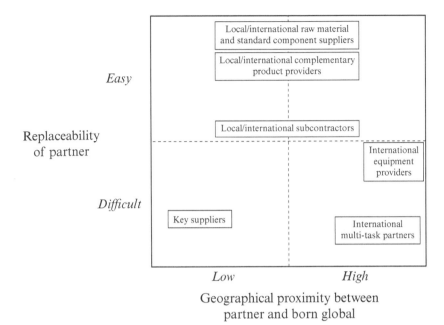

Figure 9.2   Different types of sourcing networks of born globals

Local and International Raw Material and Standard Component Suppliers

The simplest form of upstream sourcing of a born global firm is the purchasing of raw materials and standardized bulk components. The role of these actors is to provide necessary materials and components in a cost-efficient manner: 'We can purchase steel [from material suppliers] and those relationships function on a transactional basis' (CEO of BG3).

Due to the well-performing markets and high availability of these materials, these actors are very easy to replace. In addition, the location of the actors is insignificant, that is, they can be domestic or international vendors. BG3, for instance, mainly utilizes a domestic vendor but 'due to the high price level in domestic markets, we have to purchase steel also from abroad' (CEO of BG3). These actors are referred to as 'local and international raw material and standard component suppliers'.

Complementary Product Providers

A born global that focuses on its narrow core competence area and product line may find itself in a position where a customer requires more comprehensive or turnkey offerings, including other complementary products. Take BG2 as an example. As a turnkey solution provider in a project-based industry, the firm also uses a set of complementary product providers such as oil tanks and specialized vehicles. These partners are project-specific firms which simply supply products that a specific customer may want to include in the overall offering:

> The role of these complementary products is relatively marginal, it's more like we listen to the customer and find a solution . . . so, in addition to our own products, we can gather basically anything . . . if the customer requires and trusts us, we even deliver an airplane if the customer wishes so, or a light mast, or communication system . . . so, we can fulfill our customer's needs even though it's outside our competence area. (CFO of BG2)

These partners and their products are fairly easy to incorporate into the final offering. As the CFO of BG2 stated: '[The collaboration with these firms] is purely project-based . . . we can collect anything that our customer requires'. Geographically these actors can be either local or distant, since the core factors are the requirements of the customer. BG2, for instance, has local suppliers for tractors or even rubber boots as well as international suppliers for, for example, offshore oil booms. In sum, the role of these partners is to complement the offering and thus improve the customer satisfaction of the global clientele. These partners are referred to as 'complementary product providers'.

Global Equipment providers

In some cases a born global may have to build a collaboration with a set of global equipment providers. This happens when the equipment is more complex and is a part of the core product of the firm. Take BG2 as an example: 'Powerback [for the oil recovery system] is our product, it's based on our design, but it also includes an engine [manufactured by another firm]'. The crucial role of these actors is to provide cost-efficiency by providing non-core elements for the overall offering, but more interestingly, to offer the essential service and maintenance operations on a global scale. Although 80 percent of the materials and subcontracting is based in Finland, the firm also has international suppliers. In engines and hydraulic equipment, for instance, BG2 uses only a few globally recognized actors who have representatives around the world. This is mandatory in order to ensure maintenance of the equipment. Or, as the CFO of BG2 puts it: 'When we select the main engine for our powerpacks, we always select a supplier, which has a global service operations, so we don't have to be bothered by them [that is, service operations]'.

Due to the fact that the equipment is an essential part of the core product, and needs to be included in the design process, it can be argued that the equipment manufacturers are not as effortless to replace as compared to, for example, the raw material providers. However, a born global firm may still have few alternative suppliers: '[The engines of our powerbacks] can be manufactured by [large engine manufacturer x] or [large engine manufacturer y]' (CFO of BG2). These actors are referred to as 'global equipment providers'.

Local and International Subcontractors

Born globals can also delegate their manufacturing operations to a set of subcontractors: 'Our production is completely outsourced, we don't manufacture anything ourselves' (CEO of BG1). The role of the subcontractors is to mainly provide cost-efficiency, and scalability. The CEO of BG1 also commented: 'I'm really satisfied with our subcontractor network in the sense that we are able to build such a system with low capital demands . . . during the best year in our history we grew 10 times compared to the previous year, but there was still no limitations in our production'. Relying on several subcontractors also provides flexibility benefits:

> With this subcontractor network we can manufacture [our oil recovery equipment] more inexpensively but the main benefit is flexibility . . . if we had one big factory [as a partner], who would manufacture all our products, then our delivery times would be longer . . . so, in case of oil hazard, when a customer says that we need the equipment delivered here in three days, you can do miracles with this kind of subcontractor network. (CEO of BG2)

The geographical distance with these actors can vary. The production of BG1's final products, for instance, is mainly outsourced to two firms: one located in Finland and one in Estonia. BG1 has also had one project-based subcontractor in China who was responsible for production in a retrofit project in Asia. In a similar vein, BG2 has domestic subcontractors, but also a few international subcontractors, namely in China and the US.

The subcontractors are also somewhat easy to replace: '[Our two subcontractors] are replaceable [with each other] but not completely . . . it depends on the product' (CEO of BG1). 'Currently our production is delegated to two subcontractors, but we are continuously connected with a set of new potential manufacturers, who could be responsible for production in upcoming customer projects' (Marketing and Communications Coordinator of BG1). Or as CFO of BG2 states: 'There was too substantial economic risk [with company X] so we had to replace them . . . we couldn't give them [the same] responsibilities as our key suppliers'.

Thus, these network actors are referred to as 'local and international subcontractors'.

Local Key Suppliers

Born global firms often collaborate with a limited set of specific component and equipment providers. Again, the role of these partners is to improve cost-efficiency by providing non-core elements and components, but more importantly to contribute to the R&D activity of the firm.

Consider BG1 as an example. The catalytic cell manufacturers and coating suppliers of BG1 have a particularly crucial role in developing Emissiontech products: 'One critical area in our systems is a catalytic cell and we have partner X, which supplies these cells and we have really intense R&D collaboration with them' (CEO of BG1). In addition, these actors can take the responsibility for coordinating the second-tier, that is, indirect subcontractor relationships. The CFO of BG2 stated:

> In the early days when we decided that we aim for growth, we noticed that our manufacturing operations grew dramatically . . . suddenly we were a firm with no actual production capacity but had an enormous staff [for coordinating our subcontractor relationships]. That's when we got the idea of key suppliers i.e. we bundle a [key supplier] network between us and our subcontractors.

Or as the CEO of BG2 states in a business magazine: 'We've had over 200 subcontractors in Finland. Now we are selecting 5–10 key suppliers, who deliver us the complete products, which are even packaged for further shipping'.

Due to the fact that these partners contribute intensively to the R&D activity of the firm, they are extremely difficult to replace. Similarly, the in-depth collaboration requires that these partners be located in near domestic markets. These actors are referred to as 'local key suppliers'.

International Multi-task Partners

Born globals can also collaborate with large international partners operating in global target markets. The role of these international actors is to manufacture some of the components and coordinate local subcontractor networks, but also to perform the downstream or CRM activities such as marketing, selling, installation, maintenance and repair:

> We aim to seek a partner in every target market, which then acts as our front man. This started in Portugal . . . [our Portuguese] partner has the relationships and networks to manage the local activities . . . and in China we have a state-owned actor [as a partner], which is responsible for managing the customer

relationships, local subcontracting and assembly . . . so we seek out local partners in every country and do not try to enter the market by ourselves. (CEO of
BG3)

BG1 has built similar partnerships: 'In all of our retrofit projects with
customers i.e., [polluted] countries or cities, we have a local partner . . .
who manages the customer interface, as well as taking care of installation
services, certifications, and guarantees . . . and in [one project for a large
Asian city] we had a partner, who even took care of manufacturing' (CEO
of BG1).

Thus, it can be argued that the upstream and downstream networks of
born globals can overlap, that is, there may be partners who are responsible for both CRM and SCM activities. These partners have an essential
role in implementing the overall business concept, and the collaboration
is often operationalized as joint ventures. Therefore, it can be argued that
these partners are extremely difficult to replace. They are referred to as
'international multi-task partners'.

Comment

Thus, several different types of sourcing networks of born global firms are
utilized, and are distinctive in terms of their roles and contribution in the
overall business concept.

DISCUSSION AND FURTHER RESEARCH

The aim of this study is to identify different kinds of sourcing networks of
born global firms and to examine the roles of these networks in the business concept of a born global. By evaluating the upstream networks of
three born global case firms and their sourcing networks, several types of
sourcing partners were found.

Interestingly, it was found that born global firms are distinctive in
terms of utilizing international multi-task partners and international
equipment providers. These actors have a crucial role in manufacturing
and supplying components near the target markets (Kirby and Kaiser
2003), but also contribute heavily to the CRM operations of the firm.
Thus, it can be argued that born globals as small firms do not have the
resources to scale up their service operations for their globally spread customers, but need to rely on external partners to perform both upstream
and downstream activities. Theoretically, it can be proposed that the traditional distinction between upstream and downstream networks overlap

in the context of born global firms. This finding has not been reported in previous studies.

In addition, it was found that born global firms can collaborate with key suppliers, subcontractors and complementary product providers, as well as raw material and standard component suppliers. The category of complementary product providers is particularly theoretically valuable since these actors complement the resource pool of a born global firm by providing products outside the born global's competency domain and, as a consequence, satisfy the needs of a demanding global clientele. The role of key suppliers is also extremely important since they contribute to the R&D activity of the firm (Pittaway et al. 2004). This intense collaboration requires that the geographical proximity is low between the born global firm and its key suppliers.

Finally, the study found that subcontractors, complementary product providers, and raw material and standard component suppliers can easily be replaced. It can be argued that this independence is one of the main drivers why the geographical proximity between the sourcing partners and born global firms seems to be somewhat irrelevant; well-performing markets and the availability of the specific component or material enables born globals to seek cost-efficient partners regardless of where they are located. Thus, this study contributes to the literature on small born global firms and networks (Chetty and Campbell-Hunt 2003; Hoang and Antoncic 2003; Coviello 2006;) by exposing broad and vague concepts such as SME–supplier alliances (Arend 2006), inter-firm supply chain alliances (Wynarczyk and Watson 2005), and by identifying the distinctive sourcing networks for small born global firms.

This study is valuable for the managers of born global or high-growth firms. The different categories of sourcing networks can assist managers in evaluating their current network arrangements in terms of, for example, resource allocation, as well as develop their global network structures for their global operations by providing a tool for a partner selection procedure.

Born globals, or international new ventures, have been defined as 'a business organization that, from inception, seeks to derive significant competitive advantage from the use of resources and the sale of outputs in multiple countries' (Oviatt and McDougall 1994, p. 49). This chapter underlines the importance of sourcing resources and the dynamics in the supplier networks (Coviello 2006). Much more research is needed in the area of purchasing by entrepreneurial, international firms. As indicated in this chapter, supplier relations could have an important role in the development and growth of small firms.

REFERENCES

Arend, R.J. (2006), 'SME–supplier alliance activity in manufacturing: contingent benefits and perceptions', *Strategic Management Journal*, **27**(8), 741–63.

Arend, R.J. and J.D. Wisner (2005), 'Small business and supply chain management: is there a fit?', *Journal of Business Venturing*, **20**(3), 403–36.

Ayers, J. (2000), 'A primer on supply-chain management', *Information Strategy*, **16**(2), 6–15.

Bradley, P., J. Thomas, T. Gooley and J.A. Cooke (1998), 'Study finds growing interest in ERP and operations software', *Logistics Management and Distribution Report*, **37**(10), 48–50.

Brush, C.G. and P.A. Vanderwerf (1992), 'A comparison of methods and sources for obtaining estimates of new venture performance', *Journal of Business Venturing*, **7**(2), 157–70.

Buvik, A. (2001), 'The industrial purchasing research framework: a comparison of theoretical perspectives from micro economics, marketing and organization science', *Journal of Business and Industrial Marketing*, **16**(6), 439–50.

Chetty, S. (1996), 'The case study method for small- and medium-sized firms', *International Small Business Journal*, **15**(1), 73–85.

Chetty, S. and C. Campbell-Hunt (2003), 'Explosive international growth and problems of success amongst small to medium-sized firms', *International Small Business Journal*, **21**(5), 5–27.

Chetty, S. and D.B. Holm (2000), 'Internationalization of small to medium-sized manufacturing firms: a network approach', *International Business Review*, **9**(1), 77–93.

Coase, R.H. (1937), 'The nature of the firm', *Economica*, **4**, 386–405.

Coviello, N.E. (2006), 'The network dynamics of international new ventures', *Journal of International Business Studies*, **37**(5), 713–731.

Dean, A. and M. Terziovski (2001), 'Quality practices and customer/supplier management in Australian service organizations', *Total Quality Management*, **12**(5), 611–21.

Dyer, J.H. and H. Singh (1998), 'The relational view: cooperative strategy and sources of interorganizational competitive advantage', *Academy of Management Review*, **40**(2), 660–79.

Eisenhardt, K.M. (1989), 'Building theories from case study research', *Academy of Management Review*, **14**(4), 532–50.

Eisenhardt, K.M. (1991), 'Better stories and better constructs: the case for rigor and comparative logic', *Academy of Management Review*, **16**(3), 620–27.

Ellegaard, C. (2006), 'Small company purchasing: a research agenda', *Journal of Purchasing and Supply Management*, **12**(5), 272–83.

European Commission (2003), 'The new SME definition – user guide and model declaration, Enterprise and Industry Publications, available at: http.//ec.europa.eu/enterprise/enterprise_policy/sme_definition/sme_use_guide.pdf', (Accessed 28 of June 2011).

Gabrielsson, M. and M. Kirpalani (2004), 'Born globals: how to reach new business space rapidly?', *International Business Review*, **13**(5), 555–71.

Garnsey, E., E. Stam and P. Heffernan (2006), 'New firm growth: exploring processes and paths', *Industry and Innovation*, **13**(1), 1–20.

Gulati, R. (1995), 'Does familiarity breed trust? The implications of repeated ties for contractual choice in alliances', *Academy of Management Journal*, **38**(1), 85–112.

Hannan, M.T. and J. Freeman (1984), 'Structural inertia and organizational change', *American Sociological Review*, **49**(2), 149–64.

Hoang, H. and B. Antoncic (2003), 'Network-based research in entrepreneurship – a critical review', *Journal of Business Venturing*, **18**(2), 165–87.

Hoetker, G. (2005), 'How much you know versus how well I know you: selecting a supplier for a technically innovative component', *Strategic Management Journal*, **26**(1), 75–96.

Hyrsky, K. (2007), 'Entrepreneurship Survey 2007', available at: http://julkaisurekisteri.ktm.fi/ktm_jur/ktmjur.nsf/All/B348AFBDAA15B434C22573AD00276B9F/$file/jul32elo_2007_netti.pdf (accessed 13 January 2010).

Johnson, S.A. and M.B. Houston (2000), 'A reexamination of the moves and gains in joint ventures', *Journal of Financial and Quantitative Analysis*, **35**(1), 67–85.

Kaufmann, F. (1995), 'Internationalization via co-operation – strategies of SMEs', *International Small Business Journal*, **13**(2), 27–33.

Kirby, D.A. and S. Kaiser (2003), 'Joint ventures as an internationalization strategy for SMEs', *Small Business Economics*, **21**(3), 229–42.

Knight, Gary A. and S. Tamer Cavusgil (1996), 'The born global firm: a challenge to traditional internationalization theory', in Cavusgil (ed.), *Advances in International Marketing*, Vol. 8, Bingley, UK: Emerald Group Publishing, pp. 11–26.

Knight, G. and S.T. Cavusgil (2004), 'Innovation, organizational capabilities, and the born-global firm', *Journal of International Business Studies*, **35**(2), 124–41.

Knight, J., J. Bell and R. McNaughton (2001), 'The "born global" phenomenon: a re-birth of an old concept?', In proceedings of the 4th McGill Conference on International Entrepreneurship: *Researching New Frontiers*, Vol. 2, Glasgow, 21–23 September.

Kraljic, P. (1983), 'Purchasing must become supply management', *Harvard Business Review*, September–October, 109–17.

Kumar, N., L.K. Scheer and J. Steenkamp (1995), 'The effects of perceived interdependence on dealer attitudes', *Journal of Marketing Research*, **32**(3), 348–56.

Lechner, C. and M. Dowling (2003), 'Firm networks: external relationships as sources for the growth and competitiveness of entrepreneurial firms', *Entrepreneurship and Regional Development*, **15**(1), 1–26.

Lipparini, A. and M. Sobrero (1994), 'The glue and the pieces: entrepreneurship and innovation in small-firm networks', *Journal of Business Venturing*, **9**(2), 125–40.

Lu, J.W. and P.W. Beamish (2006), 'Partnering strategies and performance of SMEs' international joint ventures', *Journal of Business Venturing*, **21**(4), 461–86.

Madsen, T.K. and P. Servais P (1997), 'The internationalization of born globals: an evolutionary process?', *International Business Review*, **6**(6), 561–83.

Maurer, I. and M. Ebers (2006), 'Dynamics of social capital and their performance implications: lessons from biotechnology start-ups', *Administrative Science Quarterly*, June, 262–93.

McGee, J.E. and M.J. Dowling (1994), 'Using R&D cooperative arrangements to leverage managerial experience: a study of technology-intensive new ventures', *Journal of Business Venturing*, **9**(1), 33–48.

Miles, Matthew B. and A. Michael Huberman (1984), *Qualitative Data Analysis*, Beverly Hills, CA: Sage.

Miller, E. (2001), 'Tying it all together', *Manufacturing Engineering*, **127**(1), 38–46.

Morrissey, W.J. and L. Pittaway (2006), 'Buyer–supplier relationships in small firms', *International Small Business Journal*, **24**(3), 272–98.

Olsen, R.F. and L.M. Ellram (1997), 'A portfolio approach to supplier relationships', *Industrial Marketing Management*, **26**(2), 101–13.

Oviatt, B.M. and P.P. McDougall (1994), 'Toward a theory of international new ventures', *Journal of International Business Studies*, **25**(1), 45–64.

Parsley, C. and D. Halabisky (2008), 'Profile of growth firms: a summary of industry Canada research', available at: http://www.ic.gc.ca/eic/site/sbrp-rppe.nsf/ vwapj/ProfileGrowthFirms_Eng.pdf/$file/ProfileGrowthFirms_Eng.pdf (accessed 7 June 2010).

Pittaway, L., M. Robertson, K. Munir, D. Denyer and A. Neely (2004), 'Networking and innovation: a systemic review of the evidence', *International Journal of Management Reviews*, **5/6**(3–4), 137–68.

Quayle, M. (2002), 'Purchasing in small firms', *European Journal of Purchasing and Supply Management*, **8**(3), 151–59.

Ratti, R. (1994), 'Small and medium-sized enterprises, local synergies and spatial cycles of innovations', in Roberto Camagni (ed.), *Innovation Networks – Spatial Perspectives*, London: Belhaven Press, pp. 71–88.

Rickne, A. (2006), 'Connectivity and performance of science-based firms', *Small Business Economics*, **26**(4), 393–407.

Schutjens, V. and E. Stam (2003), 'The evolution and nature of young firm networks: a longitudinal perspective', *Small Business Economics*, **21**(2), 115–34.

Shaw, E. (2006), 'Small firm networking: an insight into contents and motivating factors', *International Small Business Journal*, **24**(1), 5–29.
Stinchcombe, Arthur L. (1965), 'Social structure and organizations', in James G. March (ed.), *Handbook of Organizations*, Chicago, IL: Rand McNally, pp. 142–93.
Storey, David J. (1994), *Understanding the Small Business Sector*, London: Routledge.
Williamson, O.E. (1975), *Markets and Hierarchies: Analysis and Antitrust Implications*, New York: Free Press.
Wynarczyk, P. and R. Watson (2005), 'Firm growth and supply chain partnerships: an empirical analysis of U.K. SME subcontractors', *Small Business Economics*, **24**(1), 39–51.
Yin, Robert (1989), *Case Study Research, Design and Methods*, Beverly Hills, CA: Sage.

10 Born global firms, internet, and new forms of internationalization
Rotem Shneor

INTRODUCTION

The phenomenon of firms quickly internationalizing from inception, while breaching the conventional evolutionary stages path of international development, has been granted various titles including the 'instant international' (Fillis 2001), 'international new venture (INV)' (Oviatt and McDougall 1994, 2005; Zahra et al. 2000; Zahra 2005; Hallbäck and Larimo 2006), the 'early internationalizing firm' (Rialp et al. 2005), 'born international' (Gabrielsson and Pelkonen 2008), and, most commonly, the 'born global' firm (Knight and Cavusgil 1996; Madsen and Servais 1997; Madsen et al. 2000; Moen 2002; Moen and Servais 2002; Andersson and Wictor 2003; Sharma and Blomstermo 2003; Gabrielsson and Kirpalani 2004; Hashai and Almor 2004; Luostarinen and Gabrielsson 2006). Here, an integrative definition of a born global (BG) firm may refer to an overall young and entrepreneurial firm aiming to enter international markets from its inception, going through a short or no domestic market period prior to international expansion, and whose majority of revenues is generated outside the home market, all while heavily relying on networks and strategic alliances as sources for learning and resources.

The reliance on hybrid forms of governance structures, such as networks and alliances, serves both as a remedy for limited resource availability and as a moderator of risk in international operations (Oviatt and McDougall 1994, 2005; Madsen and Servais 1997; Madsen et al. 2000; Gabrielsson and Kirpalani 2004). Indeed, according to Gabrielsson and Kirpalani (2004), the channels necessary for BGs to flourish are multinational corporations (MNCs) acting as system integrators or distributors, industrial and professional networks, the internet, and their various combinations.

Of particular interest, however, is the internet leg as exemplified in a growing body of literature referred to as 'internet-enabled internationalization' (IEI) (Loane et al. 2004; Loane and Bell 2007; Shneor and Flåten 2008; Shneor 2009), 'internet-enabled international entrepreneurship' (Mostafa et al. 2004), or 'global online entrepreneurship' (GOE) (Morgan-Thomas et al. 2008), specifically exploring the use of the internet in the internationalization of different firms in general, and BGs in particular.

Underlying this interest are the controversies around the internet's potential role in both speeding up and widening the scope of the international expansion process (Petersen et al. 2002; Karavdic and Gregory 2005). Such suggestions are mostly justified by the internet's theoretical capacity of leveling the playing field for all actors seeking to use the internet as a platform of international market service and growth, while overcoming knowledge gaps and resource constraints (Quelch and Klein 1996; Bennett 1997; Forsgren and Hagström 2001; Arenius et al. 2005). The purpose of the current chapter is to examine how BGs use the internet in their internationalization efforts, and, more specifically, to identify the new and unique modes through which they serve international markets online, and their defining dimensions. Such effort answers a gap in current literature, which is too often preoccupied with debating the potential and actual effects of the internet on internationalization, rather than exploring how firms are actually using it for such purposes. Hence, the current chapter answers earlier calls for research into the ways in which firms can apply the internet in their internationalization efforts (Samiee 1998a; Petersen et al. 2002; Arenius et al. 2005; Morgan-Thomas et al. 2008).

First, an introductory literature review section will highlight the main controversies around the proposed merits of IEI strategies. Second, IEI service modes will be conceptually developed by outlining their defining dimensions. Third, three cases of BGs in the software industry will be used to elaborate on the issue. Fourth, a discussion will aim to refine the concept of IEI service mode and its defining dimensions, while suggesting six propositions concerning IEI BGs' mode configurations. And, finally, conclusions will be drawn, contributions and limitations will be highlighted, and venues for future research will be suggested.

INTERNET AND INTERNATIONALIZATION

While some prophesized that the internet would lead to a revolution in the dynamics of international commerce (Klein and Quelch 1997), claiming it provides a fundamentally different environment for international marketing that requires a radically different strategic approach (Hamill 1997; Hoffman and Novak 1997), others argue that the internet should be treated only as a component of the firm's export marketing plans rather than a totally new phenomenon replacing conventional business methods (Samiee 1998a), being more evolutionary than revolutionary (Rosson

2004), and more of a 'complement to' rather than a 'cannibal of' traditional ways of competing (Porter 2001).

However, empirical evidence concerning the link between internet adoption and internationalization remains eclectic and inconsistent. Some authors find a positive link, as may be evident in Rask's (2002) study showing that the more Web experienced Danish small and medium-sized enterprises (SMEs) are, the greater the extent to which they are involved in exports. In the same spirit, Daniel et al. (2002) found that the higher the level of internet adoption in UK SMEs, the higher the level of their exports. Rosson (2004) found that internet-enabled exporting was a significant activity for Canadian SMEs, yielding positive financial results. And Hajidimitriou and Azaria (2009) found that Greek SMEs, firm-level technological infrastructure and internet capabilities had a significant positive impact on their export revenues. Moreover, in non-Western contexts, Lal (2004) found that Indian firms performed better in international markets when adopting advanced e-business tools, and Jaw and Chen (2006) showed that the degree of internationalization was positively correlated with the degree of e-commerce among Taiwanese SMEs.

More moderate and sometimes contrary findings emerged elsewhere. Moen et al.'s (2003) study of Norwegian SMEs showed that while the internet is an important tool contributing to a more rapid internationalization, it still falls short on activities involving personal sales. Morgan-Thomas and Paton's (2007) study found that using transaction-facilitating websites in UK-based SMEs does not necessarily mean international growth, and Raymond et al.'s (2005) study showed that e-business assimilation did not influence the internationalization of Canadian manufacturing SMEs.

A few explanations may be suggested for such inconsistencies. First, firms covered in these studies often had limited experience using the internet, taking into account that earliest online commercial activities only began in the mid to late 1990s, and actual common adoption even later. Second, internet technology itself continues to evolve, constantly offering more efficient, secure and user-friendly interactive systems for communication and transaction facilitation. Third, like other technologies, internet usage itself is only gradually adopted by common users. Fourth, the firm's offering's characteristics in terms of digitization potential, delivery complexity, service intensity, and levels of personalization may all impact on the internet's role in their international distribution and provisioning. And, finally, differences may result from the simple fact that various authors have been measuring different concepts with different operationalizations, while using different research methodologies, as they were studying firms operating in different temporal, spatial, and industrial contexts.

In the absence of solid proof otherwise, this chapter adopts the position that IEI at least has the potential to challenge traditional behavioral internationalization approaches, and that with time, this challenge may grow stronger and become more evident, as internet technology continuously develops and disseminates globally, and as firms become more experienced in using it in their international engagements in foreign markets.

As firms continue to experiment with IEI, and maybe even routinize it, it is equally interesting to know how this is achieved. In the next section, the defining dimensions of possible IEI modes of operations will be outlined, as part of a conceptualization effort.

INTERNET-ENABLED INTERNATIONALIZATION MODES OF OPERATION

Integrating e-commerce, export marketing, and internationalization process literatures, Shneor and Flåten (Shneor and Flåten 2008; Shneor 2009) suggested a shift from internationalization stage conceptualizations when dealing with IEI, and focusing on mode conceptualizations instead. For this purpose, modes were defined as 'strategic formats through which firms access, serve and interact (communicate and/or transact) with their clients and partners abroad' (Shneor 2009, p. 12). Such departure from a 'stage' to a 'mode' concept allows for certain flexibilities in the sense that a few modes may be employed at each stage. Hence, recognizing the possibility that clusters of modes, rather than any single mode, may be used throughout the IEI process, is quite similar to the complex reality of export management, where firms may engage in various foreign markets through a number of market entry and service modes simultaneously (Benito and Welch 1994).

In accordance with earlier studies suggesting that websites have the potential of both supplementing and replacing physical presence in foreign markets (Forsgren and Hagström 2001; Kotha et al. 2001; Hornby et al. 2002; Petersen et al. 2002; Vila and Küster 2004; Rothaermel et al. 2006; Shneor and Flåten 2008), the current chapter equates the concept of mode with firms' international websites.

The conceptualization of modes relies on identification of relevant key dilemmas emerging in the different foundation literatures, and their adoption as defining dimensions of IEI mode configurations. First, a key concern in e-adoption may be summarized as the choice between communicational and transactional functionality of online operations. Second, an important dilemma in export marketing has been identified in the strategic philosophies of global versus local orientation to international marketing activities and mix configurations. And, third, a central dilemma in internationalization revolves around foreign market operation modes and distribution channel configurations, highlighting the choices between direct and indirect foreign market service.

Accordingly, it is suggested here that all three dilemmas constitute the defining dimensions of the IEI modes: online functionality, extent of localization, and international service directness, While configuration choices are presented as dichotomous options, it is stressed here that firms usually position themselves along a continuum between the two discrete options, and that such presentation is used for simplification purposes only.

Functionality

Various conceptualizations of an e-adoption process and stages have been suggested in the e-commerce and e-marketing literatures (Daniel et al. 2002; Dou et al. 2002; Rask 2002; Rao et al. 2003; Dholakia and Kshetri 2004; Raymond et al. 2005; Saban and Rau 2005; Morgan-Thomas and Paton 2007). These all essentially suggest a four-stage process, involving the development along the information – communication – transaction – integration path, where firms evolve from having a relatively static e-presence to an interactive communications and portal engagement, further into transaction facilitation, and climaxing in dynamic enterprise integration, with cross-organizational learning and process improvements. Underlying such progression is the firm's digitization strategy, defined as the embedding of business processes in technological systems while choosing which activities to transfer online, how much to invest and which strategic objective to pursue (Morgan-Thomas and Paton 2007).

Thus, in terms of online *functionality*, firms may choose to either restrict their online activities to information provisioning and communications with clients, suppliers, partners, and other stakeholders, or enhance their communicational capabilities towards engaging in transactional exchanges through electronic means (involving online ordering, payment, billing, real-time inventory management, and so on).

Localization

International marketing scholars have been debating the standardization versus adaptation of international marketing strategy and mix for decades (Szymanski et al. 1993; Ryans et al. 2003; Theodosiou and Leonidou 2003), where proponents of standardization herald cost reduction efficiencies riding the waves of globalization and market convergence trends, while supporters of adaptation point to a complex reality of variations across country markets requiring the firm's commitments for long-term profitability. This dilemma is also relevant in the context of internet-based cross-border commercial activities, where the use of a globally uniform internet technology is constrained by the local embeddedness of commerce (Guillén 2002; Grant and Bakhru 2004; Okazaki 2004; Singh et al. 2004; Singh and Boughton 2005; Tixier 2005; Yip and Dempster 2005). This is a reality that led to a growing interest in the extent and effectiveness of local adaptation of websites, with a particular fascination with cultural issues (Luna et al. 2002; Singh et al. 2003, 2004, 2005; Singh and Baack 2004; Fletcher 2006; Sinkovics et al. 2007).

Thus, in terms of *localization*, firms may choose to either address the world as one market with target customer segments crossing national borders, hence opting for a globalized approach, or address nationally defined target markets, while accounting for relevant particularities associated with activities in each of these markets (that is, language, culture, institutional environment, and so on). Here a global approach is synonymous with standardization of online service formats across different foreign markets, while localization is synonymous with adaptation of online service formats to local market conditions, preferences, and needs.

Service Directness

Internet adoption is often associated with the elimination of process redundancies through direct interface with customers, suppliers, and strategic partners (Peterson et al. 1997; Poon and Jevons 1997; Prasad et al. 2001; Dholakia et al. 2002; Karavdic and Gregory 2005). However, a number of other authors suggest that a changing role of intermediaries is more likely than their disappearance, and that the internet has added channel intermediaries rather than displaced them (Sarkar et al. 1995; Quelch and Klein 1996; Hamill 1997; Klein and Quelch 1997; Samiee 1998b; Andersen 2005). On the one hand, the internet can connect end-users with producers directly, allowing for speedy and responsive transactions, and therefore reduce the importance of intermediaries. However, on the other hand, this may lead to inefficiencies created by information overload and the greater risks of prevailing knowledge gaps. In this situation, intermediaries may emerge as information collection, filtering, analysis, interpretation, and dissemination mechanisms; and will therefore redefine their value proposition within value chains and networks.

Therefore, in terms of international *service directness*, firms may choose to either address and serve target foreign markets directly, or do so via a variety of online and offline intermediaries, whose usage brings certain benefits to the firm such as achievement of cost efficiencies, speed to market, access to critical knowledge, access to a pool of customers, trust facilitation, and so on.

In the next section three cases drawn from BGs in the software industry will be presented, highlighting the particular representations of these dilemmas and the mode configuration combinations used to address them. Here, all firms originate from small open economies (SMOPECs), while exhibiting different internet dependence patterns, target market focus, and business model configurations.

CASES OF INTERNET-ENABLED INTERNATIONALIZING BORN GLOBAL FIRMS

An exploratory case study approach was adopted as it is an appropriate research strategy to define early stages of theory development (Eisenhardt 1989; Yin 2003; Ghauri 2004). More specifically, a multiple case approach was used as it permits replication logic (Yin 2003), where the cases are treated as a series of independent experiments that confirm or disconfirm emerging conceptual insights. However, theory and data are linked iteratively (Eisenhardt 1989; Eisenhardt and Graebner 2007). Initial theoretical assumptions and research issues are drawn from e-adoption, international marketing, and internationalization literatures, guiding empirical work and refined under the discussion section. The cases presented here are a part of a larger study into IEI practices among 16 firms from the software and travel industries. Table 10.1 describes the three cases used in this chapter. All three cases were selected based on their successful implementation of IEI strategies, their origins from SMOPEC countries (Israel and Norway), and their BG nature and orientations towards international markets – viewing the world as their market from establishment and having over 95 percent of their revenues generated outside the home market.

All information concerning these firms is adopted from Shneor's (2011) PhD dissertation, based on comprehensive data collection between 2007 and 2010 from annual reports, firm websites, press releases, and interviews with senior management. Interviews were transcribed, and together with the remaining textual sources, coded and summarized in systematic thematic tables. Case analysis reports were sent to respective managers for correction and comment.

MyHeritage.com

MyHeritage.com is an Israel-based BG start-up which was established in 2003, and officially launched in 2005. Its founding team has developed

Table 10.1   Information about studied firms

	MyHeritage.com	Opera Software	Qt Software
Type of firm	Private	Public (traded on OSE)	Public until Nokia acquisition in 2008
Specialization	Genealogy software	Web browsers	Application development framework
Internet dependency	High – web-based product and distribution	High – Internet-related product. Distribution – online and offline.	Medium – product developed online but not web based. Distribution – online and offline
Main business models	B2C for users	B2C for users B2B for integrators and distributors	B2C for developers B2B for integrators and consultancies
Revenue Models	Freemium	Revenue sharing from use + engineering and maintenance fees	Licenses for proprietary use of the Qt software
Country of origin	Israel	Norway	Norway
Year of establishment	2003 (launched 2005)	1994 (launched 1995)	1994 (launched 1996)
Annual turnover(US_m$)	Not disclosed	2007 – $53.8 2008 – $89.4	2007 – $ 27.2
	* In 2010 broke even and valued at $100		* In 2008 acquired for – $150
Number of employees	2008 – 35	2008 – 541	2006 – 232
Share of foreign sales	98%	Close to 100%	Above 95%
Main foreign markets	USA, UK, Canada, Australia	Russia, Indonesia, India, South Africa, USA	Germany, France, USA, South Korea
Foreign office	In Germany, UK, USA	In Sweden, China, Japan, India, South Korea, Poland, USA, Taiwan, Czech Republic	USA, Australia, China, Germany + Nokia international offices elsewhere

Source: www.businessweek.com/globalbiz/content/jan2008/gb2008 783831/html.

genealogy software that grew into a family-based social network for helping users create their family tree, share family photos, and organize their genealogical information online. Since its establishment, the firm has experienced an exponential growth, and by February 2010 it had established itself as the world's leading international online network for families and the second largest family history site. Currently valued at $100 million, the firm holds a registered user base of 47 million people worldwide, managing 13 million family trees, encompassing over 530 million genealogy profiles.

First, in terms of functionality, the firm's website is both the main distribution channel and the product consumption platform, hence, containing information about the product, communication tools, as well as a link to a transaction facilitating system. The software is available for download via the website, or as a web-based system, where users can create, edit, and publish their genealogy research. The product itself is offered under a 'freemium' model, where the basic version is available for free, and a premium version with advanced features is available for a subscription fee aimed at professional users and enthusiasts. The firm manages a community of people interested in genealogy research on the site, who exchange ideas and publish research results, as well as promote the software to their family members and friends. Family trees are privately managed by each user and linkages between independent family trees are suggested. In addition to the family tree builder, the firm continuously adds features based on customer feedback and research and development efforts, such as family timeline, history book, history mapping, and face recognition technologies.

Second, in terms of localization, the firm's web-based product is available in 35 languages, serving families worldwide. Although family is a general human phenomenon, it is rich with cultural particularities (for example: date and name formats). Hence, professional translations and adaptations are invested in the most important markets, while translations for other markets are the result of voluntary work by enthusiasts, which is later quality controlled by the firm's own chief translation manager. Hence, beyond a few strategically targeted markets, market performance in terms of local software adoption and extent of its viral dissemination, defines recruitment and investment policies in addressing other markets. The firm currently employs a mixture of local community managers who either are located at the firm's UK office or are part-time and freelance partners in various foreign markets abroad.

Third, in terms of service, since the value of the product is anchored in network economics logic, where the more users one has the more valuable the service becomes, and since the firm was small and resource limited for ambitious investments in international marketing, it opted to offer its products under a 'freemium' scheme. This allowed quick international adoption and dissemination based on the viral nature of the product and the community orientation of the created family tree sites. Such a situation meant opting for direct service as there were no margins to share with distribution channel partners. However, various shareware sites are updated about new versions of the software, which are made available for download indirectly through them. Other marginal initiatives have included physical distribution of CDs in selected genealogy printed publications.

In summary, for MyHeritage.com, the internet is an existential must, as the whole business model depends on internet activities and transactions, where value is created via rapid network expansion. Hence, the firm's website is the primary product, the consumption platform, as well as the marketing, sales, and distribution channel. Here, internet usage allowed for rapid international expansion, while at the same time provided real-time measurable data about market performance and trends, further enhancing operational efficiencies and strategic goal setting in localization and recruitment efforts. Reliance on a 'freemium' revenue model tilted all distribution efforts towards community and viral marketing, where the software is accessed through the firm's own site or via various shareware portals. In addition to these efforts, expansion was also achieved via acquisition of family network sites in key foreign markets, and their integration into the MyHeritage system, such as the acquisition of UK-based Kindo in 2008, and the German-based OSN Group in 2010 (itself owning leading family sites in 10 major markets including Germany, the US, Latin America, Spain, Portugal, France, and Poland).

Opera Software

Opera Software is a Norwegian-based BG software firm which was established in 1994, officially launched in 1995, and went public on the Oslo Stock Exchange (OSE) in 2004. Ever since its founding team developed a web browser while working under the Norwegian Telecom giant Telenor, the firm has been offering a constantly expanding line of web browsing products for desktop, mobile, and other devices (TV, game consoles, and so on). These developments follow its philosophy of 'One Web', according to which the Web should be made available to all people, across device types and geographies. And, indeed, since its establishment, the firm has experienced strong ongoing growth, reaching more than 100 million users worldwide by March 2010, with sales volumes nearing $100 million in 2009.

First, in terms of functionality, throughout its history the firm has been using a transaction facilitating site, where software was available for download and payments were processed via an online shop. However, through the years, the focus shifted from software sales to software dissemination, and after experiments with various revenue models, the firm eventually opted for offering its main products for free while focusing on a mix of engineering, maintenance, and revenue-sharing fees from products pre-installed on mobile phones and devices sold directly to enterprises. The firm also used a revenue-sharing model for its desktop browsers with major search engine partners such as Google.

In addition to the transaction focus, communication has also been of critical importance throughout the firm's international expansion, which manifested itself in aggressive public relations campaigns and the development of a user community site. Being a resource-limited, small Norwegian firm, the best way to market was by catching media attention via its rebel attitude in direct legal confrontation with giants such as Microsoft around competition laws. Such media coverage quickly disseminated through the internet and raised interest in the firm. Furthermore, the firm nourished its growing circle of fans and loyal users, which gradually became a large social network known as MyOpera, having over 4.5 million users by 2010 that interact, communicate, and publish blogs under the Opera brand.

Second, in terms of localization, Opera has focused on multilingual presentations in its website throughout its history, but it has done so inconsistently and to differing degrees. The main focus has always been on its English website promoting its One Web philosophy. However, recognizing a large portion of users in non-English-speaking countries, more limited texts have been offered in additional languages as well, including Japanese, Chinese, Russian, and German. Other languages went on and off the website including Polish, Dutch, and Hindi. French and Portuguese were later added, and most recently Bahasa Indonesia was added thanks to a voluntary effort by the local users' community and major growth experienced in that market. There are certain markets strategically targeted here, and some translation effort is made, but in other cases it is up to voluntary efforts by a loyal local user community with its own agendas and aspirations.

Third, in terms of service, acknowledging the need to reach critical mass for survival in the turbulent internet industry, the firm adopted a mix of direct and indirect approaches. Direct efforts are aimed at attracting users to download and try the browser from the firm's website, as well as via various shareware sites and portals. This has been done through successful public relations efforts coupled with the nourishment and development of an attractive social community site under the firm's brand. Parallel to this, the firm also created tailor branded browsers for various partners such as *Der Spiegel* in Germany. Moreover, it also used local sites for distribution such as 'Live Door' in Japan and 'Onet' in Poland. However, its main revenues are generated from relations with device manufacturers and communication service providers who use Opera browsers for creating attractive product offerings and enhancing revenues from internet connection and usage.

In summary, for Opera Software, the internet is also an existential must, but only to the extent that its products are for internet browsing. Its business model, however, is only partly dependent on internet activities and transactions, while the main source of income is generated from engineering and maintenance fees paid by enterprises integrating Opera browsers into their own bundle of products and services. Still, Opera's market share and value proposition is dependent on rapid network expansion, especially with respect to its mobile browser product line. Hence, the firm's website is a key promotions and distribution channel, both in terms of marketing communications and customer relations management. This is especially evident with respect to the nurturing, interaction, and communication with its users' community via the MyOpera site. Furthermore, to ensure that the site will not lose its vitality, the firm has been offering ever more attractive service packages for members, as well as made investments in integration efforts with other major social media and networking sites. International expansion, as such, is unsystematic and more reactive than proactive, and is evident in embracing and supporting local user communities as bridgeheads to their own national markets. More systematic efforts are done on a global scale towards key enterprise accounts rather than geographies and national markets.

Qt Software

Qt Software was established as the Norwegian BG software company 'Trolltech' in 1994, and has been on the market since 1996. In July 2006, it went public on the OSE, only to be acquired in June 2008 by the Finnish giant Nokia for $153 million, with a view to enabling Nokia to accelerate its cross-platform software strategy for mobile devices and desktop applications, and to develop its internet services business. This means that the Qt Software group within Nokia, although continuing to sell externally, now focuses its efforts on getting the software to be used by key players in a number of industries rather than on revenue generation and profitability *per se*, under a grander objective to establish Qt as the gold standard in its niche. Overall, it is estimated that over 350,000 developers are using Qt globally for numerous applications used in some 70 industries.

First, in terms of functionality, the firm is heavily influenced and guided by a philosophy viewing the market as an ongoing discussion, hence stressing the importance of online communications and the variety of tools used for enabling it, including a variety of forums, communities, open labs, IRC (Internet Relay Chat) channels, and social media. While the end customer is often an enterprise, the firm aims at attracting individual developers to try, use, and engage in the Qt development experience. Accordingly, it is using a dual licensing model, where proprietary use of the software is available for a fee and non-proprietary open source use and development of the software is available for free. The software itself is available for free download and trial through the website and various loyal open source community sites, some of which are directly supported by Qt. This implies that distribution is made primarily via the firm's own website, while proprietary licence registration forms may be filled online. The firm is currently developing its online shop and real-time transaction facilitation system.

Second, in terms of localization, markets are defined by industry segments rather than by national borders, where international presence is associated with proximity to major industry hubs and market potential estimations rather than with local adaptation efforts. Moreover, since its main target audiences are programmers using standard programming languages, such as C++, which in itself represents a public that often commands the English language, local translations are not a main international marketing concern. Having said that, a role for local adaptations is only evident in the form of language translations for certain major Asian markets, such as Japan, China, and Korea, where English proficiency remains at relatively low levels.

Third, in terms of service, the firm uses direct focused efforts towards developer communities and an identified list of major market players in various industries. Having the software available for free, and working directly with developer communities reduces commercial incentives for engagement with value-added resellers and distributors. Partnerships do exist, but these are mostly focused on technological complementarities and consultancy project agendas. Overall, Qt focuses its main effort in supporting and extending its user community, promoting transparency and product quality via various creative developer engagement initiatives, all as part of an effort towards becoming the product of choice and a gold standard in certain industries for their niche solutions.

In summary, for Qt Software, the internet is also an existential must, but only in terms of distribution to its target audience of shy and independent developers. Its business model, however, is only partly dependent on internet activities and transactions, while the main source of income is generated from proprietary license sales and projects for industry leaders. Offering an open source product also meant achieving high quality standards and a loyal community of users, which are supported and encouraged to engage in product development and its promotion among professional communities and businesses. Overall, two philosophies are guiding Qt's international development: first, a 'Qt everywhere' approach, meaning an ambition to be used across devices, industries, and countries; and, second, a view of the market as an ongoing discussion implying heavy investment in community development and direct intimate communications with professionals.

DISCUSSION

The cases presented highlight similarities and differences among the internet-enabled internationalizing BGs included in this study. Common to all cases is the concern with the three defining dimensions of IEI mode configurations, as suggested earlier – functionality, localization, and service directness (Table 10.2). Furthermore, it emerges that all firms are mainly focused on communication and community development where functionality is concerned, on language translation where localization is concerned, and on direct service where service format is concerned. However, they differ in the business and revenue models they employ, the main target markets they address, and the extent of their investment in each configuration dimension.

First, in terms of functionality, all firms seem to stress communication over transaction. This finding is supported in earlier studies examining internet adoption among exporting SMEs (Kaynak et al. 2005; Saban and Rau 2005; Loane and Bell 2007). However, this may seem counterintuitive as such small and resource-constrained firms may be more eager to generate revenues for their long-term survival and growth. Instead, survival and growth are associated with achieving a critical mass of global users rapidly, while offering products whose value increases when more users are using them. Reliance on achieving a critical mass of users is also closely connected to the niche nature of the products on offer, which are unlikely to find sufficient market potential based on domestic markets only, providing evidence for the criticality of the internet for the very existence of such firms (Quelch and Klein 1996; Hamill 1997). MyHeritage's genealogy research software derives its value to professional users from the comprehensiveness of its database; Opera Software derives value from revenue-sharing models based on the volume of actual usage patterns; and Qt Software derives value by establishing itself as a gold standard among industry leader firms and individual developers operating within its software development niche.

Table 10.2   Dimensions of IEI modes of operation

	Functionality	Localization	Service
MyHeritage.com	Communication + transaction facilitation + Integration via acquisitions Product and firm info Interactive site Communication via blog, newsletter, e-mails, and social media Product download Online payment	Language translations and minor cultural adaptations System available in 35 languages Standardized product with cultural particularities Local community managers recruited based on online market performance	Direct service and distribution as main focus. Indirect channels peripheral Direct download Direct sales Indirect distribution via shareware sites Viral and community-driven distribution
Opera Software	Communication (+ indirect transactions) Product and firm info Interactive site Product download Community site Public relations Revenue sharing with search engines based on use	Language translations Main site in English Thinner sites available in 8 languages Partnerships with local portal sites for distribution	Mixed direct and indirect distribution Direct download Indirect download from shareware sites Indirect download from local portal sites Pre-installed software on mobile phones and devices
Qt Software	Communication + Transaction Product and firm info Interactive site Lab sites Developer community sites Open source and proprietary licensing models	Language translations Main site in English Thinner sites available in 5 languages	Mainly direct distribution Direct download Direct sales Viral and community-driven distribution

Achieving critical mass enhances product development, quality, and brand awareness within target markets and segments, which are then translated into business profitability via sales interactions with selected premium and large volume paying customers. Since MyHeritage generates income from premium professional users, it is important to develop a comprehensive dataset and user-friendly tools for their research. For Opera to be the browser of choice for manufacturers and service providers, it needs to excel in feature development, device adaptations, and cross-device integration, while at the same time be popular with the end users across platforms. And for Qt to generate money it needs to excel in product quality, user friendliness and industry status, achieved through the embrace and engagement of the developer communities.

Based on these insights the following propositions are suggested:

Proposition 1(a): IEI BGs will focus on communicational rather than transactional website functionality.

Proposition 1(b): In comparison with other internationalizing firms, IEI BGs are more likely to develop online user communities for their global viral product promotions, distribution and R & D efforts.

Second, in terms of localization, all firms seem to stress translation over other forms of local adaptation. However, the firms also differ in the number of language translations being offered on the site as well as in their comprehensiveness. Common to all firms is a default global view of the world, adjoined by a practical association of market potential estimations with the willingness to invest in translations. Hence, all firms pre-specify strategically important markets towards which systematic translation efforts are directed, while other markets are addressed on a more random basis. Such randomness is associated with enthusiastic users that volunteer as translators of the site. Examples of these may be recent addition of a Catalan website for MyHeritage, a Bahasa Indonesia site for Opera, and an Arabic community site for Qt.

In this sense, if local websites are equated with virtual branches, as suggested by some authors (Forsgren and Hagström 2001; Kotha et al. 2001; Hornby et al. 2002; Petersen et al. 2002; Kim 2003; Rothaermel et al. 2006; Shneor and Flåten 2008), the reality emerging from the cases presented implies that IEI is not completely random and ignorant as suggested by some, but rather a mixture of strategic identification of key markets based on potential estimations (Forsgren and Hagström 2001), psychic and cultural distance (Rothaermel et al. 2006), as well as random market developments based on actual performance and user initiatives.

The number of languages available seems to be related to the cultural sensitivity level of the product on offer. While MyHeritage family sites are rich with cultural particularities as evident in the availability of the site in 35 languages, both Qt and Opera are available only in those languages viewed as important enough by the firm. The importance of languages in these cases is related either to major markets where overall English proficiency is low, such as Japan, China, and Korea, or to markets exhibiting relatively high levels of performance, in terms of downloads and visits, such as Russia and Indonesia in the case of Opera, and France in the case of Qt. The latter reasoning was supported in earlier research by Kotha et al. (2001), examining market entry by US internet firms.

Based on these insights the following propositions are suggested:

Proposition 2(a): IEI BGs will focus more on content language translations than on other forms of website localization.

Proposition 2(b): In comparison with other internationalizing firms, IEI BGs' website localization will be impacted to a greater extent by online performance of markets and the availability of credible translation volunteers.

Third, in terms of service, all firms seem to stress direct online distribution. Such a choice is often related to the revenue models employed by the firm, mixing distribution of basic standard versions of products for free via the website, while charging for premium and proprietary uses. Since premium and proprietary users are also professionals already familiar with the free version of the products, these are again provided directly by the firm. Under such models, resellers and distributors find little incentive in promoting the firm's product in the absence of margins for capture. The firm focuses on nourishing its customer base through interactive community sites. In the case of MyHeritage, indirect online distribution is completely absent beyond free shareware sites. Opera is the one firm that uses a certain mix of channels involving both its own site for direct distribution, as well as shareware sites, leading local market portals, and media partners, as well as various affiliate sites. Qt primarily relies on its own site and the community sites it supports, but also recently began developing an ambassador network and an affiliate program, which is still closely knit with its existing loyal user base and community members.

In this sense, the cases presented here support the notions presented earlier about disintermediation and greater provisioning of direct service via the internet (Peterson et al. 1997; Poon and Jevons 1997; Prasad et al. 2001, Dholakia et al. 2002; Karavdic and Gregory 2005), although such insights remain restricted to IEI BGs. More importantly, they extend such knowledge by highlighting the criticality of community management and development. Managing relatively low marketing budgets and offering basic versions of products for free means reliance, not only on the firm's own site, but also on leveraging its community of loyal users to disseminate knowledge about the products among their colleagues and friends, with an eventual goal of encouraging product trial and download. Once they have joined the circle, it is the community dynamics, product quality, and firm investments in the community that keep members engaged and eager to spread the word further.

Based on these insights the following propositions are suggested:

Proposition 3(a): IEI BGs will focus on direct online distribution rather than indirect online distribution.

Proposition 3(b): In comparison with other internationalizing firms, IEI BGs will rely more heavily on viral and community-based distribution.

CONCLUSION

Research suggests that BGs rely on certain channels for their rapid international development including integrator and distributor MNCs, professional and industrial networks, the internet, and their various combinations (Gabrielsson and Kirpalani 2004). In the current chapter, an effort was made at specifically examining how BGs use the internet in their internationalization efforts, while a fertile ground for such an inquiry was identified within the context of research into IEI or internet-enabled internationalization (Forsgren and Hagström 2001; Kotha et al. 2001; Petersen et al. 2002; Kim 2003; Loane et al. 2004; Rothaermel et al. 2006; Loane and Bell 2007; Morgan-Thomas and Paton 2007; Morgan-Thomas et al. 2008; Shneor and Flåten 2008; Shneor 2009).

A conceptualization of IEI modes was suggested, based on three key dilemmas underlying internet use for international development, adopted from three distinct theoretical pillars – internet adoption, international marketing, and internationalization. Namely, the question of functionality, as adopted from e-commerce literature, suggests choices along a continuum between online communications and transaction facilitation; the question of localization, as adopted from international marketing literature, suggests choices along a continuum between global standardization and local adaptation; and the question of service format, as adopted from internationalization literature, suggests choices along a continuum between purely direct and indirect market service.

This conceptualization was later confronted with evidence from three cases of BGs using the internet for their international development. Overall, it was shown that IEI BGs share some unique preferences for mode configurations. First, they invest heavily in communication features, and especially in development of interactive user communities. Second, they localize by providing textual translations in selected languages, where the number of languages available depends on the cultural sensitivity of the product, the levels of English proficiency in target markets, online market performance, and the availability of credible volunteers. Third, they serve target markets and segments directly for distribution purposes, while relying heavily on viral and community-based dissemination of product knowledge and trial. In general, one can also point out that commercial activity in B2B (business-to-business) models was mostly managed in a combined online–offline effort involving personal sales efforts, while B2C (business-to-customer) transactions were mostly concluded impersonally online.

Contribution and Implications

The main contributions arising in this chapter include the identification of IEI mode configurations unique to IEI BGs, as well as in highlighting the underlying motivations and factors leading to them. In particular, by highlighting the role of online communities as an international promotional, marketing, and distribution channel, the current chapter extends our understanding about the uniqueness of IEI dynamics and modes. Communities have been unexplored in earlier research and present a new mode of internationalization activities. Furthermore, the study also suggests that online localization is pending on the cultural sensitivity of the product on offer, that it is mostly manifesting itself in terms of translation, and that some of these translations are the result of volunteer work external to the firm. Hence, it also extends our knowledge into website localization decisions and dynamics in the context of firm internationalization process.

In terms of managerial implications, the study draws the attention of managers to the virtues and relevance of online user community development as an effective international promotion and distribution channel. Among these communities, firms may also identify potential employees for local market business development, as well as technical product research and development staff. Furthermore, successfully managed communities include a core of loyal enthusiasts which may also be used on a voluntary basis for translations, local promotional efforts, and marketing intelligence gathering. Overall, underlying community engagements is the necessity of achieving critical mass rapidly for firm growth and survival, as well as a philosophy viewing the market as an ongoing dialogue between firms and their customers. Online transactions may be more relevant for B2C's simple and relatively standardized transactions, while complex and service-intensive B2B transactions usually have a significant offline sales effort component.

Limitations and Further Research

Although generating interesting insights and extending our knowledge in areas where research is limited, the current study also has its limitations that must be acknowledged. First, the conceptual nature of the chapter leaves much room for empirical validation of the propositions it suggested. Second, since the analysis included BGs from SMOPEC countries, it is important to stress that BGs emerging in large domestic markets may exhibit different patterns. And, third, IEI mode configurations may also exhibit different patterns when investigating firms that are less reliant on the internet for conducting strategic business processes than those included in this study. Finally, as internet technology continues to evolve, its global diffusion further extended across regions, and as both firms and individuals become more experienced and comfortable using the internet for commercial purposes, one must also acknowledge the evolving nature of the phenomenon under investigation, as well as its temporal dependency. Such limitations form an attractive future research agenda in both conceptually extending the suggested dimensions of IEI mode configurations, as well as testing the validity of the suggested propositions in different firm, industry, home country, and temporal contexts.

REFERENCES

Andersen, P.H. (2005), 'Export intermediation and the internet: an activity-unbundling approach', *International Marketing Review*, **22**(2), 147–64.
Andersson, S. and I. Wictor (2003), 'Innovative internationalisation in new firms: born globals – the Swedish case', *Journal of International Entrepreneurship*, **1**(3), 249–75.
Arenius, P., V. Sasi and M. Gabrielsson (2005), 'Rapid internationalisation enabled by the internet: the case of knowledge intensive company', *Journal of International Entrepreneurship*, **3**(4), 279–90.
Benito, G.R.G. and L.S. Welch (1994), 'Foreign market servicing: beyond choice of entry mode', *Journal of International Marketing*, **2**(2), 7–27.
Bennett, R. (1997), 'Export marketing and the internet', *International Marketing Review*, **14**(4/5), 324–44.
Daniel, E., H. Wilson and A. Myers (2002), 'Adoption of e-commerce by SMEs in the UK', *International Small Business Journal*, **20**(3), 253–70.
Dholakia, Nikhilesh, Ruby Roy Dholakia and Martin Laub (2002), 'Electronic markets

and the transformation of marketing', in Nikhilesh Dholakia, Wolfgang Fritz, Ruby Roy Dholakia and Norbert Mundorf (eds), *Global E-Commerce and Online Marketing: Watching the Evolution*, Westport, CT: Quorum Books, pp. 43–60.

Dholakia, R.R. and N. Kshetri (2004), 'Factors impacting the adoption of the internet among SMEs', *Small Business Economics*, **23**(4), 311–22.

Dou, W., U.O. Nielsen and T. Chee Ming (2002), 'Using corporate websites for export marketing', *Journal of Advertising Research*, **42**(5), 105–15.

Eisenhardt, K.M. (1989), 'Building theories from case study research', *Academy of Management Review*, **14**(4), 532–50.

Eisenhardt, K.M. and M.E. Graebner (2007), 'Theory building from cases: opportunities and challenges', *Academy of Management Journal*, **50**(1), 25–32.

Fillis, I. (2001), 'Small firm internationalisation: an investigative survey and future research directions', *Management Decision*, **39**(9), 767–83.

Fletcher, R. (2006), 'The impact of culture on web site content, design, and structure: an international and multicultural perspective', *Journal of Communication Management*, **10**(3), 259–73.

Forsgren, M. and P. Hagström (2001), 'Ignorant internationalization? Internationalization patterns for internet-related firms', *Communications and Strategies*, (42), 209–24.

Gabrielsson, M. and V.H.M. Kirpalani (2004), 'Born globals: how to reach new business space rapidly', *International Business Review*, **13**(5), 555–71.

Gabrielsson, M. and T. Pelkonen (2008), 'Born internationals: market expansion and business operation mode strategies in the digital media field', *Journal of International Entrepreneurship*, **6**(2), 49–71.

Ghauri, Pervez (2004), 'Designing and conducting case studies in international business', in Rebecca Marschan-Piekkari and Catherine Welch (eds), *Handbook of Qualitative Research Methods for International Business*, Cheltenham, UK and Northampton, MA, USA: Edward Elgar, pp. 109–24.

Grant, R.M. and A. Bakhru (2004), 'The limitations of internationalisation in e-commerce', *European Business Journal*, **16**(3), 95–104.

Guillén, M.F. (2002), 'What is the best global strategy for the internet?', *Business Horizons*, **45**(3), 39–46.

Hajidimitriou, Y.A. and A.C. Azaria (2009), 'Internet and export marketing: impact of internet use on export revenues of Greek SMEs', paper presented at the the 35th European International Business Academy (EIBA) Annual Conference Valencia, Spain, December.

Hallbäck, J. and J. Larimo (2006), 'Variety in international new ventures – typological analysis and beyond', *Journal of Euromarketing*, **16**(1/2), 37–57.

Hamill, J. (1997), 'The internet and international marketing', *International Marketing Review*, **14**(4/5), 300–23.

Hashai, N. and T. Almor (2004), 'Gradually internationalizing "born global" firms: an oxymoron?', *International Business Review*, **13**(4), 465–83.

Hoffman, D.L. and T.P. Novak (1997), 'A new marketing paradigm for electronic commerce', *Information Society*, **13**(1), 43–54.

Hornby, G., P. Goulding and S. Poon (2002), 'Perceptions of export barriers and cultural issues: the SME e-commerce experience', *Journal of Electronic Commerce Research*, **3**(4), 213–26.

Jaw, Y.-L. and C.-L. Chen (2006), 'The influence of the internet in the internationalization of SMEs in Taiwan', *Human Systems Management*, **25**(3), 167–83.

Karavdic, M. and G. Gregory (2005), 'Integrating e-commerce into existing export marketing theories: a contingency model', *Marketing Theory*, **5**(1), 75–104.

Kaynak, E., E. Tatoglu and V. Kula (2005), 'An analysis of the factors affecting the adoption of electronic commerce by SMEs: evidence from an emerging market', *International Marketing Review*, **22**(6), 623–40.

Kim, D. (2003), 'The internationalization of US internet portals: does it fit the process model of internationalization', *Marketing Intelligence and Planning*, **21**(1), 23–36.

Klein, L.R. and J.A. Quelch (1997), 'Business-to-business market making on the internet', *International Marketing Review*, **14**(4/5), 345–61.

Knight, G.A. and S.T. Cavusgil (1996), 'The born global firm: a challenge to traditional internationalization theory', in S. Tamer Cavusgil (ed.), *Advances in International Marketing*, Vol. 8, Bingley, UK: Emerald Group Publishing, pp. 11–26.

Kotha, S., V.P. Rindova and F.T. Rothaermel (2001), 'Assets and actions: firm-specific factors in the internationalization of U.S. internet firms', *Journal of International Business Studies*, **32**(4), 769–91.

Lal, K. (2004), 'E-business and export behavior: evidence from Indian firms', *World Development*, **32**(3), 505–17.

Loane, S. and J. Bell (2007), 'Internet adoption by rapidly internationalising SMEs: a further challenge to staged e-adoption models', *International Journal of Entrepreneurship and Small Business*, **4**(3), 277–90.

Loane, S., R.B. McNaughton and J. Bell (2004), 'The internationalization of internet-enabled entrepreneurial firms: evidence from Europe and North America', *Canadian Journal of Administrative Sciences*, **21**(1), 79–96.

Luna, D., L.A. Peracchio and M.D. Juan (2002), 'Cross-cultural and cognitive aspects of website navigation', *Journal of the Academy of Marketing Science*, **30**(4), 397–410.

Luostarinen, R. and M. Gabrielsson (2006), 'Globalizing and marketing strategies of born globals in SMOPECs', *Thunderbird International Business Review*, **48**(6), 773–881.

Madsen, T.K., E. Rasmussen and P. Servais (2000), 'Differences and similarities between born globals and other types of exporters', in A. Yaprak and H. Tutek (eds) *Globalization, the Multinational Firm, and Emerging Economies* Advances in International Marketing, Vol.10, Bingley, UK: Emerald Group, pp. 247–65.

Madsen, T. K. and P. Servais (1997), 'The internationalization of born globals: an evolutionary process?', *International Business Review*, **6**(6), 561–83.

Moen, Ø. (2002), 'The born globals – a new generation of small European exporters', *International Marketing Review*, **19**(2/3), 156–75.

Moen, Ø., I. Endresen and M. Gavlen (2003), 'Executive insights: use of the internet in international marketing: a case study of small computer software firms', *Journal of International Marketing*, **11**(4), 129–49.

Moen, Ø. and P. Servais (2002), 'Born global or gradual global? Examining the export behavior of small and medium-sized enterprises', *Journal of International Marketing*, **10**(3), 49–72.

Morgan-Thomas, A., M.V. Jones and J. Ji (2008), 'Global online entrpreneurship: what do we know after over a decade (1997–2008) of scientific enquiriy?', paper presented at the 34th European International Business Academy (EIBA) Annual Conference, Tallinn, Estonia, 11–13 December.

Morgan-Thomas, A. and R. Paton (2007), 'Internet-enabled international growth: the impact of digitisation strategy on the international growth of UK SMEs', paper presented at the Academy of International Business (AIB) Conference, London, 13–14 April.

Mostafa, Rasha, Colin Wheeler and Pavlos Dimitratos (2004), 'Internet-enabled entrepreneurship: a conceptual model', in Marian Jones and Pavlo Dimitratos (eds), *Emerging Paradigms in International Entrepreneurship*, Cheltenham, UK and Northampton, MA, USA: Edward Elgar, pp. 155–172.

Okazaki, S. (2004), 'Do multinationals standardise or localise? The cross-cultural dimensionality of product-based websites', *Internet Research: Electronic Networking Applications and Policy*, **14**(1), 81–94.

Oviatt, B.M. and P.P. McDougall (1994), 'Toward a theory of international new ventures', *Journal of International Business Studies*, **25**(1), 45–64.

Oviatt, B.M. and P.P. McDougall (2005), 'The internationalization of entrepreneurship', *Journal of International Business Studies*, **36**(1), 2–8.

Petersen, B., L.S. Welch and P.W. Liesch (2002), 'The internet and foreign market expansion by firms', *Management International Review*, **42**(2), 207–21.

Peterson, R.A., S. Balasubramanian and B.J. Bronnenberg (1997), 'Exploring the implications of the internet for consumer marketing', *Journal of the Academy of Marketing Science*, **25**(4), 329–46.

Poon, S. and C. Jevons (1997), 'Internet-enabled international marketing: a small business network perspective', *Journal of Marketing Management*, **13**(1–3), 29–41.

Porter, M. (2001), 'Strategy and the internet', *Harvard Business Review*, **79**(3), 63–78.

Prasad, V.K., K. Ramamurthy and G.M. Naidu (2001), 'The influence of internet-marketing integration on marketing competencies and export performance', *Journal of International Marketing*, **9**(4), 82–110.

Quelch, J.A. and L.R. Klein (1996), 'The internet and international marketing', *Sloan Management Review*, **37**(3), 60–75.

Rao, S.S., G. Metts and M.A.C. Monge (2003), 'Electronic commerce development in small and medium sized enterprises: a stage model and its implications', *Business Process Management Journal*, **9**(1), 11–32.

Rask, Morten (2002), 'Evolution of web-based international marketing: patterns exhibited by Danish companies', in Nikhilesh Dholakia, Wolfgang Fritz, Ruby Roy Dholakia and Norbert Mundorf (eds), *Global E-Commerce and Online Marketing: Watching the Evolution*, Westport, CT: Quorum Books, pp. 99–110.

Raymond, L., F. Bergeron and S. Blili (2005), 'The assimilation of e-business in manufacturing SMEs: determinants and effects on growth and internationalization', *Electronic Markets*, **15**(2), 106–18.

Rialp, A., J. Rialp and G.A. Knight (2005), 'The phenomenon of early internationalizing firms: what do we know after a decade (1993–2003) of scientific inquiry?', *International Business Review*, **14**(2), 147–66.

Rosson, Philip (2004), 'The internet and SME exporting: Canadian success stories', in Hamed Etemad (ed.), *International Entrepreneurship in Small and Medium Sized Enterprises: Orientation, Environment and Strategy*, Cheltenham, UK and Northampton, MA, USA: Edward Elgar, pp. 145–77.

Rothaermel, F.T., S. Kotha and H.K. Steensma (2006), 'International market entry by U.S. internet firms: an empirical analysis of country risk, national culture, and market size', *Journal of Management*, **32**(1), 56–82.

Ryans, J.K. Jr, D. Griffith and S.D. White (2003), 'Standardized adaptation of international marketing strategy: necessary conditions for the advancement of knowledge', *International Marketing Review*, **20**(6), 588–603.

Saban, K.A. and S.E. Rau (2005), 'The functionality of websites as export marketing channels for small and medium enterprises', *Electronic Markets*, **15**(2), 128–35.

Samiee, S. (1998a), 'Exporting and the internet: a conceptual perspective', *International Marketing Review*, **15**(5), 413–26.

Samiee, S. (1998b), 'The internet and international marketing: is there a fit?', *Journal of Interactive Marketing*, **12**(4), 5–21.

Sarkar, M.B., B. Butler and C. Steinfield (1995), 'Intermediaries and cybermediaries: a continuing role for mediating players in the electronic marketplace', *Journal of Computer Mediated Communication*, **1**(3) available online.

Sharma, D.D. and A. Blomstermo (2003), 'The internationalization process of born globals: a network view', *International Business Review*, **12**(6), 739–53.

Shneor, R. (2009), 'When internet adoption meets the firm's internationalization process: the emergence of internet-enabled internationalization (IEI). paper presented at the the 35th European International Business Academy (EIBA) Annual Conference, Valencia, Spain, 13–15 December.

Shneor, R. (2011). 'Internet-enabled Internationalization modes and their configuration', doctoral dissertation 32, University of Agder, Kristiansand.

Shneor, R. and B. -T. Flåten (2008), 'The internet-enabled internationalization process: a focus on stages and sequences', *Journal of e-Business*, **8**(1–2), 44–53.

Singh, N. and D. Baack (2004), 'Website adaptation: a cross-cultural comparison of US and Mexican websites', *Journal of Computer Mediated Communication*, **9**(4), available online.

Singh, N. and P.D. Boughton (2005), 'Measuring website globalization: a cross-sectional country and industry level analysis', *Journal of Website Promotion*, **1**(3), 3–20.

Singh, N., O. Furrer and M. Ostinelli (2004), 'To localize or to standardize on the Web: empirical evidence from Italy, India, Netherlands, Spain, and Switzerland', *Multinational Business Review*, **12**(1), 69–87.

Singh, N., Z. Hongxin and X. Hu (2003), 'Cultural adaptation on the Web: a study of American companies' domestic and Chinese websites', *Journal of Global Information Management*, **11**(3), 63–80.

Singh, N., V. Kumar and D. Baack (2005), 'Adaptation of cultural content: evidence from B2C e-commerce firms', *European Journal of Marketing*, **39**(1/2), 71–86.

Sinkovics, R.R., M. Yamin and M. Hossinger (2007), 'Cultural adaptation in cross border e-commerce: a study of German companies', *Journal of Electronic Commerce Research*, **8**(4), 221–235.

Szymanski, D.M., S.G. Bharadwaj and P.R. Varadarajan (1993), 'Standardization versus adaptation of international marketing strategy: an empirical investigation', *Journal of Marketing*, **57**(4), 1–17.

Theodosiou, M. and L.C. Leonidou (2003), 'Standardization versus adaptation of international marketing strategy: an integrative assessment of the empirical research', *International Business Review*, **12**(2), 141–71.

Tixier, M. (2005), 'Globalization and localization of contents: evolution of major internet sites across sectors of industry', *Thunderbird International Business Review*, **47**(1), 15–48.

Vila, N. and I. Küster (2004), 'Marketing through internet: new strategic challenges', *Marketing Review*, **4**(3), 291–305.

Yin, Robert K. (2003), *Case Study Research: Design and Methods*, 3rd edn, Vol. 5, Thousand Oaks, CA: Sage.

Yip, G. and A. Dempster (2005), 'Using the internet to enhance global strategy', *European Management Journal*, **23**(1), 1–13.

Zahra, S.A. (2005), 'A theory of international new ventures: a decade of research', *Journal of International Business Studies*, **36**(1), 20–28.

Zahra, S.A., R.D. Ireland and M.A. Hitt (2000), 'International expansion by new venture firms: international diversity, mode of market entry, technological learning, and performance', *Academy of Management Journal*, **43**(5), 925–50.

11 Do born global SMEs reap more benefits from ICT use than other internationalizing small firms?

Noemi Pezderka, Rudolf R. Sinkovics and Ruey-Jer (Bryan) Jean

INTRODUCTION

The emergence and spread of information and communication technologies (ICTs) gave rise to speculations about their potential impact in many walks of life. Interestingly, despite the rapidly growing literature on e-commerce, research on the internet's impact on firm internationalization is comparatively limited. In a recent review of 45 empirical studies, Morgan-Thomas (2009) identifies two major streams within the 'online internationalization' literature, (a) the internationalization of e-commerce corporations and (b) the impact of the internet on the internationalization of non-internet-based firms. The present study focuses on firms which belong to the latter category.

The beginning of empirical international business (IB) research on ICT issues dates back to the seminal work of Hamill and Gregory (1997, p. 9) predicting a 'revolutionary impact on the conduct of international trade'. Macro-level studies, correlating internet access with international trade growth (for example, Freund and Weinhold 2004) seem to confirm this prediction. Furthermore, anecdotal evidence about the export opportunity-enhancing nature of the internet in developing countries (for example, Wheeler et al. 2004) was supported by empirical results indicating a higher propensity to export among firms with internet access in Eastern Europe and Central Asia (Clarke 2008). Yet, these results merely indicate that ICT, more precisely the internet, plays an important role in facilitating international trade without conveying a specific link about their contribution to export performance.

As pointed out by Anna Morgan-Thomas (2009), given the internet's unprecedented potential to reach foreign customers (Schlegelmilch and Sinkovics 1998; Yamin and Sinkovics 2006), and the trend towards increased e-enablement (Morrison et al. 2004), it is surprising how limited research is on the direct contribution of ICT to export performance.

Finding out *when* ICTs matter is even more pressing as they are approaching the end of their build-out phase (Carr 2003). This means that they are becoming widely available at affordable prices, erasing the potential for financial benefits by their mere adoption. Today, '[t]he key question is not whether to deploy Internet technology but "how" to deploy it. . .companies have no choice if they want to stay competitive' (Porter 2001, p. 64).

Furthermore, not only is the number of empirical studies on this subject matter limited, the results are highly inconsistent, calling for more investigation. In addition, while existing studies have, to varying degrees, covered ICT deployment dimensions such as 'complementary IT resources' (Morgan-Thomas 2009), 'relationship building' (for example, Morgan-Thomas and Bridgewater 2004), 'investment into IT' (ibid.); 'communication' (Raymond et al. 2005), 'online transactions' (for example, Moen, et al. 2008), 'market intelligence' (for example, Moon and Jain 2007), 'product services' (ibid.), and 'cost reduction' (for example, Lu and Julian 2007), to date there is no empirical study testing the impact of the internet as an alternative to physical foreign market entry mode on export performance. To this end, this study aims to fill this gap and to contribute to a better understanding of which internet-deployment practices actually contribute to an enhanced export performance. The question of 'how' to deploy the internet cannot be separated from the context of deployment. There is empirical evidence that young and fast-growing firms, also termed 'born globals', rely greatly on ICT as a growth facilitator (for example, Arenius et al. 2005; Servais et al. 2007; Hodgkinson 2008). However, rapid growth cannot be equated with better financial performance. Thus, the present study also aims to investigate whether ICT deployment contributes more to born global firms' export performance than to the export performance of enterprises that follow a slower internationalization pattern.

LITERATURE REVIEW

ICT Deployment and Export Performance

Following a comprehensive survey of the literature on ICT and export performance using online databases such as ABI/Inform and EBSCO, we identified nine empirical studies measuring the impact of the internet on export performance (Table 11.1). Eight of these studies directly correlated internet use with performance measures, and one study investigated the mediating impact of internet integration into marketing activities on export performance. While two of the studies operationalized internet use very broadly by measuring it as 'internet sales' and 'internet access',

Table 11.1   Empirical studies investigating the relationship between ICT use and export performance

Author/ Location of sample firms	Main research objective	ICT deployment operationalized as	Export performance operationalized as	Findings
Hodgkinson (2008) Australia	Determining the relationship between export growth performance and a series of market-oriented and internal resource variables	Internet sales	Export growth (fast/good/ modest/negative)	Fast-growth firms that are relatively small in size and have limited business and export experience are more likely to use internet sales as an early-stage entry mode
Clarke (2008) Eastern Europe and Central Asia	Does internet access affect export performance?	Internet access	Enterprise exports Exports as percent of sales for enterprises that export	Firms with internet access are more likely to export, however they do not export more than non-internet user exporters
Morgan-Thomas (2009) UK	Investigation of antecedents to online contribution to export performance (OCEP)	Complementary IT resources (advancement of IT, IT expertise of staff, investment in IT technology) Online capabilities (relationship/ transaction elements of website)	Perceived contribution of internet to: Export profits No. of foreign markets served Export sales Overall performance	Capability development effort (beta = 0.19; relational capability (0.08) have positive significant impact on OCEP Complementary IT resources and transaction capability have no significant impact on OCEP Length of export experience has a negative significant impact on OCEP

Table 11.1 (continued)

Author/ Location of sample firms	Main research objective	ICT deployment operationalized as	Export performance operationalized as	Findings
		Capability development effort (resource allocation to internet deployment)		Own export department and export intensity have a positive significant impact on OCEP
Morgan-Thomas and Bridgewater (2004) UK	Identification of the factors that influence success in using virtual channels to export markets	Investment in virtual channels Sophistication of the technology used Technological experience Transaction capability Relationship capability	Perceived impact of virtual export channels on export sales, export profit, number of markets served and overall performance	Investment and sophistication have a positive impact on virtual export channel success
Prasad et al. (2001) USA	Investigation of the extent to which the integration of the internet into marketing activities mediates the impact of market orientation on firms' marketing competencies	Customer-related marketing activities Field sales and channel member-related marketing activities Marketing research-related and management communication activities	Building awareness and image overseas Entering key markets abroad Sales growth Gaining new technology/ expertise Improve market share position Profitability	Greater integration of the internet into marketing strengthens the relationship between competitor orientation and marketing competencies, and interfunctional orientation and marketing competencies of exporting firms

Study	Purpose	Variables	Measures	Findings
Raymond et al. (2005) Canada	Investigation of the extent to which e-business assimilation contributes to the growth and internationalization of manufacturing SMEs	Communicational/informational use Business intelligence use Transactional/collaborative use	% of sales growth % of sales exported	Greater integration of the internet into marketing does not strengthen the relationship between customer orientation and marketing competencies of exporting firms There is a positive significant relationship between transaction/collaborative use of the internet and sales growth There is a significant but *negative* relationship between the use of e-business intelligence and export performance
Moon and Jain (2007) USA	Investigation of the determinants and outcomes of internet marketing activities of large and small-sized exporting firms	Internet marketing research Internet product development Internet promotion Internet distribution Internet product services	Profit Sales Market share	Internet marketing research, promotion and product services positively impact profits Internet marketing research, promotion and product services positively impact sales Internet marketing research and promotion positively impact on market share

Table 11.1 (continued)

Author/ Location of sample firms	Main research objective	ICT deployment operationalized as	Export performance operationalized as	Findings
Lu and Julian (2007) Australia	Investigation of the link between the Internet and export marketing performance	Communication Networking Market research Increasing sales volume Image enhancement Cost reduction Competitive advantage	Composite scale measure of: Economic export performance Strategic export performance Satisfaction with the performance of the export market venture	Only achieving a competitive advantage with the help of the internet has a positive significant impact on export performance
Moen et al. (2008) Denmark, Norway	Investigation of ICT use on market performance	Information search Sales activities Relationship development	New market knowledge of: Distribution channels Competitor strategies Competence development through cooperation Ability to operate in new markets Performance in international markets: Market share Sales growth Sales growth vs. competitors Profitability Overall performance assessment	No direct impact on performance, however direct and significant impact on new market knowledge Information search and relationship development positive impact on new market knowledge Sales activities negative impact on new market knowledge

respectively (see Clarke 2008; Hodgkinson 2008), the others attempted to capture internet use by devising multiple categories.

Morgan-Thomas and Bridgewater (2004) and Morgan-Thomas (2009) investigated the impact of 'complementary IT resources' and 'IT capability development' efforts on the online contribution to export performance. The former category encompasses factors such as the sophistication of IT infrastructure and IT staff as well as heavy investments in IT systems and applications. IT capability efforts include high time and resource investments into internet deployment, a high ongoing internet budget, and substantial planning of internet activities. Marketing activities replaced by the internet were measured by examining company websites. The Web contents have been classified into four categories, that is, information content, relationship-building features, online transaction features, and sophistication of the website. Prasad et al. (2001), Raymond et al. (2005) as well as Moen et al. (2008) broke down ICT deployment into three main dimensions, that is, market research, sales/transaction functions, and relationship development. In contrast to Morgan-Thomas and Bridgewater (2004) and Morgan Thomas (2009), these authors used Likert-type scale items to measure the relational dimension. While also accounting for marketing research and online transaction dimensions, Moon and Jain (2007) operationalized ICT deployment by additionally measuring the firm's dependence on the internet for new product development, advertising, and for providing product service support. Lu and Julian (2007) complemented the list of dimensions by adding 'cost reduction', 'networking', 'image enhancement', and 'competitive advantage'.

Although there seems to be a convergence in terms of the categorization of ICT deployment (information/relationship-building/transactions), the results of the studies are controversial. Seven out of the nine studies directly investigate the relationship between the transaction dimension of internet use and export performance. Contrary to expectations, only Hodgkinson (2008) found a positive significant relationship. The results indicated that fast-growth firms (born globals), tend to use e-commerce as an early-stage internationalization mode. However, in that study export performance is solely operationalized as fast/good/modest/negative export growth not accounting for the financial dimension. While Raymond et al. (2005) also found a significant positive relationship between online transactions/collaboration and sales growth, the export sales ratio (export sales/ total sales) remained unaffected.

There is only limited evidence for the relationship building potential of ICT (Morgan-Thomas 2009). Resource commitment to internet deployment in terms of allocated time, budget, and planning activities seem to positively influence export performance (Morgan-Thomas and

Bridgewater 2004; Morgan-Thomas 2009). The sophistication of the website, that is, the existence of multiple pages, regular content updates, different language versions, own domain name, as well as the registration with major search engines, also appears to have a positive impact on export success of virtual channels (Morgan-Thomas and Bridgewater 2004).

The use of the internet for business intelligence purposes yielded controversial results. While Raymond et al. (2005) found that prospecting for clients and developing competitive intelligence through online media can damage the export sales ratio, Moon and Jain (2007) identified a positive relationship between internet marketing research and export profit. However, in Moon and Jain's study, internet marketing research was operationalized because of the company's dependence on the internet for carrying out marketing intelligence as well as the quality of the company's capability to carry out marketing research on the internet. The same operationalization strategy was applied to two further constructs displaying a positive impact on export profits, that is, promotion and product support.

The review of existing empirical studies (Table 11.1) indicates that results on the contribution of ICT deployment to export performance are contradictory. These inconsistencies partially stem from differences in the operationalization of the identified dimensions. A further reason might be attributed to the timeframe of data collection. It seems that a large part of the data was gathered prior to 2005. Given the maturation and rapid expansion of the internet infrastructure, and the incorporation of IT into education systems, it can be expected that external pressure to engage in e-business is increasing rapidly. Consequently, there is need for further testing.

ICT Deployment and Born Global Firms

Although there is some empirical evidence that internet use positively correlates with firm internationalization, the causality of this relationship could not be sufficiently determined (Clarke 2008). In response to the causality question, the born global stream of the internationalization literature posits that the internet acts as an internationalization enabler. The underlying assumption is that born global firms are relatively small and limited in terms of their resource endowments (Hodgkinson 2008). Hence, there is the suggestion that they deploy the internet in order to proactively counterbalance these initial limitations (Kotha et al. 2001; Servais et al. 2007). Given the importance of technology leadership, including the reliance on ICT for the success of born globals (Knight and Cavusgil 2005), the number of empirical studies investigating their ICT deployment strategies is surprisingly limited (Gabrielsson and Gabrielsson 2010).

While Arenius et al. (2005) and Gabrielsson and Gabrielsson (2010) mainly focused on the qualities of the internet as a sales channel, Moen et al. (2003) and Loane (2005) identified a wide variety of ICT-use dimensions ranging from e-mail communication to competitor analysis. Servais et al. (2007) went beyond a simple deployment analysis and investigated the difference between born global and non-born global firms in terms of internet use. Their results show that born global firms rely on the internet more intensively than their non-born global counterparts. Other studies examined the facilitating effect of the internet on firm internationalization (for example, Kotha et al. 2001; Loane et al. 2004; Hodgkinson 2008); however, to our best knowledge, there are no studies investigating the impact of internet use on born global performance.

In this study, we define born globals as firms that internationalize within three years of their inception, have an export ratio of at least 25 percent, and operate in three or more different continents (Sundqvist et al. 2010).

CONCEPTUAL FRAMEWORK AND HYPOTHESES

The inconsistency in existing empirical results on the relationship between internet deployment practices and export performance (as pointed out above) may be due to the way these dimensions have been operationalized. By that, we primarily mean the underlying theoretical assumptions. Although no theory has been explicitly indicated, those dimensions which have been found to have a significant positive or negative impact on export performance were implicitly or explicitly connected to capability development (Morgan-Thomas and Bridgewater 2004; Moon and Jain 2007; Morgan-Thomas 2009) or to the expectation that the internet represents a resource advantage (Lu and Julian 2007).

Based on these empirical results, among the currently existing theories in international business, the resource-based view (RBV) would seem to be the one with the greatest explanatory value. However, as pointed out by Wu et al. (2006), internet use alone does not satisfy the criteria demanded by the RBV (Barney 1991). Reliance on the internet and other ICTs is more of a strategic necessity than a source of sustainable competitive advantage (Clemons and Row 1991; Powell and Dent-Micallef 1997). Powell and Dent-Micallef established that IT resources need to be embedded into an organization in order to contribute to value creation. Their results showed that 'ITs can produce competitive advantage by leveraging or exploiting Human and Business resources'(p. 392). Also building on RBV, Wu et al. (2006, p. 494) proposed and found empirical evidence that when IT technology is embedded in a firm's supply chain processes, it can contribute to the development of 'higher-order organizational capabilities . . . which are firm specific and hard to duplicate across organizations'. Similarly, Prasad et al. (2001) found evidence that the integration of internet technology into marketing activities enhances marketing capabilities, and, through these enhanced capabilities, it contributes to export performance.

In contrast to Wu et al. and Prasad et al., this study is more concerned with internet-based first-order capabilities. While, as repeatedly suggested empirically, ICT integration into business activities has the potential to enhance the development or effectiveness of higher-order capabilities (for example, Powell and Dent-Micallef 1997), they may also be influenced by a number of other factors not accounted for. In order to better understand the effect of internet integration on financial performance, it is important to investigate the relevance of first-order internet-facilitated capabilities. Consequently, we propose that those firms that develop superior capabilities in terms of communication with customers, relationship-building, reaching potential customers, bypassing costly physical presence in foreign markets, market research, being a front-runner in employing advanced export management technology, and cost reduction through internet deployment, will experience enhanced export performance.

Morgan-Thomas and Bridgewater (2004) found evidence that a high ongoing internet budget, substantial planning for internet activities, as well as high investment in terms of time and resources, led to enhanced export performance. In a later publication, using the same dataset, Morgan-Thomas (2009) renamed the construct 'web investment' as 'capability development effort'. This is in line with Porter's (2001) argument that IT investment needs to be aligned with a strategy. We take this argument a step further and propose that those firms that develop the capability to identify the most advanced technology available and integrate it into their export management process will witness higher export performance:

H1: The integration of advanced IT technology into a firm's export management processes contributes to enhanced export performance.

Although responsiveness in a world of zero-tolerance is a necessary condition to firm survival (Reeves 2000), there is no empirical evidence that using the internet for communication purposes has a direct significant impact on export performance by its own merit. However, if, through relying on internet communication, a firm achieves a competitive advantage (Lu and Julian 2007), financial benefits can be expected:

H2: A firm's internet-based communication capabilities contribute to enhanced export performance.

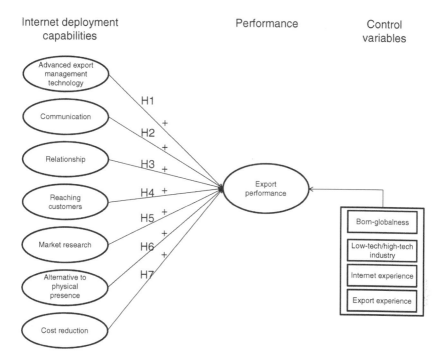

Figure 11.1   Conceptual framework

Relationship-building/maintaining capabilities have been shown to positively impact on a firm's export performance (Figure 11.1). While Morgan-Thomas (2009) focused on website features such as order tracking, online customer service, visitor recognition, and so on, Raymond et al. (2005) emphasized the collaboration function of internet technology. Moon and Jain (2007) found a positive relationship between online product service and enhanced profits. We propose that in addition to these dimensions, when a firm uses the internet as an alternative to physical market entry, it needs to be able to achieve at least the same level of customer satisfaction that it would have achieved by offline market entry:

H3: A firm's internet-based relationship-building capabilities contribute to enhanced export performance.

There seems to be an agreement in the literature regarding the internet's unprecedented potential to reach customers (Schlegelmilch and Sinkovics 1998; Yamin and Sinkovics 2006). Using the internet to generate sales leads (Bennett 1997), or setting up a website to serve as a virtual shopping window (Loane 2005) can lead to numerous possibilities. We propose that firms that identify ways to use the internet to reach more potential foreign customers will experience better export performance:

H4: A firm's capability to reach foreign customers contributes to enhanced export performance.

While there is empirical evidence that firms do carry out market research online (Bennett 1997; Loane 2005), when looking at the impact of these activities on export performance, the results are controversial. Prasad et al. (2001) found that online marketing research positively influences the development of marketing capabilities, and Raymond et al. (2005) found a negative relationship between e-business intelligence and export performance measured in terms of export sales ratio. Moon and Jain's results (2007), on the other hand, show that internet marketing research positively impacts on profits and sales, as well as on a firm's market share. This inconsistency calls for further testing. Thus we hypothesize that:

H5: Internet-based market research capabilities positively impact on a firm's export performance.

Using the internet as a direct sales channel can be used as an alternative or complement to physical market entry (for example, Gabrielsson and Gabrielsson 2010). Although there is empirical evidence that using the internet for online transactions does not have a significant direct impact on a firm's export performance (for example, Moen et al. 2008), there are no studies investigating the impact of the internet as an alternative market entry mechanism on export performance. Gabrielsson and Gabrielsson (2010) found that internet-based multiple channels can reduce the liability of foreignness and newness. Nevertheless, earlier research points to a firm's conviction that the internet is an appropriate way to counterbalance the lack of export experience (Bennett 1997). This is in line with Morgan-Thomas and Bridgewater's (2004) suggestion that the lack of extensive exporting experience in small and medium-sized enterprises (SMEs) may lead to a higher level of commitment to online internationalization. Comparable to the effects of the psychic distance paradox (O' Grady and Lane 1996), firms that are aware of their lack of export experience will attempt to compensate through the development of online capabilities:

H6: Internet-based capabilities that allow firms to avoid or reduce physical presence in a foreign market will experience enhanced export performance.

Despite the expectation that the internet can help in reducing the cost of various business activities (for example, Bennett 1997), Lu and Julian (2007) did not find a significant positive relationship between the cost-reducing use of the internet and export performance. To the best of our knowledge, there are no other studies testing this relationship, therefore, we deem the inclusion of this dimension in our study appropriate:

H7: Internet-based cost-reduction capabilities contribute to enhanced export performance.

As pointed out above, existing empirical results seem to indicate a difference in internet reliance between born globals and non-born globals (Servais et al. 2007). In addition, industry sector, export experience (Vahlne and Johanson 2002) and internet technology experience (Berry et al. 2004) may have a potential impact on the success of a firm's performance. Consequently, these factors need to be controlled for.

METHOD

Measures

As a first step, we conducted semi-structured telephone interviews with managing directors of five UK-based firms involved in active online internationalization (Yamin and Sinkovics 2006). The websites of the selected companies (i) displayed information that indicated an attempt to actively target foreign markets, for example, pricing in various currencies, website translations, cultural specific information, and (ii) were transactional rather than purely informative in nature.

These interviews have been used for scale development where no suitable measurement items were found in existing studies (Table 11.2). We used seven-point Likert-type multiple-item scales to operationalize all constructs and variables.

Sampling Frame and Data Collection

The target population was defined as UK-based SMEs involved in exporting activities and actively using a website. SMEs were determined using the definition of the European Commission, 'the category of micro, small and medium-sized enterprises (SMEs) is made up of enterprises which employ fewer than 250 persons and which have an annual turnover not exceeding EUR 50 million, and/or an annual balance sheet total not exceeding EUR

Table 11.2 Measurement scale

Original version	Adapted version*	Loading	t-value
Communication (CR = 0.7704)			
Inability to read, speak, and understand the languages of potential foreign markets (Bennett 1997)	The internet enables us to overcome difficulties in reading, speaking and understanding the languages of potential foreign export markets	0.687	7.555
Creates a good business image (Bennett 1997)	The internet allows us to effortlessly communicate a good business image to foreign customers		
Generates useful feedback from foreign customers (Bennett 1997)	The internet has helped us to gain useful feedback about our products from foreign customers	0.829	13.313
Self-developed	The internet enhances interactivity with our foreign customers	0.611	3.235
Self-developed	Using the internet, we can interact with foreign customers much quicker	0.561	2.968
Relationship-building (CR = 0.8086)			
Makes it easy for foreign customers to order goods (Bennett 1997)	The internet makes it easier for our foreign customers to order goods		
Creates ongoing relationships with customers (Bennett 1997)	The internet improves our ability to create relationships with customers in our target foreign markets	0.882	9.782
Self-developed	The internet facilitates exchange relationships with customers (e.g. feedback, comments and after-sales services)	0.802	5.030
We support customers online and customers seem happy with that (F1 L20–21**)	The internet improves foreign customer satisfaction	0.698	3.923
Self-developed	Our ability to customise products and services is dramatically improved by the internet		

198

We support customers online and customers seem happy with that (F1 L20–21)	Dealing with customers online makes it easier for us to satisfy them to our maximum potential	0.446	2.773
Reaching foreign customers (CR = 0.8491)			
Creates sales leads (Bennett 1997)	The internet improves our ability to generate foreign sales leads		
It's [the internet/our website] a very good shop window, getting our products in front of a lot more people (F1 L23–24)	The internet helps us to reach more potential foreign customers	0.834	2.393
Self-developed	Because of the internet we get unsolicited enquiries from foreign customers		
Gives the firm a competitive edge over rivals (Bennett 1997)	Using the internet to target foreign markets gives our company a competitive edge over rivals	0.884	2.683
Alternative to physical presence (CR = 0.7193)			
The net has taken some of that [need to go out to the foreign market] away though, making the world a lot more level than it used to be (F3 L73–75)	Because of the internet, country visits for exporting purposes are less important than they used to be		
Self-developed	Any future investment we might make, will go towards having an agent in our foreign markets		
Self-developed	Enhancing our physical presence in our foreign markets is our key objective		
Need to obtain foreign representation (Bennett 1997)	The internet helps us to avoid obtaining foreign representation in our export markets	0.751	5.626
The visits over there help you to see things that you weren't specifically being told about by customers (F3 L83–84)	Face-to-face contacts have given us a much better understanding of our industry in our target foreign markets	0.637	3.239

Table 11.2 (continued)

Original version	Adapted version*	Loading	t-value
Alternative to physical presence (CR = 0.7193)			
We have had some circumstances where internet could never have given us the same level of understanding of our hardware and software market and enable us to help our customers with big projects to implement our product properly. But most of the time, especially for small customers this is not the case (F5 L55–56)	When visiting foreign markets, the physical interaction allows us to see things that we wouldn't have seen via online interaction	0.537	2.235
There have been one or two occasions when we have not gained a client because we don't have a physical presence (F1 L65–67)	Our company would not have gained the customers we have, had it not been for our physical presence in our foreign market	0.566	3.205
We shouldn't ever completely ditch meeting and greeting the odd supplier or customer from time to time (F3 L96–96)	We should never completely stop meeting our foreign customers in person		
Market research (CR = 0.9303)			
Self-developed	Industry changes in our export markets are easily spotted using the internet	0.686	3.166
It [the internet] has allowed us to find out what our global competitors are doing (F3 L34)	The internet has improved our ability to find out what our foreign competitors are doing	0.688	2.762
Lack of business knowledge about competitors, clients and markets abroad (Eriksson et al. 1997)	The internet allows us to gather business knowledge about foreign clients	0.948	7.240
	The internet allows us to gather business knowledge about foreign markets	0.954	7.013
	The internet allows us to gather business knowledge about competitors abroad	0.954	7.311

Cost reduction (CR = 0.9806)			
Self-developed	The internet is an inexpensive way of communicating with customers	0.991	9.544
Lowers the cost of international marketing (Bennett 1997)	Using the internet to market our products and services internationally lowers our overall marketing cost	0.991	5.320
Lack of management time to devote to export matters (Bennett 1997)	The internet helps us overcome problems associated with lack of management time to devote to export matters	0.791	2.412
Financial costs of exporting additional to those for domestic sales (Bennett 1997)	The internet helps us to reduce the financial costs associated with exporting	0.990	4.449
Any future resources we might have will go towards that [our online business] rather than anywhere else (F3 L108–109)	In the future we will devote more resources to our online business	0.991	2.859
Advanced export management technology (CR = 0.9113)			
My business unit uses the most advanced IT for supply chain communication system (Wu et al. 2006)	Our company uses the most advanced IT systems to interact with our foreign customers	0.860	9.494
Our IT for supply chain communication system is always state-of-art technology (Wu et al. 2006)	Our IT for management of our international operations is always state-of-the-art technology	0.861	9.486
Relative to our competitors, our supply chain communication systems are more advanced (Wu et al. 2006)	Relative to our competitors, our IT for export management is more advanced	0.864	8.612
My business unit is always first to use new IT for supply chain communication system in our industry (Wu et al. 2006)	In our industry, our company is always first to use new IT for management of our international operations	0.871	8.328

Table 11.2 (continued)

Original version	Adapted version*	Loading	t-value
Advanced export management technology (CR = 0.9113)			
My business unit is regarded as an IT leader in our industry for supply chain communication system (Wu et al. 2006)	In our industry, our company is regarded as an IT leader for export management	0.625	3.205
Export performance (CR = 0.9392)			
How satisfied are you with the results of your exporting activities?			
Export sales growth (Katsikeas et al. 2000)		0.882	37.706
Export sales volume (Katsikeas et al. 2000)		0.917	61.295
Contribution of exporting to profits (Katsikeas et al. 2000)		0.806	16.473
Export market share (Katsikeas et al. 2000)		0.834	21.042
Overall export performance (Katsikeas et al. 2000)		0.903	49.961

Notes:
* 7-point Likert scale (strongly disagree =1; strongly agree =7).
** items taken directly from the interview transcripts Forbes (2006) F = Firm and L = Lines (of the interview transcript).

43 million'(European Commission 2003). In the first step, the criteria were entered into the FAME (Bureau van Dijk) database. It provides detailed, financial, descriptive, and ownership information on over 3.1 million public and private companies in the UK and Ireland. In order to determine whether the companies were involved in exporting, we examined whether their profit and loss account contained the position 'overseas turnover'. The database contained 8,605 companies corresponding to the above-mentioned specifications. We drew a random sample of 1,000 companies. The next step involved the website inspection of the selected companies. Those with non-functioning sites or with no explicit exporting activities had to be replaced. As contact person, the marketing, export or sales manager or, where these were not indicated in FAME, the managing director was selected.

Survey Response and Informant Evaluation

The first round was in the form of a postal mail-out of 1,000 questionnaires. After two weeks only 35 completed questionnaires had been returned. In order to increase the response rate, the sample companies were called one by one. By the fifth week after the mail-out, 74 responses had been returned. To further improve the response rate, a reminder e-mail was sent out to all managers who agreed on the phone to complete the survey. In total, we received back, 115 usable questionnaires accounting for a response rate of 11.5 percent.

A random sample of 82 companies was drawn from among the non-respondents (who explicitly indicated a non-willingness to respond by post, e-mail or phone) in order to test for non-response bias. The majority of non-respondents gave a shortage of time as the major reason for non-response, while only 6 percent indicated being discouraged by the length of the questionnaire (the original questionnaire had 252 scale items). Some 27 percent stated that their company policy would prohibit any participation in surveys. The remaining companies revealed their lack of interest in the topic or other reasons (for example, new manager, bankruptcy of the company, and so on) for their reluctance to reply. However, none of these was due to the substance of the questionnaire. Finally, we further assessed non-response bias by comparing selected attribute means of early respondents with those of late respondents (Armstrong and Overton 1977). The comparison of the means yielded no significant differences.

Common Method Bias

We assessed common method bias by applying two separate procedures. In a first step, we utilized the Harman one-factor test (Podsakoff and Organ

1986) by performing a principal component analysis of all the items included in the study. Since no dominant factor emerged, we conclude that there is no evidence suggesting the presence of common method bias in the study.

A more advanced step in examining comment method bias involved correlating objective data with subjective data on the same variable. The survey included a question where respondents were asked to indicate their export ratio. We subsequently downloaded the information about the selected firms' export ratio from the FAME database. The test yielded a significant and positive correlation coefficient of 0.675, again providing support for the assumption that no common method bias was limiting generalizations from our findings.

ASSESSMENT OF THE RESEARCH MODEL AND HYPOTHESES

Measurement Model Assessment

First, we examined the loadings of the individual items with their respective constructs (Table 11.3). All measurement items with loadings above 0.4 were retained (Ainuddin et al. 2007). The loadings for all measures range from 0.446 to 0.954, with most items exceeding the threshold level of 0.7 recommended by Fornell and Larcker (1981). In a second step, we examined both Cronbach's alpha and the composite reliability values for each latent variable. Both measures suggest reasonable reliability with all values exceeding the 0.7 threshold (Nunnally and Bernstein 1994).

Convergent validity was assessed by using the average variance extracted (AVE) (Table 11.3) as suggested by Fornell and Larcker (1981).

Table 11.3　Overall model evaluation

	AVE	Highest squared correlation	Composite reliability	Cronbach's alpha	*R*-square
Alt. phys. presence	0.5946	0.10896601	0.7193	0.7671	0
Cost reduction	0.9106	0.41615401	0.9806	0.9736	0
Communication	0.4618	0.32455809	0.7704	0.6636	0
Reaching new customers	0.7379	0.15031129	0.8491	0.6469	0
Export management	0.6756	0.06120676	0.9113	0.8855	0
Market research	0.7322	0.41615401	0.9303	0.9396	0
Performance	0.7560	0.06120676	0.9392	0.9187	0.3447
Relationship building	0.5268	0.32455809	0.8086	0.7014	0

Table 11.4   Company characteristics organized by industry and born-globalness of firms

Industry	Born-globalness	Internet experience (in years) Mean	Firm age (in years) Mean	Export experience (in years) Mean	Export ratio (%) Mean	Revenue (in million £) Mean
Low-tech	Non-BG	11	47	28	32.99	10.70
	BG	9	29	24	48.80	11.85
High-tech	Non-BG	10	60	29	32.22	16.66
	BG	11	31	31	63.08	9.97

Convergent validity was found satisfactory as all the values are greater than 0.5 (Henseler et al. 2009). We checked discriminant validity by using two methods, that is, the Fornell–Larcker criterion (1981) and the cross-loadings of items. As for each variable the AVE is higher than its highest squared correlation with any other variable, we can assume an adequate level of discriminant validity. This is supported by the cross-loadings. The loading of each indicator is greater than all of its cross-loadings (ibid.).

Structural Model Assessment

After ensuring that the outer model is both reliable and valid, we examined the inner path model using SmartPLS (Ringle et al. 2005). The explanatory power of a PLS model is determined by the extent of variance explained (R^2) by the endogenous latent variables (Henseler et al. 2009). The R^2 value for export performance is 0.345. Chin (1998) sets the thresholds at 0.67, 0.33, and 0.19 for substantial, moderate, and weak inner path models, respectively. Henseler et al. state that if an endogenous latent variable is explained by only one or two exogenous latent variables, already a 'moderate' R^2 value is acceptable. Although our coefficients for determination is medium, as the prediction capability of the model is sufficiently high (cv redundancy = 0.149; cv communality = 0.755) our results can be deemed as relevant and indicatory for future research. To check the prediction capability of the model, we used Stone–Geisser's Q^2 suggested in Henseler et al., applying the blindfold method (Tenenhaus et al. 2005).

Results and Discussion

Table 11.4 and Table 11.5 display the characteristics of the respondent firms. Some 50.43 percent of the respondents can be categorized as true

Table 11.5   Company characteristics

Dimension		Number of firms	Percentage of firms
Born-globalness	BG	58	50.43
	Non-BG	57	49.57
Industry	Low-tech	54	46.96
	High-tech	61	53.04
Employees	1–9	2	1.74
	10–49	27	23.48
	50–149	63	54.78
	150–250	22	19.13
Export ratio	<10m	13	11.30
	10–24.99m	18	15.65
	25–49.99m	33	28.70
	50–74.99m	30	26.09
	>75m	19	16.52
Revenue	1.00 < 1m	2	1.74
	2.00 1–4.99m	21	18.26
	3.00 5–9.99m	31	26.96
	4.00 10–24.99m	36	31.30
	5.00 25–50m	19	16.52

born globals. These firms have internationalized within three years from their establishment and are exporting more than 25 percent of their total sales to at least three continents. In terms of industry affiliation, 53.04 percent of the cases belong to the high-tech sector (for example, software, engineering, and computing) and 46.96 percent to the low-tech sector (for example, food and beverages, and clothing).

After performing a chi-square test of independence we conclude that there is no significant association between industry affiliation and born-globalness. Moreover, an independent sample *t*-test does not show differences between born globals and non-born globals in terms of their internet experience measured in years of internet use. This indicates that the comparison between born global and non-born global firms will not be affected by the firms' internet experience or industry affiliation.

The average firm age indicates that although born globals in our sample are still 'younger' than non-born globals with an average of 29 and 31 years in the low-tech and high-tech industry, respectively, they are past their start-up phase. In order to test whether this fact hampers inferences from the comparison between born globals and non-born globals, we again conducted an independent sample *t*-test which indicated that the

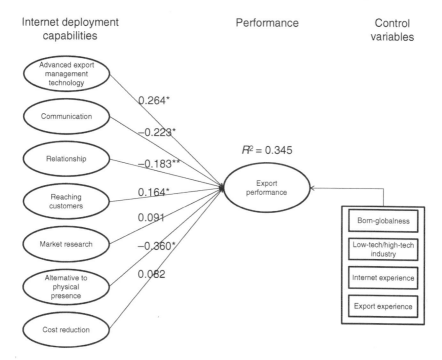

Internet deployment capabilities

Performance

Control variables

Advanced export management technology

Communication

Relationship

Reaching customers

Market research

Alternative to physical presence

Cost reduction

0.264*

−0.223*

−0.183**

0.164*

0.091

−0.360*

0.082

$R^2 = 0.345$

Export performance

Born-globalness

Low-tech/high-tech industry

Internet experience

Export experience

Note: *significant at 0.05 level; **significant at 0.10 level.

Figure 11.2 *Results of the PLS structural model* N = 115

mean difference in firm age was significant. Thus, even though some of the born global firms have already developed into more mature organizations, we are still able to find relevant differences in terms of the impact of internet-based capabilities on export performance between born globals and non-born globals.

Our overall results suggest that while certain internet-based capabilities indeed have the potential to significantly enhance firms' export performance, other internet deployment dimensions can have a negative effect. Although previous empirical findings indicated such potential damaging impact (for example, Powell and Dent-Micallef 1997), those results were not significant.

Figure 11.2 shows the results of our analysis carried out on the full sample of 115 SMEs. From our hypotheses only H1 and H4 could be fully supported. H1 stated that those firms that succeed at developing capabilities to integrate the most advanced IT technology available to their industries into their export management processes will experience enhanced export performance. In line with the literature, H4 proposed that the internet has an unprecedented potential to reach potential customers worldwide, and those firms that develop the know-how and skills to harness that potential will benefit through higher financial returns. Our findings allow us to go beyond previous inferences based on empirical evidence that ICT integration only facilitates higher-order capability development (for example, Powell and Dent-Micallef 1997; Wu et al. 2006). The results seem to confirm that the new technologies can also play an important role in the development of first-order capabilities. However, as can be seen in the case of H2 and H6, the use of ICT for active online internationalization bears its own set of risks (Pezderka and Sinkovics 2011). H2 suggested that internet-based capabilities which allow a firm to overcome language barriers, harvest consumer feedback (Sinkovics et al. 2009), and to enhance interaction with foreign customers will have an improved performance. However, contrary to our expectations, the results reveal a significant negative relationship between internet-based communication capabilities and export performance. The analysis of H6 proposing a positive relationship between the use of the internet as an alternative to a physical presence in foreign countries, and firm performance, yielded similarly negative results. One possible explanation for these disadvantageous effects may be Yamin and Sinkovics's 'virtuality trap'. This is, in essence, the managerial perception that the exploration of 'underlying market conditions' can be sufficiently carried out by the sole reliance on ICT (p. 349). H3, H5, and H7 were not supported.

In a subsequent step, we controlled for a firm's born-globalness, industry affiliation, degree of export experience, as well as internet experience, by adopting Jaccard and Turrisi's approach (2003). We measured industry affiliation by dividing our sample of 115 companies into two categories, that is, low-tech and high-tech, respectively. Export experience was operationalized using the firm's indicated export ratio. We used the number of years a firm has been using the internet as a proxy for internet experience. Table 11.6 summarizes the results.

Whereas industry affiliation and internet experience do not seem to have any significant impact on our main findings, the analysis revealed that born-globalness and export experience require closer attention.

While none of the ICT deployment dimensions had a significant contribution to non-global firms performance, in the case of born globals, internet-based communication capabilities indicated a negative significant effect.

An even more interesting finding emerged when we controlled for how the degree of export experience influences export performance. In line with our main findings before splitting the sample, firms with less export

Table 11.6 Control variables

		Control variables							
		Born globalness		Industry		Export experience (export ratio)		Internet experience (yrs)	
	Full sample	BG	non-BG	Low-tech	High-tech	Less 50%	More 50%	< 10 yrs	> 10 yrs
Export performance	N = 115 $R^2 = 0.345$	N = 58 $R^2 = 0.382$	N = 57 $R^2 = 0.141$	N = 54 $R^2 = 0.284$	N = 61 $R^2 = 0.256$	N = 65 $R^2 = 0.730$	N = 50 $R^2 = 0.434$	N = 46 $R^2 = 0.292$	N = 69 $R^2 = 0.104$
Communication	−0.223*	−0.386*	−0.063	0.064	−0.170	0.049	−0.053	0.122	−0.014
Cost reduction	0.082	0.009	−0.017	0.163	−0.120	0.042	−0.033	−0.124	−0.021
Reaching new customers	0.164*	0.238	0.143	0.082	0.146	0.061	−0.055	−0.010	0.117
Adv. export management technology	0.264*	0.183	0.210	0.109	0.189	−0.556*	0.172*	0.019	−0.009
Market research	0.091	0.141	−0.024	−0.125	0.276	0.034	−0.007	0.194	−0.028
Alternative physical presence	−0.360*	−0.238	0.260	0.464	−0.290	−0.638*	0.688*	−0.291	0.274
Relationship building	−0.183**	−0.116	−0.043	−0.078	−0.078	0.040	0.064	−0.201	−0.111

Note: *significant at the 0.05 level, **significant at the 0.10 level.

209

experience (< 50 percent export ratio) seem to suffer financial losses when relying on the internet as an alternative to physical market entry. Surprisingly, their export performance was also affected when they integrated advanced information technologies into their export management processes. Companies with more export experience (> 50 percent export ratio), on the other hand, displayed enhanced export performance for the same internet deployment dimensions.

A possible explanation for the controversial impact of IT integration may be that investment in advanced IT systems for export management needs to be aligned with the company's export intensity. In this case, the advancement of IT systems can be regarded as a proxy to the amount invested in that system. However, if firms invest more than their return on investment on that particular information technology, this will lead to losses at the profit level.

The second finding may be attributed to two issues. First, as mentioned earlier, online internationalization has its own array of risks. Despite the expectation that virtual market entry eliminates traditional international risks, most of these risks re-emerge in a transformed manner (Pezderka and Sinkovics 2011). Second, the importance of relationships in the target country (Gabrielsson and Gabrielsson 2010) can easily be underestimated due to the virtuality trap (Yamin and Sinkovics 2006). Firms with increased export experience can be expected to have developed the capabilities to manage international e-risks as well as to have found ways to counterbalance the negative effects of the virtuality trap.

CONCLUSION AND LIMITATIONS

In the 1990s, numerous papers concluded that SMEs were not deploying the internet to its full potential (for example, Hamill and Gregory 1997). After the turn of the century, research attention gradually turned to the pitfalls of overreliance on ICT such as the virtuality trap (Yamin and Sinkovics 2006), overinvestment (Carr 2003), and the lack of a clear deployment strategy (Porter 2001). This chapter set out to investigate how deploying the internet contributed to small internationalizing firms' export performance. Our findings support the relevance of these new emerging concerns. Although born globals seem to be more susceptible to falling into the communication dimension of the virtuality trap than other types of firms, a positive or negative contribution to export performance appears to be mostly influenced by a firm's export experience. Our results suggest that firms with more export experience (> 50 percent export ratio) have already developed the capabilities to transcend the virtuality trap, and thus experience enhanced export performance. On the other hand, firms with less export experience (< 50 percent export ratio), seem to overestimate the importance of IT investments and neglect the relevance of their offline/physical market experience. In summary, based on the outcome of our analysis we conclude that the internet can be best compared to a double-edged sword. It has indeed the potential to enhance the development of first-order capabilities that can contribute to enhanced export performance. Yet, when its use is not aligned with strategy (ibid.), it can lead to financial damage.

The main limitation of this study is the small sample size. Although PLS (partial least squares) is a powerful tool in dealing with small samples (Graham et al. 1994), a larger sample would allow for more variations in terms of splitting the data. A further limitation is that some of the firms that qualified as born globals are already past their start-up phase. Although we can still draw inferences from the results, future research may look into testing our findings with a subset of born globals in their infancy. Future research may also consider further investigating the circumstances under which ICT deployment directly contributes to firm performance.

REFERENCES

Ainuddin, R.A., P.W. Beamish, J.S. Hulland and M.J. Rouse (2007), 'Resource attributes and firm performance in international joint ventures', *Journal of World Business*, 42(1), 47–60.

Arenius, P., V. Sasi and M. Gabrielsson (2005), 'Rapid internationalization enabled by the internet: the case of a knowledge intensive company', *Journal of International Entrepreneurship*, 3(4), 279–90.

Armstrong, J.S. and T.S. Overton (1977), 'Estimating nonresponse bias in mail surveys', *Journal of Marketing Research*, 14(3), 396–402.

Barney, J.B. (1991), 'Firm resources and sustained competitive advantage', *Journal of Management*, 17(1), 99–121.

Bennett, R. (1997), 'Export marketing and the internet: experiences of web site use and perceptions of export barriers among UK businesses', *International Marketing Review*, 14(5), 324–44.

Berry, M., M.J. Kai-Uwe Brock and J. Kai-Uwe Brock (2004), 'Marketspace and the internationalization process of the small firm', *Journal of International Entrepreneurship*, 2(3), 187–216.

Carr, N.G. (2003), 'It doesn't matter', *Harvard Business Review*, 81(5), 41–9.

Chin, Wynne W. (1998), 'The partial least squares approach to structural equation modelling', in George A. Marcoulides (ed.), *Modern Methods for Business Research*, Mahwah, NJ: Lawrence Erlbaum, pp. 295–358.

Clarke, G.R.G. (2008), 'Has the internet increased exports for firms from low and middle-income countries', *Information Economics and Policy*, 20(1), 16–37.

Clemons, E.K. and M.C. Row (1991), 'Sustaining IT advantage: the role of structural differences', *MIS Quarterly*, 15(3), 275–92.

Eriksson, K., J. Johanson, A. Majkgård, and D.D. Sharma (1997), 'Experiential knowledge and cost in the internationalization process', *Journal of International Business Studies*, 28(2), 337–60.

European Commission (2003), 'Commission Recommendation of 6 May 2003 Concerning the Definition of Micro, Small and Medium-Sized Enterprises' (L 124/36 ed.), available at: http://europa.eu/eur-lex/pri/en/oj/dat/2003/l_124/l_12420030520en00360041.pdf (accessed 20 June 2008).

Forbes, Chloe (2006), 'Online internationalization & psychic distance – questionnaire development, measurement item generation & preliminary tests', Management: MSc dissertation, University of Manchester.

Fornell, C. and D.F. Larcker (1981), 'Structural equation models with unobservable variables and measurement error: algebra and statistics', *Journal of Marketing Research*, 18(3), 382–8.

Freund, C.L. and D. Weinhold (2004), 'The effect of the internet on international trade', *Journal of International Economics*, 62(1), 171–89.

Gabrielsson, M. and P. Gabrielsson (2010), 'Internet-based sales channel strategies of born global firms', *International Business Review*, 20(11), 88–99.

Graham, J.L., A.T. Mintu and W. Rodgers (1994), 'Explorations of negotiation behaviors in ten foreign cultures using a model developed in the United States', *Management Science*, 40(1), 72–95.

Hamill, J. and K. Gregory (1997), 'Internet marketing in the internationalization of UK SMEs', *Journal of Marketing Management*, 13(1–3), 9–28.

Henseler, J., C.M. Ringle and R.R. Sinkovics (2009), 'The use of partial least squares path modeling in international marketing', *Advances in International Marketing*, 20, 277–319.

Hodgkinson, A. (2008), 'What drives regional export performance? Comparing the relative significance of market determined and internal resource factors', *Australasian Journal of Regional Studies*, 14(1), 27–46.

Jaccard, James and Robert Turrisi (2003), *Interaction Effects in Multiple Regression* (Quantitative Applications in the Social Sciences), Thousand Oaks, CA: Sage.

Katsikeas, C.S., L.C. Leonidou and N.A. Morgan (2000), 'Firm-level export performance assessment: review, evaluation, and development', *Journal of the Academy of Marketing Science*, 28(4), 493–511.

Knight, G.A. and T.S. Cavusgil (2005), 'A taxonomy of born-global firms', *Management International Review*, 45(3), 15–35.

Kotha, S., V.P. Rindova and F.T. Rothaermel (2001), 'Assets and actions: firm-specific factors in the internationalization of U.S. internet firms', *Journal of International Business Studies*, 32(4), 769–91.

Loane, S. (2005), 'The role of the internet in the internationalization of small and medium sized companies', *Journal of International Entrepreneurship*, 3(4), 263–77.

Loane, S., R.B. McNaughton and J. Bell (2004), 'The internationalization of internet-enabled entrepreneurial firms: evidence from Europe and North America', *Canadian Journal of Administrative Sciences*, 21(1), 79–97.

Lu, V.N. and C.C. Julian (2007), 'The internet and export marketing performance', *Asia Pacific Journal of Marketing and Logistics*, 19(2), 127–44.

Moen, Ø., I. Endresen and M. Gavlen (2003), 'Use of the internet in international marketing: a case study of small computer software firms', *Journal of International Marketing*, 11(4), 129–49.

Moen, Ø., T.K. Madsen and A. Aspelund (2008), 'The importance of the internet in international business-to-business markets', *International Marketing Review*, 25(5), 487–503.

Moon, B.-J. and S.C. Jain (2007), 'Determinants and outcomes of internet marketing activities of exporting firms', *Journal of Global Marketing*, 20(4), 55–71.

Morgan-Thomas, A. (2009), 'Online activities and export performance of the smaller firm: a capability perspective', *European Journal of International Management*, 3(3), 266–85.

Morgan-Thomas, A. and S. Bridgewater (2004), 'Internet and exporting: determinants of success in virtual export channels', *International Marketing Review*, 21(4), 393–408.

Morrison, A., C. Bouquet and J. Beck (2004), 'Netchising: the next global wave?', *Long Range Planning*, 37(1), 11–27.

Nunnally, Jum C. and Ira H. Bernstein (1994), *Psychometric Theory*, 3rd edn., New York: McGraw-Hill.

O'Grady, S. and H.W. Lane (1996), 'The psychic distance paradox', *Journal of International Business Studies*, 27(2), 309–33.

Pezderka, N. and R.R. Sinkovics (2011), 'A conceptualization of e-risk perceptions and implications for small firm active online internationalization', *International Business Review*, 20(4), 408–22.

Podsakoff, P.M. and D.W. Organ (1986), 'Self-reports in organizational research: problems and prospects', *Journal of Management*, 12(4), 531–44.

Porter, M.E. (2001), 'Strategy and the internet', *Harvard Business Review*, 79(3), 62–78.

Powell, T.C. and A. Dent-Micallef (1997), 'Information technology as competitive advantage: the role of human, business, and technology resources', *Strategic Management Journal*, 18(5), 375–405.

Prasad, V.K., K. Ramamurthy and G.M. Naidu (2001), 'The influence of internet-marketing integration on marketing competencies and export performance', *Journal of International Marketing*, 9(4), 82–110.

Raymond, L., F. Bergeron and S. Blili (2005), 'The assimilation of e-business in manufacturing SMEs: determinants and effects on growth and internationalization', *Electronic Markets*, 15(2), 106–18.

Reeves, Joanna (ed.) (2000), *Business Risk*, London: Caspian.

Ringle, Christian Marc, Sven Wende and Alexander Will (2005), *Smartpls 2.0 M3*, University of Hamburg, Hamburg.

Schlegelmilch, B.B. and R.R. Sinkovics (1998), 'Marketing in the information age – can we plan for an unpredictable future?', *International Marketing Review*, 15(3), 162–70.

Servais, P., T.K. Madsen and E.S. Rasmussen (2007), 'Small manufacturing firms' involvement in international e-business activities', *Advances in International Marketing*, 17, 297–317.

Sinkovics, R., E. Penz and F.J.M. Castillo (2009), 'Qualitative analyse von online communities für neuproduktentscheidungen', *der Markt*, 48(1), 61–72.

Sundqvist, S., O. Kuivalainen and J.W. Cadogan (2010), 'Contingency factors in entrepreneurial orientation–performance relationship of firms with different levels of internationalization', in Colm Kearney (ed.), *37th Annual Conference*, Academy of International Business, UK and Chapter, Dublin, CD-ROM.

Tenenhaus, M., V.E. Vinzi, Y.-M. Chatelin and C. Lauro (2005), 'PLS path modeling', *Computational Statistics & Data Analysis*, 48(1), 159–205.

Vahlne, Jan-Erik and Jan Johanson (2002), 'New technology, new companies, new business environments and new internationalization processes?', in Virpi Havila, Mats Forsgren, and Håkan Håkansson (eds), *Critical Perspectives on Internationalization*, Amsterdam: Pergamon, pp. 209–27.

Wheeler, David, Susmita Dasgupta and Somik Lall (2004), 'Policy reform, economic growth, and the digital divide: an econometric analysis', World Bank Policy Research Working Paper 2567, Washington, DC, available at: http://papers.ssm.com/sol3/papers.cfm?abstract_id=632636.

Wu, F., S. Yeniyurt, D. Kim and S.T. Cavusgil (2006), 'The impact of information technology on supply chain capabilities and firm performance: a resource-based view', *Industrial Marketing Management*, 35(4), 493–504.

Yamin, M. and R.R. Sinkovics (2006), 'Online internationalization, psychic distance reduction and the virtuality trap', *International Business Review*, 15(4), 339–60.

12 An institutional perspective on the strategic behavior of Chinese new ventures
Huan Zou and Pervez N. Ghauri

INTRODUCTION

Over the past decades, international entrepreneurship (IE) researchers have shown great interest in understanding the growth of new and young firms that choose to compete in the international marketplace (Vahlne and Johanson 2002). Previous research acknowledges that entrepreneurs' knowledge and capabilities play a role in guiding the firm in identifying appropriate target markets, localizing the target market, and ultimately, distributing products within the newly targeted market (Sandberg and Hofer 1987; Zhu et al. 2006). However, there is insufficient knowledge about differences between international new ventures (INVs) and domestic new ventures (DNVs) (McDougall et al. 2003). With a few exceptions (for example, McDougall 1989; McDougall et al. 2003), most IE research has focused exclusively on samples of INVs (Shrader et al. 2000), or made comparisons with older internationalized firms (Reuber and Fischer 1997) and do not have direct comparisons with domestic ventures. Inspired by previous new venture research, this chapter will investigate the factors that determine and distinguish INVs' orientation from domestic ventures. Coming from an institutional perspective, two main research questions will be focused on: (i) do institutional structures between home country and host country affect entrepreneurial experience and relationship; and (ii) do entrepreneurial experience and relationship influence the strategic behavior of INVs and DNVs?

The institutional perspective suggests that strategic choices are not only driven by industry variations or firm-specific advantages, but are also a reflection of the formal and informal constraints of the particular institutional framework that entrepreneurs confront (Peng et al. 2008). The differences in social and institutional relationships and structures between domestic and international markets not only govern firms' strategic decision making, actions, and market processes, but also establish the role of individual entrepreneurs in the formation, enrolment, and manipulation of these relationships in order to proactively engage in international business activities. Thus, an entrepreneur's prior experience, personal network, and perceptions towards risk and return are a reflection of institutional structures and relationships either in home or host markets (Gao et al. 2010). However, existing studies have limited exploration on the link between institutions and strategic choices on international entrepreneurship (Teegen et al. 2004). This study asserts that institutional differences between developed and emerging markets explain variations in the entrepreneurial capabilities, resources and decision-making processes (Aldrich 1990; Gnyawali and Fogel 1994; Buckley and Casson 1998). In other words, INVs are distinguished from DNVs based on their entrepreneurial endowments, especially their experience and network capability which allow them to overcome problems associated with engaging in international business activities and enable them to compete across national boundaries and different business systems (Zou and Ghauri 2010).

This chapter examines the impact of institutional structures on strategic orientation based on three high-tech new ventures in the Chinese semiconductor industry. China was chosen as the research setting for two main reasons. First, while abundant entrepreneurship studies have been done in Western countries, there has been little research investigating international entrepreneurship in emerging markets such as China (Tan 1996; Manolova et al. 2008). There is no doubt that emerging markets, such as China, represent vast differences in the institutional structures and business environments compared with developed markets (Luo 1999; Tan and Tan 2005). This provides an exciting laboratory in which to examine the institutional-based view of internationalization strategy (Peng et al. 2008). Second, entrepreneurial firms in high-tech industries have entered a new era in which internationalization has become an important strategic consideration. Differing from large firms, these firms approach international markets, in most cases, as developed markets for their growth. Yet they are subject to the liability of newness (Stinchcombe 1965) and foreignness (Zaheer 1995). They are capable of exploiting resources to act differently in the competitive marketplace with different institutional environments in contrast to their home country. The internationalization of these firms represents potential room for 'the identification and exploitation of previously unexplored opportunities' (Hitt et al. 2001, p. 480).

This chapter offers a number of contributions to the IE literature in the context of emerging economies. An integrative framework is used within which institutional structures and entrepreneurial endowments are considered to be important factors affecting international-oriented strategy. Investigating the dimensions of institutional structures from a comparative perspective affects the strategic orientation of high-tech new ventures. Large variations in institutional structures across country boundaries are recognized as a unique opportunity to study the implications of differences in institutional environments on internationalization strategy. Furthermore, the relationship between entrepreneurial endowments and institutional structures in influencing firms' international-oriented decisions is examined as this perspective has been neglected by the existing studies. The findings of this study provide useful insights into how internal entrepreneurial endowments interact with external institutional structures, jointly affecting the internationalization strategy of firms in emerging economies.

THEORETICAL BACKGROUND AND CONCEPTUAL FRAMEWORK

Traditional explanations have rested on the resource-based view and social capital theory, emphasizing the importance of accumulating and acquiring experience and knowledge in overseas markets. However, limited studies answer the question why international entrepreneurs possess different levels of skill and expertise compared with their domestic counterparts. While extensive research focuses on characteristics of entrepreneurs, such as international experience and international entrepreneurial orientation, scholars of the institutional perspective acknowledge that the institutional environment plays a role in entrepreneurs' international behavior. Yeung (2002) investigates the important role of institutional structure in entrepreneurial endowment and resources, namely information asymmetry (Ghauri et al. 2003), business risks and opportunities, finance and capital, experience in business and management, and relationships with customers and suppliers. With the particular focus on the impact of institutional structure on entrepreneurial endowments, a framework is formed which considers the role of both of these factors in new venture growth strategies (Figure 12.1).

Entrepreneurial Endowments and New Venture Growth Strategy

In this study, entrepreneurial endowments are referred to as the capabilities, experiences, and networks the entrepreneurs have possessed. Previously gained experience and knowledge relevant for making business decisions is important for new ventures (Gilbert et al. 2006). Entrepreneurs with relevant education and background experiences are more likely to know where to obtain information needed for the venture and how to deploy the resources they obtain. Entrepreneurs' international experience, that is, they have conducted business, lived, worked, and/or studied

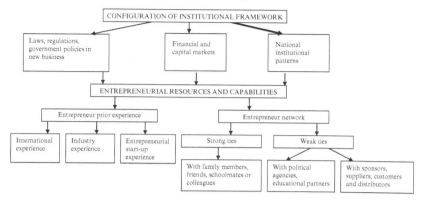

Figure 12.1   Conceptual framework

overseas (Felicitas 2005), particularly helps them identify foreign market opportunities and gives them the confidence to exploit these opportunities (McDougall et al. 2003). In addition, in emerging markets, founding members tend to have a combination of domestic and overseas background both in education and practical experience (Wright et al. 2008). Such a mixture is especially helpful in introducing new technology from global players, adapting to local business environments, expanding local and even international networks with complementary capabilities and resources, and in seizing growth opportunities for better performance. For this reason, an entrepreneur's prior experiences contribute to better strategic decisions than an entrepreneur who lacks similar experiences (McDougall et al. 1992). Therefore, it is argued that INVs can be distinguished from DNVs based on the prior relevant experience the entrepreneurs possess.

Interpersonal relationships are ubiquitous in emerging economies as the whole society is structured around webs of social relationships which are embedded in various bases of *guanxi* (Bian 1994), such as strong ties between family members, former classmates or persons coming from the same home town, contrasted with weak ties between strangers (Bian 2002; Poutziouris et al. 2002). These types of relationship contribute to the acquisition of information and new knowledge, rapid response to external threats and intense competition and further development of new entrepreneurial firms (Fu et al. 2006), depending on the intensity and depth of the relationships that entrepreneurs hold.

Many founding members of new ventures largely rely on family members, friends or schoolmates to start their business in China, showing the important role that strong ties play in organizations (Kraatz 1998).

Guanxi ties with strategic partners, that is, venture capitalists, international suppliers and customers, value chain partners, and so on, tend to be more heterogeneous and transient. Great disparity exists in terms of culture, education, technical background, managerial mindset, and even network compositions. Therefore, the ties with strategic partners can be regarded as *weak ties* due to the sparse interconnection and low level of intimacy between one entrepreneur and the other persons initially. However, in the long term such ties can have relative advantages in terms of leading to novel ideas, providing greater access to a broader base of information and resources and enabling the transfer of knowledge among individuals or teams (Uzzi 1996). This can provide growth opportunities for new ventures through learning and cooperation (Hoegl et al. 2003) when they decide to go beyond the domestic markets or product markets.

The nature of INVs in terms of newness and inexperience limits their access to resources and existing networks (Zahra 2005). To overcome barriers to entry, build links to their customers and suppliers, and attract potential customers, new ventures may benefit from entrepreneurs' prior experiences. Oviatt and McDougall (1994) note that international experiences in other INVs or multinational companies are useful in assembling resources, gaining access to existing international networks, and configuring the value chains of INVs. Other benefits of international experiences, such as gaining access to strategic partners (Reuber and Fischer 1997), have also been identified. By accumulating social capital and building linkages with international partners, new ventures can get access to information, technology, and, at times, human and financial capital (Burt 1992). In turn, learning from international network partners helps new ventures to create more value from the opportunities provided by their networks and to learn how to operate and compete in those markets.

Institutional Structure and Entrepreneurial Endowments

Following up the discussions on the links between entrepreneurial endowments and strategic orientation, it can be further argued that the value of entrepreneurial endowments will be maximized and delivered particularly when the differences in home and host institutional environments are evaluated in the strategic decision process. This argument derives from the institutional perspective, which indicates that the institutional framework or structure is 'the set of fundamental political, social and legal ground rules [that] establish the basis for production, exchange and distribution' (Davis and North 1971, pp. 6–7). It influences individuals' decision making by signalling which choice is acceptable and determining which norms and behavior individuals in a given society are socialized into.

In addition, by providing the rules of the game in which firms act and compete, the institutional structure affects the strategic choice of firms. Therefore, the institutional perspective holds the position that 'what organizations come into existence and how they evolve are fundamentally influenced by the institutional framework; in turn, they influence how the institutional framework evolves' (North 1990; p. s).

In line with the basic premise that firms are embedded in country-specific institutional arrangements, four comparative facets of institutional frameworks are examined. These concern developed and emerging markets and the influencing effects on entrepreneurial endowments, namely experiences and networks in their internationalization strategies.

First, the *regulatory framework*, which consists of laws, regulations, and government policies, provides support for new businesses, reduces the risks for individuals starting a new venture and facilitates entrepreneurs' efforts to acquire resources (Busenitz et al. 2000). For instance, the US government has provided advice and assistance for those starting new businesses and has offered grants for new technology development in small enterprises since the 1960s (SCORE 2011). Several European governments have provided small companies with financial assistance for exporting and trade development (Reynolds 1997) since the 1990s. However, the process of establishing a regulatory framework in emerging economies has just recently started and is still in progress. For example, it is only since the late 1990s that the Chinese government has been increasing fiscal fund inputs into small business in addition to setting up several funds (Chen 2006).

Scholars consider the political climate and the government sector of a country to be among favorable environmental attributes that can make the environment more munificent and thus favorable for entrepreneurial activities. The emerging economies' regulatory framework has long been described as unfavorable for entrepreneurial activities. Nevertheless, the transition from a planned to a market-based economy indicates a major environmental shift because it may disrupt established ties between firms and resources, potentially freeing resources for use by new ventures. One of the main consequences of the economic reform in emerging economies such as China is the resurgence of entrepreneurship with opportunistic and proactive behavior. Entrepreneurs are found to pursue opportunity and make decisions quickly (Tan 1996). First-mover behavior is especially favored in industries that are changing rapidly and intense levels of competition, such as high-tech sectors. In addition, entrepreneurs perceive great opportunity in overseas markets where the home regulatory framework is far less favorable than the host market and, therefore, the international-oriented strategy is preferred. Under this condition, entrepreneurial endowments provide the basis for expanded resources and capabilities stocks (Lu and Beamish 2001) to implement an effective internationalization strategy.

Second, countries with better access to *finance and capital* are more favorable to entrepreneurship (Yeung 2002) and internationalization activities. International finance researchers suggest that poor domestic environments prompt firms and investors to use international markets more intensively (Benos and Weisbach 2004; Karolyi 2004). This can be seen in entrepreneurial firms from emerging economies, because they may want to escape a poor domestic system with weak capital markets and go instead to international markets which are considered more attractive because they offer better protection to investors. Entrepreneurial activity is more likely to increase in a business system with well-developed capital markets favoring business start-ups and able to provide venture capital (Buckley and Ghauri 2004). In contrast, emerging economies have been developing their own capital markets through liberalization in the last two decades, at a cautious and moderate pace. China has relatively incomplete capital markets and insufficient sources of venture capital compared with the developed economies, resulting in 'network capital', where resources are pooled together within the 'family', as a substitute for well-developed capital markets (Yeung 2002). It is more through former schoolmates, friends or colleagues that initial funding is collected for launching a new business (Fu et al. 2006), while later growth opportunity can be constrained by the limited access to more substantial capital and funds available in emerging economies.

Third, the national institutional patterns, such as access to research and educational institutions, availability of pools of educated labor and institute-linked incubators, may determine the way in which entrepreneurial activity emerges within a country (Clarysse et al. 2005; Maura and Rodney 2006). Close linkage with research and education institutions enhances the R&D process and commercialization, facilitates problem-solving activities, and increases entrepreneurial activity (Casson 1990), especially in technology-intensive industries. In addition, the links embedded with incubators are beneficial for the establishment and development of new ventures, that is, supporting infrastructure, business resources and services, and enlarged network activities. New ventures thus have the access to needed resources through a variety of knowledge exchange among entrepreneurs and the national institutional actors. Entrepreneurial experiences and networking capabilities can even facilitate the reciprocal linkage for seeking new business opportunities such as technological development and market customization (Maura and Rodney 2006). With reference to the development of high-tech spin-out firms from universities located across Europe, Clarysse et al. (2005) conclude that firms are prompted to internationalize when benefiting from the networked institutional arrangements. These arrangements involve heavily resourced and intensive activities going on over a considerable period of time and based on world-class science. In contrast, emerging economies are still working to build up the linkages between businesses and institutes. Despite the dramatic increase in the number of incubators in China with a typical ownership structure (more in public hands), they may not have strong motivation to generate profits by helping their tenants succeed (Harwit 2002).

To summarize, the differences in the three dimensions of institutional structures between emerging economies and developed economies can affect the availability, exploitation, and the value of resources and capabilities that emerging economy new ventures require for their international growth. Emerging economy entrepreneurs may feel pressured in less favorable institutional environments despite their accumulated knowledge and capabilities and, therefore, may want to escape the environment for more business and growth opportunities in international markets (Cheng and Yu 2008).

METHODOLOGY

The objective of this study is to investigate the different strategic behavior between INVs and DNVs from an institutional perspective. Case studies in this setting can be useful in investigating the factors influencing each firm's domestic or international expansion, and in comparing strategies for internationalization under different institutional environments (Ghauri and Gronhaug 2010). Three firms were chosen to represent different strategic orientations over their history.

The integrated circuit (IC) industry in China has grown rapidly in recent years, with strong export-oriented behavior:

> In 2008, China exported 48.48 billion pieces of integrated circuit and the exports amounted to 24.32 billion USD, up by 19.1 per cent and 3.3 per cent respectively and the growth speed of the import volumes exceeding the export amounts by 15.8 percentage points, indicating that Chinese integrated circuit enterprises take the price reduction measures so as to expand the exports and strengthen the competitiveness. (CRI 2009)

Three concentrative industrial regions – Yangtze River Delta, Pearl River Delta, and Bohai Bay Rim Region – made up over 90 percent of the sales revenue of the IC industry. Large cities such as Beijing and Shanghai have witnessed the emergence of several thousand IC entrepreneurial firms in recent years. Having survived in the global financial crisis, the IC industry, especially the IC design sector in China, is claimed as one of the most promising sectors in the high-tech industries (OCN 2010). Therefore this study focused on the IC industry, using a theoretical sampling frame (Glaser and Strauss 1967). Guided by the emerging theory, heterogeneity among different types of entrepreneurial firms, that is, financial resources, product lines, and business scopes was allowed. In other words, Pettigrew's (1990) advice to go for 'polar types' was followed.

Two data sources were pursued: personal interviews and secondary sources. Data collection for each case in this study was guided by a protocol to ensure that similar procedures were followed in each and every case (Ghauri 2004). An outline of questions, statement of research purpose, and assurance of confidentiality were mailed prior to every personal interview. All informants were contacted by phone to arrange appointment times. Interviews were conducted in Beijing and Shanghai in the summers of 2006 and 2008. Each interview lasted up to one and a half hours. Secondary sources of data included feasibility study reports, company reports, articles in newspaper and trade journals, and so on. They were examined and the contents analyzed to validate the interview data regarding the strategic planning and performance.

Several rules for case analysis were followed (Yin 1993): the '24-hour rule' for the completion of detailed interview notes and impressions; the inclusion of all data regardless of its apparent importance during the interview; the addition of the investigator's own impressions at the end of each interview note; and the separation of impressions from informants' descriptions. All the interviews were analyzed by building categories, reflecting common patterns in the answers of the interview respondents and among companies (Eisenhardt 1989; Ghauri 2004). Cases were compared and contrasted in order to draw conclusions as suggested by Miles and Huberman (1994).

CASE FINDINGS

The following three cases illustrate the different ways that institutional framework and entrepreneurial resources and capabilities can explain a new venture's domestic and international strategy. Traditionally, IE scholars have investigated individual-, firm-and industry-level factors which influence international entrepreneurial activity. This study takes into account the role of national institutional structures in differentiating the behavior of INVs and DNVs. This echoes the call for an institutional approach in IE study by Young et al. (2003).

Despite the significant disparity in the three cases, there were similarities. The cases were all located in Yangpu District of Shanghai; they were all technology-intensive firms in the IC design industry; and all of them were set up by intellectual entrepreneurs with educational and engineering backgrounds in the same department at Fudan University. Therefore, the home institutional structure is controlled at a comparable level across the three cases, while the differences between the host and home environments may lead to the variations in their strategic considerations and decisions.

These firms were most characterized by their emphasis on product innovation and development. All these new ventures were between two and eight years old at the time of this research and from 2004 began launching their products and services into markets, indicating that they were finally fully involved in the market.

Case 1: Firm S

Firm S was founded by four postgraduate students majoring in microelectronic engineering from Fudan University in 1998 when the key founder was doing second-year postgraduate research at the university. The firm started with the ambition of developing circuit analysis services and software, and helping an IC design company promote competitive ability and protect IC intellectual property. In 2002, the firm obtained a $600,000 investment from a Singaporean venture capital firm. Firm S has extensive levels of involvement across a variety of foreign markets. Market coverage is also extensive. Since its first joint venture in France in October 2004, the firm subsequently acquired a Russian firm as the first overseas R&D center and established another one in Taiwan. The firm has expanded its global activities in North America, South Korea, and Japan through wholly owned enterprises and joint ventures. By collaborating with a Taiwan-based semiconductor material analysis firm, the strategic alliance provides an online platform for sales and business consultation in failure analysis, circuit analysis and EDA (electronic design automation) tools. By 2007, Firm S had grown to 140 employees globally, with sales of $1.5 million, with over 125 percent of sales growth rate due to international expansion.

Entrepreneurial endowments

Entrepreneurs of Firm S accumulated contract-based project experience in the IC design industry when they were studying at the university. Despite limited experience in marketing and sales, the entrepreneurs were quite determined to deliver innovative products and services to the market. The team focused on software design and commercialization of beta products for four years, using both their own and government-sponsored funds.

The firm was initiated by students who studied in the same department. Therefore, the entrepreneurial team was more like the previously discussed 'weak ties'. However, the firm developed networks rapidly through their first international entry. In particular, the firm recognized the great benefit from expanded business relationships in the local market. Local suppliers and buyers in France facilitated the firms' sales and product designs in order to be more tailored to local clients:

> Since our first step into the international market in 2004, we have emphasized the importance of establishing strategic networks with different markets. For instance, we have built up a strong marketing team in Russia to be in charge of promotion and after-sales service. Our R&D team in France and Taiwan have close relationships with suppliers and distributors. We know what our customers require in these markets; that's why we could upgrade our products and services and therefore get benefit from the increase in international sales.

Regulatory framework
The first foreign direct investment was initially pushed by local authority and French partners in early 2003. The entrepreneur was invited six times in one year to visit local French science incubators and high-tech firms with a view toward collaboration and alliance. Due to these visits, the entrepreneur recognized the favorable institutional environment in the host market where government support and infrastructures were strongly presented. Therefore, the firm was about to invest overseas so as to deliver their products to international markets:

> It was 'Sino-France year' in 2004 and the Shanghai municipal government facilitated industrial cooperation with French partners. I was invited to visit several science parks and incubators in Montpellier, France where I recognized business potentials to have our products sold to that market. I was quite impressed by the infrastructure and environment in that place. Firms there were able to get access to large amounts of government support in finance, personnel and management advice, creating regular communications and enabling firms to overcome obstacles in any circumstances.

Finance and capital market
Due to the heavy expenditure in R&D, the firm largely relied on government support and bank loans at that time to develop technologically advanced new products. As the initial financial capital was almost used up, Firm S faced great problems, especially in terms of insufficient operating funds in 2002:

> We survived on support from some government angels, totalling around $400,000 in bank loans over several years, but they definitely were not enough to afford our R&D investment. We had extreme financial difficulty in 2002

when we were almost forced to exit. We had to seek large amounts of external funding from venture capitalists from both domestic and international sources.

To solve the financial problem, the entrepreneur approached different sources and visited both domestic and international venture capitalists. Ultimately, he secured a $600,000 investment from a Singaporean venture capitalist who was an expert in both investment and electronic engineering industries and who valued their R&D capability and experience in this particular product area:

> We had talks with several domestic strategic investors and venture capitalists in the market. Unfortunately, they did not understand our product and industry; therefore, they were reluctant to finance us. If they had wanted to finance us, they would have required immediate returns from their investment. We finally obtained a financial injection from a Singaporean VC.

National institutional pattern

The entrepreneur comments on the limited linkage with local universities and educational institutes in the home market as compared to French incubator networks:

> Within the incubator networks, firms had frequent forums and discussions in order to do product development and marketing collectively and efficiently. The incubator also facilitated cooperation between academics in the nearby university and new businesses. In Shanghai, our relationship with Fudan seems just to be the graduates from the university and physically we were located in the university-led incubator.

Growth strategy

Firm S adopted an aggressive international growth strategy by establishing subsidiaries across different countries in Europe, Asia, and America. The firm also took over firms in Russia. The firm highlighted the importance of partnership in its internationalization strategy. Local partners provided not only access to potential customers, but also knowledge spillovers through the cluster effect and embedded networks. Therefore, the internationalization strategy which originated from international sales was restructured to augment and explore new knowledge stocks through more aggressive operational strategies such as acquisitions and wholly owned enterprises.

> Initial talks began in early 2004 after I had visited three local incubators in Montpellier. I, together with our team, believed it important to partner with a local firm in France if we wanted to sell our products there. Joint venture then became the agenda and this was highly appreciated by governments both in Shanghai and Montpellier. We also expected to sell our superior products to

the Asia-Pacific, including Japan, Taiwan, and North America, which required us to have our marketing and R&D bases in these geographical places. That's why we quickly acquired a Russian firm which was reorganized to put emphasis on marketing practices; we established an R&D center in Taiwan because we appreciated the engineers with relevant educational background and industry experience, as well as the business system in the Taiwan high-tech industry which highlighted innovation.

By 2005, Firm S had grown to 70 employees with sales of $1.1 million. After being the leading firm in its local market, Firm S has successfully grown from a local high-tech venture to a global firm able to pursue business opportunities continuously. The key founder pointed out that the sales figures began to increase, especially since 2006, with 125 per cent of sales growth due to international expansion.

Case 2: Firm M

Firm M was established by several young faculty members at State Key ASIC Lab of Fudan University in 2000. In 2002, after restructuring the firm, they began to develop a demodulator for DTV applications for local customers, which was later sold out to a NASDAQ-listed firm. Afterwards, the firm devoted itself to the development of embedded information security co-processor IP (Internet Protocol) series products, focusing on the development of silicon IPs and customer design service. Firm M's international involvement has been limited to IP licensing and contracting since 2004. This indirect entry strategy is considered to be suitable for small firms like Firm M because it does not need much initial investment or overseas commitment, but still benefits from collaboration with foreign clients during the development and testing of products. By 2007, Firm M had 15 employees with total sales of more than RMB 15 million and RMB 5 million total profits.

Entrepreneurial endowments
The founding member had run the business for two years before the corporate restructure, focusing on R&D and product customization. The entrepreneur encouraged the employees to target the right market and potential customers in addition to working on the development of products and technologies, which particularly focused on local customers by providing advanced IC solutions:

> We restructured the board which used to be dominated by university lecturers. Some people left, some people came in. We finally clarified why we worked together. By inviting some senior IC designers with overseas IC design background to join us, we could easily catch up the current market trends and

decided to develop the DTV demodulation products. We also recruited marketing experts who knew the market much better than academics.

By restructuring the firm, the entrepreneurial team was made up of both previous colleagues and new professionals. Such a mix allowed the firm to capture the latest market development as well as sustain trust and effective communication within the firm. The business deal with the US acquirer further broadened the entrepreneurial team's network with more access to international managerial knowledge and advanced technological capability:

> We later built up close relationships with multinational clients to collaboratively develop and test the new products, which later on were sold to both domestic and international markets. It was quite useful for us to accumulate more knowledge in overseas markets.

Regulatory framework

Entrepreneurs did not regard the general regulatory framework as an important issue in the firm's growth direction and strategy. Yet intellectual property policy has impacts on the firm, especially due to the nature of the industry and the market competition. Firm M had applied for a number of patents since its start-up, which protected its technological achievement in the market:

> Intellectual property protection is vital to us. It normally takes about ten months to get the patent. Compared with other countries, it is slightly quicker.

As mergers and acquisitions were not fully supported in this particular sector, the deal between the firm and the American purchaser was not disclosed to the public. The negotiation and final decision were mainly dominated by the entrepreneur and the American top management team:

> It was a bit sensitive to talk about take-over deals at that time. We would like to do it quietly. The government policy placed great emphasis on protecting domestic R&D and brands. But to our firm at that stage, it would be more important to know where the firm was about to go.

Finance and capital market

Firm M continuously invested in the second generation of QAM chip development for DTV/STB channel demodulation, which was sensitive enough to receive and transform data from weak signals. Alongside the success of this demodulator, the entrepreneurs were approached by large multinational corporations (MNCs) who were interested in expanding their share of the local market. The entrepreneurial team recognized the opportunities to get capital by selling the product line to support a new line of product development. After rounds of contacts and negotiations, Firm M decided to sell its chipsets product line to a NASDAQ-listed MNC in 2004, although the entrepreneurs highlighted the fact that the institutional environment was not supportive in terms of valuation:

> Compared with acquisitions in the same industry in developed markets, such as the U.S., the transaction value would have been at least three times that of our deal. Because we did not have a complete and transparent evaluation system and stock market here, the negotiated price might not have been the most appropriate one.

They also commented on the limitation of relying on local government financial support. Therefore, they began to both approach and negotiate with venture capitalists:

> We know the value of our product, and know how our competitors value it. That's why we'd like to talk about some big firms who were interested in us. Capital is always so important for our further development and research investment. Government innovator funds are so limited that you couldn't rely on them for the growth and expansion.

National institutional pattern

The key founder studied and worked in the university where he had good contacts with research staff and students, who were potential partners and employees for the firm. Moreover, the firm worked closely with a research center in the university and delivered a variety of products applied in information security areas:

> We had collaborative work with an information security center located in the university. Together we designed and tested a variety of micro-chips that would be applied to related fields in this sector. . . . We have employed a number of talented graduates from the lab in recent years, some of whom were my tutees in the past years. They are capable, diligent and innovative; more importantly they were passionate about the product and firm growth.

Firm M relocated the office from downtown to Zhangjiang Hi-Tech Park in 2008, which is the largest high-tech industry base in Shanghai with more than 4,000 new ventures in the IC, semiconductor lighting, information industry, and biochemical sectors. The decision was made in order to exploit the benefits of the industry cluster in the science park:

> We all know about the benefits by locating our firm in Zhangjiang. Knowledge creation is possible and we get to know much more beyond our own operations. Social activities contributed to the network building and information sharing.

But you need to work out which (resources and information) works best for you all by yourself.

Growth strategy

Firm M's strategy was mainly focused on the local market which constrained its international involvement, which had been mainly covered through IP licensing and contracting since 2004. With relatively loose international collaborative contracts, the firm expected not to overstretch its resources to overseas activities but still to benefit from collaboration with foreign clients during the development and testing of products:

> We thought it would have been a good idea to go to new markets, to compete against multinationals, and to understand how they do business in different markets, how they manage the firm, how they do product development and how they build up networks with different partners. By selling the DTV demodulator unit to the Americans, we were financially sufficient to make new breakthroughs and commercialization for the local market. We judged the risks and uncertainties and the conclusion was that we perceived great opportunities in the local market and we preferred to design, test and market these products by ourselves to serve the local market first while developing our international activities on a small scale. Therefore we aimed to excel in the local market before going abroad.

Case 3: Firm H

Firm H was established in 2004, and located close to Fudan University. Key founders were graduate students from the microelectronic engineering department at the university. Operating in the IC design industry, the firm specializes in developing and designing digital multimedia products for mass consumption in the local market. The firm has two main product lines. The first targets consumption and application markets by introducing a series of general-purpose multimedia technological solutions to local clients, such as MP3/WMA, portable video players, LCD products, plasma and flat panel televisions, DVD recorders, and high-speed video interface and storage products. The second line provides specific IC services such as security monitoring products.

Entrepreneurial endowments

The entrepreneurial team consisted of technical professionals who had previously worked for foreign IC design companies for about four to five years. Most of the team members graduated from the same department in the university, indicating close personal relationships and trust in initiating the business:

> We knew each other quite well before we started our firm. We had social activities to exchange ideas and technological development . . . when we decided to work together to start up the business, we all had abundant experience in IC design and R&D. However, we are relatively young and inexperienced in developing new products and managing the firm compared with large firms and foreign firms in this market.

Regulatory framework

Regulations and legal frameworks did not impact greatly on the firm. The firm had patents in digital multimedia processors, such as multimedia devices for automobiles in 2005. The firm had also benefited from government support in initiating the business, although to a small extent:

> Patenting is important to protect our R&D capability and core technology. Yet it is more vital for us to commercialize it and have mass production to serve the market. It is not so difficult for us to get a patent as soon as we provide all the documents to the bureaucratic department to show the value of the design and the product features. We also got some government innovator funding in support of our mini-projects. We appreciated that kind of funding because it showed that the government wanted to facilitate technological development in IC design fields.

Finance and capital market

Differing from the other two firms, Firm H obtained investment from a public IC design firm in China shortly after the firm was established. Therefore, the firm was not pressured to seek external financial investment to support in-house R&D and commercialization. With the financial back-up, Firm H developed several chips based on their multimedia processor and integrated application-specific ICs for speciality markets such as portable multimedia and multimedia communication. The firm was not too concerned about the status quo of the general financial market in China as long as the investing firm provided capital:

> We got sponsored by a domestic IC design firm. We pretty much operated under the umbrella of the investing firm. We did not need to worry about finance, marketing and customers because our sponsor did all those jobs for us. We developed products and services for local markets according to their criteria and requirements.

National institutional pattern

Having operated for three years, Firm H relied heavily on its investor firm, especially in terms of product development projects, while the connections with local research institutes were quite constrained. The business model was heavily based on the requirements of the investor firm but it tried hard to develop its technological and business capabilities. However, due to intensive market competition and the low reputation of the new venture, Firm H recognized the importance of obtaining supplement R&D and operating capabilities in order to sustain and develop its market position in a more independent manner.

Growth strategy

Recognizing its limited managerial and marketing experience, the firm targeted the domestic market instead of selling its products to international customers at the early stage. The fundamental strategic scope was constrained to the local market, due to insufficient entrepreneurial endowments as well as limited access to external institutional support. Yet the entrepreneurs addressed the likelihood of exporting, thanks to the low cost of production. Export represented a starting point for the firm to increase its sales outside the domestic market as well as to accumulate international experiences incrementally:

> Compared with firms in South Korea, Taiwan, and the U.S., we do not have our own branding valued by the domestic and global markets since we targeted low-cost product markets. Consumers are familiar with Samsung or Telechip but may have no idea about our name. Actually, most local firms targeted the same niche market as we did because we did not have sufficient financial capital and adequate research and marketing experience and knowledge to target high-end markets.

DISCUSSION

These three firms all started with internal product development by utilizing different sources of finance, personnel, and knowledge. However, the growth paths the ventures followed were very different. Firm S was facilitated to go international by perceived institutional differences and accumulated entrepreneurial endowments, while sufficient capital from venture capitals enabled the firm to decide its growth direction. In Firm H, the actual operation started after the restructuring of the firm when industry experiences were repositioned and new market opportunities were recognized. The firm then separated its core business unit and new business unit; the former was taken over by a foreign firm. The firm therefore started to serve both local and international markets by leveraging the resources and networks possessed by the entrepreneurial teams and their foreign partners. Firm H is an indigenous new venture which was sponsored by a domestic firm and mainly provided products to local customers. Table 12.1 shows some general characteristics of the three ventures.

All cases highlight the differences in institutional structure and

Table 12.1   Characteristics of the three ventures

	Firm S	Firm M	Firm H
Founding year	1998	2000	2004
No. of initial founders	4	4	2
Invention	Internally generated	Internally generated	Internally generated
Core product market	Circuit analysis solution	Information security solutions/ demodulator IP	Multi-media solutions
Capital structure	Founders' capital National innovator grant External capital (VC)	Founders' capital National innovator grant External capital (MNC)	External capital (domestic firm)
Entrepreneur educational background	Master	PhD	Master
Business model	New market discovered Internationalized to multiple countries	New market discovered Acquired by MNC Partnering with MNC	Partnering with domestic sponsor
Gross sales 2004	$ 600,000	$ 50,000	$ 0
Status winter 2004	Beginning international sales	Acquired by US firm First round of financing from US firm	Firm established First round of financing from domestic firm
Gross sales 2005	$ 11,000,000	$ 90,000	$ 8,000
No. of employees (2005)	70	17	10
Status winter 2005	Aggressive international entries to multiple markets	Beginning international sales Second round of financing from US firm New production tests completed	Domestic sales relying on sponsor's value chain
Gross sales 2007	$ 35,000,000	$ 2,000,000	$ 11,000
No of employees (2007)	130	50	11

Table 12.1   (continued)

	Firm S	Firm M	Firm H
Status summer 2007	Headquarters located in Shanghai, subsidiaries in France, Japan, Canada, Russia, Taiwan and Korea	International sales to the US market International collaborative projects (US clients)	Domestic sales relying on sponsor's value chain

entrepreneurial resources in the growth strategies of ventures. The story of Firm H particularly illustrates that a lack of experience and networks with strategic partners are major obstacles for domestic entrepreneurial activity. In contrast, the story of Firm S highlights the advanced institutional environments in developed countries in terms of government policies, capital markets, and linkages between institutions and business. In what follows, the three cases are taken as points of departure to glean three more general lessons relating to institutional structures and the role of experiences (Ghauri et al. 2005).

Role of Entrepreneurial Endowments on the Strategic Behavior of New Ventures

Obviously, experiences in relevant aspects provide knowledge on what is important, how to do things, drawing up contracts, and so on. (Stuart and Abetti 1990). New firms and their entrepreneurs, due to the liability of newness, have rather limited knowledge and experience in operations, marketing, finance, management, and other international business practices compared with large firms. This increased the difficulty of succeeding in competitive marketplaces and led to a higher failure rate (Fernhaber 2006).

Prior industry, international, and entrepreneurial experiences are all positioned differently in the three firms. It is more likely that entrepreneurial and management experiences are critical to the strategic decisions of new ventures while the international experience of Chinese entrepreneurs derived from working for multinationals is not sufficient for their international activity. More often, international experiences are accumulated when cooperating with multinationals or local firms (Firm M) and through progressive involvement in foreign operations (Firm S). Prior international experiences that refer to overseas education, residence, and employment overseas (Felicitas 2005) are not directly relevant to cross-border operations and do not enable entrepreneurs to learn how to deal with unexpected contingencies in the host countries. This leads to the following proposition:

Proposition 1: Entrepreneurial endowments, in particular entrepreneurial experiences, influence firms' growth strategies. However, international experience without direct international business knowledge may not facilitate aggressive internationalization strategy and activities.

As discussed by Fu et al. (2006), *guanxi* in Chinese high-tech industries can be categorized into strong and weak ties. Such a categorization is to differentiate the base and benefit of entrepreneur networks, which also suggests the changing nature of the networks within these small and young firms. Strong ties are largely dependent on personal relationships or social capital, composed of friends, schoolmates, and previous colleagues. They are observed especially in firms' early stages, for the purpose of starting up business, acquiring launch funding, controlling knowledge, and establishing initial contacts with potential suppliers, investors and so on (Gupta et al. 2006). However, such close ties may constrain a firm from further growth due to limited knowledge exchange with outsiders and conflicts within the firm. Network ties based on economic exchange can complement those strong ties by providing ventures with new resources and services to establish strategic networks for more market-oriented behavior. Personal and economic relations overlap as strong and weak ties evolve during the growth of new ventures, and diversified network ties turn out to be more important for the INVs.

While entrepreneurship literature (Park and Luo 2001; Yli-Renko et al. 2001; Agndal et al. 2008) highlights the important role of social ties or interactions between the firm and other partners, the dynamic of networks and relationships over time (that is, the development and change of networks ties) is still underexplored. The case findings illustrate that the changing network embeddedness affects firm growth patterns. First, entrepreneurial networks tend to change from strong tie-dominated relations to strong tie–weak tie relations or weak tie-dominated relations, given that more economic and marketing-based relationships (weak ties) provide complementary resources and an expanded market for firm growth. Second, the network evolved from a more individual-embedded one to more firm-level networks. Developing from close individual relationships at a firm's start-up stage, the network tends to be more firm-bounded with business exchanges and cooperation. Firm S started with a strong tie-based network but soon developed its network to include more economic relations.

Without previous operations in international markets, Firm S utilized the network initially possessed by its joint venture partner and transformed this into a more productive one for its own use by integrating R&D capabilities with market and value chain strengths in different regions. Firm M is another example of how the firm restructured its social networks. The firm was originally established by colleagues in the same department, shown as a strong tie-dominated network. However, the different business philosophy resulted in conflicts not just in firm growth but also product lines. Alongside the restructure, the firm's network evolved from a strong tie-dominated network to a strong tie–weak tie one by recruiting top management teams in technology, marketing, and operations. The entrepreneur also expanded the relationship to foreign partners through the business deal, and leveraged the relationship to further international collaborative projects. On the other hand, Firm H was only associated with its sponsor firm but it lacked the access to gain a wider range of relationships. Thus:

Proposition 2: Firms' networks are dynamic and changing over time, especially in emerging economies when economic relations complement personal relations in business activities. New and young firms are better able to expand weak tie-based networks at the firm level in order to get access to new resources and knowledge for growth.

Institutional Environment and Its Impact on Entrepreneurial Endowment and the Strategic Behavior of New Ventures

Different regulatory, cognitive, and normative contextual dimensions, such as those described by Busenitz et al. (2000), may explain dissimilar entrepreneurial activity across countries. Unique institutional structures guide firms' strategic activities and help determine the nature and amount of innovation that takes place within an economy (Nelson 1993). Entrepreneurs may evaluate the source of each country's strengths and weaknesses more precisely by comparing the institutional profiles between home and host countries. Globally-minded entrepreneurs may start new businesses that have an international mission from their inception (Oviatt and McDougall 1994) based on their understanding of institutional profiles across countries. Firm S devised strategies toward international sales through joint ventures and local subsidiaries and enjoyed success in countries with different profiles when it made better use of internal resources and capabilities (that is, international experience transferred from local partners, industry and marketing experience, existing incubator relationship and business partnerships with local firms), and leveraging the positive influence of governmental policies and initiatives.

It has been recognized that government support, financial and capital markets, as well as institutional linkages with business are relatively weak in China. Even though all firms received government innovator funds, they were small in amount and scale and therefore unable to generate creative innovation and marketable products. The lack of developed financial markets and capital systems forced these three firms to look at a wider range of choices to finance their further development. Firm H still turned back to its domestic sponsor while Firm S faced serious survival problems in 2002. The story of Firm S also illustrates some institutional weakness in China, such as information asymmetry, incomplete tiers of stock market, and availability of venture capital, and generally undervalued national technological capabilities. A vast disparity in China's institutional environment compared with developed markets leads to different forms of entrepreneurial activity (Acs et al. 1997; Yeung 2002). Entrepreneurs may decide where to operate based on the opportunities and challenges provided by either local or international markets for entrepreneurial activities. Hence, the entrepreneurial process in terms of location choice can be viewed largely due to the heterogeneity of capitals and resources different firms possess (Foss et al. 2007) together with the disparity in institutional arrangements across country boundaries (Yeung 2002). Therefore:

Proposition 3: A favorable host institutional environment perceived by entrepreneurs will have a 'temptation effect' for firms to escape from domestic pressures and constraints to start their internationalization activities and be more proactive in leveraging and exploiting existing experiences and capabilities and augment them for international growth.

CONCLUSIONS

This study is expected to answer the two questions: do institutional structures between home and host country affect entrepreneurial experiences and relationships, and do entrepreneurial experiences and relationships influence the strategic behavior of INVs and DNVs? Based on the collected information, this chapter concludes that disparity in home and host institutional structures influences entrepreneurial endowment, which in turn has an impact on their growth focuses (domestic versus international activities). The qualitative nature of this study has allowed the informants to provide in-depth information which they saw as critical and relevant. Through in-depth interviews of entrepreneurs in the Chinese high-tech industry, first-hand information provided insights about the relevant constructs and relationships. The overall development of the ventures and critical events are summarized in Figure 12.2.

First, by describing and analyzing the three cases, it can be seen that international entrepreneurial activities are promoted by a relatively complete and favorable regulatory environment which facilitates and supports new business. Moreover, stable financial and capital systems which finance new business are critical to their development and internationalization. Without such an institutional environment, entrepreneurs are somewhat constrained to obtain excess resources and capabilities to stimulate their business, and to access important strategic partners and investors. Second, international entrepreneurial activity tends to be more proactive in exploiting knowledge, resources, and relationships through acquisitions or joint ventures. The evolution of knowledge learning and network building facilitates new ventures' foreign operation and performance. Third, INVs highlight the importance of the international value chain to design, manufacture, distribute, and service products to multiple markets.

Firms that are capable of developing and completing their network profile are more likely to understand and serve international markets. In contrast, DNVs, due to geographical limitations and their insufficient resources and capabilities, tend to put more emphasis on their product breakthroughs and cost management.

However, additional research is needed to obtain external validity. Further analysis is required if detailed hypotheses are to be developed based on the insights gained from this study. A larger sample would allow for more concepts to emerge and a more in-depth examination of interrelationships among constructs causing INVs versus DNVs.

There are a number of implications for entrepreneurs and policy makers in emerging economies such as China. Policy makers should realize the importance of a favorable institutional structure in supporting entrepreneurial activities. As the emerging market governments are enhancing the national competitiveness in international competition, it is necessary to build up complete and regulated institutional frameworks to facilitate innovation and internationalization activities through which small and young high-tech firms can excel. For entrepreneurs, the key question on firm growth is a tough decision which requires cautious consideration and judgment. Entrepreneurs need to align their endowments with the external institutional environments in order to achieve growth and sustainable competitive advantages.

While new ventures may have their superiority in technology, they encounter a complex array of strategic decisions regarding network building, experience acquisition, and market focus. Whether to focus on

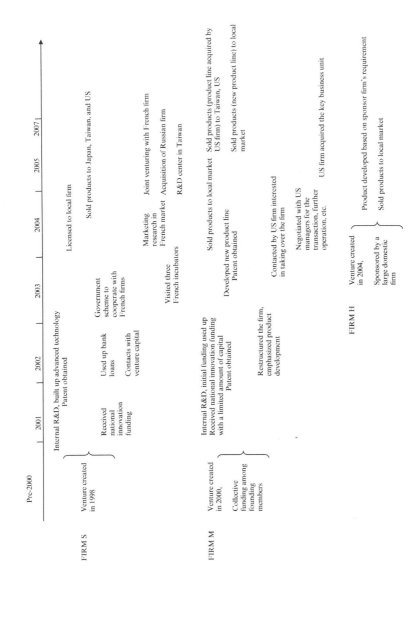

Figure 12.2   Timeline for the three ventures

domestic markets or expand into international ones depends on what resources, skills, and knowledge are the most important for entrepreneurs to marshal through a set of internal and external channels. While individual relationships have been utilized extensively in emerging economies for political networks, new ventures have to take into account the possibilities of integrating and combining knowledge and resources from different markets and get access to 'proprietary networks' (McDougall et al. 1994). Entrepreneurial experiences and networks can contribute to the establishment, maintenance, and consolidation of global value chain relationships.

REFERENCES

Acs, Z.J., R. Morck, J.M. Shaver and B. Yeung (1997), 'The internationalization of small and medium-sized enterprises: a policy perspective', *Small Business Economics*, 9(1), 7–20.

Agndal, H., S. Chetty and H. Wilson (2008), 'Social capital dynamics and foreign market entry', *International Business Review*, 17(6), 663–75.

Aldrich, H.E. (1990), 'Using an ecological perspective to study organizational founding rates', *Entrepreneurship: Theory and Practice*, 14(3), 7–24.

Benos, E. and M.S. Weisbach (2004), 'Private benefits and cross-listings in the United States', *Emerging Markets Review*, 5(2), 217–40.

Bian, Y. (1994), '*guanxi* and the allocation of urban jobs in China', *The China Quarterly*, 140, 971–99.

Bian, Yanjie, J. (2002), 'Social capital of the firm and its impact on performance: a social network analysis', in Anne S. Tsui and Chung Ming Lau (eds), *The Management of Enterprises in the People's Republic of China*, Norwell, MA: Kluwer Academic Press, pp. 275–95.

Buckley, P.J. and M.C. Casson (1998), 'Analyzing foreign market entry stategies: extending the internalization approach', *Journal of International Business Studies*, 29(3), 539–62.

Buckley, P.J. and P.N. Ghauri (2004), 'Globalisation, economic geography and the strategy of multinational enterprises', *Journal of International Business Studies*, 35(2), 81–98.

Burt, Ronald S. (1992), *Structural Holes*, Cambridge, MA: Harvard University Press.

Busenitz, L.W., C. Gomez and J.W. Spencer (2000), 'Country institutional profiles: unlocking entrepreneurial phenomena', *Academy of Management Journal*, 43(5), 994–1003.

Casson, Mark (1990), *Enterprise and Competitiveness: A Systems View of International Business*, Oxford: Clarendon Press.

Chen, J. (2006), 'Development of Chinese small and medium-sized enterprises', *Journal of Small Business and Enterprise Development*, 13(2), 140–47.

Cheng, H.-L. and C.-M.J. Yu (2008), 'Institutional pressures and initiation of internationalization: evidence from Taiwanese small- and medium-sized enterprises', *International Business Review*, 17(3), 331-348.

Clarysse, B., M. Wright, A. Lockett, E. Van de Velde and A. Vohora (2005), 'Spinning out new ventures: a typology of incubation strategies from European research institutions', *Journal of Business Venturing*, 20(2), 183–216.

CRI (China Research and Intelligence) (2009), 'Research report of Chinese integrated circuit industry', Beijing, China, April, available at: http://www.researchandmarkets.com/research/c305cf/research_report_of_Chinese_integrated circuit (accessed 29 June 2011).

Davis, Lance E. and Douglass C. North (1971), *Institutional Change and American Economic Growth*, Cambridge: Cambridge University Press.

Eisenhardt, K.M. (1989), 'Building theories from case study research', *Academy of Management Review*, 14(4), 532–50.

Felicitas, E. (2005), 'Qualitative insights into the international new venture creation process', *Journal of International Entrepreneurship*, 3(3), 178–98.

Fernhaber, S.A. (2006), 'International knowledge, reputation and new venture internationalization: the impact of intangible resources attained through internal and external sources', PhD. dissertation, Indiana University, Bloomington, IN.

Foss, K., N.J. Foss, P.G. Klein and S.K. Klein (2007), 'The entrepreneurial organization of heterogeneous capital', *Journal of Management Studies*, 44(7), 1165–86.

Fu, P.P., A.S. Tsui and G.G. Dess (2006), 'The dynamics of *guanxi* in Chinese high-tech firms: implications for knowledge management and decision making', *Management International Review*, 46(3), 277–305.

Gao, G.Y., J.Y. Murray, M. Kotabe and J. Lu (2010), 'A "strategy tripod" perspective on export behaviors: evidence from firms based in an emerging economy', *Journal of International Business Studies*, 41(3), 377–96.

Ghauri, Pervez (2004), 'Designing and conducting case studies in international business research', in Rebecca Marschan-Piekkari and Catherine Welch (eds), *Handbook of Qualitative Research Methods for International Business*, Cheltenham, UK and Northampton, MA, USA: Edward Elgar, pp. 109–24.

Ghauri, P.N. and K. Gronhaug (2010), *Research Methods in Business Studies*, 4th edn, London: FT-pearson.

Ghauri, Pervez N., Amjad Hadjikhani and Jan Johanson (2005), *Managing Opportunity Development in Business Networks*, London: Palgrave.

Ghauri, P., C. Lutz and G. Tesfom (2003), 'Using networks to solve export-marketing problems of small- and medium-sized firms from developing countries', *European Journal of Marketing*, 37(5/6), 728–52.

Gilbert, B.A., P.P. McDougall and D.B. Audretsch (2006), 'New venture growth: a review and extension', *Journal of Management*, 32(6), 926–50.

Glaser, Barney, G. and Anselm Strauss (1967), *The Discovery of Grounded Theory*, Chicago IL: Aldine.

Gnyawali, D.R. and D.S. Fogel (1994), 'Environments for entrepreneurship development: key dimensions and research implications', *Entrepreneurship: Theory and Practice*, 18(4), 43–62.

Gupta, S., J. Cadeaux and C. Dubelaar (2006), 'Uncovering multiple champion roles in implementing new-technology ventures', *Journal of Business Research*, 59(5), 549–63.

Harwit, E. (2002), 'High-technology incubators: fuel for China's new entrepreneurship?', *China Business Review*, 29(4), 26–9.

Hitt, M.A., R.D. Ireland, S.M. Camp and D.L. Sexton (2001), 'Strategic entrepreneurship: entrepreneurial strategies for wealth creation', *Strategic Management Journal*, 22(6–7), 479–91.

Hoegl, M., K.P. Parboteeah and C.L. Munson (2003), 'Team-level antecedents of individuals' knowledge network', *Decision Sciences*, 34(4), 741–70.

Karolyi, G.A. (2004), 'The role of American depositary receipts in the development of emerging equity markets', *Review of Economics and Statistics*, 86(3), 670–90.

Kraatz, M.S. (1998), 'Learning by association? Interorganizational networks and adaptation to environmental change', *Academy of Management Journal*, 41(6), 621–43.

Lu, J.W. and P.W. Beamish (2001), 'The internationalization and performance of SMEs', *Strategic Management Journal*, 22(6–7), 565–86.

Luo, Y. (1999), 'Environment–strategy–performance relations in small business in China: a case of township and village enterprises in Southern China', *Journal of Small Business Management*, 37(1), 37–52.

Manolova, T.S., R.V. Eunni and B.S. Gyoshev (2008), 'Institutional environments for entrepreneurship: evidence from emerging economies in Eastern Europe', *Entrepreneurship: Theory and Practice*, 32(1), 203–18.

Maura, M. and M. Rodney (2006), 'The networked incubator: the role and operation of entrepreneurial networking with the University Science Park incubator (USI)', *International Journal of Entrepreneurship and Innovation*, 7(2), 87–97.

McDougall, P.P. (1989), 'International versus domestic entrepreneurship: new venture strategic behavior and industry structure', *Journal of Business Venturing*, 4, 387–99.

McDougall, P.P., B.M. Oviatt and R.C. Shrader (2003), 'A comparison of international and domestic new ventures', *Journal of International Entrepreneurship*, 1(1), 59–82.

McDougall, P.P., R.B. Robinson and A.S. DeNisi (1992), 'Modeling new venture performance: an analysis of new venture strategy, industry structure, and venture origin', *Journal of Business Venturing*, 7(4), 267–89.

McDougall, P.P., S. Shane and B.M. Oviatt (1994), 'Explaining the formation of international new ventures: the limits of theories from international business research', *Journal of Business Venturing*, 9(6), 469–87.

Miles, Matthew and Michael Huberman (1994), *Qualitative Data Analysis*, 2nd edn, Thousand Oaks, CA: Sage.

Nelson, Richard R. (1993), 'A restrospective', in Nelson (ed.), *National Innovation Systems*, New York: Oxford University Press, pp. 505–24.

North, Douglass C. (1990), *Institutions, Institutional Change and Economic Performance*, Cambridge, MA: Harvard University Press.

OCN (2010), '2010–2015 China IC Industry Investment Analysis and Forecasting Report', China Investment Consulting, available at: www.ocn.com.cn.

Oviatt, B.M. and P.P. McDougall (1994), 'Toward a theory of international new ventures', *Journal of International Business Studies*, 25(1), 45–64.

Park, S.H. and Y. Luo (2001), '*Guanxi* and organizational dynamics: organizational networking in Chinese firms', *Strategic Management Journal*, 22(5), 455–77.

Peng, M.W., D.Y.L. Wang and Y. Jiang (2008), 'An institution-based view of international business strategy: a focus on emerging economies', *Journal of International Business Studies*, 39(5), 920–36.

Pettigrew, A.M. (1990), 'Longitudinal field research on change', *Organization Science*, 1(3), 267–92.

Poutziouris, P., Y. Wang and S. Chan (2002), 'Chinese entrepreneurship: the development of small family firms in China', *Journal of Small Business and Enterprise Development*, 9(4), 383–99.

Reuber, A.R. and E. Fischer (1997), 'The influence of the management teams' international experience on the internationalization behaviors of SMEs', *Journal of International Business Studies*, 28(4), 807–25.

Reynolds, P.D. (1997), 'New and small firms in expanding markets', *Small Business Economics*, 9(1), 79–84.

Sandberg, W.R. and C. W. Hofer (1987), 'Improving new venture performance: the role of strategy, industry structure, and the entrepreneur', *Journal of Business Venturing*, 2(1), 5–28.

SCORE (2011), 'Milestones in SCORE history', available at: http://www.score.org/node/147953 (accessed 29 June 2011)

Shrader, R.C., B.M. Oviatt and P.P. McDougall (2000), 'How new ventures exploit tradeoffs among international risk factors: lessons for the accelerated internationalization of the 21st century', *Academy of Management Journal*, 43(6), 1227–47.

Stinchcombe, A.L. (1965), 'Organizations and social structure', in James G. Marsh (ed.), *Handbook of Organizations*, Chicago, IL: Rand-McNally, pp. 142–93.

Stuart, R.W. and P.A. Abetti (1990), 'Impact of entrepreneurial and management experience on early performance', *Journal of Business Venturing*, 5(3), 151–62.

Tan, J. (1996), 'Regulatory environment and strategic orientations in a transitional economy: a study of Chinese private enterprises', *Entrepreneurship: Theory and Practice*, 21(1), 31–46.

Tan, J. and D. Tan (2005), 'Environment–strategy co-evolution and co-alignment: a staged model of Chinese SOEs under transition', *Strategic Management Journal*, 26(2), 141–57.

Teegen, H., J.P. Doh and S. Vachani (2004), 'The importance of nongovernmental organizations (NGOs) in global governance and value creation: an international business research agenda', *Journal of International Business Studies*, 35(6), 463–83.

Uzzi, B.D. (1996), 'The sources and consequences of embeddedness for the economic performance of organizations: the network effect', *American Sciological Review*, 61(4), 111–33.

Vahlne, Jan-Erik and Jan Johanson (2002), 'New technology, new companies, new business environments and new internationalisation processes', in Virpi Havila, Mats Forsgren and Hakan Håkansson (eds), *Critical Perspectives on Internationalisation*, London: Pergamon, pp. 209–27.

Wright, M., X. Liu, T. Buck and I. Filatotchev (2008), 'Returnee entrepreneurs, science park location choice and performance: an analysis of high-technology SMEs in China', *Entrepreneurship: Theory and Practice*, 32(1), 131–55.

Yeung, H.W.-C. (2002), 'Entrepreneurship in international business: an institutional perspective ', *Asia Pacific Journal of Management*, 19(1), 29–61.

Yin, R.K. (1993), *Applications of Case Study Research*, London: Sage.

Yli-Renko, H., E. Autio and H.J. Sapienza (2001), 'Social capital, knowledge, acquisition, and knowledge exploitation in young technology-based firms', *Strategic Management Journal*, 22(6–7), 587–613.

Young, S., P. Dimitratos and L-P. Dana (2003), 'International entrepreneurship research: what scope for international business theories?', *Journal of International Entrepreneurship*, 1(1), 31–42.

Zaheer, S. (1995), 'Overcoming the liability of foreignness', *Academy of Management Journal*, 38(2), 341–63.

Zahra, S.A. (2005), 'A theory of international new ventures: a decade of research', *Journal of International Business Studies*, 36(1), 20–28.

Zhu, H., M.A. Hitt and L. Tihanyi (2006), 'The internationalization of SMEs in emerging economies: institutional embeddedness and absorptive capacities', *Journal of Small Business Strategy*, 17(2), 1–26.

Zou, H. and P. Ghauri (2010), 'Internationalization by learning: the case of Chinese high-tech new ventures', *International Marketing Review*, 27(2), 223–44.

PART III

BORN GLOBALS: DEVELOPING LEADERS, AND TRENDS IN OTHER RESEARCH AREAS

13 Born globals: trends in developing intellectual entrepreneur founders/ managers, and in other research areas
V.H. Manek Kirpalani and Mika Gabrielsson

INTRODUCTION

Born globals (BGs) are a group of companies that promise to grow rapidly. Moreover, the successful ones are likely to become very large. The favorable impact of this on the country of origin is twofold: first is the direct and immediate economic impact through more employment; second, there will be an enhanced impact on productivity on account of the greater intellectual effect on the society skill-set through the dissemination of product creativity, and the experience of going global successfully. Therefore, it is in the self-interest of society to develop more 'global intellectual entrepreneurs' who can found and lead BGs or BG group-related firms and who can produce products and services through use of the internet which drives the growth of technological knowledge. Furthermore, these budding entrepreneurs must be capable of commercializing their skills and globalizing/internationalizing their activities.

The new information highway, the internet, is driving this technological revolution and rapid globalization. A characteristic of the revolution is the emphasis on knowledge for competitive advantage. An information- and communications-rich organizational environment is emerging. The widespread diffusion of technology is unstoppable. In such conditions, intellectual entrepreneurship arising from use of the internet has much to do. BG founders and/or leaders must learn how to take advantage of technological advances to globalize rapidly. BGs must be capable of more innovativeness than domestic small and medium-sized enterprises (SMEs) because of the foreign markets in which they must operate and succeed. But so far, little emphasis has been placed on the education needed for global entrepreneurship. The question arises, how can business schools help in the creation of what this new environment requires, that is 'global/ international intellectual entrepreneurs'? Development of the capacity to create global/international intellectual entrepreneurship arises from the intersection of three research paths: research on entrepreneurship, research in international business, and research on the development of products and services from internet use which can operate in the domain of global/international e-commerce (Kirpalani and Gabrielsson 2004). The development of BG research is causing these other three research paths to intersect with increasing frequency. This is an approach that must be nurtured. Academics have been observing accelerated globalization/ internationalization even among the smallest and newest organizations for many years, of which a number are BGs (Oviatt and McDougall 1999).

The meaning of the term 'global/international entrepreneurship' has been evolving, but consensus on definitions remains elusive. The difficulty is that the domain of entrepreneurship overlaps with the domain of other constructs such as innovation, change management, and strategic management. We now specify global/international entrepreneurship as a combination of innovative, proactive and risk-seeking behavior that leads to firms crossing international boundaries, and with the intention of creating value in organizations. The generic qualities of the global/international entrepreneur are:

- vision;
- motivation;
- implementation capability;
- ability to understand and utilize leverage; and
- creating more from less.

In today's increasingly knowledge-dependent society, vision is necessary for a global/international intellectual entrepreneur to be successful. The international business environment knowledge landscape is changing rapidly, especially as it is coupled with advances in technology across the board. Given such advances, business opportunities are burgeoning. How best is vision taught? It is vital to know the trends and their implications in order to spot the opportunities. Two general background courses should be offered: one in international business, and the other on the impact of e-commerce and role of intellectual products and services. The phenomenon of intellectual entrepreneurship is related to intellectual capital and intellectual product. Intellectual capital can be considered as capitalized knowledge – specifically, knowledge assets that are capitalized and put to productive use (Kwiatkowski and Stowe 2001). The same knowledge might also be placed on the market as a product or service of a purely, or almost purely, intellectual character, for example, consultancy or information management systems. Further, there should be a 'specific opportunities' course dealing with knowledge-based opportunities to help global/international intellectual entrepreneurs pursue particular areas (Kirpalani and Gabrielsson 2004). The emphasis throughout all these courses should be on vision generation. The methodology could be based on idea development, environmental sourcing for new ideas, and building small ideas to support some big new ideas. The global knowledge field is changing fast as new areas arise. Therefore, the new course can introduce new opportunity areas as warranted.

The teaching of motivation requires a different approach, based on participation and discovery. This approach should rely on incubators, which comprise a team with a global/international intellectual entrepreneur or product inventor and two or three persons from different business disciplines. If warranted, one designer or artist could be added. The global/ international entrepreneur will be strongly motivated and this enthusiasm should catch on among the team members. These team members could be students, managers, or senior managers who have retired from their former organization.

In group civilizations, such as Chinese and Indian, extended and/or joint families can and do contribute resources. This obviously means that global/international entrepreneurs do not need to have the same extent of risk-taking ability allied to their other foundations for motivation, or the same heightened ability to assemble resources. With regard to implementation capability, courses in computer software and use, plus an advanced course in computer applications for BG/SME firms conducting global/ international business would be useful. Additionally, courses are needed in international organization theory and behavior, international marketing, and international consumer and international industrial behavior. Furthermore, there should be standard courses in the remaining business disciplines of international accounting, decision sciences, and international finance. Finally, there must be a capstone course in international business strategy, with appropriate emphasis on cross-cultural aspects, how BGs/SMEs can leverage large multinational enterprise (MNE) channel resources, and the risks surrounding intellectual property rights.

Entrepreneurial education tends to focus on human actors and environment. The actual creation of global/international endeavors was left to the choices made by people once they were educated and on the career paths they chose to follow. If education is to foster more direct entrepreneurial action leading to the creation and growth of global/international firms, it must go further. It must teach international e-commerce courses and systematically help to construct provisions for the cognitive, social, and economic preconditions for new global/international start-ups, leading to their fusion and eventual launching. This requires a paradigm shift to an international business generating strategy (Laukkanen 2000). It should move towards an endogenous 'global/international business generating model' of self-sustaining survival and growth with four interdependent components:

- Human actors;
- Environment, which includes global/international market opportunities, regulatory and support policies;
- Intellectual products and intellectual processes; and
- Resources, including socio-cultural elements.

Resources used to be thought of as just seed or venture capital finance. Today, resources must include knowledge and social capabilities, for example, production and systems knowledge, market intimacy trust, and network relations can all be critical (Van de Ven 1993).

Entrepreneurs with technology-based firms need, at the outset, to be taught internationalization and how to participate in it. Research should also be done on whether knowledge of a foreign language is an asset that significantly affects performance. Entrepreneurs should be given the education, and thereby the chance to create successful BGs. Thus, they can contribute most to the economies in which they were created. We encourage researchers to study this educational area extensively. Such research will be most useful to other academics, many practitioners, and societal policy makers. The industry sector comprising BG and related firms is growing, and more research is needed so that valid recommendations can be made to further help its effective and rapid growth.

Another area that must not be forgotten is the strategic patterns that BGs exhibit. A central foundation underlying this group is their accelerated globalization/internationalization paths. This has a close commonality with the latecomer perspective displayed by MNEs from the BRIC (Brazil, Russia, India, China) countries and some other emerging markets. This is in contrast to the earlier approach of most MNEs and SMEs from the richer developed countries that had gradualist strategic patterns, brought out in the 'stages' and 'transaction cost' theories. The latecomer perspective stresses firms' ability to access complementary assets through internationalization and their ability to undertake organizational and strategic innovations rapidly. Furthermore, latecomer firms have flexibility, low overheads, and network based business models. These are all firm-specific advantages (Buckley et al. 2007). Many BGs exhibit these advantages as well, but as shown below, more research into how BGs can gain from networks remains to be done.

Networks

Networks of MNEs and BGs is an area that is yet to be researched fully. In Chapter 17, Vapola proposes a 'global innovative constellation' (GIC) coupled with a network framework titled the 'battleship strategy'. The

GIC approach uncovers a framework of key factors in such combinations, which can drive up added value from this form of alliance network. The suggestion is that since innovative activity is inherently uncertain, these small start-ups can test the waters and explore new technological or market opportunities. The uniqueness of the strategy lies in suggesting that the BGs can serve as scouts for MNEs. They do this service in return for the benefit of gaining access to global markets when they are part of the MNC's thrust. The key research question studied is: 'What are the key motives, strategies and structures that the two groups have for forming GICs?'. The GIC is defined as a non-equity co-opetitive multiparty alliance used to create innovations that add value relative to competition. 'Co-opetitive' is a hybrid word meaning that the parties both cooperate and compete. The GIC emphasizes competitive positioning, compared to other related concepts such as multiparty R&D alliances.

The difficulty of sustaining competitive advantage is one of the fundamental challenges facing firms in high-tech industries. Convergence between technologies leads to new products and solutions (Hitt et al. 1998). These challenges are further increased by technological, market, and regulatory uncertainties (Blomqvist 2002). Sustainability of competitive advantage is only temporary, as new technologies create new market opportunities while simultaneously destroying others in existing markets. Furthermore, Schumpeter (1934) argued that new technologies create new technologies, while simultaneously destroying others in existing markets. Therefore, sustainability of competitive advantage is only temporary. For the MNE, global learning is a critical source of competitive advantage (Doz et al. 2001). BGs focus on gaining such advantage by rapid globalization of their innovations. Since innovative activity is inherently uncertain, the scouts test the waters by exploring new technological and market opportunities. Compared to other multiparty alliances, a GIC is a non-equity co-opetitive alliance. The focus is on commercialization of possible innovations.

Due to an uncertain environment, the MNEs are constantly at risk of being overtaken by new, flexible and fast-moving entrants. Research in innovation argues that the attackers have an advantage in the era of technological change within an industry (Christensen 1997). At the advent of technological change, existing MNEs are mainly considered as followers, and thus destined to fail (Fairclough 1994). Moreover, it has been argued that the internalization of all R&D activities in MNEs is no longer a practical solution (Narula and Hagedoorn 1999).

In innovation-intensive industries, an inverted U-curve between exploitation and exploration activities and their respective performance has been identified (Uotila et al. 2009). This means that for an MNE it is not beneficial to under- or overinvest in exploring new innovations. Therefore, collaborative approaches such as the GIC system are needed. Start-ups can play multiple roles for MNEs. They can be suppliers of an innovative sub-element, a reseller through a new approach to distribution such as via the internet, a complementary solution to an MNE's offering, and also a disrupter of the technology base and a competitor.

Born Global Industries

A very interesting study has been done on selected whole industries that have become BGs. The foundation theory for whole industries that became global was set by Raymond Vernon's 'product life cycle trade theory', which was formally presented over 50 years ago (Vernon 1966). It explained how industries that are not tied to a resource base international-ize over time. This happens as technologies mature, and products can be made more cost efficient in countries with lower labor costs. Consequently, markets in advanced richer countries can be supplied by the same products produced in less developed countries that have reached an adequate stage of industrial development. Often the supplier is in fact a subsidiary or joint venture associate of the originating manufacturer whose business has grown into an MNE.

In the world of the twenty-first century, one finds that technology advances much faster, market barriers have been brought down by GATT (General Agreement on Tariffs and Trade) negotiations and WTO (World Trade Organization) efforts, and communication and transportation costs have been considerably reduced. Thus, most industries can develop their value chains so that they are globally integrated. Well-known examples of MNEs that have done this are Nike and the soft drink giants, Coke and Pepsi. Now, some BG industries have globally integrated activities from the outset. Three such industries are within the offshore renewable energy sector of wind, wave, and tidal forces. In Chapter 15, Løvdal and Aspelund show that internationalization in these three industries mani-fests in high levels of integrated operations and exchange of resources in the introduction phase of their life cycle. There is even evidence of integra-tion of the firms and their partners, and related mobility in the global value chain in the pre-introduction phase. As new theory develops in this area of BG industries, it will link with international entrepreneurship research, as BG firms are likely to be the driving force behind the growth and expan-sion of BG industries. Other characteristics include the wide availability of scientific and operational knowledge within the particular BG industry community and a large global market potential.

The economic world is at a turning point where relations between countries were previously built on trade and the establishment of subsidiaries in locations for specific advantages in a regional market. They are not built in the same way for the same purpose at present nor will they be in the future. The trend is to integrate for global/regional advantage and foreign direct investment (FDI), and products and/or intermediate components are selected for trade because of their fit in the integration network. A fact that should be emphasized is that one-third of world trade is intra-MNE. This arises by an MNE structuring its worldwide business so that it and its component suppliers and specialist providers, who could be BGs, are involved in the team on a long-term basis. Therefore, it is incumbent on researchers to study such developments, and they may well find the emergence of more BG industries.

DIFFERENT CULTURES AND BG DEVELOPMENT RESEARCH

The phenomenon of BG firms from origin, to growth path, growth rate, networking, and performance should be influenced by the home culture of the BGs, but there has been little research in this subject area. The reasons are probably threefold. First, researchers in international business working in business schools are not specifically trained in the area of culture and its influence on SMEs. Second, modern information and communication technology has only recently developed to the point where it can be taken advantage of fully by entrepreneurs who are capable of founding/managing BGs. The word 'fully' is utilized here to state the feasibility of effective use at affordable cost. Third, only relatively recently has the formation and development of BG firms begun to be seen by policy makers as having importance to their nation. Therefore, policy makers have not been involved in aiding such formation and growth, or in helping to develop programs that can utilize the cultural attributes of their people to foster formation and growth of such firms. However, there is sufficient evidence to indicate that development of BGs can be very beneficial to the economy and development of any nation.

How should the effect of culture on development of BGs be studied? One problem is that the BG has to have one or more specific and unique products that can achieve a global market. Most existing internationalizing SMEs (ISMEs) from newly industrializing countries may only be internationalizing in a few countries. However, it will be useful to the research field for them to be studied in order to discover whether their efforts were related to the influence of their different cultures. Furthermore, one has a situation in which many countries are in an emerging state in which agriculture, industry, and service are relatively underdeveloped. In such countries, it is unlikely that entrepreneurs or managers can create global products and form BGs or ISMEs. In these instances, can one relax the BG definition to include SMEs that have built up their resources and skills over time, and produced products that are successful in their domestic market? A good reason to do this is that there is some evidence that these SMEs are now ready to expand from domestic to other foreign markets, and perhaps later may be ready to go to the global market. While inclusion of such potential ISMEs is actually outside the parameters of the study of BGs themselves, it can be justified on the grounds that later, when those countries reach more developed levels, small firms from those countries may start as BGs. A definite justification is that they are already displaying indications of becoming ISMEs. Therefore, even at this stage it is worthwhile to examine the effect of culture on such potential ISMEs from least developed countries that are planning to cross borders in their pursuit of internationalization. Based on the above reasoning, a study of such ISMEs from these emerging countries may be worth researching, but certainly priority should not be accorded to such studies. A practical research approach may be for researchers from developed countries to join any promising BG/ISME research project that will be implemented by a researcher in a least developed country, especially if that researcher has been educated to an appropriate level in a developed country university.

A second problem arises in the matter of selecting the most effective way of studying the question of the effect of culture on the development of BGs. A deductive approach suggests that one first analyzes the culture of the country and then deduces its effects on the formation of BGs. It is not an easy task to correctly study the culture of a country from this perspective. To be done correctly would require considerable training in a study of culture and then in its effects on the international development of SMEs. An alternative is to adopt an inductive approach and study cases of ISMEs from such cultures. Then, through this type of study, an analysis of the effect of a culture on ISME development could be made. The decision in this handbook is to adopt this inductive approach since the unit of analysis in the book is the BG, the small firm that goes global, and related to this group are the small firms that can be classified as born-again globals, born regionals, born-again regionals, and ISMEs.

This discussion and analysis is divided into three phases. The reason for this is that each phase addresses a particular and important facet concerning the development of the BG. These important phases are all integrated into one whole to emphasize the overall importance of the BG as a unit. The three phases are the growth path for going global from origin, the growth rate of the BG in the international arena, and the factors influencing the firm's makeover from SME into a large company. In the context of this study, from origin, the major factor has to be the international growth path of the firm. From this stage what follows is the understanding of what causes the international growth rate of the firm. Finally, if the successful firm continues a high growth rate, it will obviously transform itself into a large company with concomitant large resources. In each phase mentioned, the discussion and analysis incorporates the effect of the country/region culture.

Origin

The BG literature has expanded over the last 15 years. In this literature, the subject has always been a BG, which is a new breed of SME that takes a global approach since its inception, and has a significant commitment to international business growth. One study from Portugal (Simões et al. 2009) addresses three relevant questions: the scope of what should be the definition of a BG, the relevance of the BG business model, and an adjustment in the geographic reach of the firms' internationalization. It presents research findings based on a study of a medical software service provider, and ensuing results. Then it discusses its introduction of the concept of a 'quasi-BG' having an international market that is only partially global. The authors suggest expansion of the set of BGs being analyzed to include their 'quasi-BG'. Another strong influence on BGs at birth, but a relatively unsettled issue, is the role of the entrepreneur in BG emergence and evolution. The term realistically applies to the fact that the role of the entrepreneur in making the firm focused (Nooteboom 2009), in giving it international drive (Rialp et al. 2005), and fostering networking (Gassmann and Keupp 2007) has been generally agreed upon. But what has not been looked at in depth is how entrepreneurial processes and internationalization interact and co-evolve over time (Keupp and Gassmann, 2009). This interaction and co-evolution provides an interesting focus to study. Therefore, selected studies have been included in this coverage for analysis and comment.

There seems to be an insufficient understanding of the relationship between the entrepreneur and the small firm at the earlier stages of the firm's life cycle. From a resource-based perspective one can classify the firm's intangible resources into the structural capital of the firm, and human capital, as seen in the characteristics of the founders/managers and entrepreneurial team members. However, the focus of research studies in the past has often been on the structural capital of the organization, and not on the individuals. To shift the focus to individuals, one can adopt a dynamic capabilities approach and try to identify how the BG founders'/managers' social and business networks influence BG evolution and global/international geographical penetration. External factors, which may contribute directly or indirectly, can be associated with culture and linguistic influences, the emergence of early key customers, and regulatory changes.

In Chapter 16, Simões studies six Portuguese SMEs. Some of the founders had wide networks of academic/scientific colleagues from different countries, including the USA. Further, Alcatel, a Canadian company, NASA, Nokia, and Vodaphone helped the founders seize business opportunities. This indicates that entrepreneurship is a continuing process, extending beyond creation to the internationalization trajectory followed by the firm. A common thread in the internationalization of the six SMEs was the adoption of internationalization niche strategies. The researchers also argue that the existence of a global vision at inception is not necessary for a potential BG. Rather an opportunity framing a non-geographically bound field is required, where an approach from a large international player can leverage the small firm to rapid international growth. Another point brought out by this research is how the pace and geography of internationalization is the outcome of different factors: the size of the domestic country, product characteristics, foreign market attractiveness, and the firm/founder networks.

Another study investigates the success factors in SMEs' internationalization processes among Italian firms (De Chiara and Minguzzi 2002). In particular, it concentrates on the role of support services for the internationalization of these small firms. This is an important feature of the infrastructure that encourages such small firms to internationalize, and thus take the growth path, which may lead to them becoming BGs. Some interesting research from China claims that external uncontrollable determinants of export performance have received scant research attention. The researchers examine two key external uncontrollable factors with regard to Chinese manufacturing firms: industry concentration and firm location (Zhou and Zou 2002). In addition, these researchers include as covariates other factors that are frequently studied: firm size, capital intensity, technological innovation, and industry sector. Through logistical regression and multiple regression analyses, they find that both domestic market concentration and firm location are strong predictors of Chinese firms' export intensity and export propensity. Firm location obviously becomes a strongly relevant factor when the firm has proximity to lower transport costs to external foreign markets or has powerful links with large key foreign customers. Domestic market concentration as a factor requires more valid research studies to support a conclusion about its importance. It is well known that Italian business culture has led a number of its SMEs to form industrial clusters (Porter 1990), but China has no similarly based industrial cluster culture. Moreover, a question arises as to whether domestic market concentration in China would lead to greater cooperation between the firms in that region or to greater competition. The Porter model gives the example of Italian ceramic tile industry firms which have improved their products and honed their competitive skills due to them being concentrated in a region. However, the influence on the origin of the Chinese born global firms and the role of existing support mechanisms call for further research (Vissak, Zhang and Ukrainski, Chapter 18) as they seen to be able to internationalize rapidly despite lacking experiential market knowledge, relying primarily on knowledge gained through contacts with government officials.

Another study on perceptions of growth constraints by Nigerian SMEs yielded useful information for policy makers (Mambula 2002). The study investigated perceptions of the factors that influence the growth, performance, and development of Nigerian SMEs. It then went on to analyze what implications those factors have for policy. Senior bank managers from four leading development banks were interviewed, as were a number of small business owners and/or managers. The latter group of SME owners and managers thought that the procedures for obtaining bank loans were cumbersome, bureaucratic, and had excessive collateral demands. The senior bank managers tended to agree, although for somewhat different reasons, which included the precautionary approach necessary when making loans to small businesses.

Growth Path

An empirical analysis was made of the effect of cultural distance, geographical distance, and target market size as influencing the growth path of SMEs in the software industry. The researchers examined the effect of the shift of the priorities of these firms as they approached the problem of selection of the target countries. The findings were that some 70 percent of the target country selection choices could be explained by the market size of the software market and the geographical distance alone (Ojala and Tyrvainen 2007). Further, it seemed that the SME entry priorities shifted quickly from countries within a short geographical distance to countries with high purchasing power, although the latter were at a much further geographical distance. This is a very understandable result because software is not expensive to transport. It is certainly not bulky or heavy, and in more cases than not, it can be transferred over the internet. Therefore, geographical distance has little relevance for this industry, especially versus the factor of high purchasing power. The latter factor is a strong foundation for the possibility of a better education in a relatively new product sector such as software. Now, what of international growth rates and associated risk for BGs?

International Growth Rate and Risk

In Chapter 14, Kuivalainen and Saarenketo address the lack of an integrated framework by which one can understand international pathways for software BGs. The pathway can be discovered by observation of the entrepreneur founder and the strategic actions of the BG. The foundation for the research methodology was the study of the time, scale, and scope of the BG operation. The time was presumed to be when the BG came into existence or soon after. The scale and scope were determined by the degree of internationalization at different stages of a BG's life cycle. This was in line with the thinking that 'internationalization may be captured as patterns of behaviour, formed by an accumulation of evidence manifest as events at specific reference points in time' (Jones and Coviello 2005, p. 292). Consequently, they saw that a pathway consists of several phases or stages during which a firm follows a certain behavioral pattern and these patterns can be linked to both internationalization and firm life cycles. The first is the pre-start stage, which occurred before internationalization, then the start of internationalization stage, followed by growth. During this third phase, growth was the core operation of the firm. The final stage was consolidation, when international operations became business as usual.

Another study investigated the failure of a small firm in international business even though the firm's product had advanced technological advantages (Zhang and Dodgson 2007). Usually a firm that possesses key international technical standards in a sector(s) has considerable advantages in achieving early and rapid internationalization. One of the most important innovations in mobile payments occurred when point-of-sale proximity payment solutions were introduced by Avaro, a start-up South Korean firm launched in 2000. Avaro developed and owned a critical standard in the emerging international mobile payments industry. The firm also had many other advantages that could help successful internationalization. These included attractive international market and financing opportunities, supportive international networks, a munificent national technological and business home base, and an encouraging government policy. Yet the firm's attempts at early and rapid internationalization failed. A multiplicity of factors contributed to this failure, especially specific cultural and national factors. Society's cultural values shape the orientations of the domestic social groups to which entrepreneurs relate and depend.

A stream of research into the internationalization of smaller business identifies the centrality of social ties and networks in entrepreneurship (Coviello and McAuley 1999). Such relationships encompass customers, suppliers, competitors, partners, various support agencies, family, and friends. These interactions can have specific national and cultural influences. Differing cultural traits, such as tolerance of uncertainty, and approaches to competitiveness and individualism, are found to impact on decisions firms make to form technological alliances, a feature of technology-based entrepreneurship (Steensma et al. 2000). A society's cultural values shape the orientations of the domestic social groups to which entrepreneurs relate and depend. High levels of patriotism are an example of cultural influence in Korea. Indeed, such patriotism, sometimes reflected in its extreme form of nationalism, can be 'a liability for Korean firms in globalizing their business operations' (Kim 1997, p. 76). It has been argued that, 'At the societal level, a sense of inclusion promotes strong nationalism which creates an antagonistic attitude toward foreigners' (Chung et al. 1997, pp. 136–7). The original Japanese venture capital investor in Avaro wanted to double its stake of US$10 million for 30 percent of the equity. The founder of Avaro, however, would only accept half for fear of a foreign investor taking a controlling share of his firm. He stated 'we don't want to have any dominating investors from any country apart from Korea which potentially will convert Avaro's Korean identity' (Zhang and Dodgson 2007, p. 345).

Researchers should examine the tensions in different cultures between international technological opportunity and the kinds of domestic constraints experienced by Avaro, extending beyond the limitations of individual case studies. This would provide great insight into the dynamic between the traditional and the modern as countries in Asia, such as Korea, continue to internationalize. The development and diffusion of an innovation is not just a process of technological evolution; it involves a social adaptive process, which occurs in unique institutional, social, cultural, and regulatory contexts. Further research could tease out the relationships between technology and national and corporate culture to come up with valuable insights. The relationship between a firm's behaviors, routines and leadership style, and national cultural dispositions towards issues such as hierarchy, social networks, and nationalism would improve understanding of the subtleties of the incentives and constraints on rapid and early internationalization. Such research will contribute to the understanding of the ways international business opportunities can be created by joint partnerships and/or networks involving firms in developed countries with BGs and ISMEs from different cultures.

ANNOTATED BIBLIOGRAPHY

The 'Annotated bibliography for researchers' (Chapter 19) consists of articles and other publications that we selected after a comprehensive search of the literature. We chose what we thought were the best, after taking advice from other well-known researchers. In making our selection, we consulted our peers in the discipline and relied on the opinions of the contributors to our book, most of whom are established researchers in the field, Others are younger aspirants who have just obtained a doctorate but have produced research in the field and used it to submit learned papers that were blind refereed before being accepted at major conferences. In all such cases we have heard the presentations and read their papers. Moreover, we have received comments from other researchers with regard to the submissions of these younger aspirants. We hope that the annotated bibliography will be helpful to all researchers, both experienced academics, and newcomers who want to work in this field. It should provide them with an overview of the previous work that has been done and thus enable them to launch their work from a foundation of what has already been covered. Further, it provides them with established sub-areas of work that can assist them in developing their own footprint, and gives them a base of well-thought-out ideas that might lead them to be more creative in their approach.

The following is an analysis of the overall annotated bibliography. First, as an overview, it is useful to know how many of the publications were developed in which sub-areas of the field. Some 40 percent of the publications are in the sub-area of 'rapid globalization/internationalization'. Of this 40 percent, some two-thirds directly concern born globals and one-third relate to the internationalization of SMEs. This is the largest single sub-area as was expected. This Handbook is about born globals, and fundamentally the solid core sub-area involves the rapid globalizers/ internationalizers, whether they are BGs or from the numerically much larger group of ISMEs.

The other 60 percent or so of the remaining publications from the total in the annotated bibliography have the following characteristics. There are four groups, each containing some 11 percent of the total publications: 'international entrepreneurship', 'international new ventures', 'knowledge acquisition application dissemination management' and 'strategy'. In almost all instances they relate to research done on ISMEs and not BGs in particular. Of the remaining 16 percent (100 percent minus 84 percent (40 + 4*11 = 84)), some 6 percent of the total deal with research on 'networks, joint ventures and large channels'. Then there are three groups with some 3 percent each of the total research publications: research studies in 'market orientation', 'organizational learning', and 'resources: finance and other'. The remaining 1 percent of the total publications goes to the 'internet'.

Another perspective is given by looking at the information from a somewhat different viewpoint. About 27 percent of the publications refer exclusively to BGs. Some 69 percent refer to 'internationalizing SMEs' and 1 percent each to the remaining groups of 'born-again globals', 'born regionals', 'born-again regionals', and 'born global industries'. For the BG field to grow in research and theory, the above results indicate a great need for growth in the total number of studies. In addition, one must look deeper. Only some 27 percent of the research studies were directly on BGs; the majority of the others were on 'internationalizing SMEs'. This indicates the need for far more research studies on BGs. Also it shows the paucity of studies on 'born-again globals', 'born regionals', 'born-again regionals', and 'born global industries'. Only 1 percent of the studies were done on each of these four last mentioned groups. Obviously, more studies have been carried out, but none was valid enough to be accepted in the annotated bibliography. Therefore, these groups suffer from being neglected by good researchers. Some of the neglect may have come about because these groups have never been identified as distinct groups that should be researched for the useful knowledge they can bring to bear on theory development that pertains to the whole BG-related sector.

Further, only 11 percent each of the total studies were done on 'international entrepreneurship', 'international new ventures', 'knowledge acquisition and management', and the 'strategy' sector. Obviously in all these sub-areas more studies with BGs and with ISMEs are necessary. These comments on the need for a greater number of studies are emphasized even more with regard to 'networks, joint ventures and large channels'. Only 6 percent of the studies were done in this sub-area, while it is becoming common knowledge that for BGs and ISMEs it is vital for expansion and rapid growth that they join networks, joint ventures, or otherwise link with large channels. Moreover, it is vital to find out more about the effects of market orientation, and organizational learning on the performance of BGs and ISMEs. In addition, the largest need of BGs and ISMEs is for resources, both of finance and many other kinds. Furthermore, it is surprising that there are so few published research studies on the use of the internet by BGs and ISMEs to help their performance and, specifically, the building of demand by customers for their products. The internet is generally accepted to be the wave and highway of communication technology, which is revolutionizing the way we operate generally. Its impact is all-pervasive, and touches everybody and every industry. BGs and ISMEs all have to have websites and communicate via the internet. The power of the internet as a vast, although often an unproven source of usefulness, must be researched. It is important for BGs and ISMEs to fully understand how to best use the internet. This requires many more research studies.

From a cultural standpoint, there is a third perspective. Only 23 percent of the research studies take culture into account either directly or from a location of origin distinction. Moreover, most of these studies emanate from only six regions (listed alphabetically): Australia, Israel, New Zealand, Scandinavia, Spain, and the UK Furthermore, a fact worth noting is the other potential weakness of the research stream, that research studies from these cultural regions are driven by a small number of researchers. Therefore, it is necessary to emphasize the need for more studies from regions of different culture. Research is being conducted on practitioners/actors from different cultural locations, who have launched BGs or ISMEs. All of us can learn from the effects of culturally diverse backgrounds and environments on the targets, the choice of products, and the overall performance of such firms. All of the above will be useful for the growth of theory, the research of academicians, ideas for policy makers who must want to encourage the rise of this sector of economic and technological activity, and practitioners who stand to gain from the managerial implications of such work.

DISCUSSION AND CONCLUSIONS

One very definite finding from the Zhang and Dodgson (2007) study is that the area of international entrepreneurship requires more research in order to more fully account for the particular characteristics of technology products and markets, national business systems, and enduring cultural influences to guide management practices in emerging global technology markets.

Simões's research shows that it would be very useful to have other studies done on SMEs in different countries that became BGs. First, it is important to study how the culture of different regions affects the social and business networks they create, both domestically and internationally. It will also be important to show how these networks influence the pace and geographical reach of the firm's globalization/internationalization. Second, it is important to study the effect of the size of the domestic economy, and the market attractiveness of target regions on the globalization/internationalization of the firm. A third area of study is to look at the capability of the firm/founder(s) with regard to building networks. A fourth area to study is the possibility of the product being successful globally/regionally. Finally, and perhaps most importantly, it is important to research the role of founders in the process prior to forming the SME to seizing opportunities to transform the firm into a BG once the firm comes into existence.

Research on innovation suggests that leadership strategy and innovation mainly belong to new entrants in this century of technological change (Christensen 1997). A typical reaction of existing MNEs is to broaden the set of internal innovations (Burgelman et al. 2001). However, it has been argued that the internalization of all potential R&D activities is no longer a practical solution (Narula and Hagerdoorn 1999). According to another study, an inverted U-curve between exploitation and exploration activities and performance has been identified (Uotila et al. 2009) This could mean that it is not beneficial to under- or overinvest in exploring new innovations. However, it does suggest that an incumbent MNE can use a new innovation built on top of existing know-how and systems to expand into existing markets (Vapola, Chapter 17).

REFERENCES

Blomqvist, K. (2002), 'Partnering in the dynamic environment: the role of trust in asymmetric technology partnership', PhD dissertation, Lappeenranta University of Technology, Acta Lapeenrangtaensis, 122.

Buckley, P., C. Wang and J. Clegg (2007), 'The impact of foreign ownership, local ownership and industry characteristics on spillover benefits from foreign direct investment in China', *International Business Review*, 16(2), 142–58.

Burgelman, Robert A., Modesto A. Maidique and Stephen C. Wheelwright (2001), *Strategic Management of Technology and Innovation*, 3rd edn, New York: McGraw-Hill.

Christensen, Clayton (1997), *The Innovator's Dilemma: When New Technologies Cause Great Companies to Fail*, Boston, MA: Harvard Business School Press.

Chung, Kae H., Hak Chong Lee and Ku Hyun Jung (1997), *Korean Management: Global Strategy and Cultural Transformation*, Berlin and New York: Walter de Gruyter.

Coviello, N. and A. McAuley (1999), 'Internationalization and the smaller firm: a review of contemporary empirical research', *Management International Review*, 39(3), 223–56.

De Chiara, A. and A. Minguzzi (2002), 'Success factors in SMEs' internationalization processes: an Italian investigation', *Journal of Small Business Management*, 40(2), 146–53.

Doz, Yves L., Jose Santos and Peter Williamson (2001), *From Global to Metanational: How Companies Win in the Knowledge Economy*, Boston, MA: Harvard Business School Press.

Fairclough, Gerard (1994), 'Innovation and organization', in Mark Dodgson and Roy Rothwell (eds), *The Handbook of Industrial Innovation*, Aldershot, UK and Brookfield, VT, USA: Edward Elgar, pp. 325–36.

Gassmann, O. and M.M. Keupp (2007), 'The competitive advantage of early and rapidly internationalising SMEs in the biotechnology industry: a knowledge-based view', *Journal of World Business*, 42(3), 350–66.

Hitt, M.A., B.W. Keats and S.M. DeMarie (1998), 'Navigating in the new competitive landscape: building competitive advantage in the 21st century', *Academy of Management Executive*, 12(4), 22–42.

Jones, M.V. and N.E. Coviello (2005), 'Conceptualizing an entrepreneurial process in time', *Journal of International Business Studies*, 36(3), 284–303.

Keupp, M.M. and O. Gassmann (2009), 'The past and the future of international entrepreneurship: a review and suggestions for developing the field', *Journal of Management*, **35**(3), 600–633.

Kim, Linsu (1997), *Imitation to Innovation: The Dynamics of Korea's Technological Learning*, Boston, MA: Harvard Business School Press.

Kirpalani, V.H.M. and M. Gabrielsson (2004), 'The need for international intellectual entrepreneurs and how business schools can help', *Journal of Teaching in International Business*, **16**(1), 101–18.

Kwiatkowski, Stefan and Charles R.B. Stowe (eds) (2001), *Knowledge Cafe for Intellectual Product and Intellectual Capital*, Warsaw: Academy of Management and Entrepreneurship Press.

Laukkanen, M. (2000), 'Exploring alternative approaches to high-level entrepreneurship education: creating micro mechanisms for endogenous regional growth', *Entrepreneurship and Regional Development*, **12**(1), 25–48.

Mambula, Charles (2002), 'Perceptions of SME growth constraints in Nigeria', *Journal of Small Business Management*, **40**(1), 58–65.

Narula, R. and J. Hagedoorn (1999), 'Innovation through strategic alliances: moving towards international partnerships and contractual agreements', *Technovation*, **19**(5), 283–94.

Nooteboom, Bart (2009), *A Cognitive Theory of the Firm: Learning, Governance and Dynamic Capabilities*, Cheltenham, UK and Northampton, MA, USA: Edward Elgar.

Ojala, A. and P. Tyrvainen (2007), 'Market entry and priority of small and medium-sized enterprises in the software industry: an empirical analysis of cultural distance, geographic distance, and market size', *Journal of International Marketing*, **15**(3), 123–49.

Oviatt, Benjamin M. and Patricia P. McDougall (1999), 'A framework for understanding accelerated international entrepreneurship', in Alan M. Rugman and Richard W. Wright (eds), *Research in Global Strategic Management*, 7, Stamford, CT: JAI Press, pp. 23–40.

Porter, Michael E. (1990), *The Competitive Advantages of Nations*, London: Macmillan.

Rialp, A., J. Rialp and G. Knight (2005), 'The phenomenon of early internationalizing firms: what do we know after a decade (1993–2003) of scientific inquiry?', *International Business Review*, **14**(2), 147–66.

Schumpeter, Joseph (1934), *The Theory of Economic Development*, Cambridge, MA: Harvard University Press.

Simões, V.C., P.T. Capao and R.M. Carvalho (2009), 'Quasi-born globals: do they deserve a specific approach', paper presented at the European International Business Academy 35th Annual Conference, Valencia, Spain, December 11–13.

Steensma, H.K., M.L. Steensma and P.H. Dickson (2000), 'The influence of national culture on the formation of technology alliances by entrepreneurial firms', *Academy of Management Journal*, **43**(5), 951–73.

Uotila, J., M. Maula, T. Keil and S.A. Zahra (2009), 'Exploration, exploitation and financial performance: analysis of S&P 500 corporations', *Strategic Management Journal*, **30**(2), 221–31.

Van de Ven, A.H. (1993), 'The development of an infrastructure for entrepreneurship', *Journal of Business Venturing*, **8**(3), 211–30.

Vernon, R. (1966), 'International investment and international trade in the product cycle', *Quarterly Journal of Economics*, **80**(2), 190–207.

Zhang, M.Y. and M. Dodgson (2007), 'A roasted duck can still fly away: a case study of technology, nationality, culture and the rapid and early internationalization of the firm', *Journal of World Business*, **42**(3), 336–49.

Zhou, H. and S. Zou (2002), 'The impact of industry concentration and firm location on Export propensity and intensity: an empirical analysis of Chinese manufacturing firms', *Journal of International Marketing*, **10**(1), 52–71.

14 International pathways of software born globals
Olli Kuivalainen and Sami Saarenketo*

INTRODUCTION

Over the past few decades, internationalization of small and medium-sized enterprises (SMEs) has attracted increasing attention in the international business literature. This is due to advances in communication, information, transportation technologies, a shift toward market economies, privatization and deregulation in emerging markets, the emergence of the global consumer, the availability of transnational media, and the proliferation of global products (Yip 1995). In addition, SMEs are able to grasp the opportunities of an almost borderless marketplace. For this reason, the traditional internationalization models (for example, Johanson and Vahlne 1977, 1990), have been questioned and 'newer approaches' have been offered. The emergence of, or at least a sudden increase in, born global (BG) companies is clearly a response to these rising opportunities as more and more companies are taking the step towards global markets earlier and more rapidly than similar companies did before.

Despite the importance and prevalence of BGs in most economies, scholarly research on BGs is still in its nascent stage. Although relevant research can be found in the drivers and outcomes of this phenomenon, there is a lack of an integrative framework that can help to understand the pathways that these companies typically follow in their internationalization. Furthermore, there are no established widely accepted measures to study international pathways of SMEs in a longitudinal setting (Rasmussen and Madsen 2002). These gaps in the literature limit our understanding of the internationalization behavior and process of BGs, that is, what are the various international pathways that BGs follow, why and with what outcomes?

The purpose of this chapter is twofold. First, a conceptual framework is developed based on earlier literature on international new ventures and born globals that delineates the key dimensions of an international pathway of BG companies. Second, an attempt is made to empirically examine the proposed framework in two Finnish software BGs. This study intends to advance the BG literature by laying a conceptual and empirical foundation for the future research on international pathways of BGs. While the chapter emphasizes conceptual thoughts, it also highlights the importance of longitudinal studies and focuses on the question 'what happens after the initial internationalization of software BGs?'. This is important because most previous BG operational analysis has been more or less cross-sectional by nature.

The remainder of this chapter is organized as follows. First, related literature streams pertaining to BGs and international new ventures are assessed. Second, the conceptual model is presented. Third, the research design and methodology of the study is described and the results of the empirical analysis are presented. Finally, the findings of the research and implications for theory development and managers in the software BG companies are discussed.

CONCEPTUAL FRAMEWORK: LIFE CYCLES AND MEASURES OF INTERNATIONAL PATHWAYS

A key concept in this chapter is an 'international pathway'. This term is used to describe 'stereotypical' internationalization processes or patterns of behavior which can be distinguished from one another. Along the lines of Mathews and Zander (2007, p. 398) the 'firm's internationalization is not through a strict sequence of 'stages', nor as a result of comparative static advantages, but through pathways that reflect entrepreneurial observation and strategic action'. BGs that deal with software and the conceptualization of their pathways are the focus here, and are analyzed in terms of their degree of internationalization (DOI) at various moments along the company life cycle. This is in line with Jones and Coviello (2005, p. 292) who note that 'internationalization may be captured as patterns of behaviour, formed by an accumulation of evidence manifest as events at specific reference points in time'. Consequently, it can be shown that a pathway consists of several phases or stages during which a company follows a certain behavioral pattern and these patterns can be linked to both internationalization and company life cycles. The activities and organizational structures of companies change and develop along the life cycle; activities refer to decision-making and operational processes, whereas structures refer to relationships, organizational forms and power relationships between different actors (Lester and Parnell 2008). Life-cycle models normally tend to have 3–5 stages or phases and in many cases, the internationalization process can also be linked to these evolutionary models. For software SMEs, internationalization may be seen as imperative, and BGs' internationalization life cycle, technology and product life

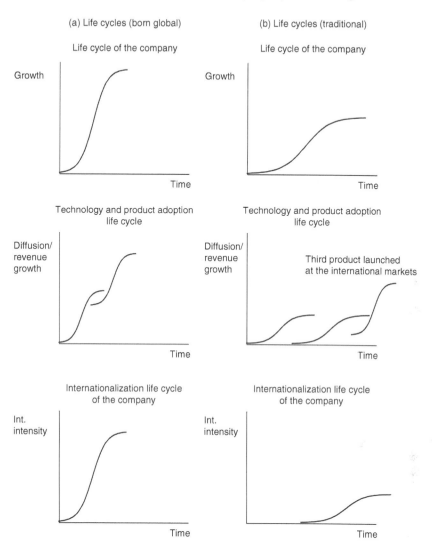

Source: Modified from Äijö et al. (2005).

Figure 14.1 Life-cycle differences between BG and 'traditional' companies

cycle, and general growth/company life cycle may follow the same temporal pattern. To illustrate this point on the importance of understanding the international pathways of BGs a comparison of the hypothetical life cycles of a BG and 'traditional' pathways are shown in Figure 14.1.

In the empirical part of the study, the internationalization life cycle of the case companies is divided into four main phases: pre-start (that is, time before the actual internationalization even before the actual founding of the company); start (that is, the phase when a company begins internationalization but it may not yet be systematic or not the core of the company's operations); growth (that is, when the internationalization is more or less the core of what the company does); and consolidation (that is, when internationalization has become 'business as usual' or there are some major changes in the industry the company operates in, such as mergers, acquisition of the company and so on).

The life-cycle approach to the internationalization process is also combined, that is, phases of internationalization, in the case of BGs. There are a number of measures which have been used to measure DOI and therefore to classify the phases of internationalization in the existing research. In his influential paper, Sullivan (1994) concludes that a company's DOI may be conceptualized using three dimensions: structural, financial, and psychological. These dimensions are important because they are related to the fact that organizing phenomena into classes or groups can be seen as a basis or a tool for systematic investigation and theory development (Hunt 1991). It is of importance that pathways can be seen as a classification scheme: companies could be classified into different internationalization paths based on their behavior and various criteria presented in the definitions related to the pathways. First, the classification is analyzed by taking the dimensions used in a well-known BG definition under scrutiny, that is, time, scale, and scope of internationalization. These three dimensions have, for example, been presented by Zahra and George (2002) in their review focusing on international entrepreneurship, and they can also be found in many other studies focusing on BGs and/or international new ventures.

Correspondingly, in line with a number of other scholars (for example, Oviatt and McDougall 1994; Knight and Cavusgil 2004; Rialph et al. 2005), this study agrees that BGs are early adopters of internationalization, that is, organizations that from or near founding, seek superior international business performance and sell their outputs in multiple countries. In this 'definition' temporal dimension ('early' and 'from or near founding') and scope dimension ('multiple countries') can be distinguished easily. The scale dimension can also be implicitly found ('sell', that is, sales). Various DOI measures and their linkages to scale and scope of internationalization can be found in Table 14.1. The information found in this table can be used as a key source to develop a conceptual framework.

Table 14.1   Exemplary indicators for the degree of internationalization

DOI indicator	Scale	Scope
No. of countries/regions where the company is present		No. of countries No. of regions
Foreign sales per total sales	FSTS (total, i.e. company level)	RSTS (regional sales to total sales) Country-level sales
Foreign assets per total assets	FATA (foreign assets to total assets)	Per region or country, e.g. RATA (regional assets to total assets)
Foreign employees to total employees	Ratio of foreign employees/all employees	Per region Per country
Existence, number of shares of subsidiaries or non-capital involvements in foreign countries	Operation modes used No. of operation modes	Per region Per country
Extent to which a company is owned and managed by non-nationals	Total/company level foreign ownership	Per region Per country; joint ventures in various countries
Share of foreign profits in total profits	Company level	Per region Per country
International experience of top managers	Company level	Per region Per country
Share of employees that spend a significant part of their time on international activities	Company level	Per region Per country

Sources: Indicators partially modified from Sullivan (1994); Rugman and Verbeke (2004, 2008); Äijö et al. (2005).

Temporal Dimension: Time as a BG Pathway Measure

Time is a hidden dimension in the internationalization footprint which makes it possible to study the actual internationalization pathway instead of static DOI (Kutschker et al. 1997). Implicitly those internationalization models which describe the traditional pathway (Johanson and Vahlne 1977) assume that internationalization activities develop incrementally in the course of time and companies establish themselves at domestic markets before entering international markets (Oesterle 1997). Although no exact timeframes have been suggested for companies following the traditional pathway, two main assumptions are implicit. First, there is a long gap between the founding of the company and subsequent internationalization, and second, it takes time for a company to reach high degrees of scale and scope of internationalization. In contrast, for BGs, 'precocity' (Zucchella et al. 2007), that is, the time lag between the founding of a company and the commencement of its international operations, is seen as a key measure by which these companies are distinguished from traditionally internationalizing SMEs. Another important measure is the speed of a company's subsequent international growth and development (Autio et al. 2000; Jones and Coviello 2005). Since BGs are the focus of this study, it is assumed that the temporal dimension is more or less preset and the focus is more on the other two dimensions, that is, scale and scope, which change and develop over time and along company and internationalization life cycles.

Scale of Internationalization of BG Companies

Scale of internationalization measures relates to the extent of a company's international operations. The 'classic' indicator of this dimension has been export intensity (foreign sales to total sales, FSTS; Sullivan 1994). This ratio has been used to study the links between multinationality and performance in a number of studies focusing especially on large multinational corporations (Contractor 2007).

For researchers focusing on traditional internationalization among SMEs, the need to define a certain specific cut-off point for export intensity has not been a decisive issue. It can be assumed implicitly, however, that if a company follows a traditional pathway and internationalizes at a slow pace, its FSTS ratio remains low during the early years of international operations. However, to make a distinction between different internationalization paths and to show that BGs are different from others, researchers focusing on rapidly internationalizing companies have utilized several FSTS ratios to be able to confirm their point. In this context, the most used is an FSTS ratio of 25 percent (see, for example, Knight, 1997; Knight and Cavusgil 2004). After more than a decade of research focusing on this issue it has been found, however, that in small countries, in which many knowledge-intensive SMEs could be expected to follow global niche strategies, this cut-off ratio is low. For example, Moen (2002) finds that the export intensity of newly established Norwegian companies is 65 percent on average. Consequently, in their more recent paper, Knight and Cavusgil (2004, p. 133) note that the 25 percent cut-off ratio for exports is 'somewhat arbitrary' and 'established in light of the exploratory goals of the research'. Following similar reasoning, the 25 percent exploratory cut-off is used here as well to select the cases, although other tighter criteria have also been recommended (for example, Gabrielsson et al. 2004, 2008). This is mainly because this ratio offers better comparability with earlier research and the companies focused on in the empirical part of the study are BGs. In any case, the increase in FSTS along the company life cycle is studied.

The fact that other indicators for the extent of internationalization could, and in many cases should, be used, such as foreign assets (for example, Rugman and Verbeke 2008), is acknowledged. Regarding the early phase of internationalization and foreign assets, however, it is clear that exporting is a dominant operation mode. In many cases SMEs cannot afford large foreign direct investments or are unlikely to make these for other reasons (for example, Dalli 1994; Brouthers and Nakos 2004). Operation modes may, however, change as the learning effects increase the capabilities of companies and when the resource and knowledge bases grow. The other interesting scale measure could be the personnel criterion, that is, how many foreigners work in the company and in what capacity, which can also be seen to reflect a psychological dimension, that is, psychic dispersion (Sullivan 1994).

Scope of Internationalization of BG Companies

In the extant literature there are two main market scope strategies, that is, market concentration – geographically narrow or limited scope – and market diversification – multiple markets or broad geographic scope (see for example, Ayal and Zif 1979; Yeoh 2004). However, in the case of scope and BG internationalization there are no exact definitions and most of the studies utilize different measures if they explicitly study the issue. The few studies that have examined the role of countries or regions in the internationalization process of small entrepreneurial knowledge-intensive companies include Reuber and Fischer (1997), Zahra et al. (2000), and McNaughton (2003).

If the issue is examined from the pathway perspective, it can be noted that a company following a traditional pathway should have a narrow market scope at the beginning of its international operations because of the lack of market knowledge (see, for example, the internationalization model presented by Johanson and Vahlne 1977), whereas one following a BG pathway must, by implication, start to operate in multiple countries on international markets almost from inception (see, for example, Oviatt and McDougall 1994).

It is essential to point out that measurement of scope is problematic as scope measures suffer from context specificity. For example, Reuber and Fischer (1997) focus on Canadian software companies and partly look at scope of operations by dividing export regions into three, that is, Canada, North America, and 'outside North America'. This type of operation would not be pertinent in a Finnish context, for example, as Finland has more neighboring countries and is a member of the European Union. One potential solution to this problem would be to state that BGs must have more markets than there are neighboring countries to be conceptually different from SMEs following a traditional internationalization pathway. There are also other suggestions: a company should operate in three main trade regions to be able to qualify as global (Ohmae 1985; Rugman and Verbeke 2004), or a company should receive more than 50 percent of sales outside its home continent (Luostarinen and Gabrielssson 2006), for example. Another aspect which could be mentioned is the scope of internationalization from the perspective of company functions. A simple measure could be the diversity of the nationalities of the company's employees.

Following this discussion of the earlier literature on BGs and international pathways, it is time to turn to a discussion of the research design.

RESEARCH DESIGN

The case study is a research strategy which focuses on the understanding of the dynamics either in multiple or single settings and it is particularly feasible when studying new areas (Eisenhardt 1989). Although the extant literature has covered BGs from many perspectives (see, for example, Rialp et al. 2005 for a review), the pathways of rapidly internationalizing SMEs are studied to a lesser extent. In particular, while the antecedents of BGs or international new ventures have been studied extensively, the dynamics of the international growth of these companies is less understood. For this reason the case method is employed for this study.

An exploratory multiple case study approach was adopted to analyze the international pathways of two Finnish software BGs. According to Pauwels and Matthyssen (2004, p. 128): '[multiple case study design] is built upon four pillars – theoretical sampling, triangulation, analytical pattern-matching logic and analytical generalization – and one roof – validation through juxtaposition and iteration'.

Regarding sampling, the software industry was chosen as a case industry because the software business is distinctive in the way that most companies operating in this field face several challenges at the same time.

These include, for example, constantly forming and growing new markets, short and rapidly changing product life cycles, existence of network externalities (that is, the value of the product often depends on the number of other users of the product) and the needs to harness emerging technologies and to adapt to collapsing markets (for example, Äijö et al. 2005). Thus, the software industry is a good example of an industry where rapid internationalization is often very important.

In the selection of cases, the general criteria on sampling SMEs used by, for example Bell et al. (2001) was followed:

- A company should be a current exporter and fulfill the requirements of BGs (that is, a company should have internationalized rapidly and operate in multiple countries, Knight and Cavusgil 1996, 2004).
- A company should employ less than 250 staff and be independent and indigenous; these criteria are in line with the EU definition for SMEs.

The selection of the companies was originally made in the spring of 2004. Both the chosen companies, which have been renamed 'Idle' and 'Trial', are BGs. However, they operated in different domains of software. Both of the companies were first analyzed independently regarding their international pathways, after which a cross-case analysis was conducted. In constructing the pathways of the case companies, multiple, both primary and secondary sources of information (that is, data triangulation, see, for example, Tellis 1997) have been utilized. These sources include longitudinal key informant interviews, Finnish business magazines, business press databases such as Talentum, presentations, company websites and so on. The key primary data collection phases were in 2004 (both), 2006 (Trial), 2008 (Idle), and 2010 (both). However, some primary data were collected for Idle in 1999 before the company as it is now was even established. In order to validate the findings and interpretations of the researchers, the assembled texts were reviewed by the managers of the focal companies who confirmed their accuracy. In the discussion section, an analytical generalization is the desired goal, presenting a model which describes international pathways of software BGs from the life-cycle perspective.

The international pathways of the two software BG case companies are discussed below. The intention is to analyze these companies to better understand their rapid internationalization, the scale and scope, and to reveal the critical incidents behind the processes. Concurrently, a framework for the following cross-case analysis will be employed.

Idle

Pre-start phase

Idle is a data-security company specializing in data-erasure applications. Its origins lie in one of the Finnish universities where both founding members were studying economics in the late 1990s. The founders of Idle actually established a predecessor of Idle in 1997 with a different business idea which proved to be less successful. This company eventually changed its name to Idle in 2000. The current product idea for Idle came from newspapers: there was discussion in the Finnish media in 1998 when computers from a hospital had been found in a dumping place although they still contained classified information about patients. A solution had to be found to remove all confidential information, and Idle invented a software program for recycling the computers efficiently. The idea was to provide solutions that enabled safe, economical, and ecological reusability.

Even before launching the first version of the product in 1999, the founders started looking for further markets abroad. The first proactive push for internationalization was participation at trade fairs from the beginning, even before the product was completely finalized. The managing director of Idle recalls: 'internationalization started in 1999 even before we had the product. I was, for example, in Amsterdam in 1999 selling the product which did not exist with "slideware" to the Dutch'. The reasons for internationalizing the company's operations were mostly rational, such as enabling growth, sharing the risk, and being geared up for international competition. The true growth potential was seen to be in international markets: in Germany, for example, the potential market was estimated to be 20 times larger than in Finland. Contacts with potential international customers were also made indirectly, through existing customers, and eventually one rather large international deal was sealed as early as 1999. Consequently, the internationalization occurred almost simultaneously with the actual founding of the company. Because of this, it is clear that concerning the temporal dimension, Idle can be seen as a BG company. Next the scale and scope of the internationalization of Idle along the life cycle of the company will be elaborated.

Start phase

In 2000, the company was renamed 'Idle'. It had three workers, a turnover of €400,000 and 4 percent of its sales came from international markets; 100,000 licenses were sold during the first one and a half years. In the same year, the company both received external funding and closed one of the biggest deals in its history with one of the world's leading investment bankers. This client led the company to have customers in 23 countries and its reference value was substantial for Idle. These events helped the financing of its international operations and new salespeople were recruited. In 2001, the company had 12 employees and 41 percent of the sales came from abroad. However, as the sales in general did not grow that rapidly, the financial result was negative during that year, and eventually Idle had to scale down its own sales force and market presence. A partnership strategy and a more detailed market strategy were developed. The key was to focus on the markets which were seen as having the most potential and direct the resources to those markets.

Although their experience on the Finnish markets and early leads from abroad gave some signals of the business potential, the managers realized that every country had its own business culture and data-erasure regulations, and experiences, as such, could not be replicated. In spite of the diversity, the basics were assumed to be the same in European countries, and countries similar to Finland were selected as key target markets. The focal market scope at the time was regional. This meant that Scandinavia (especially Sweden) and northern Europe (particularly the UK, Germany, and the Benelux countries) were selected as targets. Other countries were not excluded, but because of the limited resources of the company, the key emphasis was focused on these countries. The strategy was dynamic: having selected the target markets and the key customer groups, the management focused on creating well-functioning partnerships with the local dealers.

The partner selection proceeded quite quickly and in 2002, Idle managed to nearly eliminate losses. Nevertheless, closer cooperation with partners revealed various challenges, and in some cases, the first partner in the target market was dropped for a more effective or a more reliable one. In spite of these problems, Idle can be seen as entering the major growth phase since 2002.

Growth phase

Idle has been growing for years. There have, however been major changes in its growth strategy based on both internal and external reasons. Consequently, the growth phase of the company is divided into sub-phases in the following analysis to illustrate changes in patterns of behavior during the course of Idle's internationalization.

Early growth phase   After successful operations in its first target countries, and very rapid growth of sales, the company expanded its operations into several regions – partly because of unsolicited orders and inquiries from prospective large customers. In 2003, the company had sold a total of a million licenses, its turnover was almost €800,000 and the share of exports reached approximately 69 percent. Since 2003, Idle has also been a profit-making enterprise. The business model focused on the use of external partners, and although the turnover grew, the number of employees stayed limited. In some markets, such as Japan, Idle was the original equipment manufacturer (OEM) and the products were sold under its partners' name. In 2004, the turnover was almost €1 million of which 75 percent came from abroad, but there were still only 13 employees. The objective was to increase Idle's market share globally with the help of its local partners. However, to be able to improve the standard of the service and to be able to build the brand, the company started to develop some of the partnerships into franchise operations.

Second phase of international growth   In 2005, a clear and detailed strategy was developed for the selected market areas (Scandinavia, Germany, the UK, Benelux, Japan, and the US). The key aspect was, as mentioned before, the principal partner development in each market area with one franchising partner and a few additional other partners to make the situation competitive. The growth strategy was supported by the launch of the new product generation which had more extensive features. More detailed customer segmentation was also conducted as markets had become more competitive. Since 2006, the company has managed its international operations in a more active manner. This has meant more strategic international partnership management and better support for partners. During the last two years, Idle again changed its business model.

Third phase of international growth   Since 2009, the target has been to have full control of operations in the key markets. Idle has rapidly established several subsidiaries in Germany, Japan, the UK, the US, France, Australia, and Sweden, and more subsidiaries are being planned. This has meant that the number of employees has increased to 37 in the Finnish parent company alone. The whole Idle group consisted of 70 employees by the end of 2009, approximately half of them foreigners. The scope of nationalities was wide: there were employees from 14 different countries. Almost all the employees deal with international business issues. In addition to the new subsidiaries, the company still has an extensive partner network in more than 20 countries. Strategy is now determined by the key personnel; the external investor was bought out in 2010.

Regarding the scope of internationalization, the US has approximately 20 percent of the turnover, Germany, Japan, and the UK each make up 15 percent. The turnover comes from numbers, as the single license payments gained from different customers around the globe are rather small. In 2009, the turnover of the parent company was €3.4 million (of which approximately 90 percent came from foreign markets) and the whole group's sales were approximately €6.5 million. The company believes it is still in the growth phase, and by taking more control of the sales and marketing operations, it sees opportunities for winning more customers from the growing market, which consists of many small players. Idle sees itself as the most international player in the niche segment it operates in and has ambitious growth objectives. If there were a consolidation in the industry in the future, the aim of the company would to be a proactive operator in this development.

Trial

Pre-start phase

Trial is a company specializing in electronic patient reported outcomes solutions (electronic patient diaries and wireless data collection solutions) for the life-sciences industry. The company was officially established in August of 2000 in Helsinki, although the founders, who had experience from the telecom and medical industries and who studied at the same Finnish university, had some operations going in 1999. Its market segment comprises a very narrow niche, which it has managed to conquer in a very short time with an innovative product. The core benefit for customers was clear: clinical test result reporting, which includes lots of data, had mostly been done on paper, and Trial's process innovation shortens the time needed, diminishes costs, and enhances quality. Things moved quickly: within three months of its founding, Trial had its first product ready and soon had three customers and external funding from venture capitalists. The founders' network helped the company to attract capital. With this first round of financing, the company was able to speed up its product development, sales and internationalization. The rapid international expansion was seen as a key target from day one. One of the founders said in an interview that '[Trial] was built from the beginning with the intention of creating an international firm instead of a firm which goes abroad country after country. We sell to global customers, and the aim was to target especially top 10 pharmaceutical companies which are all global companies'. Consequently, as early as 2002, almost all revenues came from abroad. Since then all the customers have been international and Trial clearly fulfill's criteria common to BG enterprises.

Start phase

Since the company was new and the market was global, Trial needed to develop an international sales strategy. From day one, Trial has focused on direct sales for two main reasons. First, a partnership strategy was not seen as effective: the product was new; potential partners did not exist or have trust in the concept; and/or it also cannibalized the business of earlier operators in this segment. The incumbents would not have had an incentive to sell the product as there was nothing to integrate, for example. Second, as the number of operators in the selected principal target market (that is, the largest pharmaceutical companies in the world) was small, the customer segment was seen as clear and reachable using its own sales-people. Trial management decided that the sales strategy needed to be aggressive and local presence was a necessity.

By the end of 2000, Trial had established a sales office in Sweden and in the US. The selection criteria for these two locations are different. Sweden was selected because it was seen as an easy market to increase turnover and learn skills needed for further successful international operations. The US was selected as the target market based on the market potential: 90 percent of the investments for clinical trials are made in company headquarters and 90 percent of the large pharmaceutical companies are headquartered in the US.

Growth phase
In the case of Trial, it is not that easy to distinguish different sub-patterns within the growth phase: the company is a growing BG and its strategy has followed the key principles drawn in the beginning. Some interesting minor changes in patterns of behavior can be noted, however.

Early growth   The strategic decisions regarding growth and interna-tionalization and their actual implementation convinced external inves-tors. In 2001, Trial received a second round of external financing and established an office in the Czech Republic. Money was also invested in customer service development in the key markets. In 2001, for example, Trial already employed approximately 30 people. Their internationaliza-tion strategy was also supported by introducing experienced foreign board members to provide guidance. At the end of 2002, turnover was almost €3 million, and the company had approximately 60 employees, with 20–30 based in the US. Actual operative locations/offices were in Boston and San Diego, Helsinki, Dusseldorf, Stockholm, and London.

The internationalization strategy was implemented further with the third round of financing at the end of 2002, when the company received €6 million. Further new funding was received to develop a new product generation in 2003. The launch of the new product coincided with the establishment of a new American CEO, and other new international recruitments followed. From 2003 on, four out of seven members of the management team have been foreigners because Finns were seen to not have enough experience in the customer industry. In addition, from the customer relationship management perspective, it was seen as important to locate people close to customers.

Second phase of international growth   Early venture capital was used to build infrastructure; now the company used external funding mostly to maintain its presence and push forward in selected market areas. In 2004, Trial already had approximately 120 employees. However, some adjustments were made in 2005 when the company decided to rearrange its operations. Most of the European operations were moved to the UK since most of the European customers are headquartered there. By 2006, only R&D and the legal headquarters were still in Finland; everything else was done either in the US or in the UK to serve approximately 50 customers located mostly in four geographical areas: the UK, the US East Coast (New Jersey, Pennsylvania), the US West Coast (biotech cluster), and Switzerland. Based on experience gained since its inception, the company did not see any benefit in having a large geographical coverage. Restructuring was seen as an effective tool to increase the presence in the US and UK markets. The American market has always been the key market for Trial, making up 70 percent of the revenues. Europe accounts for 30 percent – the number of countries is harder to distinguish as decisions are made at the regional level. Trial's solutions, however, are currently used in more than 300 clinical trials in 68 languages and in more than 60 countries.

This decision meant that the scope of internationalization was actually scaled down based on some classic criteria for the degree of internationalization (for example, having assets in several countries). However, based on most criteria, the scale and the scope of Trial's internationalization have steadily increased. Since 2006, for example, six out of seven management team members have been foreigners, and headquarters have been moved to the US. There are approximately 120 employees of whom 10 are Finnish, 50 American, 50 British, and an additional 10 employees who are based either in London or in the US. Most of the top 20 pharmaceutical companies are Trial's customers; all the revenues (approximately €20 million) in 2009 came from foreign markets.

The company has grown continuously with the exception of two more or less stable years in 2004–05 when revenues were approximately €8 million annually. This slowdown can partly be explained by the product security debate which involved the entire pharmaceutical industry. This development was only temporary: Trial's second US-based CEO started in 2006, and after that, sales growth has been rapid and followed the forecasts. The company is still in the growth phase; it is a global leader in its field and has succeeded in the US market, which has been difficult for many Finnish start-ups. It can be expected that, in the future, when the consolidation phase is reached, investors will see a good return for the €25 million they have invested in the company.

Cross-case Analysis

The previous subsections presented two internationalization cases of Finnish software BGs. The key internationalization dimensions and the critical incidents leading the companies to proceed further along the internationalization and company life cycle are summarized in Table 14.2.

Regarding the pre-start phase before the actual internationalization, the founders of both companies had international vision and a global mindset which can be seen as key determinants for the occurrence of BGs (Madsen and Servais 1997; Nummela et al. 2004; Gabrielsson et al. 2008). Both Idle and Trial saw that the home market was too small and understood the potential of internationalization. They also spent money and resources on developing their products in the early phases when there was no direct competition. However, there are some differences: Idle was formed on the basis of the individual skills of the founders who were looking for various product ideas before succeeding; whereas Trial was formed on the basis of professional and business experience which led the founders to realize the potential of creating superior customer benefits in their chosen segment. Trial was also able to utilize its business connections and networks (for example, Crick and Spence 2005) to gain external funding early on and recruit senior external advisors to the company board to provide guidance. This enabled the company to push rapidly into international markets with its own sales force.

Idle also received external funding to provide resources for internationalization after the large reference customer became the company's client. However, as the company selected its method of growing with partners, its strategy was a little different. Idle used much less external funding than Trial to implement its strategy. When Trial established mainly its own sales offices during the early phases of international growth, Idle developed sales partnerships in various locations. It can be noted, however, that for Trial, direct sales were a much easier choice since its target segment was and is a very narrow niche. The original operational strategy is still followed with only slight adjustments; in addition, new recruitments have been made to provide more implementation skills. In contrast, Idle has changed its 'business model', making it much easier for the company to distinguish several sub-patterns in its internationalization pathway. Consequently, although Idle is a BG, it has been using several marketing and sales channel strategies for 10 years.

Both companies are still growing and both markets are still growing. Consequently, both Idle and Trial are still in the growth phase. However, as Idle's potential market and segments are much wider than Trial's, it seems to be further away from consolidation.

DISCUSSION AND CONCLUSIONS

In this chapter, we aimed to improve the understanding of the international pathways of BGs within a highly interesting and volatile software sector. To this end, a framework incorporating both the company life cycle and DOI measurements was used to study the internationalization pathways and patterns of behavior. Based on this, the classic BG measures used should be developed (a) using longitudinal (rather than cross-sectional data) and (b) in more detail by incorporating more sub-dimensions into the scale and scope measures. One motive behind this chapter was also the current disarray in conceptualization and operationalization of BGs, which makes comparison of various studies difficult. Consequently, a conceptual model based on several indicators of DOI was presented. If even the scale and scope of internationalization along the internationalization process could be selected and measured, it would be possible to analyze the internationalization process of rapidly internationalizing SMEs in a more detailed and rigorous manner.

Consequently, by utilizing longitudinal data, the scale and scope of the internationalization process of two Finnish software BGs was studied. The results from these two case studies show that although the timeframe for internationalization has been quite short for both companies, and internationalization has occurred almost in parallel with the founding of the companies, it is still possible to distinguish phases in the internationalization process and analyze critical incidents which enable these companies to move further towards deeper internationalization.

Extant literature has mostly ignored the fact that BGs experience gradually increasing commitment to foreign markets; only the length of the time span and the phases/stages are shorter than in companies following the traditional internationalization pathway through stages. There are some exceptions to this view, however. Hashai and Almor (2004), Crick and Spence (2005), and Gabrielsson et al. (2008) have noted the existence of gradual experience building even in rapid internationalization. Consequently, it is not only 'leapfrogging' (Madsen and Servais 1997) the stages that makes internationalization rapid; having a global vision and mindset, building a strategy to fit this mindset and in some cases, utilizing more resources and possessing and acquiring more skills to implement

Table 14.2 Cross-case analysis: company and international life cycles of Idle and Trial

	Idle	Trial
Pre-start	(1997–)1999 • Continuous search for innovation • 3rd product idea of the founders succeeds • Internationalization part of the plans even before the product was ready	(1999–)2000 • Vision of the global company • Processual innovation, well-defined customer segment • Connections to venture capitalists (VCs): 1st round of financing provided means for internationalization
Start	2000–2001 Scale: FSTS app. 41% Scope: customers in 23 countries, although regional focus mostly in Europe • Own sales to a few early international customers • Image and corporate branding • Venture capital to start the major push for international markets • Unsolicited order from major global customer provided a key reference • Leads followed to various places such as Hong Kong and Hungary	2001–2002 Scale: FSTS: after 2001 in practise almost 100%, 1/3 of the staff in the US Scope: some variation but in the end there were offices in the US, Finland, Sweden, Germany, and the UK; 9/20 top pharmaceutical companies as customers; customers' research sites in 31 countries • Commitment, building the presence and infrastructure on the key markets (especially in the US) • Clear customer benefit, aggressive sales • 2nd–3rd round of financing received which enabled a more ambitious future growth strategy
Growth	Early growth: 2002–2004 Scale: FSTS 69–75% Scope: more focused but also other regions than Europe included (e.g. Japan) • Growth through networks • Many customers around the globe but more focused target market strategy than before;	Early growth: 2003–2005 Scale: FSTS app. 100% Scope: Revenue app. 50% Europe and 50% USA, 13/20 top pharmaceutical companies as customers; customers' research sites in 42 countries • US markets started to take off • New product

• New US-based foreign CEO and recruiting

international operations not systematic, in some markets OEM, in most different partner types

Second growth phase: 2005–2008
Scale: FSTS 83–90%
Scope: focal areas: Europe, Japan and USA
• Launch of new product generation
• Principal partners (franchising) and others to make situation competitive; strategic partnership management

Third growth phase: 2009–
Scale: FSTS app. 90%, subsidiaries in key markets
Scope: Revenue: USA app. 20%, Germany app. 15%, Japan app. 15%, UK app. 15%, subsidiaries in key markets
• Focus on most profitable customers, more emphasis on certain markets and segments
• Control and more commitment: global network of own offices complemented by sales affiliates
• VC bought out from the company

Time ?
• Potential future incidents: mergers and acquisitions which would increase both the scale and scope

Second growth phase: 2006-
Scale: FSTS 100%
Scope: Revenue app. 30% Europe and 70% US, customers' research sites in more than 60 countries, offices in the US, the UK, and Finland
• New foreign CEO and more international outlook, e.g. headquarters moved to the US, 6/7 management team members foreign
• Key locations strengthened (UK and US); sales people travel from these locations

Consolidation

Time ?
• Potential future incidents: exit of financiers: IPO, merger or acquisition

the selected strategy also shortens some of the phases significantly. It is of great importance to study the phases/stages even if the company's life cycle is 'condensed' to be able to understand how companies become BGs and how this 'degree of born-globalness' (Kuivalainen et al. 2007) develops further. We hope that this chapter, with its two software BG case studies, will contribute to this discussion. By utilizing the life-cycle concept in addition to the traditional internationalization stages approach, the model may be more accessible to practicing managers.

NOTE

*   The authors wish to thank Jani Lindqvist, Hanna Hanninen, and Mika Ruokonen for their help in the data collection and Toivo Äijö for his help in the process of developing the ideas behind this chapter.

REFERENCES

Äijö, T., O. Kuivalainen, S. Saarenketo, J. Lindqvist and H. Hanninen (2005), *Internationalization Handbook for the Software Business*, Espoo, Finland: Centre of Expertise for Software Product Business.

Autio, E., H.J. Sapienza and J.G. Almeida (2000), 'Effects of age at entry, knowledge intensity, and imitability on international growth', *Academy of Management Journal*, **43**(5), 909–24.

Ayal, I. and J. Zif (1979), 'Marketing expansion strategies in multinational marketing', *Journal of Marketing*, **43** (Spring), 84–94.

Bell, J., R. McNaughton and S. Young (2001), 'Born-again global' firms – an extension to the "born global" phenomenon', *Journal of International Management*, **7**(3), 173–89.

Brouthers, K.D. and G. Nakos (2004), 'SME entry mode choice and performance: a transaction cost perspective', *Entrepreneurship: Theory and Practice*, **28**(3), 229–47.

Contractor, F.J. (2007), 'Is international business good for companies? The evolutionary or multi-stage theory of internationalization vs. the transaction cost perspective', *Management International Review*, **47**(3), 453–75.

Crick, D. and M. Spence (2005), 'The internationalisation of "high performing" UK high-tech SMEs: a study of planned and unplanned strategies', *International Business Review*, **14**, 167–85.

Dalli, D. (1994), 'The exporting process: the evolution of small and medium-sized firms towards internationalization', *Advances in International Marketing*, **6**, 107–15.

Eisenhardt, K.M. (1989), 'Building theories from case study research', *Academy of Management Review*, **14**(4), 532–50.

Gabrielsson, M., M. Kirpalani, P. Dimitratos, C.A. Solberg and A. Zucchella (2008), 'Born globals: propositions to help advance the theory', *International Business Review*, **17**(4), 385–401.

Gabrielsson, M., V. Sasi and J. Darling (2004), 'Finance strategies of rapidly-growing Finnish SMEs: born internationals and born globals', *European Business Review*, **16**(6), 590–604.

Hashai, N. and T. Almor (2004), 'Gradually internationalizing "born global" firms: an oxymoron?', *International Business Review*, **13**(4), 465–83.

Hunt, S. D. (1991), *Modern Marketing Theory, Critical Issues in the Philosophy of Marketing Science*, Cincinnati, OH: South-Western Publishing.

Johanson, J. and J.-E. Vahlne (1977), 'The internationalization process of the firm', *Journal of International Business Studies*, **8**(1), 23–32.

Johanson, J. and J.-E. Vahlne (1990), 'The mechanism of internationalization', *International Marketing Review*, **7**(4), 11–24.

Jones, M.V. and N.E. Coviello (2005), 'Internationalisation: conceptualising an entrepreneurial process of behaviour in time', *Journal of International Business Studies*, **36**(3), 284–303.

Knight, G.A. (1997), 'Emerging paradigm for international marketing: the born-global firm', Doctoral dissertation, Michigan State University, East Lansing, MI.

Knight, G. and S.T. Cavusgil (1996), 'The born global firm: a challenge to traditional internationalization theory', in Cavusgil (ed.), *Advances in International Marketing*, Vol. 8, Bingley, UK: Emerald Group Publishing, pp. 11–26.

Knight, G.A. and S.T. Cavusgil (2004), 'Innovation, organizational capabilities, and the born-global firm', *Journal of International Business Studies*, **35**(2), 124–41.

Kuivalainen, O., S. Sundqvist and P. Servais (2007), 'firms' degree of born-globalness, international entrepreneurial orientation and export performance', *Journal of World Business*, **42**(3), 253–67.

Kutschker, M., I. Bäurle and S. Schmid (1997), 'International evolution, international episodes, and international epochs – implications for managing internationalization', *Management International Review*, **37** (Special Issue 2), 101–24.

Lester, D. and J.A. Parnell (2008), 'Firm size and environmental scanning pursuits across organizational life cycle stages', *Journal of Small Business and Enterprise Development*, **15**(3), 540–54.

Luostarinen, R. and M. Gabrielsson (2006), 'Globalization and marketing strategies of born globals in SMOPECs', *Thunderbird International Business Review*, **48**(6), 773–801.

Madsen, T.K. and P. Servais (1997), 'The internationalization of born globals: an evolutionary process?', *International Business Review*, **6**(6), 561–83.

Mathews, J.A. and I. Zander (2007), 'The international entrepreneurial dynamics of accelerated internationalization', *Journal of International Business Studies*, **38**(3), 387–403.

McNaughton, R.B. (2003), 'The number of export markets that a firm serves: process models versus the born-global phenomenon', *Journal of International Entrepreneurship*, **1**(3), 297–311.

Moen, Ø. (2002), 'The born globals – a new generation of small European exporters', *International Marketing Review*, **19**(2), 156–75.

Nummela, N., S. Saarenketo and K. Puumalainen (2004), 'A global mindset – a prerequisite for successful internationalization?', *Canadian Journal of Administrative Sciences*, **21**(1), 51–64.

Oesterle, M.-J. (1997), 'Time span until internationalization: foreign market entry as a built-in mechanism of innovation', *Management International Review*, **37**(2), 125–49.

Ohmae, Kenichi (1985), *Triad Power: The Coming Shape of Global Competition*, New York: Free Press.

Oviatt, B.M. and P.P. McDougall (1994), 'Toward a theory of international new ventures', *Journal of International Business Studies*, **25**(1), 45–64.

Pauwels, Pieter and Paul Matthyssen (2004), 'The architecture of multiple case study research in international business', in Rebecca Marschan-Piekkari and Catherine Welch (eds), *Handbook of Qualitative Research Methods for International Business*, Cheltenham, UK and Northampton, MA, USA: Edward Elgar, pp. 125–43.

Rasmussen, E.S. and T.K. Madsen (2002), 'The born global concept', paper presented at the 28th EIBA conference, Athens, 8–10 December.

Reuber, A.R. and E. Fischer (1997), 'The influence of the management team's international experience on the internationalization behaviors of SMEs', *Journal of International Business Studies*, **28**(4), 807–25.

Rialp, A., J. Rialp and G.A. Knight (2005), 'The phenomenon of early internationalizing firms: what do we know after a decade (1993–2003) of scientific inquiry?', *International Business Review*, **14**(2), 147–66.

Rugman, A.M. and A. Verbeke (2004), 'A perspective on regional and global strategies of multinational enterprises', *Journal of International Business Studies*, **35**, 3–18.

Rugman, A. and A. Verbeke (2008), 'A new perspective on the regional and global strategies of multinational services', *Management International Review*, **48**(4), 397–411.

Sullivan, D. (1994), 'Measuring the degree of internationalization of a firm', *Journal of International Business Studies*, **25**, 325–42.

Tellis, W. (1997), 'Application of a case study methodology', *The Qualitative Report*, **3**(3), available at: http://www.nova.edu/ssss/QR/QR3-3/tellis2.html, (accessed 15 November 2005).

Yeoh, P.-L. (2004), 'International learning: antecedents and performance implications among newly internationalizing companies in an exporting context', *International Marketing Review*, **21**(4/5), 511–35.

Yip, G.S. (1995), Total Global Strategy: Managing for Worldwide Competitive Advantage, Englewood Cliffs, NJ: Prentice-Hall.

Zahra, Shaker A. and Gerard George (2002), 'International entrepreneurship: the current status of the field and future research agenda', in Michael A. Hitt, R. Duane Ireland, S. Michael Camp and Donald L. Sexton (eds), *Strategic Entrepreneurship: Creating an Integrated Mindset*, Oxford: Blackwell, pp. 255–88.

Zahra, S.A., D.R. Ireland and M.A. Hitt (2000), 'International expansion by new venture firms: international diversity, mode of market entry, technological learning and performance', *Academy of Management Journal*, **43**(5), 925–50.

Zucchella, A., S. Danicolai and G. Palamara (2007), 'The drivers of the early internationalization of the firm', *Journal of World Business*, **42**(3), 268–80.

15 Characteristics of born global industries: the birth of offshore renewables
Nicolai Løvdal and Arild Aspelund

INTRODUCTION

Raymond Vernon's (1966) product life cycle theory of trade has been central to the way that scholars have depicted internationalization of industries. By following the life cycle of a product, Vernon explains how the associated industries internationalize as a result of the actors' quest for new markets and reaction towards increased competition. Vernon's theory is cited and explained in just about every student textbook on international business and has provided clear and relevant guidelines for both international managers and policy makers on how industries gradually globalize as product offers, technologies, organizations, and competition mature.

Vernon's theory is paralleled with how the internationalization of firms has traditionally been viewed. Developed slightly later, the stage models of internationalization became the reigning paradigm of firm internationalization (Andersen 1993). The stage models depict internationalization of firms as a slow and gradual process that is initiated only after domestic maturation. They are frequently referred to as the 'Uppsala internationalization model' and the 'innovation-related model' (ibid.) depending on whether they view firm internationalization to be a learning process or an organizational change process (Aspelund and Madsen 2009). The stage models have also dominated the textbooks on firm internationalization until recently, and have provided managers and policy makers with advice on how to internationalize ventures and industries after domestic maturation.

However, the validity of the stage models has been increasingly challenged as we have seen a broad and growing literature suggesting that organizations to a lesser degree follow a gradual internationalization pattern (Rialp et al. 2005; Zahra, 2005; Aspelund et al. 2007). Some seminal studies in the early 1990s drew attention to firms that internationalized rapidly and extensively soon after inception. They established two concepts: born global firms (Rennie 1993); and international new ventures (McDougall et al. 1994; Oviatt and McDougall 1994) and gave rise to international entrepreneurship as a field of research that ultimately challenged the fundamental assertion that internationalization happens only slowly and after domestic maturation.

Scholars have argued that immediate and extensive internationalization of individual firms is possible due to favorable international market trends that are driving globalization (Knight and Cavusgil 1996; Madsen and Servais 1997). There are now also signs that even whole industries seem to violate the expectation of gradual internationalization as Vernon advocates. They become 'born global industries' – industries with globally integrated operations from the outset.

This study presents three typical examples of born global industries (BGIs) and seeks to answer the questions of what characterizes a BGI and which factors lead to their early internationalization. In order to answer these questions a descriptive study of three BGIs within the offshore renewable energy sector – wind, wave, and tidal – is analyzed. The three industries are on approximately the same level of market maturity (market introduction phase), but already highly internationalized. In order to investigate the industries, a triangulation method was used to integrate different information sources and analytic approaches of both a qualitative and quantitative nature to understand the dynamics of global industry establishment.

THEORY

Inspired by the seminal work of Everett Rogers (1962) on diffusion of innovations, many researchers have used the metaphor 'life cycle' to explain different characteristics of products as they evolve over time (Rink and Swan 1979). Different numbers and characteristics of phases are suggested in the literature, but the most common seems to be a four-stage cycle, introduction, growth, maturity, and decline (see Figure 15.1). Product life-cycle theories have also led to studies where product evolution is used as a proxy to describe industry evolution. A central research question has been what effects the industry/product life cycle has on firms. Central issues such as survival rates (Agarwal, et al. 2002), as well as business strategies and performance (Anderson 1984) seems to depend on the industry phase.

Vernon (1966) built on the life-cycle theory when he published his well-cited paper about international investment and international trade. Vernon's work became a major contribution to the field of international business as he explained how the nature of international business changed with the life cycle of the industry. He concluded that industries interna-

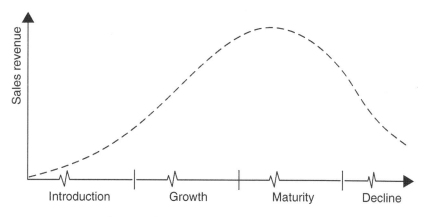

Figure 15.1 Product market life cycle

tionalize predominantly in the mature phase as competition intensified and the actors seek international markets to realize economies of scale and simultaneously look for cost reductions through production in low-cost countries.

Vernon's theory of internationalization in the mature phase fits well with what was about to become the reigning paradigm in firm internationalization – the Uppsala internationalization model (Johanson and Wiedersheim-Paul 1975; Johanson and Vahlne 1977, 1990). The Uppsala model is a stage model that depicts the internationalization pattern of a firm as a slow and incremental process where the firm spreads its activities internationally like 'rings in the water' (Madsen and Servais 1997). The model assumes firms to be risk averse, but growth seeking, and, therefore, internationalize slowly because they need to internalize experimental market knowledge from foreign markets before they fully commit firm resources abroad. Hence, based on Vernon (1966) the Uppsala scholars agreed that internationalization should predominantly happen in the *maturity* phase of an industry.

In the early 1990s, several studies were published that empirically challenged the stage models. Rennie (1993) showed that the percentage of Australian firms that internationalized right after inception was really quite high, labeling them 'born global firms'. A few years later, McDougall et al. (1994) added more empirical evidence to the phenomenon, and Oviatt and McDougall (1994) even proposed an alternative theoretical model based on transaction cost theory, entrepreneurship theory, and international business theory to explain their existence[1]. This model gave birth to the research field of international entrepreneurship (IE) and inspired a broad range of related research (for recent reviews, see Rialp et al. 2005; Zahra 2005; Aspelund et al. 2007; and Keupp and Gassmann 2009). This stream of research is interesting for the current theme because it has produced several studies that have focused on the characteristics of industries that have a tendency to give birth to born global firms.

An early study that endeavored to answer this question was Jolly et al. (1992). The authors found that born global firms, or 'global start-ups' as they called them, tended to occur in industries that went through a techno-logical shift that disrupted the dominance of the incumbents and opened the industry for fast-moving, rapidly internationalizing new ventures (INVs). One of the cases Jolly et al. studied was Logitech. Logitech used the opportunity that arose with the emerging computer peripherals market to launch a global start-up. This global market opportunity was inciden-tally a direct consequence of two other newly established firms, Microsoft and Apple, which opened the global home computer market.

Another study that focuses on internationalization in different industry contexts is Andersson (2004), who finds that internationalization strate-gies are different in growth industries and mature industries. He concludes that firms with early internationalization in growth industries are more dependent on their internal resources than on external market informa-tion. This finding is in line with what Vernon would argue, but moves the timeline for internationalization to an earlier phase.

The latter is also the case for a recent study by Fernhaber et al. (2007), who develop several propositions on the relationships between industry characteristics and the creation of INVs. Like Vernon, they propose that industry evolution has a direct effect on the tendency to nurture INVs and a moderating effect on how the industry characteristics – knowledge inten-sity, local industry internationalization, and global integration – affect the creation of INV. Fernhaber et al. (2007, p. 535) conclude that 'While tra-ditional internationalization theory, which is based on existing and mature firms, suggests firms internationalize in the mature stage of an industry, our work shows why new ventures, instead, tend to internationalize during the growth stage of an industry'. Hence, judging by the INV literature, internationalization should mainly take place in the *growth* phase of an industry.

Fernhaber et al. claim that industry evolution is the most influential industry factor affecting new venture internationalization, both directly and as a moderating factor. However, they realize the complexity of this proposition as they also note, 'An interesting observation is that while, in general, new ventures are argued to internationalize in the growth stage of an industry, it is the maturity of an industry that enhances, or positively moderates, these relationships' (p.535).

While acknowledging the various evolutionary life-cycle patterns in different industries (Rink and Swan 1979; Birkinshaw, et al. 1995), the recent understandings that the IE literature has provided on firm internationalization is inspiring, and there is evidence that the birth of GIBs are driven by born global firms (Løvdal and Aspelund 2010). However, the question is not what industry characteristics give rise to born global firms as previous literature has addressed, but rather the characteristics of industries that are born global. If the research does not find that the internationalization of firms is bounded by slow managerial processes to internationalize, why should it be expected that industries which in large part consist of firms, are bounded by the same processes?

A BGI is defined here as an industry with global integrated operations in the introduction phase of its life cycle. As will be shown, the offshore renewable energy industry fits this definition, but there is no reason to suggest that this industry is unique (it has already been suggested that the global home PC market and the PC peripherals market were similar), but it is an industry that is emerging and there is the opportunity to study it as it develops. In this study the offshore renewable energy industry is investigated in order to answer the question of what characterizes a BGI and which factors lead to early internationalization.

METHOD

This study may be described as a case study with multiple embedded cases (wind, wave, and tidal) and multiple units of analysis, industry context, and firm and manager/entrepreneur levels (Yin 2003). As suggested by Rialp et al. (2005), the study has triangulated qualitative and quantitative methods and data to ensure a rigorous examination of the internationalization processes (Gibbert 2008). The triangulation strategy adds solidity to the study because data can be accumulated and the reliability and quality of case data from different information sources is assured, and it also increases the interpretation quality from different perspectives (Jick 1979).

The study of an emerging international industry is challenging since important industry structures such as integrated value chains and sales channels are changing rapidly. Evolutionary economists often describe the early phases of an industry as dominated by start-ups with high-technology innovation capability that are able to move rapidly to secure strategic resources (Agarwal et al. 2002). Since the focus is more on technology innovations than process innovation, the business activities are often connected to resource leveraging and partnering rather than international sales (Jones 2001; Coviello 2006; Coviello and Cox 2007). Hence, to properly describe such an industry it is not sufficient to study its outputs.

To get a valid picture, the traditional focus on internal global integration in multinational companies (Hout et al. 1982; Kobrin 1991) must be changed to a broader focus where partners, investors, and other resource providers are involved. This is in line with suggestions from, for example, Bartlett and Ghoshal (1998). In order to meet this challenge the industry should be investigated on multiple levels – the industry context level, the firm level, and the managerial/entrepreneur level.

The quantitative data were gathered through a global survey sent in 2007, targeted at all the commercial actors developing technologies to harness wave or tidal energy. The companies were identified by an assessment of the International Energy Agency list (IEA 2006), internet searching, and personal networking. Finally, the survey was sent to 90 companies worldwide. Telephone contact was made at the manager level before sending the Web survey to personal e-mail addresses. Fifty companies answered the survey with sufficient quality, which gives a response rate of 56 percent of the worldwide population. The high response rate provides representative data for the worldwide population of companies within the marine energy sector.

The qualitative data were gathered through in-depth case studies of firms in the industry. Cases were chosen using a convenience sample method (Eisenhardt 1989). For this purpose, data were collected from publicly available sources (Web pages, conference papers, newspapers, magazines, annual reports, and so on) and personal interviews with managers in the different companies. Further, extensive data from institutions supporting the industry have been used. These data have been collected in the same manner as the in-depth company studies referred to above. Finally, inspired by Griliches (1990), patent data have been used as a proxy for historical innovation output.

DATA

In this section, three industries are presented – deep offshore wind, wave, and tidal energy – first in a historical perspective, thereafter through survey data and case material on the three levels: context, firm, and entrepreneur. Some characteristics are common for all industries. In these cases, data from one industry representing all three are presented. Some characteristics are more unique. In this study we focus on the differences.

Some 94 percent of the surveyed firms are start-ups. The remaining 6 percent are internal projects in larger companies. Geographical distribution of the companies is as follows: 49 percent Europe, 35 percent North America, 12 percent Oceania, 4 percent Asia.

Industry Introduction

Deep offshore wind (in the following called 'wind') is defined as technology that harnesses wind energy on the oceans by using floating structures on water depth deeper than 60 meters (EWEA 2009). The industry is a spin-off from the fast-growing onshore and bottom-fixed[2] wind industry. The offshore aspect represents opportunities for other actors than those dominating the onshore market. The first grid connected floating wind turbine was commissioned in Norway in 2009.

Wave energy ('wave') is defined as technology that harnesses the movement in ocean waves. This can be done through various principles (see, for example, Cruz 2008). No single design has turned out to be dominant yet. In 2008 the first grid-connected commercial wave park was installed in Portugal (IEA 2009).

Tidal stream ('tidal') is defined as technology that harnesses the kinetic energy from moving water caused by rise and fall of sea levels from the combined effects of the rotation of the earth and the gravitational forces. As with wave energy, this energy might be harnessed even though this industry has born a dominant design and various principles are in use (see, for examples, Myers et al. 2009). The first grid-connected tidal stream turbine was installed in Norway in 2003.

A common thread for all the industries is that the technologies and projects are resource demanding. The technological issues are complex, they are capital intensive with most of the cost occurring upfront, they require large-scale infrastructure in the sea, and demand large installations. Another common issue is that none can enjoy a ripe market, but all benefit from high market expectations. Basic calculations show that there are millions of megawatts to harness and the industries are expected to grow into multi-billion industries.

Industry History

As change in industry landscapes is a slow process (Cunningham 1969), we must go back to the 1970s to get an understanding of the three industries' pre-introduction phase. Figure 15.2 summarizes the industries' history.

In 1973, the Yom Kippur war led to a global oil crisis and revealed the reality of oil as a scarce resource. This kick-started a number of innovation activities worldwide. Both wave and wind enjoyed national-funded research programs on new energy sources in several countries as a reaction to the oil crisis (for example, Germany, Sweden, the UK, Norway, Italy, Japan, and the US). Despite various demonstration projects and scattered involvement from industrial players, these projects did not transform into

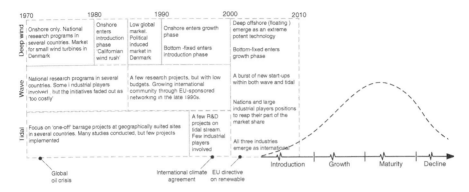

Figure 15.2   Historical development in the three industries

industries and more or less diminished when the oil price fell in the early 1980s.

In the 1980s, California introduced tax incentives to boost a domestic industry for onshore wind. This resulted in more than 12,000 installed wind turbines, but from an unexpected number of foreign players (Germany, Belgium, Denmark, the Netherlands, Ireland, Japan, and the UK). In 1985, Danish suppliers delivered more than 50 percent of the turbines installed in the US. The same year, the Californian tax regime was changed and the market dried out (Righter 1996). This internationalization experience was instrumental for the Danish onshore wind industry, which got the volume they needed to professionalize their value chains (Auken 2002). This was the first significant evidence of how differences in national innovation systems (Lundvall 2007; Bergek et al. 2008) would drive internationalization within renewable energy industries. The 1990s were a breakthrough for onshore wind, driven by tailormade political support schemes in European nations. Motivated by limited land areas, and opposition to increased noise and visual impact, a few bottom-fixed offshore wind projects were commissioned in Europe during the 1990s.

Wave energy did not experience any 'Californian rush' as wind did. As a result, wave energy was left to small research teams in a limited number of countries, with low funding. Tidal energy deviates from the wind and wave industry during the 1970s and 1980s as the technological solution was, except for a few research projects, limited to barrages along the shoreline (Charlier and Finkl 2009). Studies were conducted on barrage projects in several countries (Argentina, Australia, Korea, Japan, India, England, Wales, Bangladesh, Egypt, Russia, and Singapore), but only France, Canada, Russia, and China (small scale) built any (ibid.). These 'one off-projects', with heavy environmental impact, had low potential for cost reductions. In 1995 the first tidal stream technology was tested in the UK, but as with wave energy, the activities were basically left to small research teams in a limited number of countries.

In the 2000s, all three industries in focus received substantial interest from commercial actors. Wave and tidal energy experienced a techno-logical leap and deep sea wind emerged as a new industry. There are now more than 100 companies worldwide which pursue commercialization of devices to harness energy from the sea. They include 64 wave concepts from 19 different countries, 48 tidal energy concepts from 14 different countries, and five deep offshore wind concepts originating from four different countries.

Industry Context Characteristics

In Figure 15.2, two political incidents representing the underlying con-textual drivers of the three industries are shown, the UN Kyoto Protocol adopted in 1997 (UN 1998) and an EU directive on renewable energy in 2001 (CEC 2001). The Kyoto Protocol was the first intergovernmental agreement that obliged nations to lower their emission of greenhouse gases (mainly CO_2 from fossil fuel), and the EU directive stated that renewable energy was an important part of the EU's energy mix and gave specific targets for each member country. Both represent fundamental drivers towards more renewable energy and inspired many nations to design tailormade support systems to facilitate renewable energy tech-nologies. Such major intergovernmental events lead to media attention and may influence the direction of search for established firms and new entrepreneurs (Bergek et al. 2008). An assessment of media coverage of offshore renewable energy revealed a 36 percent growth since 2000.[3]

The UK and Portugal, two of the countries with the most attractive national support schemes (IEA 2006), are foreseen by the survey respond-ents to be the countries with the highest value creation from the marine energy industry 10 years from now. The UK is the country with the most firms and highest market expectation, and is about to become the global hot spot for offshore renewable industries. According to our survey data, a proactive government is rated as the most important factor for compa-nies when they consider doing a demo or full-size park project abroad. National support schemes include not only direct financial measures, but also institutional efforts such as concession procedures or infrastructure such as subsea cables and test centers.

The US-based wave energy developer Ocean Power Technologies may serve as an example of how important the context in a foreign country may be when a company decides to go international. In their first real move in

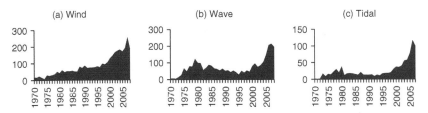

Note: Search strings, (WIND AND (OFFSHORE OR FLOAT+))/BI/ICLM and PRD1>=1970, ((WAVE)/BI/ICLM and (F03B-013)/IC) and PRD1>=1970, ((TIDAL OR TIDE)/BI/ICLM and (F03B-013)/IC) and PRD1>=1970.

Figure 15.3   Patent history in the three industries

Europe, they went public on the London AIM stock exchange in the UK. According to the CEO,

> [T]he London capital markets were more knowledgeable about . . . the wave energy arena. This was due in part to the UK having had several wave power companies gaining press coverage, and because the UK government had identified wave energy as an important, strategic source of electrical power. . . . it makes perfect sense to look further afield where the political and investor audiences are potentially more receptive, while maintaining a broad international scope. (Taylor 2006, p. 67)

Figure 15.3 shows the global development of key patents within the three industries.[4] As the graphs show, all industries have a history of activities picking up early in the 1970s and accelerated innovation rates from around 2000. Europe has been the dominating geographical market for all three industries, but the three most innovative countries measured by issued patents are all outside Europe: Japan, the US, and China. The industries are knowledge intensive. Within the wave and tidal industries the average number of patents is 4.1 per firm.

While the output from offshore renewable energy devices (electricity) is standardized, there is an ongoing battle of dominant design on the various technologies. Both may be important drivers for internationalization. Work has been done to develop guidelines and standards that could facilitate the technology development. One example is the EU-funded program EquiMar (Myers et al. 2009). The aim of EquiMar is to 'deliver a suite of protocols for the equitable evaluation of marine energy converters'. This program involves a consortium from 11 countries representing universities, technology developers, and certification agencies. To build confidence in early phases, some companies utilize existing standards for other offshore technology, for example, from the oil and gas industry.

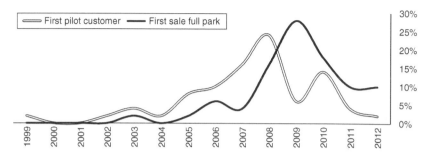

Figure 15.4   First experienced or expected market access (wave and tidal)

Firm-level Characteristics

Despite a long patent history, it was not until the recent decade that the technologies gained acceptance on the marketplace through pilot customers and power parks (Figure 15.4). In total, 49 percent of the wave and tidal firms had a confirmed pilot customer in 2007, and 14 percent reported to have reached agreement to deliver to the first full-scale park.

We have analyzed several case companies to reveal the characteristics of the ongoing global integration, some of which are briefly presented in Table 15.1. In immature industries it is not international sales that is the dominating international activity. There are still, however, several international transactions taking place. Figure 15.5 shows that 38 percent of the firms will carry out their demo projects in a foreign country and more than half of them expect the first sale to be abroad. To get a further indication on how far the companies intended to use internationalization as a strategy they were asked to rate the statement, 'We would move our main office to a foreign country if needed'. Some 58 percent of the respondents agreed with this statement.

The case examples in Table 15.1 serve as good illustrations of how start-ups and multinational companies act across borders and between continents to find needed resources, exploit attractive support schemes and national innovation systems, be present in hot spots, and position themselves for growth. The activities are often done in partnership between start-ups and incumbents. This is also found in the survey data. When asked which business activities were planned to do in-house and which were planned to do through external firms, all activities, except research, development and sale, contain more than 10 percent external content (Figure 15.6).

Companies within all industries show intentions to include partners both upstream (technology related) and downstream (market related).

Table 15.1 Examples of international integration

Company (industry)	Internationalization	Case characteristics
Atlantis Resources (tidal)	Australian start-up. Attracted by low cost and high-quality R&D capabilities and moved HQ to Singapore. Signed a deal with a US investment bank. Established a subsidiary in London to access the European market. Sold shares to Statkraft, a large energy company from Norway. Developing projects in Scotland, Australia and India.	• Moving HQ • Exploiting foreign attractive innovation system • Foreign subsidiary in hot spot • International investors
Ponte di Archimede (tidal)	Established in Italy. Developed and tested a tidal energy device in Italy. Cooperating with the UN on demonstration projects in China, Indonesia and the Philippines.	• Demo project in developing country
Statoil (wind)	Oil and gas company controlled by the Norwegian government. Developed the world's first operating floating wind turbine. Invited by the state of Maine in the US to establish a demo project.	• State attracting leading firms • MNC diversifying
Principle Power (wind)	Start-up from the US with a floating wind concept. Concept tested in model size in wave tanks. Agreed with the Portuguese energy company EDP to establish a phased project incl. a full-scale demo in Portugal. Received investments from Portuguese manufacturer.	• Foreign investors • Foreign manufacturer • Foreign pilot customer • Exploiting foreign attractive support schemes

XEMC (wind)	Large manufacturing complex from China. Acquired the Dutch start-up Darwind which designs wind turbines specialized for offshore use.	• Firm from developing countries acquires innovative start-up
General Electric (wind)	MNC with HQ in the US. Acquired the Norwegian offshore wind turbine manufacturer Scanwind. Establishing cooperative R&D center for offshore wind in Norway.	• MNC acquires innovative start-up • R&D facilities to tap into a foreign innovation system
AWS (wave)	Dutch start-up. Established demo project in Portugal. Moved HQ to the UK. Attracted local and international investors. Accessed several rounds of funding and support programs from the UK and Scottish governments.	• Moving HQ to hot spot • Internationalization to access resources • Exploiting foreign attractive innovation system
Pelamis (wave)	World leading start-up from Scotland. Sold the world's first commercial wave park to a customer in Portugal. Published a press release stating that it was not them that chose Portugal; it was Portugal that chose the wave energy industry – by establishing attractive political support schemes. Shortly after, the support schemes in Scotland were significantly improved.	• Exploiting foreign attractive support schemes • Pressure on home country's politicians to improve support schemes

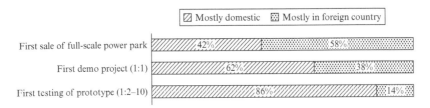

Figure 15.5   Historical or expected location of some milestone activities

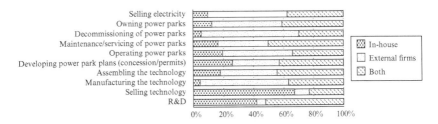

Figure 15.6   Planned business model

Upstream, more than 50 percent of the wave and tidal companies reported to have three or more foreign nationalities among their consultancies, suppliers, and the research institutions with whom they cooperated.

Downstream we see a good match between technology developers in all three industries, with large utility companies who seek to secure options in these new industries. According to the Norwegian utility company Statkraft (2008), more than 50 percent of the top 20 European energy companies have taken positions in new wave and tidal technology through investments in start-ups. All the major deep offshore wind consortiums include one or more energy companies. These partnerships serve as internationalization vehicles for innovations and, typically, materialize as pilot sales in a foreign market.

Most of the technology developers are start-ups. As we know from previous research, start-ups are resource constrained and seek access and leverage resources through hybrid structures (Gabrielsson and Kirpalani 2004). However, there are also other reasons for going international. Figure 15.7 shows a rated list of factors motivating internationalization, and reveals that internationalization is both need based and opportunity driven.

On average, 27 percent of the total development costs were reported to be covered by governmental funding, and 73 percent were covered by private funding. In total, 52 percent report that they have shareholders from two or more countries; only 20 percent of the firms are backed by

Foreign opportunities attracts us — 80%
It allows for survival in a competitive market — 71%
Setting the standard worldwide — 69%
Desire to increase the speed of internationalization — 65%
Achieve more at a lower cost — 63%
Pre-empt competition worldwide — 58%
Mitigation against limited resources (funding, knowledge, etc.) — 49%
Avoid domestic market inertia — 47%
Bad domestic conditions — 40%

Figure 15.7   Factors explaining international activities

venture capital. While 28 percent had not received any governmental funding, more than 30 percent had received governmental funding in more than two nations.

What about expected future sale? Each firm was also asked to imagine that they had sold technology to 100 parks and to provide their expected geographical distribution of those parks. The summarized result gave 4 percent in Africa, 10 percent in South America, 10 percent in Oceania, 15 percent in Asia, 23 percent in North America, and 39 percent in Europe. None of the firms expected to sell technology within only one continent.

Entrepreneurial Level

'For me it is a necessity – I thrive on the unknown', says Alla Weinstein, CEO of Principle Power (Weinstein 2009). Weinstein is a good example of how a person's experience and orientation drives the internationalization of a company. Weinstein grew up in Moscow, but moved to the US and worked for the technology and manufacturing conglomerate Honeywell International. After 20 years with Honeywell, she ventured into the wave energy business with a concept acquired from Sweden. Her company developed internationally with activities in Denmark, Ireland, South Africa, the US and Portugal. She served as the first President of the European Ocean Energy Association. In 2007, she left the wave energy company and co-founded Principle Power in the USA. After only 16 months she entered into a pilot customer agreement with a Portuguese energy company worth €20 million, with a phased plan for building large power parks.

The survey data reveal that those with very strong international experience (32 percent) are more agreed on statements such as 'It is important for our company to internationalize rapidly' and 'ten years from now I believe my company will be one of the dominating companies worldwide'. They are less concerned about theft of technology and cultural problems, and they are more willing to internationalize before the technology is proven. An increasing number of nationalities represented in the team correlate with the urge for rapid internationalization.

All three industries seem to be born out of international communities of practice, but with slightly different histories. Wave energy is born out of an international research community. Tidal energy is somewhat similar, but on a smaller scale and with a community focusing on barrage technologies. The first international Symposium on Wave Energy Utilization was held in Sweden in 1979. In 1993, the first European Wave Energy Symposium was held with support from the European Commission to invite the international community to discuss results from various national research projects. This has today become the European Wave and Tidal Energy Conference and has since been held eight times in different countries. Some 84 percent of the respondents report to have participated in international conferences or something similar. With a basis in the international culture and network developed between the researchers, a community evolved where new industrial players could interact through international conferences, research projects, and publicly funded networks. In this sense, the international industrial network was, and still is, shaped through the relations and culture that already existed in the research communities. Deep offshore wind differs, as it is a spin-off from the onshore and bottom-fixed industry. As described above, the onshore industry experienced a rapid internationalization during the Californian wind rush and since then has gradually grown more international.

Survey data shows that companies which are members of an international industry organization (52 percent of the respondents) are more oriented towards rapid internationalization and even show more willingness to move the main office to a foreign country.

DISCUSSION

The three industries described above are all typical examples of BGIs. Hence, they are all examples of industries where there are high levels of internationally integrated operations and exchange of resources in the introduction phases of their life cycle. Moreover, there is evidence that internationalization in terms of integration of resources and mobility of firms occurs even in the pre-introduction phase (see Figure 15.8). These findings lead to the conclusion that BGIs are pushing the limits of existing international business theory and that earlier work on the internationalization of industries, both in the international business, and the international entrepreneurship literature, needs to be reassessed.

However, the study also shows the relevance of the international entrepreneurship literature as born global firms are found to be the most pertinent driving force behind the emergence of BGIs. As scholars in the

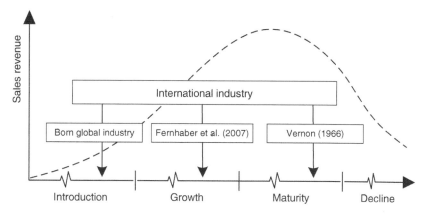

*Figure 15.8   Revised positions of industry internationalization in the
product market life cycle*

area we need to ask ourselves the question of whether the emergence of
BGIs is driven by the same globalization trends as international firms. If
so, BGIs could very well become as commonplace as born globals are in
the modern economy today.

The main questions of this study are what characterizes a BGI and what
facilitates its rapid internationalization. Some general propositions stated
below based on the findings from the offshore renewable industries, may
begin the discussion to answer these questions.

The first proposition concerns the long incubation time that can be seen
in all three industries. During the pre-introduction phase, the awareness
of potential business opportunities grew among individuals, firms, and
nations. However, in this phase governmentally funded research activities
were far more common than commercial activities. Following the nature
of the scientific community, the knowledge that was generated was globally distributed through scientific publications, conferences, and patents.
When the market was ready, latent innovations existed around the world
and relevant research knowledge was internationally available. Therefore,
the first proposition is:

P1: BGIs are characterized by long incubation.

All three industries build their business propositions on offering new
renewable energy. This is demanded to avoid global warming and to
secure a supply of energy, but also as a contribution towards a sustainable economical growth. Only a handful of nations have access to
abundant reserves of fossil fuel, and offshore energy sources are globally

distributed. Global demand facilitates globalization of the industry – between both developed and developing countries. Global demand also spurs a globalization of the media coverage, which again affects the global awareness of the business opportunity. All three industries have the potential to become big industries and this seems to be a precondition in order to attract the large amount of investments that are needed to spur these industries into multiple markets simultaneously. This leads us to the second proposition:

P2: BGIs are characterized by global business opportunities with vast market potential.

However, global industries include activities in all parts of the value chain, including sourcing. Although there is the possibility that a global industry might be initiated from one country alone, the data say otherwise. The case industries suggest that the origin of patents and companies are spread all over the triad. It can also be noted that nations with the best market conditions were not necessarily the nations with the most patents. This creates a global supply side of innovations which may facilitate earlier globalization of the industry. Hence, the third proposition:

P3: BGIs are characterized by international origin of technologies, patents, and firms.

Different nations have different industry structures and will make different efforts to secure their part of the value creation potential from new and promising industries. It happened in the home computer industry (Encamation and Wells 1986) and it happens in the offshore renewable energy industries. Some nations are aiming to become global hot spots (Porter 1990; Pouder and Caron 1996). This leads to heterogeneity in national support schemes and market attractiveness. The data suggest that this observed market heterogeneity is driving internationalization on the firm level. This leads to the fourth proposition:

P4: BGIs are characterized by heterogeneity in national support schemes or market attractiveness.

Due to heterogeneity in market attractiveness there is a tendency for geographical hot spots or lead markets to be established in the early days of an industry. As can be seen in the case industries, presence in lead markets is regarded as important in order to be able to win the battle for dominant designs and be well positioned for the growth phase of the industry. The data suggest that the quest to establish the dominating design is driving internationalization. Therefore, the fifth proposition:

P5: BGIs are characterized by an ongoing battle to establish the dominant design.

In the case industries, the end product is electricity, which is a highly standardized product. Standardization is regarded as having both positive and negative effects on global integration (Birkinshaw et al. 1995), but it can be seen from the data that the standardized end product greatly facilitates internationalization of the industry. There are two reasons for this. First, global standards of the end product mean little need for local market adaptation and hence lower costs of international expansion. These lower costs and lower demands for local adaptation significantly reduce the risk for firms, technology developers, investors and customers alike. This leads to the sixth proposition:

P6: BGIs are characterized by homogeneous global demand and end products.

The case industries predominantly consist of newly established companies, and these companies are also the most important source of new innovations. It can be observed that many of these start-ups are willing to forge highly international strategies very early in their life cycle to develop and commercialize their technologies. Therefore, the seventh proposition:

P7: In the early phases, BGIs are primarily characterized by innovative start-ups with international strategies and high international mobility.

Start-ups might be the dominating source of innovations in BGIs, but from former research it is known that multinational corporations (MNCs) play a vital role in getting the innovations to the market (Gabrielsson and Kirpalani 2004). The most important partners for start-ups in the wave, tidal, and deep offshore wind industries are energy companies. They provide resources, reputation, network, and political influence, and are often pilot customers. Energy companies have traditionally been state-owned, domestically focused companies. However, the energy industries have been extensively deregulated in the last two decades. As a result, the energy companies have developed international orientation and growth strategies. Herewith, the eighth proposition:

P8: BGIs are characterized by incumbents with established or emerging internationalization strategies.

Before an industry reaches the point where commercial sales are the dominant income source, the main focus of the firms is to source and integrate resources (finance, technologies, knowledge, physical assets, organizational assets, and so on) in order to position the company well for future sales growth. The data suggest that these activities are carried out across national boundaries. The data particularly show that start-ups bounded by resource constraint are actively seeking resources and partnership with potential manufacturers and/or customers in foreign countries. This leads to the ninth proposition:

P9: BGIs are characterized by international sourcing and integration of resources in order to position ventures for future sales.

More and more managerial talent in the world has international experience, international education (Madsen and Servais 1997; Bartlett and Ghoshal 1998), or takes part in international communities of practice. This is something that is clearly shown in the data, and its consequence is stronger international orientation on behalf of the ventures that are created. It can also be observed that international communities of practice such as scientific communities serve as arenas where international business opportunities are recognized by potential entrepreneurs and where they can establish international relations that are valuable for their ventures. It is likely that industries dominated by managers with international experience, international networks, and international orientations will experience rapid internationalization. Therefore, the tenth proposition:

P10: BGIs are characterized by entrepreneurs with international experience, international business relations, and international orientation.

Having proposed these characteristics of BGIs, the primary call is for more research on these emerging industries. First, there is a need to establish how common BGIs are. Is the emergence of BGIs just a natural consequence of the globalization trends that can be seen in international business, as has been suggested above, or are the industries that have been studied here only exceptional cases that have emerged due to global climate change hysteria? Second, it would be good to see the propositions above tested for their validity in a broader range of industries.

The next question that naturally arises is what are the consequences for international business theory? In this study a narrow range of literature and projected former research on rapid firm internationalization into an industry perspective has been studied. Former research on globally integrated industries has focused on more mature industries and taken an MNC perspective. Birkinshaw et al. (1995) found three forces to be dominating in global industries, (i) the potential for economies of scale in value-adding activities; (ii) differences in comparative advantages across countries; and (iii) standardized market demand across countries.

We have defined a BGI as an industry with globally integrated operations in the introduction phase of its life cycle. The data give good insights into the highly international and dynamic interplay between nations, start-ups, and MNCs during the incubation period and the introduction phase of an industry. The findings are in line with former studies, but a development of new measures is in order to be better able to monitor internationalization processes in industries in early phases.

Gabrielsson and Kirpalani (2004) show how start-ups may internationalize rapidly in partnership with MNCs. Aaker and Day (1986) discuss when larger companies should enter new industries and Bartlett and Ghoshal (1998) consider strategies for larger firms to become transnational firms. Encamation and Wells (1986) discuss the rationale for host countries to attract foreign firms and Porter (1990), examines the competitiveness of different nations. Various combinations of these perspectives with focus on early industry phases will give room for valuable research contributions with far-reaching implications for global economic development.

If one could point to one significant implication for managers based on the current study, it would be to emphasize the competitive advantage of mobility in the early stages of BGI establishment. The findings suggest that this increases international competitiveness, firm value, and the probability of long-term survival.

On a policy level, the most powerful implication is that the rise of the BGI phenomenon may represent an era where global integration, and therefore also global competition, takes place right from the start in new industries. National policy must be designed accordingly and short-sighted protectionism seems to be unwise. Instead, policy should be designed to capture the value through attracting strategic industries and facilitating rapid internationalization among local firms.

CONCLUSIONS

The study concludes that the international activities in the pre-establishment phases are extensive and that these international activities lay the foundation for the establishment of 'born global' industries – an industry with global integrated operations in the introduction phase of its life cycle. These findings have important implications for international business theory, practitioners, and policy makers. First, in terms of scholarly thought, a reassessment of the dynamics that are asserted by Raymond Vernon needs to be made. Apparently, the internationalization of these industries is more rapid than the product life cycle advocates and it is driven by other factors. On the practitioner's level, a similar reassessment needs to be made. Under the traditional model, managers had more time and resources to establish profitable domestic ventures before considering internationalization and international competition. This is no longer the case. Rather, managers should be proactive in establishing international relations and activities as early as possible in the venture's life cycle. Moreover, they should nurture mobility as it appears to be a key success factor in the early phases of a BGI. The findings also have implications for policy makers. This is primarily because increased mobility of new industries makes traditional path dependency of domestic industry development less reliable. That is, it is unlikely that the traditional approach of supporting and protecting early-stage development of industries will provide the basis for long-term domestic industry growth. With increased mobility and early global competition, a longer-term perspective on how to establish a favorable environment for industry growth should be considered.

NOTES

1. McDougall et al. established the term 'international new ventures'. There are slight differences in definitions between international new ventures and born global firms, but these are not relevant for the discussion here. Therefore, the terms will be used interchangeably.
2. To avoid any misunderstanding, the expression 'bottom-fixed' instead of 'offshore' is used for turbines installed on depths less than 60 meters.
3. Based on a search on the keywords marine energy, ocean power, wave power, and tidal power in Factiva.
4. In this case the wind graph includes bottom-fixed turbines.

REFERENCES

Aaker, D.A. and G.S. Day (1986), 'The perils of high-growth markets', *Strategic Management Journal*, **7**(5), 409–21.
Agarwal, R., M.B. Sarkar and R. Echambadi (2002), 'The conditioning effect of time on firm survival, an industry life cycle approach', *Academy of Management Journal*, **45**(5), 971–94.

Andersen, O. (1993), 'On the internationalization process of firms, a critical analysis', *Journal of International Business Studies*, **24**(2), 209–31.

Anderson, C.R. (1984), 'Stage of the product life cycle, business strategy, and business performance', *Academy of Management Journal*, **27**(1), 5–24.

Andersson, S. (2004), 'Internationalization in different industrial contexts', *Journal of Business Venturing*, **19**(6), 851–75.

Aspelund, A. and T.K. Madsen (2009), 'The role of innovative and entrepreneurial behavior in internationalization processes', *Advances in International Marketing*, **20**, 155–76.

Aspelund, A., T.K. Madsen and Ø. Moen (2007), 'International new ventures, review of conceptualizations and findings', *European Journal of Marketing*, **41**(11/12), 1423–74.

Auken, S. (2002), 'Answers in the wind, how Denmark became a world pioneer in wind power', *Fletcher Forum on World Affairs*, **26**, 149–57.

Bartlett, Christopher A. and Sumantra Ghoshal (1998), *Managing across Borders: The Transnational Solution*, Boston, MA: Harvard University Press.

Bergek, A., S. Jacobsson, B. Carlsson, S. Lindmark and A. Rickne (2008), 'Analyzing the functional dynamics of technological innovation systems: a scheme of analysis', *Research Policy*, **37**(3), 407–29.

Birkinshaw, J., A. Morrison and J. Hulland (1995), 'Structural and competitive determinants of a global integration strategy', *Strategic Management Journal*, **16**(8), 637–55.

CEC (Commission of the European Communities) (2001), Directive 2001/77/EC of the European Parliament and of the Council of 27 September 2001 on the promotion of electricity produced from renewable energy sources in the internal energy market, *Official Journal of the European Communities*, Brussels.

Charlier, Roger Henry and Charles W. Finkl (2009), *Ocean Energy, Tide And Tidal Power*, Berlin: Springer.

Coviello, N.E. (2006), 'The network dynamics of international new ventures', *Journal of International Business Studies*, **37**(5), 713–31.

Coviello, N.E. and M.P. Cox (2007), 'The resource dynamics of international new venture networks', *Journal of International Entrepreneurship*, **4**(2–3), 113–32.

Cruz, Joao (ed.) (2008), *Ocean Wave Energy, Current Status and Future Perspectives*, Berlin and Heidelberg: Springer.

Cunningham, M.T. (1969), 'The application of product life cycles to corporate strategy, some research findings', *European Journal of Marketing*, **3**(1), 32–44.

Eisenhardt, K.M. (1989), 'Building theories from case study research', *Academy of Management Review*, **14**(4), 532–50.

Encamation, Dennis J. and Louis T. Wells Jr (1986), 'Competitive strategies in global industries: a view from host governments', in Michael E. Porter (ed.), *Competition in Global Industries*, Boston, MA: Harvard Business School Press, pp. 267–90.

EWEA (European Wind Energy Association) (2009), 'Oceans of Opportunity – Harnessing Europe's largest domestic energy resource', EWEA.

Fernhaber, S.A., P.P. McDougall and B.M. Oviatt (2007), 'Exploring the role of industry structure in new venture internationalization', *Entrepreneurship: Theory and Practice*, **31**(4), 517–42.

Gabrielsson, M. and V.H.M. Kirpalani (2004), 'Born globals, how to reach new business space rapidly', *International Business Review*, **13**(5), 555–71.

Gibbert, M. (2008), 'What passes as a rigorous case study?', *Strategic Management Journal*, **29**(13), 1465–74.

Griliches, Z. (1990), 'Patent statistics as economic indicators, a survey', *Journal of Economic Literature*, **28**(4), 1661–707.

Hout, T., M.E. Porter and E. Rudden (1982), 'How global companies win out', *Harvard Business Review*, **60**(5), 98–108.

IEA (2006), 'Review and Analysis of Ocean Energy Systems Development and Supporting Policies', International Energy Agency, Paris.

IEA (2009), *Annual Report: International Energy Agency Implementing Agreement on Ocean Energy Systems (IEA–OES)*, edited by A. Brito-Melo and G. Bhuyan, Paris: IEA.

Jick, T.D. (1979), 'Mixing qualitative and quantitative methods: triangulation in action', *Administrative Science Quarterly*, **24**(4), 602–11.

Johanson, J. and J.-E. Vahlne (1977), 'The internationalization process of the firm – a model of knowledge development and increasing foreign market commitments', *Journal of International Business Studies*, **8**(1), 23–32.

Johanson, J. and J.-E. Vahlne (1990), 'The mechanism of internationalization', *International Marketing Review*, **7**(4), 11–24.

Johanson, J. and F. Wiedersheim-Paul (1975), 'The internationalization of the firm – four Swedish cases', *Journal of Management Studies*, **12**(3), 305–22.

Jolly, V.K., M. Alahutha and J.P. Jeannet (1992), 'Challenging the incumbents, how high technology start-ups compete globally', *Journal of Strategic Change*, **1**(1), 71–82.

Jones, M.V. (2001), 'First steps in internationalisation – concepts and evidence from a sample of small high-technology firms', *Journal of International Management*, **7**(3), 191–210.

Keupp, M.M. and O. Gassmann (2009), 'The past and the future of international entrepreneurship, a review and suggestions for developing the field', *Journal of Management*, **35**(3), 600–633.

Knight, G.A. and S.T. Cavusgil (1996), 'The born global firm: a challenge to traditional internationalization theory', in S. Tamer Cavusgil (ed.), *Advances in International Marketing*, **8**, 11–26.

Kobrin, S.J. (1991), 'An empirical analysis of the determinants of global integration', *Strategic Management Journal*, **12**(1), 17–31.

Løvdal, Nicolai S. and A. Aspelund (2010), 'International entrepreneurship in the offshore renewable energy industry', in Rolf Wustenhagen and Robert Wuebker (eds), *Handbook of Research on Energy Entrepreneurship*, Cheltenham, UK and Northampton, MA, USA: Edward Elgar, pp. 121–44.

Lundvall, B.A.M. (2007), 'National innovation systems – analytical concept and development tool', *Industry and Innovation*, **14**(1), 95–119.

Madsen, T.K. and P. Servais (1997), 'The internationalization of born globals, an evolutionary process?', *International Business Review*, **6**(6), 561–83.

McDougall, P.P., S. Shane and B.M. Oviatt (1994), 'Explaining the formation of international new ventures, the limits of theories from international business research', *Journal of Business Venturing*, **9**(6), 469–87.

Myers, L.E., A.S. Bahaj, F. Gardner, C. Bittencourt and J. Finn (2009), 'Device Classification Template: Equitable Testing and Evaluation of Marine Energy Extraction Devices in terms of Performance, Cost and Environmental Impact', EquiMar, European Commission.

Oviatt, B.M. and P.P. McDougall (1994), 'Toward a theory of international new ventures', *Journal of International Business Studies*, **25**(1), 45–64.

Porter, Michael E. (1990), *The Competitive Advantage of Nations*, New York: Free Press.

Pouder, R. and H.S.J. Caron (1996), 'Hot spots and blind spots, geographical clusters of firms and innovation', *Academy of Management Review*, **21**(4), 1192–225.

Rennie, M.W. (1993), 'Global competitiveness, born global', *The McKinsey Quarterly*, **(4)**, 45–52.

Rialp, A., J. Rialp and G.A. Knight (2005), 'The phenomenon of early internationalizing firms, what do we know after a decade (1993–2003) of scientific enquiry', *International Business Review*, **14**(2), 147–66.

Righter, Robert W. (1996), *Wind Energy in America, A History*, Norman, OK: University of Oklahoma Press.

Rink, D.R. and J.E. Swan (1979), 'Product life cycle research, a literature review', *Journal of Business Research*, **7**(3), 219–42.

Rogers, Everett (1962), *The Diffusion of Innovations*, New York: Free Press.

Statkraft (2008), 'Does the industry have enough knowledge and skills?', paper presented at the International Conference on Ocean Energy, Brest, France, 15–17 October.

Taylor, G.W. (2006), 'AIM admission opens doors to investment community', *Infrastructure Journal*, Spring, 66–8.

UN (1998), '*Kyoto Protocol to the United Nations Framework Convention on Climate Change*', United Nations, New York.

Vernon, R. (1966), 'International investment and international trade in the product cycle', *Quarterly Journal of Economics*, **80**(2), 190–207.

Weinstein, A. (2009), Interview with MSNBC.com, April 22. Available at: www.msnbc.msn.com/id/29497494/ns/us/news-environment/t/gut-check-green-jobs-hope-or-hype.

Yin, Robert K. (2003), *Case Study Research: Design and Methods*, Newbury Park, CA: Sage.

Zahra, S.A. (2005), 'A theory of international new ventures, a decade of research', *Journal of International Business Studies*, **36**(1), 20–28.

16 Portuguese born globals: founders' linkages, company evolution, and international geographical patterns
Vitor Corado Simões

INTRODUCTION

There is a burgeoning literature on born globals[1] (BGs). This topic is gaining increasing relevance in today's international business (IB) research. Academic concern with this phenomenon is not surprising, since BG firms play a growing role in the present stage of the globalization process.

Much has been done since the seminal contribution on international new ventures by Oviatt and McDougall (1994). There is wide agreement in the literature about a host of features that characterize BGs. To the original innovativeness, proactiveness, and risk-taking features noted (ibid.), other 'orientations' and characteristics have been considered: global vision at inception[2] (Gabrielsson et al. 2008), international entrepreneurial and marketing orientations (Lee et al. 2001; Knight and Cavusgil 2004, 2005; Weerawardena et al. 2007), learning (Autio et al. 2000; Dimitratos and Plakoyiannaki 2003; Gabrielsson et al. 2008), networking (Coviello and Munro 1995; Dimitratos and Plakoyiannaki 2003; Coviello 2006; Gassmann and Keupp 2007), and unique products (Gassmann and Keupp 2007; Gabrielsson et al. 2008).

An unsettled issue is the role of the entrepreneur in BG emergence and evolution. There is agreement about the key role of the entrepreneur or the entrepreneurial team[3] in shaping the firm as a cognitive focusing device (Nooteboom 2009), in providing it with an international drive (Oviatt and McDougall 1994; Rialp et al. 2005a) and in fostering networking (Gassmann and Keupp 2007; Rialp et al. 2005a). Keupp and Gassmann (2009, p. 613) note, however, that 'there is a serious gap in our knowledge regarding how the process of entrepreneurially driven internationalization evolves'. In particular, 'the study of the early, entrepreneurship-driven stages of internationalization could be an opportunity to achieve a more general understanding of how entrepreneurial processes and internationalization interact and co-evolve over time' (p. 614).

Such a gap is, in our opinion, due to an insufficient understanding of the relationships between the entrepreneur and the firm at early stages in its life cycle. While recognizing the role of the entrepreneur(s) in the process of founding and giving initial direction to the firm, constructs of entrepreneurial orientation tend to focus on firms' top management at the time of inquiry, (see, for example, Knight and Cavusgil 2004, 2005), not at the time of their birth, Weerawardena et al. (2007) being an exception. The resource-based framework put forward by Rialp et al. (2005a) classifies firm intangible resources into structural capital (of the firm) and human capital (managers and entrepreneurial team characteristics). Unfortunately, they fail to acknowledge the fact that, at early stages, human capital shapes structural capital to a large extent. Of course, there are exceptions (Shrader et al. 2000; Jones and Coviello 2005; Coviello 2006; Dominguinhos 2006; Mathews and Zander 2007). In general, however, the BG literature focuses on the organization, not on the individual. In our opinion, this may be inappropriate. At very early stages of firm creation and internationalization, organizations are largely shaped by their founders, especially founder-managers, as well as by the early challenges and opportunities faced, often unexpectedly (Crick and Spence 2005). The firm's identity is still being formed: to borrow from De Geus (1997), the 'persona' of the firm is still in the making. This chapter is intended to address the above-mentioned gap. It is aimed at identifying how founders' social and business networks influence BG evolution and geographical spread.

The theoretical basis for our endeavor is the dynamic capabilities approach, though with a twist to accommodate the fact that the borderline between firms' and entrepreneurs' capabilities in early life-cycle stages is fuzzy. An evolutionary perspective will become evident throughout the chapter. Drawing on Oviatt and McDougall (1994) and Knight and Cavusgil (2004), BGs are defined as firms that, since their founding or early in their life, seek superior IB performance from the use of resources and the sale of outputs in multiple countries. The empirical analysis will be based on a set of six in-depth case studies of Portuguese BGs, working in technology-intensive fields.

The remainder of the chapter is organized as follows. In the next section a theoretical perspective of the evolutionary interaction between founders and company resources and capabilities is developed, leading to the identification of the main research question. Then, a methodological section addresses the procedures followed in the empirical research and provides a summary table with the key features of the cases studied. The main findings are presented next. Then, a discussion of the findings is undertaken, against the background of extant literature. The presentation and discussion of the findings are organized along three interrelated themes:

founders' networks in sensing and seizing business opportunities; the interaction among founders' moves, external environment, and company evolution; and the geography of internationalization. The chapter ends with a brief concluding section.

LITERATURE REVIEW: FOUNDERS' ROLE IN EARLY FIRM EVOLUTION

The dynamic capabilities approach (Teece et al. 1997; Eisenhardt and Martin 2000; Helfat et al. 2007; Teece 2009) is strongly influenced by the evolutionary theory of economic change of Nelson and Winter (1982). According to Teece (2009, p. 206), dynamic capabilities include: (i) the capability to sense opportunities; (ii) the capability to seize opportunities; and (iii) the capacity to manage threats through the combination, recombination, and reconfiguring of assets inside and outside the firm's boundaries. This immediately suggests a link to entrepreneurship research, as David Teece himself acknowledges. However, to our best knowledge, the use of dynamic capabilities in studying the BG is still scarce (Mort and Weerawardena 2006; Gassmann and Keupp 2007; Weerawardena et al. 2007).

From an entrepreneurship perspective, it may be argued that the processes of sensing and seizing capabilities pre-exist firm birth. The very creation of the firm is due to entrepreneurs' capabilities to sense and seize opportunities, and to organize assets to respond to those opportunities. Whether taking a Schumpeterian or a Kirznerian perspective, the entrepreneurial process is based on the interaction between three elements: the entrepreneur, the opportunity, and the project (Simões and Dominguinhos 2006). The entrepreneur senses a business opportunity, and strives to create a new firm to seize it. Individual (and/or group) characteristics, competences, attitudes and motivations will lead, through a conjecturing process, to the framing of a project. This will require the combination of a bundle of resources, from additional technological, marketing, and managerial knowledge (often involving the setting up of an entrepreneurial team with complementary experience) to finance (Laanti et al. 2007; Gabrielsson et al. 2008). International entrepreneurial dynamics (Mathews and Zander 2007) recognizes the key role of the prospective entrepreneur in sensing opportunities.[4]

As Jones and Coviello (2005) suggested, international entrepreneurship is a process of behavior in time. Interestingly, this process starts before the entrepreneurial event of firm birth, and does not come to an end with it. On the contrary, the *ex ante* framing of opportunities and project design may not be fully validated *ex post*, thereby requiring adjustments and additional resources, a process in which the entrepreneurs still have an important role to play. To use a biological image, the 'baby' is too small to walk alone, and still needs strong support from the 'parents'. The entrepreneur still has to nurture the firm after inception. Consequently, the new-born firm will draw significantly from entrepreneurs' capabilities and networks (Coviello 2006). Only gradually will the firm develop its own capabilities and routines, and acquire its identity. In spite of the later emergence of a firm's dynamic capabilities, the founder's heritage is likely to have a long-lasting influence on the future of the firm (Bartlett and Ghoshal 1989). Therefore, we concur with Coviello (2006) and Gabrielsson et al. (2008) in stressing the convenience of identifying phases of BG development. We argue, in particular, that there is 'life' before birth and that there is an 'infant' phase where individual founders' capabilities may be stronger than a firm's capabilities.

In the case of BGs, the founders' influence is felt in different dimensions: the business model, the type of products/services delivered, the organizational atmosphere, inter-organizational linkages and alliances, and, of course, the geographical spread of operations. It is suggested that founders' international professional and social networks will be mobilized to promote the firm's initial international growth. This argument has already been mentioned by other scholars (Oviatt and McDougall 1994; Coviello and Munro 1995; Yli-Renko et al. 2001; Sharma and Blomstermo 2003; Coviello 2006; Mathews and Zander 2007; Kudina et al. 2008).

What deserves to be further investigated, in our opinion, is the role of founders in both the pre-birth and the 'infant' phases of the BG, and the interaction between founders and firm capabilities in forging internationalization. Such an interaction is also influenced by external factors, which may contribute to shape the BGs' geography of internationalization. Such external factors may be associated with cultural and linguistic issues as well as critical events (emergence of early key customers, customers' challenges, regulatory changes).

Therefore, our research question will be formulated as follows: how do founders' capabilities and networks contribute to shape BGs' evolution and early internationalization patterns?

METHOD

To address the above research question, we shall draw on different pieces of research carried out on Portuguese BGs in which we have participated or supervised. Six case studies were selected. Case studies are appropriate to answer 'How?' questions, as well as to study recent and under-researched phenomena (Eisenhardt 1989; Ghauri et al. 1995; Yin 2009). Since the focus is on processes, the option for case studies, based on histories and experiences of entrepreneurs and on the evolution of the interactions with the environment, is warranted (Gummerson 2000). Our approach is also intended to respond to Coviello and Jones's (2004) quest for developing further case studies to understand social phenomena in BGs.

The cases were selected on the basis of their potential contribution to answer the research question and their relevance for addressing the process of firm creation and internationalization. The concern in case selection was relevance rather than representativeness (Stake 1994). The purpose was to address 'rich' cases, whose analysis might provide insights for enhancing our knowledge about the issues at hand. This approach is relatively common in BG research (Mort and Weerawardena 2006; Gassmann and Keupp 2007).

Information was collected through semi-structured interviews with the members of the initial entrepreneurial team,[5] supplemented by a thorough analysis of websites, magazines, and the press. In five cases, the companies' CEOs at the time were also interviewed (in three cases, these were among the entrepreneurial team). The interviews typically lasted between 90 and 120 minutes. In four cases, there were two rounds of interviews. Questions about firm antecedents, the opportunity framing process, and early company development were asked. More specifically, entrepreneurs' previous experience, knowledge levels, and personal and business relationships were key issues for information collection. Information about international activities, such as geographical range of activities, entry modes, strategy formation, and the timeframe for entering international markets, was also collected.

The main elements of the six case studies are presented on Table 16.1.

FINDINGS

The main findings of the comparative analysis of the case studies may be clustered around three themes:

1. founders' networks in sensing and seizing business opportunities;
2. founders, external environment, and company evolution; and
3. geography of internationalization.

These themes will also be used to structure the discussion.

Table 16.1 Entrepreneurs' background and firms' geography of internationalization

Case	Entre-pren. team	Academic background	Professional experience	Professional/social network	Initial busin. partners/ triggering factors	Geography of internationalization
A Software for call centers	1	Post-graduate in engineering	Employee in MNE (working experience abroad). University teacher	MNEs (IBM, Alcatel). Former business partners. University colleagues	Sydney Olympics	Americas, Australia, Europe, Asia, Africa Exports: Above 60%.
B Biotech-nology	2	PhDs in biotech-nology	None	Colleagues in UK (one of them was co-founder of the venture), Denmark and USA Contacts with MNEs		America, Europe Exports: 88%
C Software to manage critical events	3	Doctoral studies in information systems	Previous work in Portugese companies (employment in Scotland and the Netherlands in one case)	University colleagues (Coimbra) Training course of the University of Austin Partners in European research projects Colleagues at MNCs (Siemens . . .)	Canadian company NASA (Jet Propulsion Laborat.) ESA Trigger: NASA contact	Europe, America, Asia, Africa, Oceania Exports: 62% Subsidiaries: Brazil Romania, UK, and USA
D Geo-referen-tiation software	5	PhD in engineering	University professors Researchers	MIT Media Lab. Partners in European research projects University colleagues	Vodafone Alcatel Siemens Trigger: Stay at MIT Media Lab	Europe, America, Asia Exports: 35% Offices in Brazil, Spain, and USA

Table 16.1 (continued)

Case	Entre-pren. team	Academic background	Professional experience	Professional/social network	Initial busin. partners/ triggering factors	Geography of internationalization
E Optical fibers monitoring	5	2 PhDs in electr. engineering 2 PhDs in physics 1 engineer	Researchers Employee in MNE (working experience in USA; Italy and Brazil)	Applied Optics Group (Univ. Kent, UK) Partners in European research projects Worldwide instruments business Colleagues in USA (Univ. Illinois) and Spain Research center colleagues.	Brazilian and USA partners to market company products	Americas, Europe, Asia Exports: 80% Strategic alliances: Brazil, USA, Spain
F Paperless hospitals	1 (+1)	PhD in molecular biology (+ degree in bus. administr.)	None	Colleagues at Stanford Other former colleagues in the USA Academic contacts in Europe Winner of Research Prize	Hospitals in Portugal and Spain Trigger: visit to USA	Europe, Americas, Asia Exports: 60% Subsidiaries: Brazil, the Netherlands, Singapore, Spain, UK and USA

Sources: Simões and Dominguinhos (2001, 2005 and 2006), Dominguinhos (2006), Sá (2009), Simões et al. (2009), COTEC (2010), Business Press and interviews with company founding teams.

Founders' Networks in Sensing and Seizing Business Opportunities

The first remark is that, in most cases, companies were created by an entre-preneurial team, and not by a single individual. However, there is often (namely in Case B and Case D) a leader or a 'champion' who plays a key role, namely with regard to external relationships. Case C is somewhat an exception, because for a long period after company inception, there was a strong commitment to collective management, and the CEO job was assigned on a rotational basis.

Initially, founders' networks were mainly academic/scientific. Such networks were forged in the context of post-graduate education and research projects. In Case B, there was a wide network of schoolmates in the UK, Denmark, and the USA. This network was used, in the first instance, to attract a co-founder, and then to help assess the business idea. This network also enabled the establishment of contacts with foreign companies, namely multinational enterprises (MNEs), since some PhD colleagues became employed by MNEs. In Case D, there was a significant exposure to the international scientific community. A post-doc research grant of the 'champion' founder at the MIT Media Lab was the triggering factor for company creation. In Case E, again, scientific linkages abroad, namely in the UK, were instrumental in sensing and evaluating the busi-ness opportunity. In both Case D and Case E, there has been an interac-tion between foreign and domestic networks, since the founders were members of research teams in Portugal, at the university and/or research centers, which were mobilized for the entrepreneurial project. Case C has some similarities, since the founders were carrying out their PhD studies abroad, while maintaining strong contacts with the Portuguese Alma Mater. It is, however, different to the extent that the main triggering factor for sensing and seizing the opportunity came from outside the network: an inquiry following a publication in an international journal. Cases A and F are different for several reasons. In both cases, domestic research networks were not strong, although academic and social networks played a role. Case A is unique, since it is the only one where a business network was already in place. The founder had wide professional experience in MNEs in Portugal, and had previous experience of company creation. The business network was instrumental in sensing the opportunity, since this emerged due to a challenge raised by Alcatel.

From the above description, it becomes clear that the process of oppor-tunity framing does not show any one single pattern. The role of the founders' networks in sensing and seizing opportunities is different from case to case. There is, however, a similar thread that pervades most cases (namely C, D, E, and F): the interaction between foreign and domestic academic/research networks. The first occurs in the foreground, as it provides the perception of an international business opportunity, as well as a test of its business logic and feasibility. The second is largely in the background, although it is relevant for enabling an operational basis as well as funding/providing incubation facilities. In all cases, except A, scientific/academic and social networks pre-exist business networks. These emerge and gain importance only at later stages, but their role, as will be shown below, may be decisive for accelerated internationalization.

Founders, External Environment, and Company Evolution

The cases show that the conjectures leading to firm creation are often not fully validated *ex post*. The external environment, namely early customers, plays a key role in the *ex post* business opportunity validation process. Some early customers are behind the redefinition and stabilization of firms' products. In general, such a redefinition requires a strong commitment by the founders. In some cases, it may even amount to the creation of a new corporate entity.

Case A is particularly interesting in that respect, since the framing of the business opportunity stemmed from an outside challenge. In the first company founded by the entrepreneur, a software company, customers were found to face bill collection problems, and software was developed to enable faster telephone connections and bill collection. Aware of this through business networks, the Portuguese subsidiary of Alcatel invited the company to develop a solution to enable an integrated telemarketing approach for a Brazilian customer. The product developed was considered to have a significant market potential, leading the founder to launch a new company, just to develop this business on a worldwide scale.

The role of foreign organizations in helping the founders to sense and seize business opportunities is also clear in Case C. The inquiry from a Canadian company following an academic article of the potential entrepreneurs, and the interest shown by the NASA Jet Propulsion Laboratory in a technology developed by them, were instrumental in defining the initial product offer of the company. The relationship with NASA also led to the decision to locate at a virtual business incubator in California. However, the founders were very committed to increasing the company's product portfolio, often as a response to customers' challenges. The founders recognized that the company initially followed an 'opportunistic' approach. They envisaged that approach as an important instrument to ensure company sustainability and growth.

Similar processes were apparent in the evolution of Case D. Telecel, a joint venture between Vodafone and Portuguese partners, was the first key business customer. Starting from the development of maps, the company entered the video-games business with Telecel/Vodafone. From here, the company enlarged the customer scope to include Nokia, and developed its geo-referentiation competencies further. Although displaying a relatively large business scope, video games have continued to be a key product.

Business interactions have also influenced the evolution of Cases B and E. These were, however, less relevant than in the other cases. Case B had, since inception, a clear intention to develop a patent portfolio to license at different maturation stages. However, the path was much longer and thornier than expected. In the early phase, between 1996 and 2000, it acted mainly as a consultancy firm (Dominguinhos 2006). The purpose was to earn money from contracts with MNEs and with the EU (FP research projects[6]), in order to enable the development of company patents. Meanwhile, after opening up to venture capitalists, the company was able to get a few patents and strived to develop biopharmaceutical products. The firm presents itself as a 'development company', and licensing out became more important. Case E followed a different path by entering an internet trading platform, and setting up strategic alliances with 'peer' small companies abroad, both to market its products and to learn. In this case, the role played by large partners has been less relevant, and the changes in company trajectory were not so evident.

In contrast, the change in the entrepreneur's perception of the opportunities offered by the external environment in Case F, was essential to a strategic turnaround, instilling in the company a global approach that was not apparent beforehand. During the first four years, the company was focused on the Iberian market. The change occurred when the founder decided to visit the USA to assess with his former colleagues at Stanford how innovative the company approach was. The result was surprising: its software had a tremendous international potential. The triggering factor was not customer orders, but rather the 'validation' of the company approach with a scientific (and, indirectly, business) network. Without it, the company would probably have followed a more traditional internationalization trajectory.

To sum up, business opportunities are often unveiled in a manner different from that anticipated by the founders when they created the company. The emergence of foreign customers was instrumental in shaping development paths in Cases A, C, and D. They opened opportunities not envisaged beforehand, leading the company to adapt. The perception of the external environment opportunities was essential for Case E's turnaround. In addition, in Case B, though a change process was already anticipated, it turned out to be different from expected. This suggests that entrepreneurship cannot be envisaged, even in BGs, as a process that ends with company creation. Entrepreneurs' role continues to be very relevant in shaping the business model and adapting the product scope in the early years of the firm. This also has significant implications for the internationalization trajectory followed by the company.

Geography of Internationalization

Although there are different internationalization patterns, early linkages established with multinational and/or foreign customers were often instrumental in enabling internationalization moves and in shaping internationalization trajectories. This does not mean that company founders and management efforts were not important. Sometimes the very linkages mentioned above stemmed from their efforts, drawing upon academic/scientific networks. What is remarkable is how such linkages shaped the company business scope and internationalization.

Since the pre-establishment phase, there has been a perception that the business opportunity was not bound to the national market. In some instances, namely Cases B, C, D, and E, it was clear that, given the niche characteristics of the firm's products, the Portuguese market was too small for the company to grow and prosper.[7]

Case A had the most-developed business network. As mentioned above, the triggering factor for internationalization (and even for company creation) was the approach by Alcatel. The firm's software solutions were integrated into Alcatel products. Then, a global partnership was set up with IBM for worldwide marketing of the firm software. At a third stage, to promote the diffusion of its call centers and CRM software, partnerships were established with consultancy companies (Accenture, CapGemini/Ernst&Young). Internationalization was therefore leveraged by linkages, and extended globally at a fast pace. Foreign inquiries were also decisive in Case C. The relationship with NASA implied an early location in the USA, and this was the first relevant market abroad. The links with the European Space Agency (ESA), fostered by Portugal's accession to ESA only emerged later. These early links shaped the firm business portfolio, at that time very much oriented towards aerospace and defense. In this context, an office was opened in London, six years after inception, to further explore the European market. One year later, the company entered China. All these steps were led by the founding team. Multinational links were also paramount in Case D's early stage. The fact that Telecel/Vodafone Portugal was the first large customer for video games meant that the company was forging a channel to supply Vodafone worldwide. The early strategy also included the setting up of product development partnerships at a global level with other European MNEs.

In contrast, MNEs' role in the internationalization of Companies E and F was minor, if any. Case F was originally focused on the Iberian market, entering Spain one month after getting the first contract in Portugal. Several years elapsed, however, before it changed its name and went outside the Iberian Peninsula, to set up a subsidiary in the USA. As mentioned, support from the founder's scientific/social network in the USA was very relevant for this decision. Then, in less than three years, the firm was able to get contracts for setting up 'paperless hospital' software all around the world, from the Netherlands, Italy, and the UK, to Malaysia and Brazil. Interestingly, this accelerated internationalization in a closely regulated business was possible due to a strategy of product 'adaplication' (Simões et al. 2009), combining replication with adaptation. Case E had a global vision since inception: an English name, and an international website domain. Before launching the firm, an advisory board, involving scientists (from the USA, the UK and Spain) and company executives was set up. It had two main purposes: to keep the company abreast of recent scientific and 'operational' developments in the optical fibers field, and to provide an international reputation. The company had developed, since inception, an international strategy with three main vectors: marketing, through the presence in web platforms and agency relationships; product range complementariness, with 'peer' partners in the USA, Brazil, and Switzerland; and long-term learning partnerships with international agencies/associations and potential customers (Sá 2009). Five years since inception, Case B is present in Europe (nine countries), the Americas (USA, Brazil, and Colombia), and the Far East (Australia, China, and Taiwan).

There is a common thread in the internationalization of the six companies: the adoption of international niche strategies. Regarding the pace, the entry modes, and the geographical pattern, however, the differences are clear. Most companies exhibit a fast internationalization since inception, but there is one case where accelerated internationalization, with a global spread, only emerged later. For several cases, the establishment of early relationships with MNEs or foreign agencies was instrumental in enabling a fast geographical spread. Interestingly, in forging such linkages, the founders' scientific/academic and professional networks played an important role. The entry modes varied from indirect (through MNEs) and direct exports to direct investments, through licensing out and strategic alliances. There were no general rules: every firm followed an idiosyncratic, path-dependent pattern, very much influenced by founders' networks, early customers, and emerging opportunities. With regard to the geographical spread, diversity is again the norm. However, a few national markets are common to the majority of the cases surveyed: Brazil, Spain, the USA, and the UK.

DISCUSSION

Founders' Networks' Role in Sensing and Seizing Business Opportunities

The cases studied show that founders' networks play an important role in framing opportunities. They contribute to develop a project leading to company creation. They are envisaged as a source of ideas and resources as well as a means to proceed to an *ex ante* validation of the business idea. Our findings confirm the arguments of Gulati et al. (2000), and are in line with those of Coviello and Munro (1995), Andersson and Wictor (2003), and Sharma and Blomstermo (2003) regarding the relevance of early relationships in the launching of new international ventures. More importantly, they are convergent with those of Coviello (2006) concerning the role of networks before company creation.

Interestingly, in most of the cases surveyed, the social and academic/scientific networks precede the emergence of business networks. This is the consequence of two factors. The first concerns the very characteristics of the BGs considered in this study, most of them created by individuals with academic backgrounds. The second is related to the relevance of those networks in the *pre*-company creation stage. From this perspective, our research confirms the argument of Hite and Hesterly (2001) that network focus will change from mainly 'identity based' to mainly 'calculative'. This should not be given a negative connotation. When the company starts, it needs to generate resources from the market, and the business network gradually develops and strengthens. In fact, in our sample, when founders have a stronger early reliance on academic/scientific networks, the chances of confirming the conjectures and expectations that led to firm creation appear to be lower. Of course, there are initiatives to develop planned networks (Ellis 2000; Dominguinhos 2006), mostly after firm creation. But in several cases the market did not validate the *ex ante* sensing of opportunities. It is suggested that an appropriate sensing and seizing of opportunities requires a stronger involvement by founders in relevant business networks. These may provide the 'practical' knowledge and the resources needed for the new company to be sustainable and grow internationally. This is convergent with recent ideas of Johanson and Vahlne (2009) about the 'liability of outsidership'.

To overcome such a liability, the role of founders is very relevant. To some extent, they lend credibility and reputation to a company project that is still in the making. They use their academic/scientific network as a basis to enter business networks and improve their position there. Our research indicates, however, that this process may not be that easy. Being able to explore 'bridging' opportunities requires additional learning and may be time-consuming. Additionally, the adaptation to customers' needs may entail significant changes at the company level, namely regarding administrative procedures, business model, product scope, and market focus. For some companies, this was a hard learning process. The founders' nurturing and stabilizing role became essential: they kept the firm together while the focus was changing to better respond to 'real' customer requirements. Mathews and Zander's (2007) perspective of internationalization as a process of entrepreneurial discovery and strategizing under uncertainty, is, therefore, confirmed by our research.

As the involvement in business networks is enhanced, the opportunities to exploit the interactions between the academic/scientific and business networks improve. The founders may then act as 'bridges' between both types of networks, a finding already identified by Gassmann and Keupp (2007) regarding BGs in biotechnology. Such a 'bridging' role has, at least initially, a positive effect on the founders' reputation. They have a double 'domain-specific familiarity' (Fan and Phan 2007), with both company and academic specialists, enabling them to bridge structural holes (Burt 1992). This fact might be likely to make accelerated internationalization easier, as suggested by Fan and Phan.

Founders, External Environment, and Company Evolution

The above comments indicate that the entrepreneurial process goes much further than what Jones and Coviello (2005, p. 293) call 'the entrepreneurial event'. In fact, such a process includes pre-birth opportunity framing and resource bundling, company inception, and early company evolution. While important, company creation is an event in a longer process. To fully understand BGs, one should not focus only on the traditional 'three-year after inception' perspective. As Madsen and Servais (1997) remarked, one is dealing with an evolutionary process.

Furthermore, our findings and earlier research (Simões and Dominguinhos 2005; Simões et al. 2009) indicate that, contrary to Gabrielsson et al. (2008), for a company to become a BG, the existence of 'a global vision at inception' is not needed. From our analysis, what is required is a non-geographically bound opportunity framing. This condition is weaker than that argued by Gabrielsson et al. (2008). In fact, the key reason behind accelerated internationalization may be an approach from an international player, which levers the company to fast international growth earlier than anticipated. Some of our case studies show that unelicited, early, and often challenging contacts from those players open unexpected avenues for company internationalization, thus making those companies BGs.[8] As discussed by Gabrielsson and Kirpalani (2004), our research confirms that MNEs may play different roles in providing early internationalization channels: systems integrators (Case D), distribution channels (Case A), and technology and marketing partners (Case C). This puts in motion learning processes, as Autio et al. (2000), Autio (2005), and Zahra (2005) stressed. Learning provides 'a balance between unintended occurrences and intended design' (Coviello 2006, p. 725).

It was noted above that international learning and leveraging processes are not without pain for the new-born company. In fact, the contacts and requests often entail a change in company opportunity framing. In some cases, it may even go to the redesign of the whole company, to appropriately seize the opportunity. Paraphrasing Pirandello's play, new technology-based firms correspond to (technological) capabilities looking for a customer. There are technological capabilities, but the applications demanded do not exactly correspond to what the company has antici- pated. Responding to challenging customers' orders may not just enable fast internationalization, but also pave the way for the future. In other words, it spurs the process of transforming capabilities into homogene- ous, internationally marketable products (Gassmann and Keupp 2007). Customer requests for internationally driven products provide focus, and may help the company to mature and to find a clear international value- added niche (Nooteboom 2009; Simões et al. 2010).

In this process, the founder plays a central role. A parallel with Vygotsky's (1934 [1962]) language learning process seems to be warranted. Early customers are voicing themes that the company has to integrate itself, but the founders (as parents) have to nurture the company (the 'baby') to better understand the new words, as well as to set up a linkage between thinking and action. As mentioned above, the founders provide the internal and external credibility and reputation needed to ensure company change. They are also important to assemble and orchestrate the resources needed to seize the new opportunity (McDougall et al. 1994). It may happen, however, that the founder has to be 'sacrificed' for the company to grow and stabilize, changing from a dominant exploration model to an increased exploration–exploitation mix, where required lead- ership capabilities are different (March 1991; Nooteboom 2009).

Geography of Internationalization

This issue is not independent from the two addressed above. As men- tioned, internationalization is sometimes leveraged by contacts from early international customers. Networks matter as well. Business networks appear to be more relevant than social ones, a finding that is in line with Coviello (2006). This does not mean, however, that the findings of Ellis

(2000) and Harris and Wheeler (2005) are completely excluded. In fact, in some instances, as our cases show, academic/scientific and social networks are important, insofar as they enable a checking of opportunities and provide referrals. Case F is a good example: these networks fulfilled both roles, and were instrumental in the move to the USA and from there to Malaysia. The trick seems to be the forging of links between social and scientific/academic networks, on the one hand, and business networks, on the other.

Drawing on McEvily and Zaheer (1999), one of the main conclusions is that resource development and internationalization pathways are firm specific. These are influenced by unintended occurrences, including approaches by international customers which contribute in different ways for the international diffusion of company products (Ellis and Pecotich 2001; Coviello 2006). This is evident in some cases studied. For instance, without an approach from NASA, Case C would not have located in the USA so early.

Nevertheless, looking at the IB pattern as a whole, it becomes clear that company decisions of network development, resource allocation, and market search are no less important. The companies surveyed are simultaneously reactive and proactive in their international development (Johanisson 1998; Coviello 2006). The factors behind company internationalization decisions are related to different factors, besides the overcoming of the 'liability of outsidership' (Johanson and Vahlne, 2009). The analysis of our cases suggests that there are two key factors in the decision to enter a foreign market: learning opportunities and, most importantly, market attractiveness. Learning opportunities are mainly related to the country's trend-setting features and industry-specific clusters. For these reasons, some firms have decided to set up offices or to undertake direct investments in the United States. Being in the United States was perceived as essential to enhance learning. Another consideration has to do with reputation and achieving a 'global' status. The main factor, however, is market attractiveness. This is assessed as the result of two main considerations: founders' perception of psychic proximity, and market characteristics, namely size. The latter is self-explanatory. The first stems from a mix of cultural proximity, living experience, language mastering, and former networking. This is not so much based on general cultural considerations, but rather on the founders' subjective perception. This explains, on the one hand, decisions to go to Brazil or Spain, and, on the other, the choice to go to the USA, the UK, or the Netherlands.

The accelerated internationalization phenomenon is, from another perspective, associated with the existence of a unique, internationally homogeneous product. This lends confirmation to the findings of Knight and

Cavusgil (2004) and Gassmann and Keupp (2007). However, at inception, this perception may not exist or, alternatively, there is a bet on a product that proves not to be appropriate. The involvement of customers is then central for the company to develop the 'right' product and/or to become aware of the world market potential of existing products.

To sum up, the pace and geography of internationalization are the outcome of different factors, dealing with the shallowness of the domestic country, the characteristics of the product, market attractiveness, and company and founder networks.

CONCLUSIONS

This research was aimed at answering the following question: how do the founders' capabilities and networks contribute to shape BGs' evolution and early internationalization patterns?

Based on the analysis of six case studies of Portuguese BGs, evidence was provided to help us answer the above question. The evidence collected is sound enough to support a set of interesting conclusions. These are, to a significant extent, convergent with extant literature on BGs. A process perspective is highlighted. In contrast, they illuminate aspects that have been under-researched so far. The conclusions are organized around four themes.

The first concerns the need to deepen our understanding of the relationships between the entrepreneurial project and early company life. Global reach and accelerated internationalization are to some extent anchored on pre-birth features, namely, how the business opportunity is framed. But they are also dependent on later events, stemming from company initiatives and from unexpected customer approaches. The main thread linking 'pre' and 'post' firm creation is provided by the founders. Their role does not decline when the firm is born. On the contrary, they are essential for the company to overcome initial 'teething' difficulties.

A second conclusion is that entrepreneurial projects are bound to change *ex post*, as a consequence of market exposure. Such a change appears to be more common when firm creation is undertaken by researchers/academics. The development of a business network, enabling the process of market validation of entrepreneurial ideas, is very important for a company's early growth and sustainability. The new-born firm has to adapt to customer requirements. Simultaneously, these may open new, unexpected, development paths. Again, the founders play a role in lending credibility to the company, and in forging relevant business connections.

The third conclusion is that bridging networks may become an important leverage factor. When scientific/academic and business networks do exist, academic company founders may play a bridging role, combining insights from both fields. This has a positive impact on company development. However, moving between the two fields requires learning and the development of trust. This is a time-consuming process, particularly in an international context.

The fourth conclusion concerns the geography of internationalization. The shallowness of the Portuguese domestic market encourages companies to try to internationalize. However, the existence of a 'body of understanding' (Pavitt 1998), anchored in scientific knowledge, may not be enough to ensure fast internationalization. The triggers for this may come from international customers, namely multinational players, who provide levers and networks for expanding in the international space. Having internationally homogeneous products is important insofar as they enable faster market expansion. However, they are not a necessary condition as our research suggests: when the firm is able to follow an 'adaplication' approach, combining adaptation and replication, fast internationalization processes may also be achieved.

This chapter was intended to enhance our knowledge about the role of founders in early company evolution, based on a set of case studies of Portuguese BGs. It made some contributions, but more is still to be done. The role of founders in the process of going from pre-birth sensing of opportunities to post-birth seizing (or not) deserves further study. Particularly relevant is the process of company revision of *ex ante* projects and adaptation to unexpected challenges. The individual/team/ organizational dialectics over time is central to better understand the emergence and early development of BGs. A particularly fruitful, though difficult, research stream would be the comparison of 'intended' BGs with 'realized' BGs to identify the factors, other than luck, which lead to either outcome.

NOTES

1. Although I am aware of the multitude of labels to denote the firms that early in their life cycles develop significant outward business activities (see, for instance, Rialp et al. 2005b, and Svensson and Payan 2009) and have raised criticisms to some conceptualizations of born globals (Simões et al. 2009), I think that this label is the most appropriate to capture the key features of those firms.
2. I do not fully share this perspective, since sometimes the global vision is not present at inception, but emerges at a later stage, though still early in the firm's life cycle, (see Simões and Dominguinhos 2005; Simões et al. 2009). More on this later.
3. For the sake of economy, the terms 'entrepreneur' and 'founder' will be used

interchangeably. We are aware, however, that in most cases there is not just one individual behind the venture, but rather a team of entrepreneurs or founders.
4. Mathews and Zander (2007) refer to 'the discovery of opportunities'. We prefer 'seizing', since discovery implicitly assumes that the opportunity pre-exists the entrepreneur, while we argue, in line with Weick (1995), that in entrepreneurial processes, entrepreneurs make sense of opportunities. See Simões and Dominguinhos (2006).
5. In one case this has not been possible. However, an interview was conducted with a close collaborator, who was also involved in the firm's early stage.
6. Seventh Framework Programme of the European Community for Research, Technological Development and Demonstration Activities.
7. For Case B, there wasn't even a market in Portugal.
8. As noted above, the process may not be easy for the company, often entailing significant changes.

REFERENCES

Andersson, S. and I. Wictor (2003), 'Innovative internationalization in new firms: born globals – the Swedish case', *Journal of International Entrepreneurship*, **1**(3), 249–76.

Autio, E. (2005), 'Creative tension: the significance of Ben Oviatt's and Patricia McDougall's article 'Toward a theory of international new venture', *Journal of International Business Studies*, **36**(1), 9–19.

Autio, E., H. Sapienza and J. Almeida (2000), 'Effects of age at entry, knowledge intensity, and immitability on international growth', *Academy of Management Journal*, **43**(5), 909–24.

Bartlett, Christopher A. and Sumantra Ghoshal (1989), *Managing Across Borders: The Transnational Solution*, Boston, MA: Harvard Business School Press.

Burt, Ronald S. (1992), *Structural Holes*, Cambridge, MA: Harvard Business School Press.

COTEC (2010), Rede PME Inovação, available at: (http://www.cotecportugal.pt/index.php?option=com_content&task=blogcategory&id=58&Itemid=179 (accessed October 1, 2010).

Coviello, N.E. (2006), 'The network dynamics of international new ventures', *Journal of International Business Studies*, **37**(5), 713–31.

Coviello, N.E. and M. Jones (2004), 'Methodological issues in international entrepreneurship research', *Journal of Business Venturing*, **19**(4), 485–508.

Coviello, N.E. and H. Munro (1995), 'Growing the entrepreneurial firm: networking for international market development', *European Journal of Marketing*, **29**(7), 49–62.

Crick, D. and M. Spence (2005), 'The internationalization of 'high performing' UK high-tech SMEs: a study of planned and unplanned strategies', *International Business Review*, **14**(2), 167–85.

De Geus, Arie (1997), *The Living Company: Growth, Learning and Longevity in Business*, London: Nicholas Brealey.

Dimitratos, P. and E. Plakoyiannaki (2003), 'Theoretical foundations of an international entrepreneurial culture', *Journal of International Entrepreneurship*, **1**(2), 187–215.

Dominguinhos, P. (2006), 'Born globals – Da formatação da oportunidade à aprendizagem global', PhD dissertation, ISEG, Lisbon.

Eisenhardt, K.M. (1989), 'Building theories from case study research', *Academy of Management Review*, **14**(4), 532–50.

Eisenhardt, K.M. and J.A. Martin (2000), 'Dynamic capabilities: what are they?', *Strategic Management Journal*, **21**(Special issue October–November), 1105–21.

Ellis, P. (2000), 'Social ties and foreign market entry', *Journal of International Business Studies*, **31**(3), 443–69.

Ellis, P. and A. Pecotich (2001), 'Social factors influencing export initiation in small and medium-sized enterprises', *Journal of Marketing Research*, **38**(1), 119–30.

Fan, T. and P. Phan (2007), 'International new ventures: revisiting the influences behind the "born-global" firm', *Journal of International Business Studies*, **38**(7), 1113–31.

Gabrielsson, M. and V.H.M. Kirpalani (2004), 'Born globals: how to reach new business space rapidly', *International Business Review*, **13**(5), 555–72.

Gabrielsson, M., V.H.M. Kirpalani, P. Dimitratos, C.A. Solberg and A. Zucchella (2008), 'Born globals: propositions to help advance the theory', *International Business Review*, **17**(4), 385–401.

Gassmann, O. and M.M. Keupp (2007), 'The competitive advantage of early and rapidly internationalizing SMEs in the biotechnology industry: a knowledge-based view', *Journal of World Business*, **42**(3), 350–66.

Ghauri, Pervez, Kjell Gronhaug and Ivar Kristianslund (1995), *Research Methods in Business Studies*, Hemel Hempstead, UK: Prentice-Hall.

Gulati, R., N. Nohria and A. Zaheer (2000), 'Strategic networks', *Strategic Management Journal*, **21**(3), 203–15.

Gummerson, Evert (2000), *Qualitative Methods in Management Research*, 2nd edn, London: Sage.

Harris, Simon and Colin Wheeler (2005), 'Enterpreneurs' relationships for internationalization: function, origins and strategies', *International Business Review*, **14**(2), 187–207.

Helfat, Constance E., Sydney Filkenstein, Will Mitchell, Margaret A. Peteraf, Harbir Singh, David J. Teece and Sidney J. Winter (2007), *Dynamic Capabilities: Understanding Strategic Change in Organizations*, Malden, MA: Blackwell.

Hite, J.M. and W.S. Hesterly (2001), 'The evolution of firm networks: from emergence to early growth of the firm', *Strategic Management Journal*, **22**(3), 275–86.

Johanisson, B. (1998), 'Entrepreneurship as a collective phenomenon', paper presented at the Rank XII Conference, Lyons.

Johanson, J. and J.-E. Vahlne (2009), 'The Uppsala internationalization process model revisited: from liability of foreignness to liability of outsidership', *Journal of International Business Studies*, **40**(9), 1411–31.

Jones, M.V. and N. Coviello (2005), 'Internationalization: conceptualizing an entrepreneurial process of behaviour in time', *Journal of International Business Studies*, **36**(3), 284–303.

Keupp, M.M. and O. Gassmann (2009), 'The past and the future of international entrepreneurship: a review and suggestions for developing the field', *Journal of Management*, **35**, 600–633.

Knight, G.A. and S.T. Cavusgil (2004), 'Innovation, organizational capabilities, and the born-global firm', *Journal of International Business Studies*, **35**(2), 124–41.

Knight, G.A. and S.T. Cavusgil (2005), 'A taxonomy of born-global firms', *Management International Review*, **45**(3), Special issue, 15–35.

Kudina, A., G. Yip and H. Barkema (2008), 'Born global', *Business Strategy Review*, **19**(Winter), 38–44.

Laanti, R., M. Gabrielsson and P. Gabrielsson (2007), 'The globalization strategies of business-to-business born global firms in the wireless technology industry', *Industrial Marketing Management*, **36**(8), 1104–17.

Lee, C., K. Lee and J.M. Pennings (2001), 'International capabilities, external networks, and performance: a study on technology-based ventures', *Strategic Management Journal*, **22**(6–7), 615–40.

Madsen, T.K. and P. Servais (1997), 'The internationalization of born globals: an evolutionary process?', *International Business Review*, **6**(6), 561–93.

March, James (1991), 'Exploration and exploitation in organizational learning', *organization Science*, **2**, 71–87.

Mathews, J.A. and I. Zander (2007), 'The international entrepreneurial dynamics of accelerated internationalization', *Journal of International Business Studies*, **38**(3), 387–403.

McDougall, P.P., S. Shane and B.M. Oviatt (1994), 'Explaining the formation of international new ventures: the limits of theories from international business research', *Journal of Business Venturing*, **9**(6), 469–87.

330 *Handbook of research on born globals*

McEvily, B. and A. Zaheer (1999), 'Bridging ties: a source of firm heterogeneity in competitive capabilities', *Strategic Management Journal*, **20**(12), 1113–56.
Mort, G.S. and J. Weerawardena (2006), 'Networking capability and international entrepreneurship: how networks function in Australian born global firms', *International Marketing Review*, **23**(5), 549–72.
Nelson, Richard R. and Sidney G. Winter (1982), *An Evolutionary Theory of Economic Change*, Cambridge, MA: Harvard University Press.
Nooteboom, Bart (2009), *A Cognitive Theory of the Firm: Learning, Governance and Dynamic Capabilities*, Cheltenham, UK and Northampton, MA, USA: Edward Elgar.
Oviatt, B.M. and P.P. McDougall (1994), 'Towards a theory of international new ventures', *Journal of International Business Studies*, **25**(1), 45–64.
Pavitt, K. (1998), 'Technologies, products and organisation in the innovating firm: what Adam Smith tells us that Joseph Schumpeter doesn't', *Industrial and Corporate Change*, **7**(3), 433–51.
Rialp, A., J. Rialp and G. Knight (2005a), 'The phenomenon of early internationalizing firms: what do we know after a decade of research (1993–2003) of scientific inquiry', *International Business Review*, **14**(2), 147–66.
Rialp, A., J. Rialp, D. Urbano and Y. Vaillant (2005b), 'The born-global phenomenon: a comparative case study research', *Journal of International Entrepreneurship*, **3**(2), 133–71.
Sá, F.N.A. (2009), 'Parcerias e internacionalização numa start-up portuguesa: Estudo de caso', Case written for the course on 'International aspects of technology and innovation', ISEG, Lisbon.
Shrader, R.C., B.M. Oviatt and P.P. McDougall (2000), 'How new ventures explore trade-offs among international risk factors: lessons for the accelerated internationalization of the 21st century', *Academy of Management Journal*, **43**(6), 1227–47.
Sharma, D. and A. Blomstermo (2003), 'The internationalization process of born globals: a network view', *International Business Review*, **12**(6), 739–53.
Simões, V.C., P.T. Capão and R.M. Carvalho (2009), 'Quasi-born globals: do they deserve a specific approach?', paper presented at the 35th EIBA Conference, Valencia, December.
Simões, V.C. and P. Dominguinhos (2001), 'Portuguese born globals: an exploratory study', paper presented at the 27th EIBA Conference, Paris, December.
Simões, V.C. and P. Dominguinhos (2005), 'An exploratory study on opportunity framing process', paper presented at the 31st EIBA Conference, Oslo, December.
Simões, V.C. and P. Dominguinhos (2006), 'Empreendedor, oportunidade, projecto: o trinómio do empreendedorismo', *Comportamento Organizacional e Gestão*, Special issue, 43–69.
Simões, V.C., V.S. Roldão, P. Bento, N.J. Crespo, G. Cardoso, H.P. Sousa, M.M. Godinho, P. Camilo, R.M. Cartaxo and S. Mendonça (2010), *Estudo de caracterização da actividade desenvolvida pelas empresas que constituem a Rede PME Inovação*, Lisbon: ISCTE/ISEG.
Stake, Robert E. (1994), *The Art of Case Research*, Newbury Park, CA: Sage.
Svensson, Göran and Janice M. Payan (2009), 'Organizations that are international from inception: terminology and research constellations – "academic protectionism" or "academic myopia"?', *Journal of Small Business and Enterprise Development*, **16**(3), 406–17.
Teece, David J. (2009), *Dynamic Capabilities and Strategic Management*, Oxford: Oxford University Press.
Teece, D.J., G. Pisano and A. Shuen (1997), 'Dynamic capabilities and strategic management', *Strategic Management Journal*, **18**(7), 509–33.
Vygotsky, Lev S. (1934/ [1962]), *Thought and Language*, Cambridge, MA: MIT Press.
Weerawardena, J., G.S. Mort, P.W. Liesch and G. Knight (2007), 'Conceptualizing accelerated internationalization in the born global firm: a dynamic capabilities perspective', *Journal of World Business*, **42**(3), 294–306.
Weick, Karl (1995), *Sensemaking in Organizations*, Thousand Oaks, CA: Sage.
Yin, Robert K. (2009), *Case Study Research – Design and Methods*, 4th edn, Newbury Park, CA: Sage.

Yli-Renko, H., E. Autio and H.J. Sapienza (2001), 'Social capital, knowledge acquisition, and knowledge exploitation in young technology-based firms', *Strategic Management Journal*, **22**, 587–613.

Zahra, S.A. (2005), 'A theory of international joint ventures: a decade of research', *Journal of International Business Studies*, **36**, 20–28.

17 Battleship strategy for managing MNC–born global innovation networks
Terhi J. Vapola

INTRODUCTION

This research explores the use of global innovation constellations[1] between multinational corporations (MNCs) and globally oriented start-ups in high-tech industries. In particular, it uncovers a framework of key factors that are used in driving the added value from this particular type of alliance network. This framework is labeled the 'battleship strategy'.

The battleship strategy can be well illustrated by a metaphor. A battleship[2] is large and powerful. It has strong firepower and powerful engines that propel it forward, but it takes time for its engines to get started or to change its course. Therefore, it uses small and agile fighter jets to scout its environment. The uniqueness of the battleship strategy lies in the suggestion that start-ups can serve as scout planes for MNCs. Since innovative activity is inherently uncertain, start-ups may test the waters and explore new technological or market opportunities outside the MNC's normal operations, while the start-ups benefit from gaining access to global markets as a part of the MNC's solutions.

Despite its fundamental importance, global innovation constellations between MNCs and a large number of innovative start-ups in the high-tech industries have received surprisingly little attention in international business research. There does not yet appear to be sufficient theoretical understanding of how the challenges of constant innovative change in dynamic industries, and the resulting pressures on the sustainability of competitive advantage in the global markets, can be addressed by using global innovation constellations. In particular, previous research has overlooked the problem of asymmetry between MNCs and start-ups, which the managers need to account for in structuring global innovation constellations in ways that add value for all participants in high-tech markets. Alvarez and Barney (2001) argue that a start-up might not gain economic returns from participating in alliances with large firms, while other researchers are equally concerned that an MNC cannot gain returns *ex post* from innovations that are beyond its own boundaries. Therefore, it seems appropriate to explore this problem in greater detail from the

332

perspective of the added value for participating firms. The *research question* is stated as follows: what are the key motives, strategies and structures that MNCs and start-ups have for forming global innovation constellations?

Turning to definitions, an *alliance constellation* is a set of firms linked together through alliances that compete in a particular competitive domain (Gomes-Casseres 1996). In other words, it has multiple participants and it is considered as a tool for competitive advantage when positioning it against other similar multiparty alliances. For the purposes of this research, this is narrowed further. In this research, a *global innovation constellation* is defined as a loose, non-equity opportunity-seeking co-opetitive multiparty alliance that spans across the world and is used in order to create innovations that add value to participants relative to competition.

Compared to related concepts, such as multiparty R&D alliances, the notion of a global innovation constellation emphasizes the competitive positioning against similar alliance groups. The primary focus is on the business opportunity creation, and, therefore, technological advances of the innovation are not the core issue, rather the primary focus is given to the commercialization of the innovation. This is aligned with Schumpeter's (1912[1934]) definition of innovation.

The two key types of players of this research are MNCs and start-up firms (or born globals). An MNC is defined as a large multinational firm with significant tangible and intangible assets and hence the capacity to operate widely across the globe, with global learning as a critical source of competitive advantage (Bartlett and Ghoshal 1989; Doz et al. 2001). The expression 'MNC' is used as a generic term referring to an MNC as a whole, including headquarters and subsidiaries. In this research, 'start-up firms' are considered to be similar to Oviatt and McDougall's (1994) definition of born globals, with limited resources but yet focusing on gaining competitive advantage by seeking rapid globalization of their innovations.

After this introduction, the theoretical foundation of this research is presented. This is followed by the research design. The findings are consolidated next. Finally, the central contributions and the implications of the research are laid out. The limitations are stated, leading to suggestions for future research directions.

THEORETICAL FOUNDATION

Turning to the theories providing the basis for approaching this research, this section reviews the theoretical perspectives relevant to this research.

Perspectives on Innovation

The difficulty of sustaining competitive advantage is one of the fundamental challenges facing firms in today's global high-tech industries. The pace of technological change is intense, and industry structures and power positions of individual firms are constantly changing (Moriarty and Kosnik 1989; McGrath 1995; Hitt et al. 1998). Convergence between technologies leads to new products and solutions (Hacklin et al. 2009). These challenges are further increased by technological, market, and regulatory uncertainties (Blomqvist 2002).

Change, uncertainty, and an emphasis on the entrepreneurial discovery, are the cornerstones of the Schumpeterian perspective to innovation. The resurgence of neo-Schumpeterian theories and models is a clear sign of the significance of his theoretical works on the dynamics of economic change as a result of innovative activities (Parayil 1991; Rothaermel and Hill 2005; Diamond 2009). Schumpeter (1912 [1934]) argues that new technologies create new market opportunities while simultaneously destroying others in existing markets. Therefore, sustainability of competitive advantage is only temporary (ibid.; Brown and Eisenhardt 1998).

Further, Schumpeter was the first to state that innovative change generates competition (Brunner 1994). Innovation introduces imperfect competition and disequilibrium into the economic system; for a firm this introduces the possibility of a temporary monopoly situation, with high unit profit margins and prices in those markets where it possesses the greatest performance advantage over other competing alternatives (Hagedoorn 1989). This competition works for the benefit of innovatively advanced firms (Brunner 1994), and hence innovations from other firms affect their own results.

Due to an uncertain environment, the MNCs are constantly at risk of being overtaken by new, flexible, and fast-moving entrants (Foster 1986; Anderson and Tushman 1990; Christensen 1997; Almor and Hashai 2004; Rothaermel and Hill 2005; Stieglitz and Heine 2007). Disruptions occur when new entrants that start in a niche segment use innovations and, as they improve, displace incumbent technologies from mainstream segments (Adner and Zemsky 2006). Research on innovation argues that the attackers have a natural advantage in the era of technological change within an industry (Foster 1986; Christensen 1997). Thus, leadership strategy and innovation are mainly attached to the new entrants that have a higher comparative return by engaging in disruptive technological change. This implies that existing firms are mainly considered as followers at the advent of a technological change, and thus destined to fail (for example, Fairclough 1994).

When realizing the risk of followership, a typical way of becoming less vulnerable to attacks from new technology-based entrants is by broadening the set of internal innovation (Burgelman et al. 2001). Rothaermel and Hill (2005) argue that having a strong R&D capability as a means to overcome the innovative drawback may mitigate the negative performance effect caused by the innovations of start-ups. However, Narula and Hagedoorn (1999) argue that the internalization of all potential R&D activities is clearly no longer a practical solution. An inverted U-curve between exploration and exploitation activities and their respective performance has been identified, and this relationship is more pronounced in innovation-intensive industries (Uotila et al. 2009). In other words, it is not beneficial to under- or overinvest in exploring new innovations. Furthermore, rapid change means that firms have a shorter time to recover their investments (Narula and Hagedoorn 1999).

However, when previous research has examined the impact of innovation on a firm's competitive advantage, it may have overlooked the nature of technology, and the collaboration that frequently occurs between firms when introducing the new innovations into vast global markets.

First, it is more likely for an incumbent MNC to ensure the continuation of its power position if new innovation is built on top of existing know-how and systems, and if the new innovation expands into the existing market (Vapola 2000). While the incumbent MNC still needs the new innovation, the base investments in the old technology are not lost. The internalization of all potential new innovations, however, still poses a serious challenge to MNCs (Narula and Hagedoorn 1999). Therefore, in addition to internal R&D activities, collaborative approaches with other original innovators are needed.

Second, Christensen (2005) argues that the odds are low for creating new start-ups with a sustaining, leap-beyond-the-competition strategy. Small start-ups may lack the capabilities to commercialize their innovations quickly into global markets (Gabrielsson and Kirpalani, 2004). Commercialization for global markets is a costly process, where the interest of small entrants may well suggest collaborating with incumbent MNCs.

Strategic alliance research suggests that complementarity also plays an important role in driving the added value of inter-firm relationships (Harrigan 1988; Nielsen 2004; Stieglitz and Heine 2007; Hallikas et al. 2008; Lunnan and Haugland 2008). Extant research recognizes the high degree of partnerships exhibited particularly between large MNCs and new entrants in high-tech industries, and the paramount importance of these partnerships for innovation-related performance improvements (Rothaermel and Hill 2005).

Innovation-driven Competitive Advantage

In order to address the impact of innovation on firms in the industry, it is important to discuss the concept of competitive advantage and its key factors. It is suggested that resource ownership or control may no longer be the necessary condition for competitive advantage. Autio and Yli-Renko (1998) and Chesbrough (2003) suggest an open innovation approach between large companies and entrepreneurial start-ups, which allows innovation to traverse the firm's boundaries. Consequently, it is not sufficient to rely only on the MNC's internal global knowledge sensing, mobilizing, and operationalizing capabilities (Doz et al. 2001). Hence, while recognizing both the risk of trusting and relying on their partners (Becerra et al. 2008), and the limiting impact of external innovation on internal learning by doing (Weigelt 2009), it appears rational to complement an internal innovation strategy by external innovation.

Innovations affect competitive advantage by shifting existing cost and benefit positions, and also potentially, by increasing rivalry. Further, start-ups as new players in the value net need to be added to the framework. Schumpeter (1912[1934]) considers the economic profitability to be the incentive that stimulates entrepreneurship and thereby innovation. Innovative globally oriented start-ups tend to create competitive advantage by exploring and developing new technologies or businesses (Sharma and Blomstermo 2003; Almor and Hashai 2004; Gabrielsson and Kirpalani 2004; Vapola et al. 2008). Innovation can complement or replace an MNC's current core technologies (Vapola 2000). Furthermore, while start-ups can initially provide complementary peripheral technologies, these peripheral technologies may become core technologies in the future (Burgelman et al. 2001; Adner and Zemsky 2006).

By considering the impact of external and internal innovation, and the logic of how innovative start-ups affect other firms' competitive advantage, a new conceptual extension to the generic competitive advantage concept appears. As illustrated in Figure 17.1, the impact of innovation can be derived in three distinct ways. First, both external and internal innovation may affect the benefit position of the firm relative to its competitors, because new ideas may create new needs and preferences. Hence, innovation may affect the willingness to pay of customers in a given product market. Second, when an innovation affects the relative cost structure, the competitive advantage of a firm may change relative to the firm with the cost affecting innovation. Third, should an external innovation provide its inventor with the means to enter the market, a

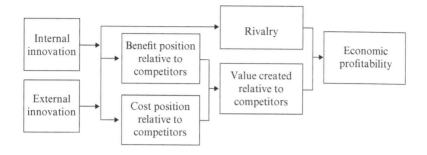

Source: Besanko et al. (1996).

Figure 17.1 Impact of innovation on a firm's competitive advantage

firm will experience increased rivalry in its markets. This threat is especially valid in an extreme case; when an innovative start-up changes the dominant design (Anderson and Tushman 1990). In each of these three different ways, the start-up affects the firm's competitive advantage (Vapola et al. 2008).

Drawing on Adner and Zemsky (2006), the net competitive advantage of a firm is the sum of its differentiation (dis)advantage and its cost (dis)advantage after the substitution threat of new innovation. Innovations originating in start-up firms contribute positively to competitive advantage if MNCs have access to them and succeed in integrating them.

Drawn from Vapola et al. (2008), and aligned with co-opetitive theory (Brandenburger and Nalebuff 1996), an MNC's access to start-up originated innovation is subject to the role a start-up chooses to play. For this reason, the research presented in this chapter highlights the fact that start-ups can play multiple roles for MNCs. For example, a start-up can be a supplier of an innovative sub-element of an MNC's offering. A start-up can also be a reseller of an MNC's products and services through a new approach to distribution, such as the internet. A start-up can also disrupt the technology base and become a competitor to an MNC. And, finally, a start-up can provide a complementary solution to an MNC's offering. According to an argument in the industrial economics stream of thought, the logic expressed above addresses exactly the purpose of alliances: firms with dissimilar capabilities can coordinate creation of complementary products (Gomes-Casseres 2006). The shift from providing a competing solution to a complementary solution can be very small; in principle it might be the same innovation, which is just positioned on the market in different ways.

RESEARCH DESIGN

This chapter explores conceptually (Whetten 1989) the variables that shape the motivations of participants in global innovation constellations, describes the logic of the game in the global innovation constellations using both a metaphor of a battleship as well as applying the value net (Brandenburger and Nalebuff 1996) to the research context. It uses empirical examples from case studies (Eisenhardt and Graebner 2007).

The unit of analysis is the groups of firms that are being analyzed: the MNCs and the start-ups. Since the aggregated level as the unit of analysis is not directly observable, the unit of observation needs to be different from the unit of analysis. Therefore, this research relies on data from the firm level, which is then aggregated to describe the larger phenomenon of the two types of firms in the context of new opportunity creation resulting from interacting in global innovation constellations in high-tech markets. Thereafter, with respect to global innovation constellations, the properties of these two types of firm are explored and also their strategies for participating in constellations. The chapter identifies the variables of internal strategy and external structure for such constellations.

Although it is clear that the research needs to address both the firm and the inter-firm level of analysis, an exploratory approach allowed for a multilevel analysis to be applied in the research. The chapter addresses both the interaction between the two types of firm as well as the internal management questions of the types of firms by addressing the analytical properties of strategy and structure.

The main focus of this research is the area of dynamic high-tech industry. In particular, the mobile telecommunications and software industries were selected as the main empirical context for researching global innovation constellations between start-ups and MNCs. The reasons for this selection are the characteristics of innovation-driven change, the proliferation of global innovation constellations, the entrepreneurial approach, and global presence. Hence, these industries provide a rare and rich case research setting to investigate the key factors relating to MNCs' and start-ups' participation in global innovation constellations.

Empirically, Nokia and Hewlett Packard (HP) were used as main case MNCs, and the global innovation constellations were operationalized as Forum Nokia and HP Bazaar. In Nokia's case, at the time of empirical research, there were over 400 categorized as PRO members, and in HP's case there were over 600 partners in the constellation. Additionally, case data from 14 Finnish software start-ups was used. Semi-structured interviews, observation, and secondary research were used to collect data.

Data analysis was started shortly after data collection, and was carried out in parallel with further data collection. Incidents describing the phenomenon were sought, that is, illustrations, statements, and actions that were explicitly related to the investigation. The next phase of the analysis was the concern with how the various conceptual factors that had been identified could be linked into a coherent framework explaining the phenomenon. Various iterations were carried out. Comparison of cases helped to increase the robustness of the models. Table 17.1, summarizes the methodological choices.

FINDINGS

This research questions how global innovation constellations are utilized to contribute to competitive advantage of its asymmetric participants. It explores the value creation and appropriation strategies and the structures of respective constellations among the two types of firm. Noting that the individual focus areas are covered in their respective articles, the main focus of this present chapter is to draw conclusions in the form of an emergent framework.

Implications of Asymmetry between MNCs and Start-ups

In global high-tech industries, new innovations affect firms' competitive advantage. Recently, there has been a significant increase in the formation of large non-equity multiparty alliances focusing on innovative activities. For example, advanced high-tech MNCs such as Nokia and HP have formed global innovation alliances with hundreds of small developers.

Empirical insights from the global high-tech industry suggest different approaches that start-ups and MNCs use for collaborating with each other. For example, Finnish software start-ups use different large value chain partners such as system suppliers (for example, Nokia), large system integrators, and large telecommunications operators in their efforts to commercialize their innovations in international markets. On the other hand, an MNC example is when Nokia's partnerships help the firm to execute its strategic intent of transforming itself from the world's leading mobile phone manufacturer into an internet solutions firm. The number of Nokia's internet partnerships has grown tremendously over recent years. In addition to large strategic partnerships, this portfolio consists of a large number of small software developers across the world.

The empirical insights suggest that the different types of firm also have rather different motivations, capabilities, and approaches to global innovation constellations which managers need to account for, both internally

Table 17.1 Summary of methodology

Focus area	Focus of analysis	Cases in this research	Method of data collection	Data sources	Data types
1. Performance	Categorization of membership in global innovation constellation and having the respective product launched in the market	Case firms (=27): Entire population of mobile operators in Belgium, France, Germany, Netherlands, Taiwan, USA Case global innovation constellation: Global i-mode Alliance	Data through secondary research in 2005	Natsuno (2003), public announcements in the NTT DoCoMo website, and analyst reports: CurrentAnalysis, Jupiterresearch, Gartner, Ovum, Yankee Group Analysys Research	List of members and non-members in their respective countries
	Analysis of performance	Same as above	Same as above	EMC cellular subscriber database, Yankee, Merrill Lynch	Database of each firm's subscriber and ARPU during 1999–2004 (included). N = 81
2. Motivations, initial conditions and strategies	Conceptualization of Battleship strategy and structure: Analysis of incidents describing the phenomenon, and the linkages between its factors	Case MNCs: Nokia and Hewlett-Packard Case global innovation constellations and case firms (incl. above): Forum Nokia with partner number of over 400 developers and HP Bazaar with over 600 partners in 2005	Semi-structured interviews in 2004–05 Data from secondary archival research and observation in 2004–06	Interviews of most important informants: directors in charge or the founders of constellations, observation over several years Secondary data from corporate websites, annual reports, industry brochures, press releases	Qualitative data from sources and multiple iterations of the conceptual frameworks over 2004–8
	Various iterations				

3. Partner attraction	Identification of characteristics, which start-ups perceive driving the attractiveness of their partners	Case firms: 14 globally oriented Finnish case start-ups in the software industry	Semi-structured interviews in 2005. Data from secondary archival research in 2008-09	14 senior managers, plus websites, press releases, annual reports, potential partners	Database of responses from 47 dyadic relationships each with 53 structured questions, and complementary unstructured data. Plus archival data
4. Alliance portfolio management	Category of international strategy	Case MNCs: Honkarakenne, Nokia, Wärtsilä, Perlos, Kone. Case alliances: all alliances that were publicly referred to	Semi-structured interviews	34 senior managers (Director to Sr. VP level)	Cross-sectional data: 65 hours of tape-recorded transcripts
	Strategic alliance orientation	Same as above	Data from above. Secondary archival research spanning years 1997-2007	Above, plus business journals (Kauppalehti, Optio), websites, press releases, annual report	Database of 9,000 data points incl. codified primary interview data and longitudinal archival data
	Portfolio management characteristics	Same as above	Same as above	Same as above	Same as above

and in structuring a global innovation constellation in ways that add value for differing participants. Solution accounting for the asymmetry between global innovation constellation participants is crucial, because both types of parties are making their choices independently.

First, the difference in characteristics of MNCs and start-ups given an asymmetric importance for partner attraction and selection. From the MNC's point of view, portfolio logic suggests that the MNC add more partners to its constellation in order to maximize its chances of getting access to successful innovation. A case MNC highlighted the importance of third-party innovation and ecosystem partners. Having global innovation constellations with a large number of partners may allow the MNC to externalize part of its innovation activities, while gaining competitive advantage through ideas developed by other firms. A decision to add one additional partner may not be very strategic. For example, during an interview, a manager participating in founding a global innovation constellation at HP said that for him, the more critical question was how to get innovative start-ups to approach them, out of all the potential MNC partners, rather than approaching other MNCs that might be that particular MNC's competitors.

Another manager from a different case MNC stated that the biggest challenge is not to find the great external innovation, but to actually know internally what is of highest interest to the firm. The capability to evaluate and decide upon a larger number of innovations and companies is crucial. On the other hand, start-ups with the most sought-after innovations may be in the position of choosing their partners, and in this case, the MNC's indecisiveness might negatively influence the start-up's choice of the global innovation constellation.

Small entrepreneurial start-ups benefit from partnerships with large global partners providing that they gain access to international markets, but they cannot spread their limited resources to engage in very many partnerships at a given time. For example, many CEOs of small high-tech firms said that they are very eager to partner with large MNCs and participate in global innovation constellations, but were concerned about the complexity and resource consumption of these financially uncertain early activities. Therefore, small firms tend to choose a small number of partner MNCs with whom they will invest the necessary time and effort for setting up the new partnership.

For small firm managers, the choice of a partner that really brings added value in the form of global business can be a question of survival. If the returns are delayed or are not realized, the financial leverage of the small start-up might be used up by then. For this reason, start-ups may prefer a constellation where multiple potential partners are present. Because of a scarcity of resources, start-ups can get many allies through a single alliance network.

Due to the nature of MNCs and start-up firms, when looking from both perspectives, a significant asymmetry in the question of partner attraction is presented. This makes it fundamentally different from establishing relationships with similar types of firms. The challenge is especially relevant in high velocity industries; due to constant change in the market, pressure is put on quickly finding and attracting the right partners to commercialize the innovations on a global scale.

Second, the difference in characteristics of MNCs and start-up firms places asymmetric importance on the portfolio management of the alliance. From the viewpoint of a small start-up, the alliance portfolio management may be a non-issue, as it can be flexible in managing its small number of partners without heavy processes and governance issues. However, from the perspective of a large MNC, this may be a significant issue. MNCs such as Nokia and HP may have hundreds of individual partners of different types. Some of these individual partners may be a part of multiparty alliances. Alliances may have formed for multiple purposes. They may address different geographies, or span around the world. Case MNCs are managing the collaboration with these innovators through direct and indirect relationships. As third-party innovation and partnerships have become central to the MNC's strategy, firms have found themselves dealing with issues relating to the management of large alliance portfolios. Therefore, the method by which the MNC manages geographical and functional differences via the portfolio of strategic alliances affects its competitiveness. Consequently, alliance portfolio management has become an important issue for MNCs.

Taken as a whole, this research argues that differing motivations and needs between MNCs and start-up firms place dissimilar management factors in positions of critical importance for value capture. Consequently, this research suggests that start-ups emphasize partner selection, and MNCs emphasize alliance portfolio management in their pursuit of capturing performance gains from these constellations. Further, this suggestion also provides insights into the particular issues of asymmetric partners of a given firm, which will enable the managers to structure the relationships in ways accounting for these differences in needs. This is important, because the successful partnerships of firms that freely choose their partners must provide benefits for all participants.

Emergent Framework: Battleship Strategy for Global Innovation Constellations

In order to demonstrate the inter-linkages of key concepts related to the boundary spanning of MNCs and start-ups via global innovation constellations, the key concepts are identified and the reasoning is explained. First, drawing on findings addressing motivation, strategies, and constellation structures, it is suggested that an MNC possesses a wide access to global markets, while start-ups are constrained in terms of this parameter. This suggests higher complementarity between the two types of firm. Further, this research assumes that the innovation activities of an MNC emphasize (but are not limited to) exploitation of innovations, while the innovation activities of start-ups emphasize (but are not limited to) exploration of innovations. Again, this suggests higher complementarity between the two types of firm. Hence, it is suggested that the higher the complementarity between MNCs and start-ups, the higher is the motivation for firms to participate in global innovation constellation with the other types of partners.

Second, if these two types of firm can benefit from access to each other's complementary capabilities in a synergistic manner, then this forms a motivation for such firms to participate in a global innovation constellation with partners of the other type. Continuing to draw on findings, higher complementarity will increase the likelihood that the strategic goal of MNCs through global innovation constellation partnership is to gain access to explorative external innovations, and higher complementarity will increase the likelihood that the strategic goal for start-ups through the global innovation constellation partnership is to gain fast innovation commercialization opportunities on a global basis.

Third, MNCs tend to have a large stock of resources, while start-ups tend to have a limited stock, which suggests differing needs for the number of partners with which to interact in the global innovation constellation. Furthermore, the MNC is expected to seek a large number of partners with the help of its large stock of resources, while the start-up is expected to limit itself to a small number of partners due to its limited stock. Hence, they also have differing needs in terms of what is critical in structuring the global innovation constellation. Therefore, start-ups are expected to focus managerial attention on choosing the right partners, while MNCs are expected to focus managerial attention on alliance portfolio management.

Fourth, the start-ups are attracted to the partners providing high financial returns, wide access to global markets, brand and reputation association, and industry leadership externalities. Hence, as start-ups are assumed to act in ways that maximize their own profits, it is suggested that the more the start-up optimizes the management of its partner selection, the higher is the positive effect of a global innovation constellation on the start-up's performance.

Fifth, MNCs are considered to optimize their partner portfolio manage-

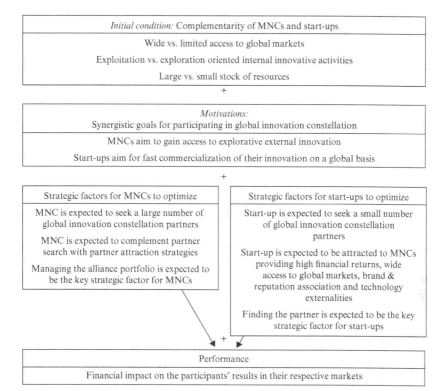

*Figure 17.2   Battleship strategy framework for global innovation
constellations*

ment with respect to internal strategic orientation. Hence, as MNCs are assumed to act in ways that maximize their own profits, the more an MNC optimizes its alliance portfolio management and its strategic orientation, the higher the positive effect of global innovation constellation on that MNC's performance.

Finally, if the premises listed above are true, then it is expected that the participating firms will gain added value from their participation in global innovation constellation. Optimizing the entire logic of the respective key management factors, as described above, is expected to yield beneficial financial results for the participating asymmetric firms. The chain of arguments described above illustrates the interaction of the key concepts of this research. As stated previously, the objective of this research is to create a framework capturing the strategic logic of using global innovation constellations. This emergent framework, conceptualized in the Figure 17.2, identifies the key factors for both MNCs and start-up firms related to global innovation constellations. Further, it also shows the inter-connections of the key factors.

The identification of factors and their linkages to each other are impor-tant, because this enables both MNCs and start-up firms to effectively utilize the framework for driving the added value from global innovation constellation. The data in Figure 17.2 contribute to the new extension to the theory, and thereby present a synthesis in the form of a new emergent framework for the battleship strategy that drives the added value accrued from global innovation constellations for its asymmetric partners.

Connecting the findings from the research into a single theoretical framework shows that the different constructs explored in this research interact with one another beyond the boundaries of participating firms. This is important, as no single interaction occurs in a vacuum, but rather influences, and is influenced by, all factors within the participating firms, and the value net it is embedded in, in complex and unpredictable ways. Internal choices affect the firm's external partnering opportunities, choices of other players affect the firm's partnering opportunities, and the nature of each firm and its strategic orientation affect the joint value creation.

DISCUSSION AND CONCLUSIONS

This research has important implications for our understanding of strategic alliances. It explored the critical dimensions of MNC–start-up global high-tech innovation constellations from the perspective of its asymmetric par-ticipants. It approached these focus areas from the added-value perspective in order to address the unique needs and distinct contributions of differing participants, and placed an emphasis on the novel MNC perspective.

Theoretical Contributions

This research offers explorative results that focus on global innovation constellations between MNCs and up to hundreds of start-ups. Several theoretical contributions emerge from the research. A key contribution is the new emergent framework. This has important implications for our understanding of managing the added value accruing from global innova-tion constellations. The framework that emerges is labeled the 'battleship strategy'.

This research argues that the high complementarities between the two types of firms, MNCs and start-ups, provide a solid basis for joint value creation. Simultaneously, the differing motivations and needs between MNCs and start-up firms pose dissimilar management factors of critical

Table 17.2   *Summary of contributions to different literature streams*

Research stream	Authors	Contribution of this research
Strategic alliance research on large non-equity multiparty alliances	Hagedoorn and Duysters (1999), Doz et al. (2001), Sakakibara (2002), Rothaermel and Deeds (2004), Cassiman et al. (2009)	Sheds light on less researched global innovation constellations between asymmetric types of firm. In particular, explores motivations of these two types of firm
International business research on MNC–start-up relationships	Oviatt and McDougall (1994), Coviello and Munro (1997), Alvarez and Barney (2001), Blomqvist (2002), Gabrielsson and Kirpalani (2004), Coviello (2006)	Covers seldom-covered start-up partnerships. Provides evidence on this phenomenon from the MNC's perspective. Identifies motivations and strategies of MNCs to enter into these relationships. Suggests solutions accounting for the asymmetry and complementarity. Places the start-up in the role of the primary actor in pursuing growth through MNCs, which is well aligned with these concepts of entrepreneurial orientation and global vision
Other international business research	Dunning (2001)	Explores the MNC's management of market assets in global competition
	Ricart et al. (2004)	Explores global strategies of MNCs and start-ups
	Brandenburger and Nalebuff (1996) Brandenburger and Stuart (1996)	Suggest less utilized theoretical perspectives for future international business research

importance for value capture. Specifically, the chapter sheds light upon the factors of motivation from the perspective of its asymmetric participants: it suggests that MNCs are motivated by gaining access to explorative external innovations, while start-ups are motivated by addressing fast innovation commercialization opportunities on a global basis. It shows evidence that participating in global innovation constellations adds value to the participating firms. The key contributions are summarized in Table 17.2.

Managerial Implications

As for the managers in high-tech industries, there is an increasing strategic need to facilitate the large number of relationships with external firms, in order to foster and gain access to external innovation. A key implication of this research is that global innovation constellations influence the competitive advantage of the firm, and may yield financial returns (Vapola and Seppälä 2007). The frameworks and models provide effective tools for addressing and managing the critical strategic factors. While the high complementarities between the two types of firm provide a solid basis for joint value creation, the differing motivations and needs between these two types of firm raises different management issues that are of critical importance. Specifically, in the pursuit for capturing financial gains from these constellations, this research suggests that start-ups emphasize the search for an attractive partner that has the potential to provide fast commercialization on a global basis, and that MNCs emphasize the optimization of their alliance portfolio management approaches in order to manage a large number of partnerships efficiently.

Moreover, as there may be thousands of firms and multiple innovation constellations in a given industry on a global basis, a competitive game for attracting ideas and products from the most interesting partnerships arises. Innovations are typically new combinations and reconfigurations of existing knowledge by different interacting parties (Schumpeter 1912 [1934]). Therefore, strategic motivation, entrepreneurial approach, and facilitating loose structures for interactions are needed. Another key issue is to be able to identify where and when to anticipate difficulties and what kind of response strategies may be introduced.

The managerial challenges are to optimize the factors in the battleship framework for value creation in ways that sufficient value can be captured not only for themselves but also for other players. According to game theory, partners will only come forward if it is their best choice to maximize their own private value capture. The effective use of global innovation constellations involves both the giving and receiving aspects of it, as the interactions must add the highest value for all parties involved, compared to their other strategic alternatives for operations. The game recurs over time, so previous choices will affect future opportunities.

Note that global innovation constellations are not to be used in all circumstances or relied upon alone, but this should be a part of a wider palette of strategy methods, all of which have their advantages and disadvantages. In other words, global innovation constellations provide a complementary approach in the pursuit of competitive advantage.

Policy Implications

From the policy perspective, a key question is to consider how to foster cooperation between start-ups and MNCs. Structures need to equip both types of firm with good identification mechanisms of potential partners, incubation structures that not only help to nurture the early inventions but also provide links to potential globalization partners, and hence open doors, and finally provide governmental financial instruments for early commercialization and growth phases.

Limitations and Future Research

The limitations of this research guide suggestions for future research directions. First, owing to the research approach and setting, this theory is constrained by the consideration of only two specific types of firm, and is most applicable to the global high-tech market context. Hence, it is likely to be most applicable to the new opportunity creation phase in the global high-tech market context. Second, the empirical parts are conducted using multiple methods, and apply multiple case studies as the source of data. While the cases provide insights into the phenomenon, the extent to which the frameworks can be applied across a wider population of firms still needs to be tested.

Nevertheless, the overarching aim of the research is to build theory, a consideration that is reflected by the selected methodologies and their application scope. The resulting framework is a new extension to the theory that bridges rich in-depth case evidence with mainstream research. Therefore this research provides an appropriate contribution to this important topic. Hence, with future research the new emergent framework and the research propositions can now be tested in a wider empirical context.

NOTES

1. A global innovation constellation refers to a set of MNCs and start-ups linked together by a loose non-equity multiparty innovation alliance that competes in a particular competitive domain, and where relationships for participating firms are facilitated by creating new value-adding opportunities on a global basis.
2. A more correct military term would be an aircraft carrier. However, as the term is used here only as a metaphor for the purposes of illustrating the business concept, this notion could also very well refer to the imaginary sci-fi battleships used in space wars between people in their respective star constellations. Therefore it was decided that the battleship simply sounds better for the context of this research.

REFERENCES

Adner, R. and P. Zemsky (2006), 'A demand-based perspective on sustainable competitive advantage', *Strategic Management Journal*, **27**(3), 215–39.

Almor, T. and N. Hashai (2004), 'Competitive advantage and strategic configuration of knowledge-intensive small and medium sized multinationals: a modified resource based view', *Journal of International Management*, **10**(4), 479–500.

Alvarez, S. and J. Barney (2001), 'How entrepreneurs can benefit from alliances with large firms', *Academy of Management Executive*, **15**(1), 139–48.

Anderson, P. and M.L. Tushman (1990), 'Technological discontinuities and dominant designs: a cyclical model of technology change', *Administrative Science Quarterly*, **35**(4), 604–33.

Autio, E. and H. Yli-Renko (1998), 'New, technology-based firms as agents of technological rejuvenation', *Entrepreneurship and Regional Development*, **10**(1), 71–92.

Bartlett, C.A. and S. Ghosal (1989), *Management across Borders: The Transnational Solution*, Cambridge, MA: Harvard Business School Press.

Becerra, M., R. Lunnan and L. Huemer (2008), 'Trustworthiness, risk, and the transfer of tacit and explicit knowledge between alliance partners', *Journal of Management Studies*, **45**(4), 691–713.

Besanko, D., D. Dranove and M. Shanley (1996), *Economics of Strategy*, New York: John Wiley.

Blomqvist, K. (2002), 'Partnering in the dynamic environment: the role of trust in asymmetric technology partnership', PhD dissertation, Lappeenranta University of Technology, Acta Universitatis Lappeenrantaensis 122.

Brandenburger, Adam M. and Barry J. Nalebuff (1996), *Co-opetition*, New York: Currency Doubleday.

Brandenburger, A.M. and H.W. Stuart (1996), 'Value-based business strategy', *Journal of Economics and Management Strategy*, **5**(1), 5–24.

Brown, Shona L. and Kathleen M. Eisenhardt (1998), *Competing on the Edge: Strategy as Structured Chaos*, Boston, MA: Harvard Business School Press.

Brunner, H.P. (1994), 'Technological diversity, random selection in a population of firms, and technological institutions of government', in L. Leyesdorff and P. Van Den Besselua (eds), *Evolutionary Economics and Chaos Theory, New Directions in Technology Studies*, London: Pinter, pp. 33–43.

Burgelman, R.A, M.A. Maidique and S.C. Wheelwright (2001), *Strategic Management of Technology and Innovation*, 3rd edn, New York: McGraw-Hill.

Cassiman, B., M.C. Di Guardo and G. Valentini (2009), 'Organising R&D projects to profit from innovation: insights from co-opetition', *Long Range Planning*, **42**(2), 216–33.

Chesbrough, H.W. (2003), 'The era of open innovation', *MIT Sloan Management Review*, **44**(Spring), 35–41.

Christensen, Clayton M. (1997), *The Innovator's Dilemma: When New Technologies Cause Great Companies to Fail*, Boston, MA: Harvard Business School Press.

Christensen, C. (2005), 'The ongoing process of building a theory of disruption', *Journal of Product Innovation Management*, **23**(1), 39–55.

Coviello, N.E. (2006), 'The network dynamics of international new ventures', *Journal of International Business Studies*, **37**(5), 713–31.

Coviello, N. and H. Munro (1997), 'Network relationships and the internationalisation process of small software firms', *International Business Review*, **6**(4), 361–86.

Diamond, A.M., Jr (2009), 'Schumpeter vs. Keynes: "In the long run not all of us are dead"', *Journal of the History of Economic Thought*, **31**(4), 531–41

Doz, Yves L., Jose Santos and Peter Williamson (2001), *From Global to Metanational: How Companies Win in the Knowledge Economy*, Boston, MA: Harvard Business School Press.

Dunning, John H. (2001), 'An evolving paradigm of the economic determinants of international business activity', in Joseph Lap-Chiu Cheng and Michael A. Hitt (eds), *Managing*

Multinationals in a Knowledge Economy: Economics, Culture, and Human Resources, Amsterdam, London: JAI Press, Elsevier, pp. 3–28.

Eisenhardt, K.M and M.E. Graebner (2007), 'Theory building from cases: opportunities and challenges', *Academy of Management Journal*, **50**(1), 25–32.

Fairclough, Gerard (1994), 'Innovation and organisation', in Mark Dodgson and Roy Rothwell (eds), *The Handbook of Industrial Innovation*, Aldershot, UK and Brookfield, VT, USA: Edward Elgar, pp. 325–36.

Foster, Richard N. (1986), *Innovation: The Attacker's Advantage*, Letchworth, UK: Garden City Press.

Gabrielsson, M. and V.H.M. Kirpalani (2004), 'Born globals: how to reach new business space rapidly', *International Business Review*, **13**(5), 555–71.

Gomes-Casseres, Benjamin (1996), *The Alliance Revolution: The New Shape of Business Rivalry*, Cambridge, MA: Harvard University Press.

Gomes-Casseres, Benjamin (2006), 'How alliances reshape competition', in Oded Shenkar and Jeffrey J. Reuer (eds), *Handbook of Strategic Alliances*, Thousand Oaks, CA: Sage, pp. 39–53.

Hacklin, F., C. Marxt and F. Fahrnia (2009), 'Coevolutionary cycles of convergence: an extrapolation from the ICT industry', *Technological Forecasting and Social Change*, **76**(6), 723–36.

Hagedoorn, John (1989), *The Dynamic Analysis of Innovation and Diffusion: A Study in Process Control*, London and New York: Pinter.

Hagedoorn, J. and J. Duysters (1999), 'Learning in dynamic inter-firm networks – the efficacy of multiple contacts', MERIT working papers, August 1–42.

Hallikas, J., J. Varis, H. Sissonen and V.-M. Virolainen (2008), 'The evolution of the network structure in the ICT sector', *International Journal of Production Economics*, **115**(2), 296–304.

Harrigan, K.R. (1988), 'Joint ventures and competitive strategy', *Strategic Management Journal*, **9**, 141–58.

Hitt, M.A., B.W. Keats and S.M. DeMarie (1998), 'Navigating in the new competitive landscape: building strategic flexibility and competitive advantage in the 21st century', *Academy of Management Executive*, **12**(4), 22–42.

Lunnan, R. and S.A. Haugland (2008), 'Predicting and measuring alliance performance: a multidimensional analysis', *Strategic Management Journal*, **29**(5), 545–56.

McGrath, Michael (1995), *Product Strategy for High-Technology Companies: How to Achieve Growth, Competitive Advantage and Increased Profits*, New York: McGraw-Hill.

Moriarty, R. and T. Kosnik (1989), 'High-tech marketing: concepts, continuity, and change', *Sloan Management Review*, **30**(4), 7–17.

Narula, R. and J. Hagedoorn (1999), 'Innovating through strategic alliances: moving towards international partnerships and contractual agreements', *Technovation*, **19**, 283–94.

Nielsen, B.B. (2004), 'The role of knowledge embeddedness in the creation of synergies in strategic alliances', *Journal of International Business Research*, **58**(9), 1194–204.

Oviatt, B.M. and P.P. McDougall (1994), 'Toward a theory of international new ventures', *Journal of International Business Studies*, **25**(1), 45–64.

Parayil, G. (1991), 'Schumpeter on invention innovation and technological change', *Journal of the History of Economic Thought*, **13**(01), 78–89.

Ricart, J.E., M.J. Enright, P. Ghemawat, S.L. Hart and T. Khanna (2004), 'New frontiers in international strategy', *Journal of International Business Studies*, **35**(3), 175–200.

Rothaermel, F.T. and D.L. Deeds (2004), 'Exploration and exploitation alliances in biotechnology: a system of new product development', *Strategic Management Journal*, **25**(3), 201–21.

Rothaermel, F.T. and C. Hill (2005), 'Technological discontinuities and complementary assets: a longitudinal study of industry and firm performance', *Organization Science*, **16**(1), 55–70.

Sakakibara, M. (2002), 'Formation of R&D consortia: industry and company effects', *Strategic Management Journal*, **23**(11), 1033–50.

Schumpeter, Joseph (1912 [1934]), *The Theory of Economic Development*, Cambridge, MA: Harvard University Press.

Sharma, D.D. and A. Blomstermo (2003), 'The internationalization process of born globals: a network view', *International Business Review*, **12**(6), 739–53.

Stieglitz, N. and K. Heine (2007), 'Innovations and the role of complementarities in a strategic theory of the firm', *Strategic Management Journal*, **21**(1), 1–15.

Uotila, J., M. Maula, T. Keil and S.A. Zahra (2009), 'Exploration, exploitation, and financial performance: analysis of S&P 500 corporations', *Strategic Management Journal*, **30**(2), 221–31.

Vapola, T. (2000), 'Technological leadership and competitive strategy: a case of shaping the future', MSc thesis, Helsinki School of Economics.

Vapola, Terhi J. and Tomi T. Seppälä (2007), 'The performance impact of membership in a global alliance: evidence on the revenue growth rate of mobile operators', in Progress in International Business Research, Gabriel Benito and Henrich Greve (eds), London: Macmillan, pp. 119–38.

Vapola, T.J., P. Tossavainen and M. Gabrielsson (2008), 'The battleship strategy: the complementing role of born globals in MNCs' new opportunity creation', *Journal of International Entrepreneurship*, **6**(1), 1–21.

Weigelt, C. (2009), 'The impact of outsourcing new technologies on integrative capabilities and performance', *Strategic Management Journal*, **30**, 595–616.

Whetten, D.A. (1989), 'What constitutes a theoretical contribution?', *Academy of Management Review*, **14**(4), 490–95.

18 Successful born globals without experiential market knowledge: survey evidence from China

Tiia Vissak, Xiaotian Zhang and Kadri Ukrainski*

INTRODUCTION

Internationalization processes have received considerable research attention for the last five decades. As a result, many approaches have emerged. Some of them – such as the Uppsala model and the innovation-related internationalization models – have demonstrated the importance of (experiential) knowledge. These models stated that the lack of experiential knowledge may force firms to internationalize slowly by using simple foreign operation modes – such as indirect exporting – and entering culturally and geographically closest countries first. Firms were able to enter other countries and use other modes only after acquiring the necessary knowledge. Some other research streams – including the network approach to internationalization and the studies on born globals, international new ventures, and other fast internationalizers – have shown that knowledge can be acquired by several other means besides experience. As a result, some firms may use more advanced entry modes and enter far markets – even other continents – soon after establishment.

Unfortunately, the current literature has paid little attention to the knowledge acquisition of born globals and its impact on their internationalization. Several authors (for example, Mitra and Golder 2002; Morgan et al. 2003; Bengtsson 2004; Ling-yee 2004; Pedersen and Petersen 2004; Saarenketo et al. 2004; Weerawardena et al. 2007; Brennan and Garvey 2009; Casillas et al. 2009; Freeman et al. 2010; Zou and Ghauri 2010) have emphasized the importance of this issue. China is an especially interesting country for studying this subject: after the period of reforms and opening up – private enterprises were allowed in China in 1978 – many Chinese firms became successful born globals without having any experiential knowledge, and several of them also lacked other market knowledge. Liu et al. (2008) and Naudé

(2009) pointed to some shortcomings of current research streams and concluded that (experiential) knowledge is not always necessary for fast internationalization.

This chapter aims to show that Chinese born globals have internationalized successfully despite having less experiential market knowledge than other internationalizers. (In this chapter, born globals are defined as firms that have entered at least two other continents besides their home continent and also achieved at least a 25 percent export share per turnover within three years of their founding.) We start with a literature review of studies on the importance of experiential market knowledge for fast internationalization and those on foreign market knowledge acquisition. After a methodology section, survey evidence from China is presented and analyzed. Following a discussion of the results, the chapter presents some managerial and research implications.

LITERATURE REVIEW

Literature on the Importance of Experiential Foreign Market Knowledge for Internationalization

This subsection gives an overview of the literature on slow internationalization and shows how it has emphasized the importance of experiential foreign market knowledge for internationalization. It continues with an overview of the research on born globals, international new ventures, and other fast internationalizers, and explains why some firms – despite lacking such knowledge – still internationalize very fast.

The architects of the Uppsala (U-) model – including Johanson and Wiedersheim-Paul (1975), Johanson and Vahlne (1977, 1990), and Vahlne and Johanson (2002) – assumed the following:

1. Experiential market knowledge (mainly acquired through foreign operations) drives the internationalization process, reduces market risk and uncertainty, and generates business opportunities.
2. As the acquisition, integration, and use of such knowledge are gradual and slow, firms internationalize slowly and incrementally. This characterizes their whole internationalization process but also activities in individual countries.
3. As firms lack knowledge about foreign countries and wish to avoid uncertainty, they first enter neighboring or otherwise comparatively well-known and similar countries. They also pass through steps from having no regular export activities to exporting via independent

representatives (agents), establishing overseas sales, and production/ manufacturing units.

Some exceptions to the model (Johanson and Vahlne 1990) can also explain why born globals emerge: (i) internationalization is easier for large or resourceful enterprises; (ii) if market conditions are stable, firms can obtain relevant market knowledge in other ways; and (iii) a firm with considerable experience in similar markets may use it in other countries.

Innovation-related internationalization (I-) models agree that internationalization is incremental and depends on firms' experiential learning and uncertainty regarding their internationalization decisions (Fina and Rugman 1996; Morgan and Katsikeas 1997), but these models show that other factors besides knowledge also influence internationalization. For instance, foreign-owned firms internationalize faster if the headquarters take the initial decision to start exporting and organize sales through their own global marketing network (Wiedersheim-Paul et al. 1978).

The Finnish model agrees that at first, internationalization may be slow (Welch and Luostarinen 1988; Luostarinen 1989; Luostarinen and Welch 1997). It emphasizes the importance of foreign market knowledge and other competencies but acknowledges that some knowledge can be acquired from other sources (Welch and Luostarinen 1988; Chetty 1999), for instance, through importing. This may reduce risk and uncertainty regarding outward internationalization (Karlsen et al. 2003). As a result, several firms 'leapfrog' some stages and internationalize rapidly (Chetty 1999).

Born globals, international new ventures, and other fast internationalizers have been actively studied since the early 1990s. Several definitions have been used. For example, Madsen and Servais (1997, p. 579) emphasized such firms' interest in seeking to 'derive significant advantages from the use of resources from or the sale of outputs to multiple countries/ continents right from their legal birth'. Kuivalainen et al. (2007), in turn, claimed that true born globals' turnover from abroad should reach at least 25 percent and they should enter culturally distant foreign countries during the first three years since establishment, while Gabrielsson et al. (2004) stressed that they should generate at least 50 percent of total sales from outside their home continent in 15 years or less since starting operations.

Although different definitions and classifications have been used, scholars have agreed that these companies are usually young and small and their markets can be very volatile (Oviatt and McDougall 1994). As they are growth oriented, flexible, and ready to take risks (Spence and Crick 2009), they internationalize very quickly: some born globals even start exporting before generating any domestic sales (Bell 1995).

Several success factors of born globals have been identified: having a narrow (but critical) skill set (Wolff and Pett 2000), focusing on relatively narrow niches (Saarenketo et al. 2004), and using their founders' and/or owners' pre-existing knowledge (Weerawardena et al. 2007), business and personal relationships (Saarenketo et al. 2004), and international business experience (McDougall et al. 2003; Zucchella et al. 2007). They may also learn from other relationships (Saarenketo et al. 2004; Zhou et al. 2007) or create new ones (Casillas et al. 2009; Freeman et al. 2010). In addition, they may hire internationally experienced staff (Wolff and Pett 2000; McDougall et al. 2003; Spence and Crick 2009), and cooperate with export consultants (Zucchella et al. 2007) or internationally experienced distributors (Spence and Crick 2009), but even these measures will not automatically guarantee born globals long-term success or survival (Pajunen and Maunula 2008; Naudé 2009).

Literature on Foreign Market Knowledge Acquisition

Slater and Narver (1995) identified three sources of information: direct (own) experience, others' experience, and organizational memory. Eriksson et al. (2000) distinguished between three experiential knowledge types: business knowledge (about foreign market conditions, customers, and competitors), institutional knowledge (about the foreign country's norms, rules, values, government, and institutional frameworks), and internationalization knowledge (about the firm's own capabilities and resources for internationalization). This subsection shows how to acquire knowledge.

The network approach to internationalization has stated that internationalization is accompanied by establishing and developing business relationships in foreign networks (Johanson and Mattsson 1988). Through network relationships, a firm can use its partners' knowledge without having to experience the same (Eriksson et al. 1998; Brennan and Garvey 2009). It can also learn about their capabilities, strategies, and needs, and obtain knowledge about their business conditions and other networks (Johanson and Johanson 1999). By joining the nets, it can expand in leaps (Hertz 1996), but network relationships do not always guarantee internationalization success: they can even inhibit it (Ford 1998; Ling-yee 2004).

The relationships between foreign direct investment (FDI) and host country exports have received substantial research interest. Several authors have shown that foreign subsidiaries export more than locally-owned firms because: (i) they have better marketing and management skills, technology and international business contacts, more general know-how, and they may use their parents' brand names; and (ii) the owners can help them to establish a distribution network, follow consumer tastes, safety standards and industrial norms, shape a new product image, and deal with distribution, servicing, product design, and packaging (Blomström 1990; Dunning 1994; Lauter and Rehman 1999; Hadley and Wilson 2003).

Firms can also use other ways to acquire foreign market knowledge: conduct market research; make pre-entry visits (Eriksson et al. 1997; Pedersen and Petersen 2004; Zou and Ghauri 2010); hire other firms' former expatriates (Downes and Thomas 1999), foreign immigrants (Pécoud 2002) or people from other firms active on a specific market (Bengtsson 2004; Brennan and Garvey 2009); and acquire firms in the target country (Pajunen and Maunula 2008) or cooperate with them (Bengtsson 2004). Moreover, firms can acquire knowledge and other assistance from trade missions (Seringhaus and Mayer 1988), industry associations, and governmental organizations (Hadley and Wilson 2003; Child and Rodrigues 2005). It is also possible to acquire some (near-) market knowledge by attending exhibitions and trade fairs (Liu et al. 2008), from a firm's subsidiaries in economically similar and culturally close countries (Mitra and Golder 2002) and, sometimes, even unintentionally discover interesting information about internationalization (Bengtsson 2004).

Based on the literature review, the following can be concluded: (i) the lack of foreign market knowledge may slow down internationalization and increase firms' preference towards selecting closest countries and simplest market entry modes first; (ii) direct market experience is not the only way of acquiring foreign market knowledge: firms can also hire people possessing such knowledge, cooperate with other firms, and use several other methods; and (iii) having sufficient foreign market knowledge may considerably speed up a firm's internationalization, but does not guarantee success.

METHODOLOGY AND SURVEY EVIDENCE

Methodology

In the following subsection, survey evidence from 104 Chinese born globals and 276 other firms is provided. In this study, born globals were defined as firms that have entered at least two other continents besides their home continent and reached a 25 percent export share within three years of their founding. This definition, therefore, follows those by Madsen and Servais (1997) and Kuivalainen et al. (2007), rather than the one by Gabrielsson et al. (2004) to encompass the speed of these firms' initial internationalization.

The authors developed the questionnaire based on the theoretical part of the chapter. Its first part concerned firms' general data – such as the foundation year, turnover, and number of employees – and the characteristics of their internationalization: the start of foreign activities, the selection of foreign markets, and foreign operation methods, but also the export share per turnover and the year it reached 25 percent. The respondents were then asked to assess their knowledge sources before the beginning of internationalization, and also the knowledge of their first foreign market.

In total, 18,353 firms from four Chinese provinces – Anhui, Guangdong, Jiangsu, and Zhejiang – were contacted in December 2010 and January 2011, as the firms from these provinces were active internationalizers. The potential respondents were identified mainly through the lists of exporting firms obtained from the local authorities and import/export associations, but some were also recommended by contacted managers and owners. In addition to receiving 355 completed surveys, 65 firms were interviewed using the same questionnaire and their data were added to the survey results. As it was intended to compare born globals with other internationalized firms, the data of 40 firms without any international activities were excluded and the resulting sample size was 380. The authors acknowledge that the response rate is low and that the resulting sample may be biased towards highly international firms as the questions also concerned activities on continents outside Asia.

For assessing differences in firm characteristics and born globals and other internationalized firms' market knowledge, the simple one-way analysis of variance (ANOVA) model was used and estimated with SPSS (Statistical Package for the Social Sciences). The means of different firm characteristics and market knowledge variables were used for testing the null hypothesis $H_0 = \mu_{BG} = \mu_{NBG}$ where μ_{BG} was the mean of born global firms and μ_{NBG} the mean of other firms. The F-statistic was calculated by dividing the variation among the sample means by the variation within the samples. A large F-statistic shows that the former exceeds the latter: thus the null hypothesis – that born globals and other firms' means are similar – can be rejected.

To perform the ANOVA, the samples have to be normally distributed, the variances within the samples equal (homogeneous) and all observations independent. To assess whether or not the standard deviations varied significantly across the two groups, Levene's test (Levene 1960) was conducted. This test has been considered unduly sensitive, especially if the data are not normally distributed, so the recommendations of Tabachnick and Fidell (1996) were followed. If p was smaller than 0.001 (instead of Levene's original 0.05), we concluded that the standard deviation or vari-

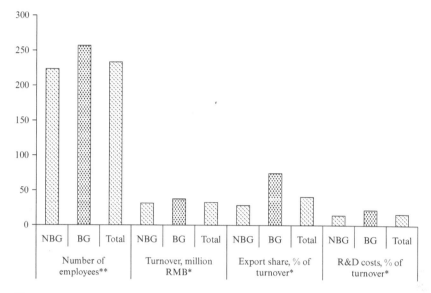

Notes:
*   Difference in means is significant at the 0.05 level.
**   Difference in means is significant at the 0.1 level.

Figure 18.1   Firm characteristics (mean values, data from 2010)

ances varied significantly across the groups and thus there was a violation of the assumption of homogeneity of variance. On the other hand, if p was larger than 0.001, we concluded that insufficient evidence was available for proving that the standard deviation or variances varied significantly across the groups. With our data, the violation of the homogeneity of variance requirement existed; therefore the more robust Brown–Forsythe (Brown and Forsythe 1974) and Welch (Welch 1951) tests were also used for assessing the equality of means. The null hypothesis (assuming the similarity of born globals and other firms) was rejected when F-statistics were large.

Survey Evidence

The sample firms had on average 230 employees, an export share of 39 percent and a share of R&D costs from turnover of 14 percent (see also Figure 18.1 and Appendix Table 18A1.1). The average establishment year was 1996 (varying between 1983 and 2005). The establishment years of born globals and other internationalized firms did not differ considerably. However, while born globals started exporting on the average in

1997 and made first FDI in 1999, the other firms followed on average in 2001 and 2002, respectively. This can be a very important difference as in 1999–2001, internet services were expanded considerably in China. For those born globals that entered foreign markets earlier, it was thus harder to obtain foreign market knowledge than for other firms that internationalized later. The survey results also reveal that in general born globals had a larger turnover, a higher export share and larger R&D costs than other firms (the differences in means were statistically significant; see Appendix Tables 18A2.1 and 18A3.1). The mean of the number of employees did not differ at the 0.05 level, but did at the 0.1 level, implying also that born globals had a slightly higher productivity (turnover per employee).

Most firms selected the USA as their first foreign market for exporting or making FDI (55.3 and 32.9 percent of all respondents, respectively). The second popular choice was Germany (11.3 and 6.1 percent, respectively). Born globals were even more inclined toward selecting the USA as their first foreign market – 72 percent of them started their internationalization from there. Their next popular choices were Canada and Germany with 7 and 6 per cent, respectively, of the sample. Only three firms selected an Asian country as their first foreign market. Other firms also started their foreign activities mainly from the USA – 49 per cent of them selected it as their first foreign market. Their next most popular choices were Germany and the UK with 13 and 6 percent of the sample, respectively. Only 18 of these firms selected an Asian country as their first foreign market.

It is interesting that before entering the first foreign market, born globals assessed the prior knowledge of the market near to 'no knowledge at all': their mean scores were between 1 and 1.5 in all aspects on the scale where 1 meant 'not at all' and 7 'very much'. At the same time, the mean scores for other internationalized firms were between 2.5 and 3.5 (see Figure 18.2 and Appendix Table 18A1.2) and the difference was statistically significant (see Appendix Tables 18A2.2 and 18A3.2). Firms knew the most about their business partners – suppliers and customers – while they were slightly less knowledgeable of the target market's formal and informal institutions.

Figures 18.3 and 18.4 demonstrate that born globals had very little experiential knowledge before internationalization and they hardly used any other ways for acquiring such knowledge. Their most popular source for acquiring knowledge was contacting governmental organizations – about half of born globals obtained knowledge through them. This channel was even more popular among other internationalized firms – about 79 percent used it – but for them, it was even more important to have direct experience from working in international firms or studying in the target country. In most categories, except for participating in trade fairs and expositions or conferences and seminars (these two differences were not statistically

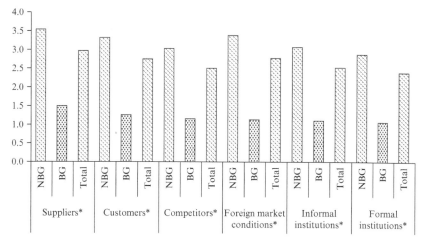

Notes:
* Difference in means is significant at the 0.05 level.
Rated from 1 to 7, 1 means 'not at all' and 7 means 'very much'.
Informal institutions: foreign country's norms, rules and values.
Formal institutions: foreign country's government, laws, and institutional frameworks.

Figure 18.2   Knowledge of the firm's first foreign market before entering it

significant), born globals' means were considerably lower than other firms' means (these differences were smaller and thus not statistically significant except in the case of getting knowledge from industry associations; see also Appendix Tables 18A1.3, 18A2.3, and 18A3.3). These results can be related to born globals' earlier internationalization and the absence of possibilities to obtain such knowledge from some of these sources at that time.

DISCUSSION, CONCLUSIONS, AND IMPLICATIONS

The authors of the U- and I-models showed that the speed of internationalization may depend on firms' possession of experiential foreign market knowledge, but the literature on born globals, the network approach to internationalization, and the literature on relationships between FDI and host country exports demonstrated that experience is not always necessary: even very young firms may internationalize rapidly. The sources of acquiring market knowledge were identified in several studies, but some authors also showed that the fact of having knowledge in itself will not guarantee successful internationalization.

The empirical evidence of this study demonstrated that born globals

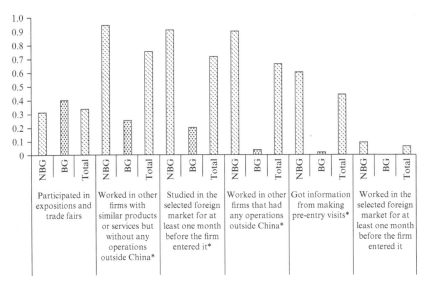

Notes:
*   Difference in means is significant at the 0.05 level.

Firms answered either 'yes' (1) or 'no' (0).

It was not possible to test the last knowledge acquisition form – 'worked in the selected foreign market for at least one month before the firm entered it' – because this value was 0 in the case of born globals as none of them had used this knowledge acquisition form.

Figure 18.3   Foreign market knowledge and experiential forms of its acquisition before starting foreign activities

internationalized rapidly despite having less experiential knowledge and also less knowledge about their first foreign market than slower internationalizers. This supports the findings of Naudé (2009), who discovered a negative impact of foreign experience on the internationalization decision and also the conclusion by Liu et al. (2008) that experiential knowledge may be helpful for internationalization, but it is not always necessary for initiating it. The authors also checked whether born globals evaluated their strengths – lower prices, better quality, faster delivery times, more advanced/innovative products/services, better customer service, better connections in foreign countries, better design, strong financial support from the owner(s), better production technology, skilled employees, greater flexibility, managers' stronger interest in internationalization, stronger governmental support or a well-known brand name – differently from other firms. The firms had to rate these strengths from 1 to 7, where 1 meant 'not at all' and 7 'very much'. The only significant difference concerned flexibility (if the Welch statistic was used) and according to the

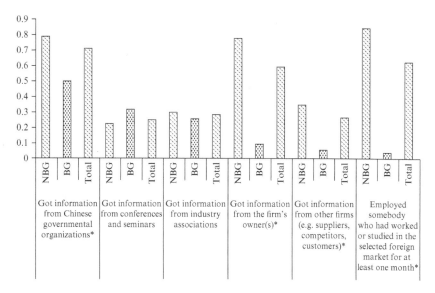

Notes:
* Difference in means is significant at the 0.05 level.
Firms answered either 'yes' (1) or 'no' (0).

Figure 18.4 *Foreign market knowledge and non-experiential forms of its acquisition before starting foreign activities*

results, born globals considered themselves less flexible than others: means were 4.58 and 4.76, respectively. Thus, it would be interesting to study further what caused these firms' faster internationalization compared to other companies.

Although the chapter demonstrated that firms can internationalize rapidly despite lacking experiential market knowledge, these results do not fully contradict with the U- and I-models as it was shown that born globals were slightly larger, and Johanson and Vahlne (1990) considered larger size an exception to their model. Moreover, the results showed that other internationalizers also lacked knowledge (although they had more knowledge than born globals and this difference was statistically significant) when they entered their first foreign market. At the same time, there is a contradiction in terms of market selection: 93 percent of other internationalizers also selected a market from outside Asia as their first foreign market. It should be studied further whether this result could have been caused by the questionnaire design or a low response rate or whether this tendency also characterizes other Chinese internationalizers. (Zou and Ghauri (2010) also noted Chinese firms' tendency to prefer culturally different countries for initial internationalization but they concentrated on high-tech firms while our sample also included low-tech firms.)

Although the studied born globals were not particularly active in obtaining foreign market knowledge through different channels (except in the case of governmental organizations – Child and Rodrigues (2005) also emphasized this aspect in their study about Chinese internationalizers – this does not mean that other firms' managers should necessarily follow their example. Although the lack of knowledge was not an impediment to these firms' successful internationalization, it cannot be concluded that having knowledge would automatically slow down internationalization or even harm it (according to Naudé (2009), knowledge could make firms more cautious toward foreign entry, but increase their survival rate). On the other hand, managers should also understand that acquiring foreign market knowledge in itself will also not automatically guarantee successful internationalization. Internationalization success may also depend on many other factors that were not studied in this chapter.

As this chapter was based only on the data of 380 firms from four Chinese regions, of which only 104 were born globals, it cannot be stated that this sample fully represents these regions, let alone the whole of China, or the entire world. The means of foreign market knowledge acquisition and their impacts on born globals and other firms' internationalization should be studied further. More firms, regions, and countries should be examined and the results compared by industry, firm size, location, and other characteristics: for example, if Asian born globals have more or less knowledge than European born globals, or if smaller born globals use more or fewer knowledge sources than larger ones. More attention should be paid to the use of different knowledge sources and the impacts of each of these on internationalization: for instance, if it is more or less important to get knowledge from governmental agencies than from foreign immigrants or other firms' former expatriates. Another area to study would be whether more successful firms obtain knowledge differently from less successful ones and how this influences internationalization success.

It would also be interesting to study whether the preferred ways of knowledge acquisition differ depending on the type of necessary foreign market knowledge. The costs and benefits of foreign market knowledge acquisition, but also the factors leading to failures of knowledge acquisition and internationalization, also need research attention. This would enable researchers to put forward more specific managerial implications, and make recommendations to governmental organizations responsible for export promotion and advancing other forms of internationalization.

NOTE

* This research was financed by the Estonian Science Foundation's Grants Nos 7405, 8580 and 8546 and target financing of the Estonian Ministry of Education and Research No. 0180037s08.

REFERENCES

Bell, J. (1995), 'The internationalization of small computer software firms: a further challenge to "stage" theories', *European Journal of Marketing*, 29(8), 60–75.

Bengtsson, L. (2004), 'Explaining born globals: an organisational learning perspective on the internationalisation process', *International Journal of Globalisation and Small Business*, 1(1), 28–41.

Blomström, Magnus (1990), *Transnational Corporations and Manufacturing Exports from Developing Countries*, New York: United Nations.

Brennan, L. and D. Garvey (2009), 'The role of knowledge in internationalization', *Research in International Business and Finance*, 23(2), 120–33.

Brown, M.B. and A.B. Forsythe (1974), 'Robust tests for the equality of variances', *Journal of the American Statistical Association*, 69(2), 364–7.

Casillas, J.C., A.M. Moreno, F.J. Acedo, M.A. Gallego and E. Ramos (2009), 'An integrative model of the role of knowledge in the internationalization process', *Journal of World Business*, 44(3), 311–22.

Chetty, S. (1999), 'Dimensions of internationalisation of manufacturing firms in the apparel industry', *European Journal of Marketing*, 33(1/2), 121–42.

Child, J. and S.B. Rodrigues (2005), 'The internationalization of Chinese firms: a case for theoretical extension?', *Management and Organization Review*, 1(3), 381–410.

Downes, M. and A.S. Thomas (1999), 'Managing overseas assignments to build organizational knowledge', *Human Resource Planning Journal*, 22(4), 33–48.

Dunning, J.H. (1994), 'Re-evaluating the benefits of foreign direct investment', *Transnational Corporations*, 3(1), 23–51.

Eriksson, K., J. Johanson, A. Majkgård and D.D. Sharma (1997), 'Experiential knowledge and cost in the internationalization process', *Journal of International Business Studies*, 28(2), 337–60.

Eriksson, Kent, Jan Johanson, Anders Majkgård and D. Deo Sharma (1998), 'Time and experience in the internationalization process', in Anders Majkgård (ed.), *Experiential Knowledge in the Internationalization Process of Service Firms*, Uppsala, Sweden: Department of Business Studies, pp. 185–217.

Eriksson, K., A. Majkgård and D.D. Sharma (2000), 'Path dependence and knowledge development in the internationalization process', *Management International Review*, 40(4), 307–28.

Fina, E. and A.M. Rugman (1996), 'A test of internalization theory and internationalization theory: the Upjohn Company', *Management International Review*, 36(3), 199–213.

Ford, David (1998), 'Two decades of interaction, relationships and networks', in Peter Naudé and Peter Turnbull (eds), *Network Dynamics in International Marketing*, Oxford: Elsevier, pp. 3–15.

Freeman, S., K. Hutchings, M. Lazaris and S. Zyngier (2010), 'A model of rapid knowledge development: the smaller born-global firm', *International Business Review*, 19(1), 70–84.

Gabrielsson, M., V. Sasi and J. Darling (2004), 'Finance strategies of rapidly-growing Finnish SMEs: born internationals and born globals', *European Business Review*, 16(6), 590–604.

Hadley, R.D. and H.I.M. Wilson (2003), 'The network model of internationalisation and experiential knowledge', *International Business Review*, 12(6), 697–717.

Hertz, S. (1996), 'The dynamics of international strategic alliances', *International Studies of Management and Organization*, 26(2), 104–30.

Johanson, Jan and Martin Johanson (1999), 'Developing business in Eastern European networks', in Jan-Åke Törnroos and Jarmo Nieminen (eds), *Business Entry in Eastern Europe: A Network and Learning Approach with Case Studies*, Helsinki: Kikimora Publications, pp. 46–71.

Johanson, Jan and Lars-Gunnar Mattsson (1988), 'Internationalization in industrial systems – a network approach', in Neil Hood and Jan-Erik Vahlne (eds), *Strategies in Global Competition*, London: Croom Helm, pp. 287–314.

Johanson, J. and J.-E. Vahlne (1977), 'The internationalization process of the firm: a model of knowledge development and increasing foreign market commitments', *Journal of International Business Studies*, 8(1), 23–32.

Johanson, J. and J.-E. Vahlne (1990), 'The mechanism of internationalization', *International Marketing Review*, 7(4), 11–24.

Johanson, J. and F. Wiedersheim-Paul (1975), 'The internationalization of the firm: four Swedish cases', *Journal of Management Studies*, 12(3), 305–22.

Karlsen, T., P.R. Silseth, G.R.G. Benito and L.S. Welch (2003), 'Knowledge, internationalization of the firm, and inward–outward connections', *Industrial Marketing Management*, 32(5), 385–96.

Kuivalainen, O., S. Sundqvist and P. Servais (2007), 'Firms' degree of born-globalness, international entrepreneurial orientation and export performance', *Journal of World Business*, 42(3), 253–67.

Lauter, G.P. and S.S. Rehman (1999), 'Central and East European trade orientation and FDI flows: preparation for EU membership', *International Trade Journal*, 13(1), 35–52.

Levene, Howard (1960), 'Robust tests for equality of variances', in Ingram Olkin, Sudhist G. Ghurye, Wassily Hoeffding, William G. Madow and Henry B. Mann (eds), *Contributions to Probability and Statistics: Essays in Honor of Harold Hotelling*, Palo Alto, CA: Stanford University Press, pp. 278–92.

Ling-yee, L. (2004), 'An examination of the foreign market knowledge of exporting firms based in the People's Republic of China: Its determinants and effect on export intensity', *Industrial Marketing Management*, 33(7), 561–72.

Liu, X., W. Xiao and X. Huang (2008), 'Bounded entrepreneurship and internationalisation of indigenous Chinese private-owned firms', *International Business Review*, 17(4), 488–508.

Luostarinen, Reijo (1989), *Internationalization of the Firm: An Empirical Study of the Internationalization of Firms with Small and Open Domestic Markets, with Special Emphasis on Lateral Rigidity as a Behavioral Characteristic in Strategic Decision-making*, Helsinki: Kyriiri OY.

Luostarinen, Reijo and Lawrence Welch (1997), *International Business Operations*, Helsinki: Kyriiri.

Madsen, T.K. and P. Servais (1997), 'The internationalisation of born globals: an evolutionary process?', *International Business Review*, 6(6), 561–83.

McDougall, P.P., B.M. Oviatt and R.C. Shrader (2003), 'A comparison of international and domestic new ventures', *Journal of International Entrepreneurship*, 1(1), 59–82.

Mitra, D. and P.N. Golder (2002), 'Whose culture matters? Near-market knowledge and its impact on foreign market entry timing', *Journal of Marketing Research*, 39(3), 350–65.

Morgan, N.A., S. Zou, D.W. Vorhies and C.S. Katsikeas (2003), 'Experiential and informational knowledge, architectural marketing capabilities, and the adaptive performance of export ventures: a cross-national study', *Decision Sciences*, 34(2), 287–321.

Morgan, R.E. and C.S. Katsikeas (1997), 'Theories of international trade, foreign direct investment and firm internationalization: a critique', *Management Decision*, 35(1/2), 68–78.

Naudé, W. (2009), 'Rushing in where angels fear to tread? The early internationalization of indigenous Chinese firms', *Journal of Chinese Economic and Foreign Trade Studies*, 2(3), 163–77.

Oviatt, B.M. and P.P. McDougall (1994), 'Toward a theory of international new ventures', *Journal of International Business Studies*, 25(1), 45–64.

Pajunen, K. and M. Maunula (2008), 'Internationalisation: a co-evolutionary perspective', *Scandinavian Journal of Management*, 24(3), 247–58.

Pécoud, A. (2002), '"Weltoffenheit schafft jobs": Turkish entrepreneurship and multiculturalism in Berlin', *International Journal of Urban and Regional Research*, 26(3), 494–507.

Pedersen, T. and B. Petersen (2004), 'Learning about foreign markets: are entrant firms exposed to a "shock effect"?', *Journal of International Marketing*, 12(1), 103–23.

Saarenketo, S., K. Puumalainen, O. Kuivalainen and K. Kyläheiko (2004), 'Dynamic knowledge-related learning processes in internationalizing high-tech SMEs', *International Journal of Production Economics*, 89(3), 363–78.

Seringhaus, F.H.R. and C.S. Mayer (1988), 'Different approaches to foreign market entry between users and non-users of trade missions', *European Journal of Marketing*, 22(10), 7–18.

Slater, S.F. and J.C. Narver (1995), 'Market orientation and the learning organization', *Journal of Marketing*, 59(3), 63–74.

Spence, M. and D. Crick (2009), 'An exploratory study of Canadian international new venture firms' development in overseas markets', *Qualitative Market Research: An International Journal*, 12(2), 208–33.

Tabachnik, Barbara G. and Linda S. Fidell (1996), *Using Multivariate Statistics*, New York: Harper Collins.

Vahlne, Jan-Erik and Jan Johanson (2002), 'New technology, new companies, new business environments and new internationalisation processes?', in Virpi Havila, Mats Forsgren and Håkan Håkansson (eds), *Critical Perspectives of Internationalisation*, Amsterdam: Pergamon, pp. 209–27.

Weerawardena, J., G. Sullivan Mort, P.W. Liesch and G. Knight (2007), 'Conceptualizing accelerated internationalization in the born global firm: a dynamic capabilities perspective', *Journal of World Business*, 42(3), 294–306.

Welch, B.L. (1951), 'On the comparison of several mean values: an alternative approach', *Biometrika*, 38(3–4), 330–36.

Welch, L.S. and R. Luostarinen (1988), 'Internationalization: evolution of a concept', *Journal of General Management*, 14(2), 34–57.

Wiedersheim-Paul, F., H.C. Olson and L.S. Welch (1978), 'Pre-export activity: the first step in internationalization', *Journal of International Business Studies*, 9(1), 47–58.

Wolff, J.A. and T.L. Pett (2000), 'Internationalization of small firms: an examination of export competitive patterns, firm size, and export performance', *Journal of Small Business Management*, 38(2), 34–47.

Zhou, L., W.-P. Wu and X. Luo (2007), 'Internationalization and the performance of born-global SMEs: the mediating role of social networks', *Journal of International Business Studies*, 38(4), 673–90.

Zou, H. and P.N. Ghauri (2010), 'Internationalizing by learning: the case of Chinese high-tech new ventures', *International Marketing Review*, 27(2), 223–44.

Zucchella, S., G. Palamara and S. Denicolai (2007), 'The drivers of the early internationalization of the firm', *Journal of World Business*, 42(3), 268–80.

APPENDIX 18A.1   DESCRIPTIVE STATISTICS

Table 18A1.1   Firm characteristics (mean values, data from 2010)

		No of firms	Mean	Std dev	Std error	95% confidence interval for mean	
						Lower bound	Upper bound
Turnover,	NBG	276	30.50	18.592	1.119	28.29	32.70
million	BG	104	35.67	21.133	2.072	31.56	39.78
RMB	Total	380	31.91	19.430	0.997	29.95	33.87
Number	NBG	276	222.48	156.419	9.415	203.94	241.01
of	BG	104	256.63	173.192	16.983	222.94	290.31
employees	Total	380	231.82	161.670	8.293	215.52	248.13
Export	NBG	276	26.89	19.595	1.179	24.57	29.21
share,	BG	104	72.63	15.155	1.486	69.69	75.58
% of	Total	380	39.41	27.532	1.412	36.63	42.19
turnover							
R&D	NBG	201	11.78	7.650	0.540	10.71	12.84
costs,	BG	102	19.34	6.016	0.596	18.15	20.52
% of	Total	303	14.32	7.979	0.458	13.42	15.22
turnover							

Table 18A1.2   Knowledge of the firm's first foreign market before entering

		No of firms	Mean	Std dev	Std error	95% confidence interval for mean	
						Lower bound	Upper bound
Knowledge about customers	NBG	276	3.30	1.251	0.075	3.16	3.45
	BG	104	1.26	0.654	0.064	1.13	1.39
	Total	380	2.74	1.444	0.074	2.60	2.89
Knowledge about competitors	NBG	275	3.02	1.154	0.070	2.88	3.16
	BG	104	1.15	0.478	0.047	1.06	1.25
	Total	379	2.51	1.312	0.067	2.37	2.64
Knowledge about suppliers	NBG	275	3.54	1.253	0.076	3.39	3.69
	BG	104	1.48	0.574	0.056	1.37	1.59
	Total	379	2.97	1.440	0.074	2.83	3.12
Knowledge about foreign market conditions	NBG	276	3.38	1.177	0.071	3.24	3.52
	BG	104	1.13	0.516	0.051	1.02	1.23
	Total	380	2.76	1.446	0.074	2.62	2.91
Knowledge about the foreign country's government, laws and institutional frameworks	NBG	275	2.88	1.302	0.078	2.73	3.04
	BG	104	1.09	0.397	0.039	1.01	1.16
	Total	379	2.39	1.384	0.071	2.25	2.53
Knowledge about the foreign country's norms, rules and values	NBG	275	3.06	1.208	0.073	2.92	3.21
	BG	104	1.11	0.481	0.047	1.01	1.20
	Total	379	2.53	1.373	0.071	2.39	2.66

Note: Rated from 1 to 7, 1 means 'not at all' and 7 means 'very much'.

Table 18A1.3 Foreign market knowledge (acquisition) before starting foreign activities

		No of firms	Mean	Std dev	Std error	95% confidence interval for mean	
						Lower bound	Upper bound
Worked in other firms with similar products or services but without any operations outside China	NBG	276	0.95	0.227	0.014	0.92	0.97
	BG	104	0.25	0.435	0.043	0.17	0.33
	Total	380	0.76	0.430	0.022	0.71	0.80
Worked in other firms that had operations outside China	NBG	276	0.91	0.293	0.018	0.87	0.94
	BG	104	0.04	0.193	0.019	0.00	0.08
	Total	380	0.67	0.471	0.024	0.62	0.72
Worked in the selected foreign market for at least one month before the firm entered it	NBG	276	0.09	0.282	0.017	0.05	0.12
	BG	104	0.00	0.000	0.000	0.00	0.00
	Total	380	0.06	0.244	0.012	0.04	0.09
Studied in the selected foreign market for at least one month before the firm entered it	NBG	276	0.91	0.288	0.017	0.88	0.94
	BG	104	0.19	0.396	0.039	0.12	0.27
	Total	380	0.71	0.453	0.023	0.67	0.76
Employed somebody who had worked or studied in the selected foreign market for at least one month	NBG	275	0.84	0.364	0.022	0.80	0.89
	BG	104	0.04	0.193	0.019	0.00	0.08
	Total	379	0.62	0.485	0.025	0.57	0.67
Got information about the selected foreign market from other firms (e.g. suppliers, competitors, customers)	NBG	276	0.34	0.476	0.029	0.29	0.40
	BG	104	0.06	0.234	0.023	0.01	0.10
	Total	380	0.27	0.442	0.023	0.22	0.31

		N					
Got information about selected foreign market from the firm's owner(s)	NBG	276	0.78	0.418	0.025	0.73	0.82
	BG	104	0.09	0.283	0.028	0.03	0.14
	Total	380	0.59	0.493	0.025	0.54	0.64
Got information about the selected foreign market from making pre-entry visits	NBG	276	0.61	0.490	0.029	0.55	0.66
	BG	104	0.02	0.138	0.014	−0.01	0.05
	Total	380	0.44	0.498	0.026	0.39	0.49
Got information about the selected foreign market from industry associations	NBG	276	0.30	0.453	0.028	0.24	0.35
	BG	103	0.25	0.437	0.043	0.17	0.34
	Total	379	0.28	0.452	0.023	0.24	0.33
Got information about the selected foreign market from Chinese governmental organizations	NBG	276	0.79	0.408	0.025	0.74	0.84
	BG	103	0.50	0.502	0.050	0.40	0.59
	Total	379	0.71	0.454	0.023	0.66	0.76
Got information about the selected foreign market from conferences and seminars	NBG	276	0.22	0.416	0.025	0.17	0.27
	BG	104	0.32	0.468	0.046	0.23	0.41
	Total	380	0.25	0.432	0.022	0.20	0.29
Got information about the selected foreign market from exhibitions and trade fairs	NBG	276	0.31	0.462	0.028	0.25	0.36
	BG	104	0.39	0.491	0.048	0.30	0.49
	Total	380	0.33	0.471	0.024	0.28	0.38

Note: BG: born globals, NBG: other internationalized firms. Firms answered either 'yes' (1) or 'no' (0).

APPENDIX 18A.2   RESULTS OF ANOVA

Table 18A2.1   ANOVA: firm characteristics

		Sum of squares	df	Mean square	F	Sig.
Turnover, million RMB	Between groups	2,019.307	1	2,019.307	5.411	0.021
	Within groups	141,058.633	378	373.171		
	Total	143,077.941	379			
Number of employees	Between groups	88,075.942	1	88,075.942	3.391	0.066
	Within groups	9,817,903.245	378	25,973.289		
	Total	9,905,979.187	379			
Export share, % of turnover	Between groups	158,040.058	1	158,040.058	462.224	0.000
	Within groups	129,242.963	378	341.913		
	Total	287,283.022	379			
R&D costs, % of turnover	Between groups	3,865.698	1	3,865.698	75.752	0.000
	Within groups	15,360.420	301	51.031		
	Total	19,226.118	302			

Table 18A2.2   ANOVA: knowledge of the firm's first foreign market before entering

		Sum of squares	df	Mean square	F	Sig.
Knowledge about customers	Between groups	315.814	1	315.814	251.626	0.000
	Within groups	474.425	378	1.255		
	Total	790.239	379			
Knowledge about competitors	Between groups	262.286	1	262.286	254.556	0.000
	Within groups	388.448	377	1.030		
	Total	650.734	378			
Knowledge about suppliers	Between groups	319.426	1	319.426	259.360	0.000
	Within groups	464.311	377	1.232		
	Total	783.736	378			
Knowledge about foreign market conditions	Between groups	384.255	1	384.255	355.627	0.000
	Within groups	408.429	378	1.081		
	Total	792.684	379			
Knowledge about the foreign country's government, laws and institutional frameworks	Between groups	243.708	1	243.708	191.214	0.000
	Within groups	480.498	377	1.275		
	Total	724.206	378			
Knowledge about the foreign country's norms, rules and values	Between groups	288.726	1	288.726	256.851	0.000
	Within groups	423.786	377	1.124		
	Total	712.512	378			

Table 18A2.3 *ANOVA: foreign market knowledge (acquisition) before*
first foreign activities

		Sum of squares	df	Mean square	*F*	Sig.
Worked in other firms with similar products or services but without any operations outside China	Between groups	36.555	1	36.555	410.205	0.000
	Within groups	33.685	378	0.089		
	Total	70.239	379			
Worked in other firms that had operations outside China	Between groups	56.824	1	56.824	784.014	0.000
	Within groups	27.397	378	0.072		
	Total	84.221	379			
Studied in the selected foreign market for at least one month before the firm entered it	Between groups	38.845	1	38.845	377.568	0.000
	Within groups	38.889	378	0.103		
	Total	77.734	379			
Employed somebody who had worked or studied in the selected foreign market for at least one month	Between groups	48.922	1	48.922	459.685	0.000
	Within groups	40.123	377	0.106		
	Total	89.045	378			
Got information about this country from other firms (e.g. suppliers, competitors, customers)	Between groups	6.201	1	6.201	34.492	0.000
	Within groups	67.955	378	0.180		
	Total	74.155	379			
Got information about this country from the firm's owner(s)	Between groups	35.841	1	35.841	240.662	0.000
	Within groups	56.294	378	0.149		
	Total	92.134	379			

Table 18A2.3   (continued)

		Sum of squares	df	Mean square	F	Sig.
Got information about the selected foreign market from making pre-entry visits	Between groups	25.925	1	25.925	144.294	0.000
	Within groups	67.914	378	0.180		
	Total	93.839	379			
Got information about the selected foreign market from industry associations	Between groups	0.150	1	0.150	0.732	0.393
	Within groups	77.075	377	0.204		
	Total	77.224	378			
Got information about the selected foreign market from Chinese governmental organizations	Between groups	6.515	1	6.515	34.322	0.000
	Within groups	71.559	377	0.190		
	Total	78.074	378			
Got information about the selected foreign market from conferences and seminars	Between groups	0.700	1	0.700	3.780	0.053
	Within groups	70.047	378	0.185		
	Total	70.747	379			
Got information about the selected foreign market from exhibitions and trade fairs	Between groups	0.562	1	0.562	2.540	0.112
	Within groups	83.659	378	0.221		
	Total					

APPENDIX 18A.3 TESTS OF HOMOGENEITY OF VARIANCES AND ROBUST TESTS OF EQUALITY OF MEANS

Table 18A3.1 Tests of firm characteristics

	Test of homogeneity of variances					Robust tests of equality of means			
	Levene's statistic	df1	df2	Sig.		Statistic[a]	df1	df2	Sig.
Turnover, million RMB	3.240	1	378	0.073	Welch Brown–Forsythe	4.820 4.820	1 1	166.534 166.534	0.030 0.030
Number of employees	1.843	1	378	0.175	Welch Brown–Forsythe	3.092 3.092	1 1	170.030 170.030	0.080 0.080
Export share, % of turnover	5.526	1	378	0.019	Welch Brown–Forsythe	581.267 581.267	1 1	238.238 238.238	0.000 0.000
R&D costs, % of turnover	4.461	1	301	0.036	Welch Brown–Forsythe	88.438 88.438	1 1	249.813 249.813	0.000 0.000

Note: [a] Asymptotically F distributed.

Table 18A3.2   Tests of data about foreign market knowledge of the firm's first foreign market before entering

	Test of homogeneity of variances					Robust tests of equality of means			
	Levene's statistic	df1	df2	Sig.		Statistic[a]	df1	df2	Sig.
Knowledge about customers	67.640	1	378	0.000	Welch Brown–Forsythe	241.089 241.089	1 1	124.742 124.742	0.000 0.000
Knowledge about competitors	43.053	1	377	0.000	Welch Brown–Forsythe	1123.904 1123.904	1 1	279.706 279.706	0.000 0.000
Knowledge about suppliers	62.374	1	377	0.000	Welch Brown–Forsythe	284.500 284.500	1 1	145.828 145.828	0.000 0.000
Knowledge about foreign market conditions	124.642	1	378	0.000	Welch Brown–Forsythe	771.344 771.344	1 1	336.784 336.784	0.000 0.000
Knowledge about the foreign country's government, laws and institutional frameworks	126.822	1	377	0.000	Welch Brown–Forsythe	60.868 60.868	1 1	352.847 352.847	0.000 0.000
Knowledge about the foreign country's norms, rules and values	92.276	1	377	0.000	Welch Brown–Forsythe	338.711 338.711	1 1	273.410 273.410	0.000 0.000

Note: [a] Asymptotically *F* distributed.

Table 18A3.3 Tests of data about foreign market knowledge (acquisition) before first foreign activities

	Test of homogeneity of variances					Robust tests of equality of means			
	Levene's statistic	df1	df2	Sig.		Statistic[a]	df1	df2	Sig.
Worked in other firms with similar products or services but without any operations outside China	131.057	1	378	0.000	Welch	241.089	1	124.742	0.000
					Brown–Forsythe	241.089	1	124.742	0.000
Worked in other firms that had operations outside China	14.208	1	378	0.000	Welch	1123.904	1	279.706	0.000
					Brown–Forsythe	1123.904	1	279.706	0.000
Studied in the selected foreign market for at least one month before the firm entered it	28.453	1	378	0.000	Welch	284.500	1	145.828	0.000
					Brown–Forsythe	284.500	1	145.828	0.000
Employed somebody who had worked or studied in the selected foreign market for at least one month	50.242	1	377	0.000	Welch	771.344	1	336.784	0.000
					Brown–Forsythe	771.344	1	336.784	0.000
Got information about this country from other firms (e.g. suppliers, competitors, customers)	320.233	1	378	0.000	Welch	60.868	1	352.847	0.000
					Brown–Forsythe	60.868	1	352.847	0.000

	Statistic	df1	df2	Sig.		Statistic[a]	df1	df2	Sig.
Got information about this country from the firm's owner(s)	51.158	1	378	0.000	Welch Brown–Forsythe	338.711 338.711	1 1	273.410 273.410	0.000 0.000
Got information about the selected foreign market from making pre-entry visits	1170.696	1	378	0.000	Welch Brown–Forsythe	326.227 326.227	1 1	360.386 360.386	0.000 0.000
Got information about the selected foreign market from industry associations	3.213	1	377	0.074	Welch Brown–Forsythe	0.765 0.765	1 1	190.985 190.985	0.383 0.383
Got information about the selected foreign market from Chinese governmental organizations	51.823	1	377	0.000	Welch Brown–Forsythe	28.436 28.436	1 1	154.943 154.943	0.000 0.000
Got information about the selected foreign market from conferences and seminars	12.680	1	378	0.000	Welch Brown–Forsythe	3.397 3.397	1 1	167.877 167.877	0.067 0.067
Got information about the selected foreign market from expositions and trade fairs	7.700	1	378	0.006	Welch Brown–Forsythe	2.405 2.405	1 1	176.000 176.000	0.123 0.123

Note: [a] Asymptotically *F* distributed.

19 Annotated bibliography for researchers

Acedo, F.J. and M.V. Jones (2007), 'Speed of internationalization and entrepreneurial cognition: insights and a comparison between international new ventures, exporters and domestic firms', *Journal of World Business*, **42**(3), 236–52.
Researchers interviewed top managers of various small and medium-sized enterprises for this study. The study concluded that an international orientation corresponded to a higher degree of proactivity and a lower perception of risk.

Albaum, G. and D.K. Tse (2001), 'Adaptation of international marketing strategy components, competitive advantage, and firm performance: a study of Hong Kong exporters', *Journal of International Marketing*, **9**(4), 59–81.
The authors use a sample of 183 export firms in Hong Kong to develop and test hypotheses and propositions about the impact of adaptation decisions on a firm's competitive position and performance in foreign markets.

Andersson, P. and L. Mattsson (2006), 'Timing and sequencing of strategic actions in internationalization processes involving intermediaries: a network perspective', *Advances in International Marketing*, **17**(16), 287–315.
The article analyzes a study of the benefit of timing and sequencing of strategic actions in a firm's internationalization process. The intermediaries between exporters and end-users are a particular focus.

Andersson, S. (2000), 'The internationalization of the firm from an entrepreneurial perspective', *International Studies of Management and Organization*, **30**(1), 63–92.
This study develops the concept of three different kinds of entrepreneurs and how they pursue international strategies: the marketing entrepreneur, the technical entrepreneur, and the structure entrepreneur.

Armario, J.M., D.M. Ruiz and E.M. Armario (2008), 'Market orientation and internationalization in small and medium-sized enterprises', *Journal of Small Business Management*, **46**(4), 485–511.

Using an empirical study of a multi-industry sample of Spanish small and medium-sized enterprises, the relationships between market orientation, knowledge acquisition, and market commitment to the enterprises' performance is examined.

Aspelund, A. and T.K. Madsen (2009), 'The role of innovative and entrepreneurial behavior in internationalization processes', *Advances in International Marketing*, **20**, 155–76.
The authors explore how international entrepreneurship studies and the innovation-related internationalization model have contributed to the current understanding of the internationalization processes of firms.

Aspelund, A., T.K. Madsen and Ø. Moen (2007), 'A review of the foundation, international marketing strategies, and performance of international new ventures', *European Journal of Marketing*, **41**(11/12), 1423–48.
This article both provides a review of the literature on born global firms, or 'international new ventures' (INVs) and suggests that linear models of analysis do not apply to born globals, rather non-traditional models and theories will give a better analysis of the born global phenomenon.

Autio, E. (2005), 'Creative tension: the significance of Ben Oviatt's and Patricia McDougall's article 'Toward a theory of international new ventures', *Journal of International Business Studies*, **36**(1), 9–19.
The authors discuss the impact of Oviatt and McDougall's theory of international entrepreneurship on earlier process theories of internationalization.

Autio, E., H.J. Sapienza and J.G. Almeida (2000), 'Effects of age at entry, knowledge intensity and imitability on international growth', *Academy of Management Journal*, **43**(5), 909–24.
International growth in entrepreneurial firms is examined by looking at both the effect of knowledge intensity and the effect of imitable technologies. Unexpected findings indicate that imitable technologies lead to fast growth much the same as greater knowledge intensity.

Bell, J., D. Crick and S. Young (2004), 'Small firm internationalization and business strategy: an exploratory study of 'knowledge-intensive' and 'traditional' manufacturing firms in the UK', *International Small Business Journal*, **22**(1), 23–56.
Using a qualitative approach interviewing 30 key decision makers in internationalizing small firms, the links between overall business

strategies and their patterns, processes and pace of internationalization were explored.

Bell, J., R. McNaughton and S. Young (2001), 'Born-again-global firms – an extension to the born-global firm', *Journal of International Management*, **7**(3), 173–89.
This article discusses the phenomena of established firms doing business in domestic markets suddenly and rapidly embracing internationalization. Case studies are used to analyze the motivations and triggers that lead firms to be born-again globals.

Bell, J., J. McNaughton, R. Young and D. Crick (2003), 'Towards an integrative model of small firm internationalization', *Journal of International Entrepreneurship*, **1**(4), 339–62.
The differences in internationalization strategies of born global firms and born-again global firms are examined. The authors propose a model that recognizes and encompasses these different internationalization 'pathways'.

Birkinshaw, J., A. Morrison and J. Hulland (1995), 'Structural and competitive determinants of a global integration strategy', *Strategic Management Journal*, **16**(8), 637–655.
This study looks at how structural and competitive factors impact on global integration strategies and concludes that it varies greatly among different industries. In addition, the study looked at the connection between a business's global integration strategy and its overall performance and found similar industry variations.

Boehe, D.M. (2009), 'Brazilian software SME's export propensity: bridging 'born global' and stage approaches', *Latin American Business Review*, **10**(2/3), 187–216.
Using 76 software SMEs based in Brazil's Northeastern region, this study tests a path model using the partial least squares (PLS) technique and PLS-Graph software and concludes that the more restrictive Penrosian theory of firm growth is compatible with the more proactive Schumpeterian view of entrepreneurship.

Bradley, F. and M. Gannon (2000), 'Does the firm's technology and marketing profile affect foreign market entry?', *Journal of International Marketing*, **8**(4), 12–36.
Using data from 105 firms in four European countries, the authors test hypotheses to determine the influence of technology and marketing profiles on entry into foreign markets.

Brannback, M., A. Carsrud and M. Renko (2007), 'Exploring the born global concept in the biotechnology context', *Journal of Enterprising Culture*, **15**(1), 79–100.
Interviews and multiple industry cluster surveys, among other information-gathering techniques, were used to fully explore the concept of 'born global'.

Brouthers, L.E., G. Nakos, J. Hadjimarcou and K.D. Brouthers (2009), 'Key factors for successful export performances for small firms', *Journal of International Marketing*, **17**(3), 21–38.
Using a sample of small firms from Greece and several Caribbean countries, the authors find that emphasizing international sales and restricting exports to a few foreign markets results in superior export performance.

Bürgel, O. and G. Murray (2000), 'The international market entry choices of start-up companies in high-technology industries', *Journal of International Marketing*, **6**(2), 33–62.
The entry mode to international sales decision process is analyzed by looking at the choices made by 246 technology-based start-ups with global activities.

Casillas, J.C., A.M. Moreno, F. Acedo, M.A. Gallego and E. Ramos (2009), 'An integrative model of the role of knowledge in the internationalization process', *Journal of World Business*, **44**(3), 311–22.
The integration of the influence of knowledge on international business behavior is proposed through a model that tracks several phases that knowledge progresses through in an organization.

Chetty, S. and H. Agndal (2007), 'Social capital and its influence on changes in internationalization mode among small and medium-sized enterprises', *Journal of International Marketing*, **15**(1), 1–29.
Ten New Zealand and ten Swedish small and medium-sized enterprises are examined to see how social capital influences their move to internationalization mode.

Chetty, S. and C. Campbell-Hunt (2003), 'Explosive international growth and problems of success amongst small to medium-sized firms', *International Small Business Journal*, **21**(1), 5–27.
Small and medium-sized businesses in New Zealand are examined from the business network perspective to see how rapid growth as a result of internationalization is handled.

Chetty, S. and C. Campbell-Hunt (2004), 'A strategic approach to internationalization: a traditional versus a 'born-global' approach', *Journal of International Marketing*, **12**(1), 57–81.
Using 16 in-depth case histories of New Zealand firms, this article looks at both traditional and born global approaches to analyze the internationalization process and how the strategies differ and lead to differences in the rapidity in which international growth is realized.

Chiara, A.D. and A. Minguzzi (2002), 'Success factors in SMEs' internationalization processes: an Italian investigation', *Journal of Small Business Management*, **40**(2), 146–53.
Small and medium-sized enterprises in Italy are looked at to see how the role of support services impacts on internationalization, among other factors.

Contractor, F.J. (2007), 'Is international business good for companies? The evolutionary or multi-stage theory of internationalization vs. the transaction cost perspective', *Management International Review*, **47**(3), 453–75.
This article looks at the multinationality/performance (M/P) link in a business's successes or failures, concluding that internationalization creates more benefits than problems.

Coviello, N.E. (2006), 'The network dynamics of international new ventures', *Journal of International Business Studies*, **37**(5), 713–31.
Using multi-site case research to advance a set of propositions on the network dynamics of early-stage international new ventures, this study builds on arguments that network theory and analysis are basic to international entrepreneurship.

Coviello, N.E. and M.P. Cox (2007), 'The resource dynamics of international new venture networks', *Journal of International Entrepreneurship*, **4**(2–3), 113–32.
Three case studies are used to look at how networks facilitate resource development in international new ventures. Using the conception, commercialization and growth stages as a base, four propositions relating to the dynamics of organizational, human, physical, and financial and social capital are developed.

Crick, D. and M.V. Jones (2000), 'Small high-technology firms and international high-technology markets', *Journal of International Marketing*, **8**(2), 63–85.

Technologically oriented small and medium-sized firms located in the UK are analyzed, leading the authors to challenge the incremental approach to internationalization based on their findings of the rapid internationalization of the studied technology-oriented firms and their success in entering the global market.

Dí Gregorio, D., M. Musteen and D.E. Thomas (2008), 'International new ventures: the cross-border nexus of individuals and opportunities', *Journal of World Business*, **43**(2), 186–96.
This article examines the importance of location of enterprises on country borders and how the cross-border aspect influences the resources and markets in becoming international firms.

Falay, Z., M. Salimäki, A. Ainamo and M. Gabrielsson (2007), 'Design-intensive born globals: a multiple case study of marketing management', *Journal of Marketing Management*, **23**(9/10), 877–99.
This study looks at how designers enter the international marketplace and concludes that designers would benefit from a partnership with a marketing professional to maximize their success as a born global enterprise.

Fan, T. and P. Phan (2007), 'International new ventures: revisiting the influences behind the 'born-global' firm', *Journal of International Business Studies*, **38**(7), 1113–31.
This article rethinks the importance of 'born global' in terms of the impact this concept has on the movement of an enterprise to enter the international market.
The authors conclude that a firm that goes global close to inception is not necessarily a distinct breed, but rather factors such as size of the local market and production capacity as well as others play a role in internationalization.

Fernhaber, S.A., P.P. McDougall and B.M. Oviatt (2007), 'Exploring the role of industry structure in new venture internationalization', *Entrepreneurship: Theory and Practice*, **31**(4), 517–42.
Drawing on literature from industrial economics, international business, and entrepreneurship to identify industry structure variables within the theoretical framework of international new ventures, the authors propose several theories about how the variables both separately and together can influence the viability of new venture internationalization.

Fletcher, D. (2004), 'International entrepreneurship and the small business', *Entrepreneurship and Regional Development*, **16**(4), 289–305.

This study looks at the differences between small businesses that enter the international market immediately (born global) and those that enter the international market a few years after start-up. The study concludes that the late starters tend to use the same strategies they developed locally when going to the international market, whereas born globals do not have that strategy because they enter the international market virtually upon inception.

Francis, J. and C. Collins-Dodd (2000), 'The impact of firms' expert-orientation on the export-performance of high-tech small and medium-sized enterprises', *Journal of International Marketing*, **8**(3), 84–103.
Multiple measures of export performance of small and medium-sized Canadian high-tech firms are analyzed with the conclusion that proactive export strategies have a more positive impact on export success than conservative export strategies.

Freeman, S. and S.T. Cavusgil (2007), 'Toward a typology of commitment states among managers of born-global firms: a study of accelerated internationalism', *Journal of International Marketing*, **15**(4), 1–40.
The attitudinal orientations of senior management with young entrepreneurial firms that are operating in a global environment are the focus of this article. The aim is to assist managers in rapidly creating an international and global enterprise.

Freeman, S., R. Edwards and B. Schroder (2006), 'How smaller born-global firms use networks and alliances to overcome constraints to rapid internationalization', *Journal of International Marketing*, **14**(3), 33–63.
This article focuses on how smaller born global firms use technology and networking to overcome their lack of economies of scale.

Freeman, S., K. Hutchings, M. Lazarius and S. Zyngier (2010), 'A model of rapid knowledge development: the smaller born-global firm', *International Business Review*, **19**(1), 70–84.
To address the failure of existing models to properly explain the rapid internationalization of firms, the authors extend current theory to argue that born global managers can use newly formed relationships in addition to pre-existing relationships in quickly and proactively developing new knowledge leading to the rapid commercialization of products. Technological experience is emphasized as shared technological knowledge fosters rapid transfer and development of new knowledge.

Gabrielsson, M. (2005), 'Branding strategies of born globals', *Journal of International Entrepreneurship*, **3**(3), 199–222.

This article focuses on the branding strategies used by 30 Finnish small and medium-sized 'born global' enterprises. One conclusion of the research is that branding strategies are dependent on the degree of globalization.

Gabrielsson, M. and V.H.M. Kirpalani (2004), 'Born globals: how to reach new business space rapidly', *International Business Review*, **13**(5), 555–71.
This study proposes that born globals must use the large channels provided by MNCs, networks, and/or the internet to rapidly receive cash flow and substantial revenues. Born globals from Israel and Finland selling similar products are used in the study.

Gabrielsson, M., V.M. Kirpalani, P. Dimitratos, C.A. Solberg and A. Zucchella (2008), 'Born globals: propositions to advance the theory', *International Business Review*, **17**(4), 385–401.
Using empirical evidence, this study looks at three phases that born globals go through: introductory, growth and resource accumulation, and break-out to independent growth as a major player in the international market. Based on the evidence, the authors conclude that the process is very different for born globals and traditional enterprises and that much can be learned by studying these differences.

Gabrielsson, M., V. Sasi and J. Darling (2004), 'Finance strategies of rapidly-growing Finnish SMEs: born internationals and born globals', *European Business Review*, **16**(6), 590–604.
This article looks at the influence of financing strategies and the finance management capabilities on the globalization of small and medium-sized Finnish enterprises. Born global enterprises proved to have more access to financial resources and financial managerial resources from the beginning as compared to born internationals.

Gleason, K.C. and J. Wiggenhorn (2007), 'Born globals, the choice of globalization strategy, and the market's perception of performance', *Journal of World Business*, **42**(3), 322–35.
A logistic regression analysis is used to study 124 newly public firms in the US that undertake 261 international joint ventures or acquisitions in the first six years of their existence.

Hashai, N. and T. Almor (2004), 'Gradually internationalizing 'born global' firms: an oxymoron?', *International Business Review*, **13**(4), 465–83.
Knowledge-intensive born global firms based in Israel are studied to

challenge the theory that born globals contradict the stages theory. Findings show that born global firms, while not necessarily following the classic stages theory, can have a gradual increase in foreign market entry.

Hitt, M.A., L. Bierman, K. Uhlenbruck and K. Shimizu (2006), 'The importance of resources in the internationalization of professional service firms: the good, the bad, and the ugly', *Academy of Management Journal*, **49**(6), 1137–57.
Human capital and relational capital derived from relations with both corporate clients and foreign governments are analyzed. The study shows that human and relational capital tended to have a positive influence on internationalization, but corporate client relational capital needed strong human capital to have that influence.

Ireland, R.D. and J.W. Webb (2007), 'Strategic entrepreneurship: creating competitive advantage through streams of innovation', *Business Horizons*, **50**, 49–59.
This article explores the importance and necessity of being nimble and adaptive in the current environment where technologies are increasingly changing and evolving.

Jantunen, A., N. Nummela, K. Puumalainen and S. Saarenketo (2008), 'Strategic orientations of born globals – do they really matter?', *Journal of World Business*, **43**, 158–70.
A total of 299 Finnish companies representing a broad spectrum of industrial sectors were analyzed to test the hypothesis that there is a connection between a firm's strategic orientation and its international performance.

Johanson, J. and J.-E. Vahlne (2009), 'The Uppsala internationalization process model revisited: from liability of foreignness to liability of outsidership', *Journal of International Business Studies*, **40**, 1411–31.
With the changes in business practices and theoretical advances made since the original Uppsala model was created in 1977, the business environment is now viewed as a web of relationships or networks rather than the neoclassical market of independent suppliers and customers. While the change mechanisms are essentially the same, the authors added trust-building and knowledge creation to recognize that new knowledge is developed in relationships.

Jolly, V.K., M. Alahutha and J.P. Jeannet (1992), 'Challenging the incumbents: how high technology start-ups compete globally', *Journal of Strategic Change*, **1**(1), 71–82.

Based on a study of four high-tech companies established since 1982 from four different countries, the authors propose that a global strategy is not necessarily preceded by a global presence. In the case of the four companies studied, a global strategy and a global presence occurred together, unlike the situation with large multinational companies.

Jones, M.V. and N.E. Coviello (2005), 'Internationalization: conceptualizing an entrepreneurial process of behavior in time', *Journal of International Business Studies*, **36**(3), 284–303.
Three potential models of internationalization are developed by the authors to address the call for a unifying direction for research in the new field of international entrepreneurship. The authors draw on both classic approaches to internationalization and insights from considering entrepreneurship as a separate and distinct field of study.

Kalantaridis, C. (2004), 'Internationalization, strategic behavior, and the small firm', *Journal of Small Business Management*, **42**(3), 245–62.
Using the findings from a survey of 1,000 enterprises doing business internationally located in the main urban areas of England, this article compares small firms to their medium and large-sized counterparts to see how strategy development compares. The study concludes that while strategies are similar regardless of the size of the firm, the strategic behavior increases for medium and large-sized enterprises as their international operations grow more complex, but similar behavior is not seen in smaller enterprises.

Karra, N. and N. Phillips (2004), 'Entrepreneurship goes global', *Ivey Business Journal*, **69**(2), 1–6.
This study concludes that entrepreneurs with particular talents and ambitions are looking to sell their products around the world – not just in the limited location where they are based; they are the new breed of born global entrepreneurs.

Karra, N., N. Phillips and P. Tracey (2008), 'Building the born global firm: developing entrepreneurial capabilities for international new venture success', *Long Range Planning*, **41**(4), 440–58.
Using an in-depth case study of a successful entrepreneur and the two international ventures he founded, the authors propose three entrepreneurial capabilities important for successful international new venture creation: international opportunity identification, institutional bridging, and a capacity and preference for cross-cultural collaboration.

Katsikeas, E.S., M. Theodosiou and R.E. Morgan (2005), 'Export market expansion strategies of direct-selling small and medium-sized firms: implications for export sales management activities', *Journal of International Marketing*, **3**(2), 57–92.
Punctuated equilibrium theory is used for the framework to analyze small and medium-sized UK exporters who adopt an export market expansion strategy: market concentration or market expansion. Specifically, the authors look at the characteristics of export sales managers and how their behavior impacts on export sales strategies.

Katz, J. and W. Gartner (1988) 'Properties of emerging organization', Academy of management Review, **13**(3), 429–41.
This article explores the characteristics of emerging organizations and suggests that emerging organizations can be identified by four properties: intentionality, resources, boundary and exchange. The authors make suggestions for selecting samples for research on emerging organizations and the implications for research and theory on new and emerging organizations are discussed.

Knight, G. (2000), 'Entrepreneurship and marketing strategy: the SME under globalization', *Journal of International Marketing*, **8**(2), 12–32.
Small and medium-sized enterprises (SMEs) are investigated to determine the relationships between entrepreneurial orientation, marketing strategy and tactics, and firm performance in SMEs affected by globalization. The author's findings and conclusions seek to help SME managers understand the critical roles of marketing and entrepreneurship in successful global enterprises.

Knight, G.A. and S.T. Cavusgil (1996), 'The born global firm: a challenge to traditional internationalization theory', in S. Tamer Cavusgil (ed.), *Advances in International Marketing*, Vol.8, Bingley, UK: Emerald Group Publishing, pp. 11–26.
The authors discuss the new phenomenon of born global firms, rapidly internationalizing firms strategically focusing on the size of the market and their ability to lead in the market, rather than entering new markets based on psychic distance. The authors state that to qualify as a born global, rapid internationalization must take place within three years of the firm's inception. In addition, the rapid internationalization is achieved by focusing on niche markets and entrepreneurial thinking. The born global phenomenon requires new thinking on the internationalization process.

Knight, G.A. and S.T. Cavusgil (2004), 'Innovation organizational capabilities and the born-global firm', *Journal of International Business Studies*, **35**(2), 124–41.
The authors highlight the critical role of innovative culture, knowledge, and capabilities in the ability of born global firms to enter into the international market immediately or early on in their existence. Case studies and survey-based studies lead the authors to conclude that born global firms employ a unique mix of orientations and strategies that drive their international success.

Knight, G.A. and S.T. Cavusgil (2005), 'A taxonomy of born-global firms', *Management International Review*, **45**(3), 15 35.
The authors develop a taxonomy to facilitate the understanding of 'born global' firms. Among other findings, the study indicates that entrepreneurial orientation and technological leadership are factors in successful international business performance.

Knight, G., T.K. Madsen and P. Servais (2004), 'An inquiry into born-global firms in Europe and the USA', *International Marketing Review*, **21**(6), 645–65.
Data from case and survey-based studies in Denmark and the USA are used to investigate 'born global' enterprises. A structural model representing key factors in international success is used to test various hypotheses.

Kocak, A. and T. Abimbola (2009), 'The effects of entrepreneurial marketing on born global performance', *International Marketing Review*, **26**(4/5), 439–52.
Based on interviews conducted with five born global firms, the authors conclude that organizational structure, the entrepreneurial processes adopted in creating firms, and marketing and learning orientation are all critical ingredients in the successful early internationalization of enterprises based in emerging economies.

Kuivalainen, O., S. Sundqvist and P. Servais (2007), 'Firms', degree of born-globalness, international entrepreneurial orientation and export performance', *Journal of World Business*, **42**, 253–67.
This article looks at the relationship between entrepreneurial orientation (EO) and two born global strategies – those firms that are true born globals and those firms that are apparently born global (born international). Based on their study of 185 Finnish exporting firms, the authors conclude, among other things, that true born globals had better export performance.

Kundu, S.U. and J.A. Katz (2003), 'Born-international SMEs: bi-level impacts of resources and intentions', *Small Business Economics*, **20**, 25–47.
The authors use the Katz and Gartner (1988) model to explain the early lives of born international firms. Based on a sample of 47 young born international firms from the software industry in India, the authors used the boundary property to define the central sampling framework. Resources and intention were evaluated on their impact of the fourth property of exchange. Findings suggest that in the early stages of firm development, owner characteristics have a greater impact on performance than firm characteristics.

Laanti, R., M. Gabrielsson and P. Gabrielsson (2007), 'The globalization strategies of business-to-business born global firms in the wireless technology industry', *Industrial Marketing Management*, **36**(8), 1104–17.
The globalization process of business in the wireless technology industry is examined to determine how a rapidly growing industry changes strategies for born global businesses.

Lituchy, T.R. and A. Rail (2000), 'Bed and breakfasts, small inns and the internet: the impact of technology on the globalization of small businesses', *Journal of International Marketing*, **8**(2), 86–97.
Using a survey the authors developed, small inns and bed and breakfast establishments in Canada and the United States were examined to determine how these businesses use the available technologies and what they considered to be the pros and cons of these technologies. The article looks at how the internet can help small and medium-sized enterprises enter the global market.

Loane, S., J. Bell and R. McNaughton (2007), 'A cross-national study on the impact of management teams on the rapid internationalization of small firms', *Journal of World Business*, **42**(4), 489–504.
A cross-national study conducted in Australia, Canada, Ireland, and New Zealand is the basis of this article which examines the impact of top management teams on rapid internationalization of new enterprises.

Lopez, L.E., S.K. Kundu and L. Ciravegna (2009), 'Born global or born regional? Evidence from an exploratory study in the Costa Rican software industry', *Journal of International Business Studies*, **40**(7), 1228–38.
Based on data collected from interviewing 40 CEOs or founders of Costa Rican software companies, the authors found that few of the companies were born global. Rather, most companies gradually entered the interna-

tional market. The few that did export soon after their inception, according to the authors, were born regional, not global.

Lu, Y., L. Zhou, G. Brunton and L. Weiwen (2010), 'Capabilities as a mediator linking resources and the international performance of entrepreneurial firms in an emerging economy', *Journal of International Business Studies*, **41**(3), 419–36.
Using a large sampling of Chinese entrepreneurial firms, the authors study the relationships between capabilities, resources, and international performance. Findings indicate that capabilities have a mediating role in the relationship between resources and international performance.

Luostarinen, R. and M. Gabrielsson (2006), 'Globalization and marketing strategies of born globals in SMOPECs', *Thunderbird International Business Review*, **48**(6), 773–801.
This study looks at the challenges managers and entrepreneurs of companies originating in small and open economies (SMOPECs) face when their firms undergo instant or rapid globalization.

Madsen, T.K., E. Rasmussen and P. Servais (2000), 'Differences and similarities between born globals and other types of exporters', in A. Yaprati and H. Tutek (eds), *Globalization the Multinational Firm and Emerging Economies*, Advances in International Marketing, Vol. 10, Bingley, UK: Emerald Group Publishing, pp. 247–265.
Using Danish companies born global after 1976 and more traditional Danish exporters, the authors compare various models of internationalization for similarities and differences in the two groups.

Madsen, T.K. and P. Servais (1997), 'The internationalization of born globals – an evolutionary process', *International Business Review*, **6**(6), 1–14.
This article summarizes the empirical evidence reported about born globals, interprets the phenomena of born globals at a deep theoretical level, and suggests a new conceptualization of the research issue. The authors conclude that born globals grow in a way which may be in agreement with evolutionary thinking.

Mambula, C. (2002), 'Perceptions of SME growth constraints in Nigeria', *Journal of Small Business Management*, **40**(1), 58–65.
Since Nigeria's independence, the Nigerian government has put a great deal of money into small business development and entrepreneurial programs. This article looks at what factors have influenced these enterprises and how these factors might influence policies.

Manolova, T., I.M. Manev and B.S. Gyoshev (2009), 'In good company: the role of personal and inter-firm networks for new-venture internationalization in a transition economy', *Journal of World Business*, **45** (3), 257–65.
Using a large sampling (*n* = 623) of entrepreneurial ventures in Bulgaria, the authors find that domestic personal networks have a positive effect on internationalization. The study concludes that the earlier a new venture engages in inter-firm collaboration, the higher the degree of its internationalization. Managerial practice and public policy implications are also discussed.

Mathews, J.A. and I. Zander (2007), 'The international entrepreneurial dynamics of accelerated internationalization', *Journal of International Business Studies*, **38**, 387–403.
The authors attempt to delineate an emerging field of international business (IB) scholarship, using the appearance of international new ventures and the phenomenon of accelerated internationalization they feature to identify a specific set of issues that are not included in most existing IB frameworks. The authors propose a framework found at the intersection of entrepreneurial and internationalization perspectives, which they label 'international entrepreneurial dynamics'.

Mayrhofer, U. (2004), 'International market entry: does the home country affect entry-mode decisions?', *Journal of International Marketing*, **12**(4), 71–96.
Using 26 empirical studies on home-country effects on a firm's choice of entering the international market, the author concludes that a company's nationality is likely to have an impact on strategy but that some cultural and economic factors are more relevant than others.

McDougall, P.P. and B.M. Oviatt (2000), 'International entrepreneurship: the intersection of two research paths', *Academy of Management Journal*, **43**(5), 902–6.
This article discusses how international business researchers are expanding their focus to include entrepreneurial firms in their research agendas.

McDougall, P.P., B.M. Oviatt and R.C. Shrader (2003), 'A comparison of international and domestic new ventures', *Journal of International Entrepreneurship*, **1**, 59–82.
Using a sample of 214 new ventures, the authors found that international new ventures were significantly different from domestic new ventures in their entrepreneurial team experience, strategy, and industrial structure.

There was a higher level of previous international and industry experience in the international new ventures as well as more aggressive strategies and use of more channels of distribution than domestic new ventures.

McDougall, P.P., S. Shane and B.M. Oviatt (1994), 'Explaining the formation of international new ventures: the limits of theories from international business research', *Journal of Business Venturing*, **9**(6), 469–87. The authors use 24 case studies of international new ventures (INVs) to demonstrate that existing international business theories do not adequately explain the formation process of INVs. The authors suggest that three questions must be answered to attempt to explain the formation process of INVs: (i) who are the founders; (ii) why do they choose to compete internationally rather than just in their home markets; and (iii) what is the form of their international business activities?

McNaughton, R.B. (2003), 'The number of export markets that a firm serves: process models versus the born-global phenomenon', *Journal of International Entrepreneurship*, **1**, 297–311. The author uses both process models and existing literature about born global firms to identify possible influences on the number of export markets served by a firm. Using the results of a survey of micro-exporters, the study concludes that the number of export markets is positively associated with firm age, proprietary and knowledge-intensive products, industries that are internationalized, and small domestic markets.

Melén, S. and E.R. Nordman (2009), 'The internationalization modes of born globals: a longitudinal study', *European Management Journal*, **27**(4), 243–54. Eight biotechnology born globals are divided into three groups – low committers, incremental committers, and high committers – describing their initial and continued internationalization modes. The authors determine that the biggest difference in the three groups is the speed at which the firms commit resources to foreign markets.

Michailova, S. and H.I. Wilson (2008), 'Small firm internationalization through experiential learning: the moderating role of socialization tactics', *Journal of World Business*, **43**(2), 243–54. The authors use insights from socialization tactics literature to determine how social aspects impact on a firm's internationalization. Moen, Ø. (2002), 'The born globals – a new generation of small European exporters', *International Marketing Review*, **19**(2), 156–75. Taking information from an empirical study of small firms in Norway and France, the authors found that more than half of exporting firms established since 1990 could be classified as born globals, indicating that the born global phenomenon is not limited to just a few firms but includes the majority of newly established exporting firms. This study found that a firm is either born global or 'born as local', implying that decisions made during the establishment process of a firm may be more important to future export development than might have been expected. The authors recommend that export assistance programs focus on newly established and highly involved exporters.

Moen, Ø., I. Endresen and M. Gavlen (2003), 'Executive insights: use of the internet in international marketing: a case study of small computer software firms', *Journal of International Marketing*, **11**(4), 129–49.
Using six case studies of software firms, the authors conclude that the internet is used for finding information about customers, distributors, and partners. The internet, however, does not replace personal sales, but is important for product reviews and image building.

Moen, Ø. and P. Servais (2002), 'Born global or gradual global? Examining the export behavior of small and medium-sized enterprises', *Journal of International Marketing*, **10**(3), 49–72.
Small and medium-sized firms from Denmark, France, and Norway are used in this study to determine how gradual development of a global market compares with the rapid development of born global firms.

Mort, G.S. and J. Weerawardena (2006), 'Networking capability and international entrepreneurship: how networks function in Australian born global firms', *International Marketing Review*, **23**(5), 549–72.
Using six exemplar case studies from low and high-tech industry sectors, the focus of this research is on how the role and characteristics of entrepreneurial owner-managers compares with the development of networking capability.

Nordman, E.R. and S. Melén (2008), 'The impact of different kinds of knowledge for the internationalization process of born globals in the biotech business', *Journal of World Business*, **43**(2), 171–85.
This study looks at different kinds of knowledge bases – born industrials and born academics. The study concludes that the founders and managers of businesses and their varying technological and international knowledge have an effect on the firms' behavior – either proactive or reactive – in discovering foreign market opportunities.

Ojala, A. and P. Tyrvainen (2007), 'Market entry and priority of small and medium-sized enterprises in the software industry: an empirical analysis of cultural distance, geographic distance, and market size', *Journal of International Marketing*, **15**(3), 123–49.
This study is based on the market entry of small and medium-sized firms in the software industry. The findings indicate that around 70 percent of country choices for entering global markets can be explained by two factors: the size of the software market in the country and the geographical distance.

Oviatt, B.M. and P.P. McDougall (1994), 'Toward a theory of international new ventures', *Journal of International Business Studies*, **25**(1), 45–64.
The authors present a framework that explains the phenomenon of international new ventures by integrating international business, entrepreneurship and strategic management theory. The framework describes four elements for the existence of international new ventures: (i) organizational formation through internationalization of some transactions; (ii) strong reliance on alternative governance structures to access resources; (iii) establishment of foreign location advantages; and (iv) control over unique resources.

Oviatt, B.M. and P.P. McDougall (1995), 'Global start-ups: entrepreneurs on a worldwide stage', *Academy of Management Executive*, **9**(2), 30–44.
Based on the start-up process of Logitech, Inc., the authors studied 12 similar start-ups to determine whether Logitech had a unique experience or whether a pattern could be found in the creation dynamics and success characteristics of global start-ups.

Oviatt, B. and P. McDougall (2000), 'International entrepreneurship: the intersection of two research paths', *Academy of Management Journal*, **43**(5), 902–6.
The authors discuss the growing phenomenon of the research paths of international business and entrepreneurship intersecting and how international business researchers are broadening their focus to include entrepreneurial firms in their research agenda, as well as entrepreneurship researchers including cross-border business activity in their studies.

Oviatt, B. and P. McDougall (2005), 'Defining international entrepreneurship and modeling the speed of internationalization', *Entrepreneurship: Theory and Practice*, **29** (5), 537–53.
The authors propose a reformulated definition of international

entrepreneurship and present a model of how the speed of entrepreneurial internationalization is influenced by various forces including the enabling forces of technology, the motivating forces of competition, the mediating perceptions of entrepreneurs, and the moderating forces of knowledge and networks.

Oviatt, B. and P. McDougall (2005), 'The internationalization of entrepreneurship', *Journal of International Business Studies*, **36**(1), 2–8.
This article looks back at the authors' award-winning article of 1994 – 'Toward a theory of international new ventures' and explains the personal and intellectual origins of the work. In addition the definitions of 'international new ventures' and 'international entrepreneurship' are highlighted and the authors respond to concerns about the importance of international business scholarship by showing their research as a successful exportation of international business scholarship into adjacent disciplines.

Oviatt, B.M., P.P. McDougall, M. Simon and R.C. Shrader (1993), 'Heartware International Corporation: a medical equipment company 'born international' Part A', *Entrepreneurship: Theory and Practice*, **18**(2), 111–28.
Looking at one medical equipment company founded in New Jersey in 1988, the article focuses on Heartware International's expansion into the international market.

Pedersen, T. and B. Petersen (2004), 'Learning about foreign markets: are entrant firms exposed to a "shock effect"?', *Journal of International Marketing*, **12**(1), 103–23.
Different predictions of how foreign-market familiarity changes when firms first enter the international market are subjected to empirical examination using data from managers of international firms in Denmark, Sweden, and New Zealand. The study concludes that managers of firms entering the international market tend to experience a greater 'shock effect' when entering border markets than when entering more distant markets.

Rennie, M.W. (1993), 'Global competitiveness: born global', *McKinsey Quarterly*, **4**, 45–52.
Using a McKinsey study of Australia's high-value-added manufacturing exporters showing the rise of many small to medium-sized companies that successfully compete from their inception against large established players, the author asserts that they went against popular wisdom of

slowly building their way into international trade and were instead, born global.

Reuber, A.R. and E. Fischer (1997), 'The influence of the management team's international experience on the internationalization behavior of SMEs', *Journal of International Business Studies*, **28**(4), 807–25.
The authors examine the role of the management teams' international experience as a mechanism for rapid internationalization looking at Canadian software product firms. The authors show that internationally experienced management teams are more likely to develop foreign strategic partners and to delay less in obtaining foreign sales after start-up, leading to a higher degree of internationalization.

Rialp, A. and J. Rialp (2006), 'Faster and more successful exporters: an exploratory study of born global firms from the resource-based view', *Journal of Euromarketing*, **16**(1/2), 71–86.
This paper analyzes the effect of several firm resources that have an intangible character to determine whether these resources have had an impact on entry into the international export activity from the firm's inception. Conclusions from the study indicate that human and organizational capital resources have a major impact on successful born global firms.

Rialp, A., J. Rialp and G.A. Knight (2005), 'The phenomenon of early internationalizing firms: what do we know after a decade (1993–2003) of scientific inquiry?', *International Business Review*, **14**(2), 147–66.
The authors analyze 38 studies from the last decade that deal with global start-ups, born global firms and international new ventures using the criteria of main objective and type of research; theoretical framework/s of reference; methodological issues; and main findings and/or conclusions. In doing so, the authors aim to reveal the most relevant contributions and benefits as well as potential drawbacks of previous studies.

Rialp, A., J. Rialp, D. Urbano and Y. Vaillant (2005), 'The bornglobal phenomenon: a comparative case study research', *Journal of International Entrepreneurship*, **3**, 133–71.
Several firms involved in exporting, both born global and more traditional firms located in a region of Spain, are investigated for comparative purposes. Results indicate that both have two distinctive and consistent patterns of international development. In addition, the born global firms seem to be more entrepreneurial in their export entry into foreign markets than the more traditional firms.

Rialp-Criado, A., I. Galván-Sánchez and S.M. Suárez-Ortega (2010), 'A configuration-holistic approach to born-global firms' strategy formation process', *European Management Journal*, **28**(2), 108–23.
The authors apply an integrated strategic management perspective to look at how born globals use different strategies depending on specific factors impacting their international development and specific phases in their international development processes.

Schwens, C. and R. Kabst (2009), 'Early internationalization: a transaction cost economics and structural embeddedness perspective', *Journal of International Entrepreneurship*, **7**(4), 323–40.
The authors develop and test a framework for the determinants of early internationalization. Their results indicate that asset specificity is negatively related to early internationalization, while prior international experience of the management team and international network contacts have a positive impact on early internationalization.

Shrader, R.C., B.M. Oviatt and P.P. McDougall (2000), 'How new ventures exploit trade-offs among international risk factors: lessons for the accelerated internationalization of the 21st century', *Academy of Management Journal*, **43**(6), 1227–47.
Using 212 foreign market entries by 87 new ventures based in the US, the authors look at how the risks of accelerated internationalization can be managed. Findings include the use of simultaneous trade-offs among foreign revenue exposure, risk of the country being entered, and the mode in which entry commitment is made in each country all contribute to the firm's ability to manage strategic risks.

Styles, C. and T. Genua (2008), 'The rapid internationalization of high technology firms created through the commercialization of academic research', *Journal of World Business*, **43**(2), 146–57.
The effect of networks and entrepreneurial orientation is explored via the internationalization of high-technology firms created through the commercialization of academic research. The authors use the framework for international entrepreneurship developed by Jones and Coviello (2005).

Sullivan, D. (1994), 'Measuring the degree of internationalization of a firm', *Journal of International Business Studies*, **25**, 325–42.
To address the lack of reliability of measuring the degree of internationalization of a firm, the authors collected data on nine attributes of 74 American manufacturing MNCs. Analysis revealed a linear

combination of five variables with a reliability coefficient of 0.79 as a measure of the degree of internationalization of a firm.

Vapola, T.J., P. Tossavainen and M. Gabrielsson (2008), 'The battleship strategy: the complementing role of born globals in MNC's new opportunity creation', *Journal of International Entrepreneurship*, **6**(1), 1–20.
The impact of new innovations on multinational companies' (MNCs') competitive advantage are explored to see why and how MNCs form strategic alliances with smaller and more innovative born globals.

Weerawardena, J., G.S. Mort, P.W. Liesch and G. Knight (2007), 'Conceptualizing accelerated internationalization in the born global firm: a dynamic capabilities perspective', *Journal of World Business*, **42**, 294–306.
To address what they see as a gap in existing approaches to explaining rapid internationalization of born global firms, the authors look at the knowledge building undertaken by the firms and their founders prior to the actual establishment of the firm. They propose that a set of dynamic capabilities that are built and nurtured by internationally-oriented entrepreneurial founders enable their firms to develop cutting-edge knowledge-intensive products leading to accelerated market entry.

Westhead, P. and M. Wright (2001), 'The internationalization of new and small firms: a resource-based view', *Journal of Business Venturing*, **16**(4), 333–58.
The authors present information on a study about the factors that encourage small and medium-sized enterprises to export their products, looking at both human and financial capital.

Wolff, J.A. and T.L. Pett (2000), 'Internationalization of small firms: an examination of export competitive patterns, firm size and export performance', *Journal of Small Business Management*, **38**(2), 34–47.
The impact on size of 157 small firms with active export markets outside of the US is examined. The authors use three size divisions – larger small firms, medium small firms, and smaller small firms – and found differences based on these divisions.

Yeoh, P. (2000), 'Information acquisition activities: a study of global start-up exporting companies', *Journal of International Marketing*, **8**(3), 36–60.
The author looks at information source use and information search effort to find out how it impacts on export performance. The findings conclude

that those firms that engage in more information search and information sources tend to have higher performance levels.

Yip, G.S., J.G. Biscarri and J.A. Monti (2000), 'The role of the internationalization process in the performance of newly internationalizing firms', *Journal of International Marketing*, **8**(3), 10–35.
Based on a study of 68 newly internationalized US firms, the conclusion is that generally, there is no systematic approach that is followed, however, firms that do use a systematic approach enjoy better performance.

Zahra, S.A. (2005), 'A theory of international new ventures: a decade of research', *Journal of International Business Studies*, **36**, 20–28.
This article reviews Oviatt and McDougall's original propositions about the validity and usefulness of existing theory, in particular the Uppsala process model of internationalization, highlighting their important contributions to the field. The author also highlights the progress made in research using Oviatt and McDougall's framework, the major debates that persist about the nature and role of INVs, and the source of their competitive advantages.

Zahra, S.A., R.D. Ireland and M.A. Hitt (2000), 'International expansion by new venture firms: international diversity, mode of market entry, technological learning, and performance', *Academy of Management Journal*, **43**(5), 925–50.
This study focuses on how firms use the technological learning gained through internationalization – specifically the effects of international expansion as measured by international diversity and the method of market entry on the firm's technological knowledge and how that knowledge impacts on financial performance.

Zhang, M.Y. and M. Dodgson (2007), '"A roasted duck can still fly away": a case study of technology, nationality, culture and the rapid and early internationalization of the firm', *Journal of World Business*, **42**(3), 336–49.
This study looks at the failure of a start-up Korean company, Avaro, to succeed in the international market even though it appeared to have many of the factors in its favor that normally contribute to a successful entry. The study concludes that the intricacies of national business systems, and cultural influences, among other things can have a negative impact on entry into international markets.

Zhao, H. and S. Zou (2002), 'The impact of industry concentration and firm location on export propensity and intensity: an empirical analysis

of Chinese manufacturing firms', *Journal of International Marketing*, **10**(1), 52–71.
While much research has focused on the internal and controllable factors involved in export performance, this study focuses on two key external uncontrollable factors–industry location and industry concentration – to determine whether these two factors have a large impact on a firm's performance.

Zhou, L. (2007), 'The effects of entrepreneurial proclivity and foreign market knowledge on early internationalization', *Journal of World Business*, **42**(3), 281–93.
Using survey data from international entrepreneurial firms in mainland China, this study tests and supports a mediating mechanism of foreign market knowledge as it relates to the pace and performance of firms that go through early internationalization.

Zhou, L., W.-P. Wu and X. Luo (2007), 'Internationalization and the performance of born-global SMEs: the mediating role of social networks', *Journal of International Business Studies*, **38**(4), 673–90.
The authors propose that home-based social networks play an important mediating role in the relationship between inward and outward internationalization and firm performance. Using survey data on small and medium-sized enterprises in the emerging economy of China, they found support for this in the form of *guanxi*, implying that international business managers should consider social networks as an efficient means of helping internationally oriented SMEs to go international more rapidly and profitably.

Zucchella, A., S. Danicolai and G. Palamara (2007), 'The drivers of the early internationalization of the firm', *Journal of World Business*, **42** (3), 268–80.
The authors look at the early start of international activities in a sample of 144 small and medium-sized enterprises using a theoretical framework with the aim of integrating a fragmented literature body. The role of the previous experience of the entrepreneur, in particular the entrepreneur's international experience, was found to be significant. This positive association between early start of international activities and niche positioning of the business enforces the relevance of entrepreneurship.

Index